Lecture Notes in Computer Science 8378

Commenced Publication in 1973
Founding and Former Series Editors:
Gerhard Goos, Juris Hartmanis, and Jan van Leeuwen

Nelly Bencomo   Robert France
Betty H.C. Cheng   Uwe Aßmann (Eds.)

Models@run.time

Foundations, Applications, and Roadmaps

 Springer

Volume Editors

Nelly Bencomo
Aston University
School of Engineering and Applied Science
Birmingham, B4 7ET, UK
E-mail: nelly@acm.org

Robert France
Colorado State University
Department of Computer Science
Fort Collins, CO 80523, USA
E-mail: france@cs.colostate.edu

Betty H.C. Cheng
Michigan State University
Department of Computer Science and Engineering
East Lansing, MI 48824, USA
E-mail: chengb@cse.msu.edu

Uwe Aßmann
Technische Universität Dresden
Institut für Software- und Multimediatechnik
01062 Dresden, Germany
E-mail: uwe.assmann@tu-dresden.de

ISSN 0302-9743   e-ISSN 1611-3349
ISBN 978-3-319-08914-0   e-ISBN 978-3-319-08915-7
DOI 10.1007/978-3-319-08915-7
Springer Cham Heidelberg New York Dordrecht London

Library of Congress Control Number: 2014942560

LNCS Sublibrary: SL 2 – Programming and Software Engineering

Typesetting: Camera-ready by author, data conversion by Scientific Publishing Services, Chennai, India

Printed on acid-free paper

Springer is part of Springer Science+Business Media (www.springer.com)

Preface

Traditionally, research on model-driven engineering (MDE) has mainly focused on the use of models at the design, implementation, and verification stages of development. This work has produced relatively mature techniques and tools that are currently being used in industry and academia. However, software models also have the potential to be used at runtime, to monitor and verify particular aspects of runtime behavior, and to implement self-* capabilities (e.g., adaptation technologies used in self-healing, self-managing, self-optimizing systems). A key benefit of using models at runtime is that they can provide a richer semantic base for runtime decision-making related to runtime system concerns associated with autonomic and adaptive systems. The research topic models@run.time has been explored since the first international workshop of the same name in 2006 with novel research results. The need for advancing the research in this area motivated the organization of the Dagstuhl Seminar 11481 on models@run.time that was held from November 27 to December 2, 2011. The seminar comprised valuable discussions about the foundations, techniques, mechanisms, state of the art, research challenges, and applications for the use of runtime models. The seminar also provided an exceptional opportunity to bring together different communities in order to share insights and to expand and strengthen the cross-fertilization and momentum that had been initiated at previously organized workshops on models@runtime.

This book is one of the outcomes of the Dagstuhl Seminar. The book comprises four research roadmaps and seven research papers from experts in the area. The four roadmap papers were developed by groups of Dagstuhl participants that detail the issues discussed during the five-day Dagstuhl Seminar and provide insights to key features of the use of runtime models. All the papers in this book were peer reviewed including the roadmap papers. The roadmap papers were written by the original participants of the Dagstuhl Seminar over the course of two years following the seminar.

The first part of the book consists of the four roadmap papers. The roadmap papers elaborate on the research challenges for runtime models identified by each of the four working groups of the Dagstuhl Seminar: the need for a reference architecture, uncertainty tackled by runtime models, mechanisms for leveraging runtime models for self-adaptive software, and the use of models at runtime to address assurance for self-adaptive systems.

The first roadmap paper by Aßmann, Götz, Jézéquel, Morin, and Trapp, titled "A Reference Architecture and Roadmap for Models@run.time Systems," outlines a reference architecture for systems that use models@run.time. The authors highlight as a key property of this kind of system their use and provision of manageable reflection to overcome the limitation of reflective systems used in the past. The chapter also presents a roadmap comprising short- and long-term research challenges for the area, an overview of enabling and enabled technologies, and several application fields and use cases.

The second roadmap paper by Bennaceur, France, Tamburrelli, Vogel, Mosterman, Cazzola, Costa, Pierantonio, Tichy, Akşit, Emmanuelson, Gang, Georgantas, and Redlich, titled "Mechanisms for Leveraging Models at Runtime in Self-Adaptive Software," elaborates on challenges associated with developing mechanisms that leverage models at runtime to support runtime software adaptation. Specifically, the paper discusses challenges associated with developing effective mechanisms for supervising running systems, reasoning about and planning adaptations, maintaining consistency among multiple runtime models, and maintaining fidelity of runtime models with respect to the running system and its environment. The paper also describes related problems, state-of-the-art mechanisms, and open research challenges in the area.

The third roadmap paper by Giese, Bencomo, Pasquale, Ramirez, Inverardi, Wätzoldt, and Clarke, titled "Living with Uncertainty in the Age of Runtime Models," explores the role of runtime models as a means to cope with uncertainty. The chapter introduces a terminology suite for models, runtime models, and uncertainty, which is followed by a state-of-the-art summary on model-based techniques for addressing uncertainty both at development and runtime. Using a case study about robot systems, the chapter discusses how current techniques and the MAPE-K loop can be used together to tackle uncertainty. The chapter proposes possible extensions of the MAPE-K loop architecture with runtime models to further handle uncertainty at runtime. Key challenges and enabling technologies for using runtime models to address uncertainty are identified.

The fourth roadmap paper by Cheng, Eder, Gogolla, Grunske, Litoiu, Muller, Pelliccione, Perini, Qureshi, Rumpe, Schneider, Trollmann, and Villegas, titled "Using Models at Runtime to Address Assurance for Self-Adaptive Systems," explores the state of the art for using models at runtime to address the assurance of self-adaptive software systems. It defines what assurance information can be captured by models at runtime and puts this definition into the context of existing work according to different categories of assurance techniques. The chapter also outlines key research challenges for using models to address assurance at runtime. The chapter concludes with an exploration of selected application areas where models at runtime could provide significant benefits beyond existing assurance techniques for adaptive systems.

Part two of this book comprises the following research papers.

The first paper by DeLoach, Ou, Zhuang, and Zhang, titled "Model-Driven, Moving-Target Defense for Enterprise Network Security" presents the design and initial simulation results for a prototype moving-target defense (MTD) system, whose goal is to exponentially increase the difficulty of attacks on enterprise networks. The novelty of the presented approach lies in the use of runtime models that explicitly capture a network's operational and security goals, the functionality required to achieve those goals, and the configuration of the system. The MTD system reasons over these models to determine how to make changes to the system that are invisible to legitimate users but appear chaotic to an attacker.

The presented system uses these runtime models to analyze both known and unknown vulnerabilities to ensure that the necessary adaptations occur in the right areas to protect the system against specific attacker profiles.

The second paper by Autili, Ruscio, Inverardi, Pelliccione, and Tivoli, titled "ModelLAND: Where Do Models Come from?," presents the thesis that there is the need of explore techniques to automatically extract models from existent software. The chapter proposes a general overview of the motivating problem and shows two different techniques, tailored to specific domains, to automatically build models of different nature from software artefacts.

The third paper by Yu, Tun, Bandara, Zhang, and Nuseibeh, titled "Model-Driven Software Development Processes to Problem Diagnoses at Runtime," discusses the problem of the existing gap between templates and runtime-adapted models. In order to tackle this problem, the paper presents a generalization from concrete problematic examples in model-driven software development (MDSD) processes to a model-based problem diagnosis. The chapter presents a procedure that separates the automated fixes from those runtime gaps that require human judgments.

The fourth paper by Redlich, Blair, Rashid, Molka, and Gilani titled "Research Challenges for Business Process Models at Runtime" examines the potential role of business process models at runtime by discussing the state of the art of both business process modeling and models@run.time, reflecting on the nature of business processes at runtime, and highlighting key research challenges that need to be addressed to enable their use.

The fifth paper by Cazzola, Rossini, Bennett, Pradeep, and France, titled "Fine-Grained Semi-Automated Runtime Evolution," describes an approach to updating Java software at runtime through the use of runtime models consisting of UML class and sequence diagrams. Changes to models are transformed to changes on Java source code, which is then propagated to the runtime system using the JavAdaptor technology. In particular, the presented approach permits in-the-small software changes, i.e., changes at the code statement level, as opposed to in-the-large changes, i.e., changes at the component level. The chapter presents a case study that demonstrates the major aspects of the approach and its use, including results of a preliminary evaluation of the approach.

The sixth paper by Cazzola, titled "Evolution as Reflections on the Design," revisits the role that reflection and design information have in the development of self-evolving artefacts. Moreover, the author summarizes the lesson learned using a high-level reflective architecture to support dynamic self-evolution in various contexts and shows how some of the existing frameworks adhere to such architecture and how the evolution affects their structure.

The seventh paper by Trapp and Schneider titled "Safety Assurance of Open Adaptive Systems - A Survey" presents a survey that analyses the state-of-the-art of models at runtime from a safety engineering point of view in order to assess the potential of this approach and to identify gaps that have to be filled in future research to yield a safety assurance approach for open adaptive systems.

While the papers in this book cover a wide range of topics regarding the use of runtime models, additional research challenges and related research topics still exist for further investigation. For example, the following topics are prime areas for further study: (1) synthesis of software during execution using runtime models, (2) inference of new knowledge during runtime based on, for example, machine learning techniques, should be further studied to enable the incorporation of new information during the execution of the system, (3) the use of runtime models that embody distributed and composable abstractions that can be leveraged by complex forms of systems, such as cyber-physical systems, or systems of systems. Nevertheless, as organizers of the Dagstuhl meeting and editors of this collection of papers, it is our hope that this book will prove useful for both researchers and practitioners who work in the area of runtime models as guidance and a stepping-stone for future research with models@run.time.

Finally, we would like to thank all the authors of the chapters of this book for their excellent contributions, and we also thank the participants of the Dagstuhl Seminar 11481 on "Models@run.time" for their dynamic participation during the meeting and their diligent efforts afterwards in completing the roadmap chapters. Special thanks to Prof. Gordon S. Blair for the support and help in the organization of the Dagstuhl Seminar and this book. Thanks also to Alfred Hofmann and his team at Springer for helping us to publish this book. Last but not least, we deeply appreciate the great efforts of the following expert reviewers who helped us ensure that the contributions are of high quality: Thais Batista, Gordon Blair, Franck Chauvel, Peter Clarke, Laurence Duchien, Sebastian Götz, Paul Grace, Marin Litoiu, Brice Morin, Liliana, Pasquale, Patrizio Pelliccione, Rui Moreira, Vítor E. Silva Souza, Arnor Solberg, Hui Song, Matthias Tichy, Mario Trapp, Norha M. Villegas, Yijun Yu, and Gang Huang.

April 2014

Nelly Bencomo
Robert France
Betty H.C. Cheng
Uwe Aßmann

Table of Contents

A Reference Architecture and Roadmap for Models@run.time Systems

Uwe Aßmann[1], Sebastian Götz[1], Jean-Marc Jézéquel[2],
Brice Morin[3], and Mario Trapp[4]

[1] Technische Universität Dresden, Germany
uwe.assmann@tu-dresden.de, sebastian.goetz@acm.org
[2] IRISA, University of Rennes 1, France
jezequel@irisa.fr
[3] SINTEF, Norway
brice.morin@sintef.no
[4] Fraunhofer IESE, Germany
mario.trapp@iese.fraunhofer.de

Abstract. The key property of models@run.time systems is their use and provision of manageable reflection, which is characterized to be tractable and predictable and by this overcomes the limitation of reflective systems working on code, which face the problem of undecidability due to Turing-completeness. To achieve tractability, they abstract from certain aspects of their code, maintaining *runtime models* of themselves, which form the basis for reflection. In these systems, models form abstractions that neglect unnecessary details from the code, details which are not pertinent to the current purpose of reflection. Thus, models@run.time systems are a new class of reflective systems, which are characterized by their tractability, due to abstraction, and their ability to predict certain aspects of their own behavior for the future. This chapter outlines a reference architecture for models@run.time systems with the appropriate abstraction and reflection components and gives a roadmap comprised of short- and long-term research challenges for the area. Additionally, an overview of enabling and enabled technologies is provided. The chapter is concluded with a discussion of several application fields and use cases.

1 Introduction

The term "adaptive software system" is somehow a pleonasm, because software has been first invented to make hardware more flexible and adaptable to varying situations in its environment. Software has then evolved according to different paradigms. Object orientation, combined with design patterns, already provides organized means to customize or even adapt software systems (*e.g.*, Strategy pattern [GHJV95]). Current programming languages (like Java), component-based platforms (like Fractal [BCL+03] or OpenCOM [CBG+08]) or SOA platforms (e.g., OSGi [OSG12]) offer reflection APIs, which enable even more powerful dynamic adaptation (*e.g.*, based on dynamic class loading).

N. Bencomo et al. (Eds.): Models@run.time, LNCS 8378, pp. 1–18, 2014.

Traditionally the development of software systems, adaptive or not, used to be split in distinct steps with a clear distinction between design activities and runtime execution [BBF09][1]. The more critical the system is, the more choices will be made at design-time in order to reduce the reconfiguration options to a set of predictable configurations. For example, safety-critical embedded systems are designed and intensively validated at design-time (e.g., model checking) before they are actually deployed [AG93, ELLSV02]. At runtime, they have a predictable behavior, time and resource consumption, which enables *certification bodies* to approve these systems. There is, however, a growing need for more flexible adaptive systems, able to cope with unanticipated situations, still without jeopardizing safety properties. This is typically the case of Cyber-Physical Systems (CPS) as described in Section 6. Hence, new approaches are needed to enable unanticipated adaptations while ensuring guarantees. This is, in our opinion, the ultimate purpose of models@run.time.

The central advance of models@run.time systems is their use and provision of manageable reflection. In general, a reflective software system is causally connected with its code, i.e., when the code changes, the system changes too. Such a system can inspect its code (introspection), can generate new code (code generation), or even change its code (intercession). Because in most cases, Turing-complete programs are reflected about, the problems to be solved by a reflective system are undecidable and unpredictable, even at a checkpoint at runtime. Models@run.time systems improve on this problematic situation. They abstract from certain aspects of their code, maintaining *runtime models* of themselves. In these systems, models form abstractions that neglect unnecessary details from the code and from the environment, i.e., details which are not pertinent to the current purpose of reflection. In these steps, care has to be taken. In general, several models are formed and maintained at runtime, in order to cope with the information loss of abstraction. Also, it has to be ensured that abstractions work correctly, i.e., are faithful with regard to the real behavior of the software system. However, if these precautions are ensured, a models@run.time system is able to perform tractable reflection, due to the faithful abstractions, and it may predict certain aspects of its own behavior for the future. Therefore, models@run.time systems provide and use manageable reflection, which is characterized to be tractable and predictable and by this overcomes the limitation of classic reflection on code, which faces the problem of undecidability.

Taking this definition into account, models@run.time software systems turn out to be a new class of reflective systems, which are characterized by their tractability and predictability. All application domains utilizing reflective systems benefit from this advancement. In addition, two currently hot application domains, especially benefit from the advancement of models@run.time systems:

– **Cyber-Physical Systems.** Models@run.time systems reflecting upon virtual as well as physical processes in comparison to models@run.time systems, which are meant to reflect on a pure virtual system (i.e., information system).

---

[1] See in particular the side note by Finkelstein.

- **Safety-Critical Systems.** Systems, which demand for verification and certification (e.g., due to their ability to endanger the safety of human beings) in comparison to systems, which do not have such requirements.

Both application domains face the limitation of current reflective systems: undecidability. Models@run.time enable both domains to abstract all concerns of interest to reflection to the information required for the respective decisions. By this, reflection becomes manageable due to abstraction. Furthermore, both domains demand for predictive reflection, i.e., the ability to reflect upon possible future states of the system in comparison to reflect only upon the current system state (and structure).

To summarize, the key advantage of models@run.time systems over reflective software systems, achieved by modeling and separation of concerns principles, is decidability and tractability. By approaching the capabilities of intelligent thinking, we believe models@run.time is the next step in the evolution of software. Models@run.time allow to "mentally" build several potential models of reality and to mentally evaluate these models by means of what-if scenarios [BBF09][2]: *what* **would** *happen if I* **would** *do this action*? During this mental reasoning, the manipulation of the model does not impact the reality, until an acceptable solution has been found. Then, this solution is actually realized, which has an impact on the real world. In other words, the mental model is re-synchronized with the reality. In the case where a relevant aspect of the reality changes during the reasoning process, the model is updated and the reasoning process should re-build mental models, ideally by updating already existing models. This characterizes predictive reflection based on abstraction, i.e., manageable reflection. Models@run.time enable systems to reason about alternatives to reach their goals and consequences of the particular actions in comparison to classical systems which basically learn and react (*i.e.*, animal-like behavior). This includes that the system is able to justify why it takes a certain decision or not. Models@run.time have, thus, the potential to provide both flexibility and assurance, instead of a mere trade off. It can reconcile users, domain experts, engineers (aware of the obvious need for runtime adaptivity), with certification bodies (which need stringent guarantees).

In the following section we discuss, which technologies form the prerequisite for systems following the models@run.time paradigm and how models@run.time enable the development of modern software systems. Next, in section 3, we present a reference architecture for models@run.time to expose the key advancements of models@run.time over reflective systems. We summarize related work as instantiation of this reference architecture and discuss associated communities in section 4. In section 5, we provide a roadmap for models@run.time by a discussion of central, open research questions on the uses and purposes of models@run.time systems. Finally, we conclude the chapter and present compelling applications in section 6.

---

[2] See in particular the side note by Selic.

2   Enabled and Enabling Technologies for Models@run.time

In the following, we will first discuss the technologies forming the basis for models@run.time systems and then discuss the technologies enabled by models@run.time in turn.

2.1   Technologies Required by Models@run.time

Systems, according to the models@run.time paradigm, are based on the reflection principles, as defined by Bobrow *et al.*:

> *The ability of a program to manipulate as data something representing the state of the program during its own execution. There are two aspects of such manipulation: introspection and intercession. Introspection is the ability of a program to observe and therefore reason about its own state. Intercession is the ability of a program to modify its own execution state or alter its own interpretation or meaning.* [BGW93]

In practice however, reflection is a powerful yet hazardous process (see for example the drawbacks of the Java reflection API, clearly reported by Oracle[3]), since it provides no support to "preview" what will be the result of an adaptation. Basically, erroneous adaptation based on reflection can only be detected *a posteriori*, or even *post mortem* if the rollback mechanisms were not able to put the system back to a safe state. The fundamental idea behind models@run.time is to complement classic reflection with strong modeling foundations as defined by Rothenberg:

> *Modeling, in the broadest sense, is the cost-effective use of something in place of something else for some cognitive purpose. It allows us to use something that is simpler, safer or cheaper than reality instead of reality for some purpose. A model represents reality for the given purpose; the model is an abstraction of reality in the sense that it cannot represent all aspects of reality. This allows us to deal with the world in a simplified manner,* **avoiding the complexity, danger and irreversibility of reality**. [RWLN89]

The key characteristic of a models@run.time system is then its ability to project some aspects of the reality (its context, its behavior, its goals, etc.) to the modeling space in order to enable tractable decisions, in a safe space, to produce decidable plans. This is basically separation of concerns [Dij82] applied in a disciplined way at runtime, and to some extent, how human thinking works.

> *What to my taste is* **characteristic for all intelligent thinking**. *It is, that one is willing to study in depth an aspect of one's subject matter in isolation for the sake of its own consistency, all the time knowing that*

---

[3] http://docs.oracle.com/javase/tutorial/reflect/

one is occupying oneself only with one of the aspects. It is "the separation of concerns". It does not mean ignoring the other aspects, it is just doing justice to the fact that from this aspect's point of view, the other is irrelevant. It is being one- and multiple-track minded simultaneously. [Dij82]

We perceive reflection, modeling and separation of concerns as the three main pillars to achieve models@run.time and make future software systems able of *intelligent thinking*, i.e., abstract, predictive reflection.

2.2 Technologies Enabled by Models@run.time

Models@run.time as a technology enables various further technologies. Of particular interest is the possibility to realize *safe adaptive systems*. The key problem of such systems is the contradiction between safety and adaptivity. To ensure safety, all variants of the system have to be checked against possible threats, usually at design time. In highly adaptive systems, the number of system variants usually grows exponentially and, thus, prolongs the safety check to an unfeasible degree. The reasoner of models@run.time systems allows for postponing safety checks to the runtime of the system as has been shown in [ST11]. In consequence, only those variants of the system have to be checked, which are reachable from the current variant. This significantly lowers the amount of variants to be considered and, thus, enables the realization of safe adaptive systems.

Furthermore, models@run.time enable the realization of *Cyber-Physical Systems (CPS)*, which are adaptive systems integrating the virtual and physical world. A central requirement for CPS is safety, due to the physical part of the system. This is because the physical actions of a CPS are able to threat human life, the environment or the system itself. In addition, CPS are adaptive systems, because they naturally adjust themselves continuously to the their environment. In consequence, models@run.time is the key enabling technology for CPS, because models@run.time enable the realization of safe adaptive systems.

Besides these two particular application domains, all domains, which already make use of reflection, benefit from the advancements by models@run.time.

3   A Reference Architecture for Models@run.time Systems

The goal of this section is to understand how models@run.time are key enablers for modern software systems, to clarify their typical use cases and fundamental interests, as well as to define a reference architecture for models@run.time. Based on our recent experiences (*e.g.*, in the DiVA project [FS09, MBNJ09] and the MQuAT approach [GWCA11, GWCA12]), we propose the generic reference architecture (RA) depicted in Figure 1, which provides a generic framework for models@run.time, and which is meant to be instantiated for different domains.

According to the reference architecture, a models@run.time system always interfaces with a managed system, which is monitored and controlled by the

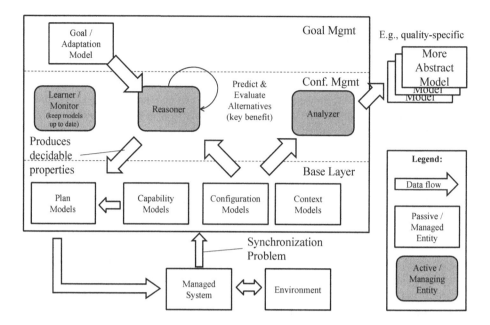

Fig. 1. Reference Architecture for models@run.time Systems

managing models@run.time system. Notably, a models@run.time system is not directly interfaced to the environment. Instead, the managed system's sensors and actuators are utilized for this purpose. The managed system can be any observable and controllable system (e.g., a personal computer, a wireless sensor network, a robot or a managing models@run.time system again). Each models@run.time system comprises three layers, comparable to the layers of Kramer and Magee [KM09]. From bottom to top these are:

- a base layer comprising models of the managed system,
- a configuration management layer comprising active components of the system realizing the feedback loop on the managed system and
- a goal management layer comprising models of the system's goals, realizing an internal feedback loop between the goal management layer as managing element and the configuration management layer as managed element.

3.1   Runtime Models of the Base Layer

The *base layer* comprises four types of models, which are abstractions of specific aspects of the system for a given purpose:

Context Models contain relevant information about the current state of the managed system's environment, *e.g.*, the current temperature, or higher level context information such as an alert information derived by aggregating or interpreting the information of different sensors. The interpretation of context information is context-dependent itself. For example, a temperature of 50 °C will be interpreted as "hot" as a room temperature, but as "cold" for a furnace. To keep this type of model synchronous to the environment, the sensors of the managed system are utilized. Context models do not cover information about the managed system, but only of the environment's observable state.

Configuration Models express the current configuration of the managed system, i.e., its current state. Current models@run.time approaches usually provide an architectural view on the managed system (i.e., which services are currently deployed and running on which resources). Both, configuration and context models, cover the abstracted runtime state subject to tractable, predictive reflection.

Capability Models describe the features available to influence the managed system (*e.g.*, whether software components can be added/removed and rebound, whether parameters of system components can be adjusted), which actuators are available and how they can affect the environment. Typically this model is rather static and depends on the underlying infrastructure. However, this model can be updated, *e.g.*, after a new actuator has been added in the system.

Plan Models describe a set of actions (according to the capability models) to be performed by the system to realize an adaptation. They represent reconfiguration or action scripts, which describe how the managed system shall be reconfigured and how the actuators of the managed systems shall be used to effect the environment.

3.2 The Configuration Management Layer

The *configuration management layer* contains the active entities of a models@run.time system, which make use of the models of the base layer. This layer typically comprises a reasoner, an analyzer and optionally a learner.

The **reasoner's** evaluates alternative future configurations of the system. This includes (1) to realize the predictive reflection, (2) to identify the best configuration w.r.t. the goals specified on the top layer, and (3) to derive reconfiguration or action plans to establish the envisioned system configuration. To evaluate possible future configurations, the reasoner uses the information provided by the context and configuration models, representing the managed system and its environment's state, and derives possible variations of them, which are reachable in the future, based on the capabilities of the managed system covered by the capability models. To identify the best future configuration w.r.t. the system's goals, the reasoner evaluates each possible future system variant against the goal models of the top layer. To derive reconfiguration plans, the system compares the current system configuration with the envisioned system configuration and deduces a sequence of actions to be taken based on the capability model of the base layer. By these means, the reasoner creates the plan models of the base layer.

The **analyzer** has two tasks. First, the analyzer has to detect whether the whole system (i.e., managed and managing system) should be re-evaluated. To do so, the current system state has to be evaluated against the system's goals. If the current system state deviates from the goals, the analyzer will trigger the reasoner, to compute a reconfiguration plan. Second, the analyzer further abstracts the information contained in the models of the base layer. This raises the level of abstraction of the models and, in turn, to lower the complexity of predictive reflection. The analyzer has to abstract the context, configuration and capability models of the base layer to ensure the existence of a capability model on the same level of abstraction for the abstracted context and configuration models. Based on this, models@run.time systems can manage models@run.time system too. The analyzer realizes the bridge between the models@run.time system on lower and higher abstraction level.

The **learner** has two tasks, too. On the one side, the learner is responsible to keep the models of the base layer synchronized with the system. Thus, the learner utilizes the managed systems sensors to capture the environment's state and continuously observes the managed system itself to update the context and configuration model on the base layer. On the other side, the learner can observe the reasoner to detect, whether the decisions of the reasoner are beneficial on the long run or not. Thus, whereas the reasoner evaluates possible future scenarios based on the current system's state, the learner takes into account the system's history to deduce, whether the comparably shortsighted decisions of the reasoner are meaningful and correct on the long run. Based on this, the learner can provide the reasoner with additional (historical) information, to improve the quality of decision making over time.

3.3   The Goal Management Layer

Finally, the *goal management layer* comprises **goal models** of the system, which are used by the reasoner to evaluate the alternative future configurations with respect to the fulfillment of the specified goals. Notably, these goal models can and should be able to change over time, because changes in the context of the system could require adjustments to the goals. This depicts the need for the last feature of the reference architecture: as models@run.time systems are systems themselves, they can be stacked. That is a models@run.time system could monitor and control another models@run.time system. As each models@run.time system realizes a feedback loop, the proposed reference architecture allows for the development of layered feedback loops as has been shown in the Collaborative Research Centre 614 [ADG+09], which focused on self-optimizing systems in mechanical engineering. The proposed architecture is represented as an operator-controller-module (OCM), which realizes three layers of feedback loops. The bottommost layer contains the controller, which directly controls the physical system. On top of the controller, the reflective operator is situated, which is capable of operation scheduling. That is—in contrast to the controller layer— the reflective operator is able to plan the future behavior of the physical system. Finally, the topmost layer comprises the cognitive operator, which is capable of more complex planning methods and utilizes techniques from machine learning. Thus, from bottom to top, the models of the system, utilized by the layers, get more and more abstract, but the applicable techniques get more and more powerful.

In summary, the key advancements over state of the art of models@run.time systems are realized by the reasoner and the analyzer respectively:

1. **Predictive Reflection.** The ability of reasoning about *future* configurations of the system is the advance of models@run.time systems over reflective systems, which are able to reason on the current, but not on future configurations of a system.
2. **Tractability by Abstraction.** The ability of the analyzer to abstract the information used by the reasoner (possibly multiple times) allows for reduction of the reasoning task's complexity and, thus, to get decidability and, finally, tractability of the overall system.

4   Literature Review

4.1   Instantiations of the Reference Architecture

The DiVA project proposes a reference architecture which leverages models@run.time to support dynamic variability [MBNJ09, MBJ+09]. A feature model describes the variability of the system. A reasoner component takes this variability model as input, as well as a model of the context, to compute a set of features well suited to the current context (not necessarily the best). A weaver component then composes these features to produce an architectural model, describing the configuration. This configuration is checked at runtime (since it is not possible to check all possible configuration at design time) and the system is automatically adapted to reflect this architectural model. If the model is invalid, the reasoner computes another configuration.

In [FMS11], the DiVA reference architecture has been instantiated in a different way to fit the need of low-power embedded systems (8-bits, 16MHz, 1Kb RAM). In this setup, the adaptation logic is fully simulated at design-time, so the number of configurations to be addressed by such a small node remains tractable. The adaptation process is compiled into a state machine, which is then merged with the core logic (also expressed as a state machine). The resulting state machine is finally compiled into C code to be deployed on the micro-controller.

The multi-quality auto-tuning (MQuAT) approach [GWCA11, GWCA12] developed in the collaborative research center 912 and preceding projects particularly focuses on self-optimizing systems following economic principles by multi-objective optimization (i.e., the system is optimized w.r.t. the optimal tradeoff between multiple objectives, which represent either cost or utilities). The main constituents of MQuAT are: (1) the cool component model (CCM) and the quality contract language (QCL), which are meta-model defined concepts to be used to specify self-optimizing systems, and (2) the runtime environment THEATRE (THE Auto-Tuning Runtime Environment), which comprises resource managers to monitor and control the target system and control loop managers, which realize the reasoner component by means of an adaptive multi-objective optimizer (i.e., various implementations of the optimizer exist, whereof continuously the best is chosen, based on the current context). A key characteristic of MQuAT is the application of quality contracts, which cover dependencies between non-functional properties of system components (both software and hardware), to reduce the amount of system configurations, which need to be considered during optimization.

In [SCG+12] the MQuAT reference architecture has been instantiated for multi-tenant applications—applications hosted in the cloud, which are configured by tenants, whose customers use the application. This type of application introduces a further restrictions on possible system configurations, due to tenant constraints like the exclusive use of a single server or the restriction to only use servers within a certain country.

A further reference architecture is ConFract [CCOR06], which particularly focuses on self-healing systems. In this approach functional contracts are used to specify how a valid system is characterized and to initiate self-healing in case of contract violations. The developer is able to explicitly specify resource usage profilers as part of the system. In consequence, the functional contracts, which use data generated by these profilers, can be used as non-functional contracts, so dependencies between non-functional properties can be expressed too.

In [CGK+11], Calinescu et al. present QoSMOS–a generic architecture for adaptive service-based systems (SBS). The central constituents of QoSMOS are formal specifications of QoS requirements (using probabilistic temporal logics) including the specification of dependencies between QoS requirements, model-based QoS evaluation using verification techniques, learning monitoring of QoS properties and reasoning techniques, based on high-level, user-specified goals and multi-objective utility functions. QoSMOS is an instance of our proposed reference architecture, which focuses specifically on SBS comprised of a set of web services under the control of a workflow engine.

4.2   Relevant Communities

Models@run.time are relevant to several research communities as depicted in Fig. 2. Among them two types of communities can be distinguished. First, communities which provide fundamental techniques for models@run.time. Second, communities which benefit from the advancements by models@run.time and provide use cases in turn.

Three communities are relevant to models@run.time in particular: the **self-adaptive systems** (SAS), the **autonomous computing** and **middleware** community. The first two communities investigate systems, which adjust themselves according to changes in their environment. The middleware community covers, among others, the problem how to coordinate multiple independent systems. Whereas the SAS community focuses on a top-down approach w.r.t. the coordination of multiple systems, the autonomous computing community focuses on bottom-up approaches (self-organization), where the coordination originates from each individual system [ST09]. For this purpose, all three communities rely on reflection to observe and adjust the systems they manage or coordinate. Hence, the advanced reflection mechanisms of models@run.time enable

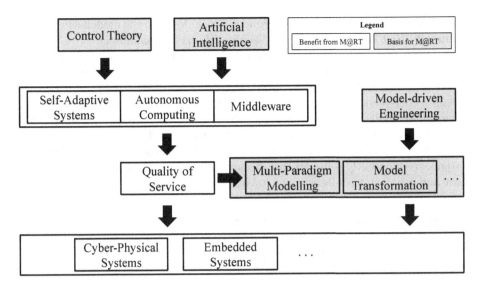

Fig. 2. Research Communities Relevant to Models@run.time

advancements in these communities, which provide use cases to models@run.time in turn.

All three communities rent many concepts from the **control theory** and the **artificial intelligence** community. Whereas control theory covers systems adjusting themselves to external influences in general, artificial intelligence provides, among others, planning and analysis techniques to coordinate autonomous systems.

Another set of communities relevant to models@run.time are those focusing on **quality-of-service** optimization and assurance. This includes various specialized communities which cover particular non-functional properties. For example, *performance, fault-tolerance, safety, physical dynamics* and *energy*. Each community requires means to model the (non-functional) behavior of a system subject to optimization or assurance w.r.t. the specific non-functional property of interest. To realize optimization or assurance, again reflection is used as a basis. Especially, the prediction capabilities of models@run.time are beneficial for these communities. In turn, they provide use cases to models@run.time.

The **model-driven engineering** community provides fundamental techniques to models@run.time. Besides general modeling techniques, solutions to particular problems for models@run.time are addressed by this community. For example, model evolution, model transformation, model synchronization and model-based diagnostics, where each problem usually forms its own community.

To cover multiple aspects of a system's non-functional behavior, modeling techniques from different domains are to be integrated or bridged. This challenge is addressed by the **multi-domain/multi-paradigm** modelling community.

Hence, this community provides fundamental techniques to the models@run.time community that can be useed by the *quality-of-service* community.

Moreover, especially the **cyber-physical systems** community demands for multi-domain modelling (physical dynamics combined with computational models). It is yet another community, which makes use of models@run.time. This is because cyber-physical systems are self-adaptive or autonomous systems, where a particular challenge is the management of multiple non-functional properties from different domains. This includes the **embedded systems** community, which starts to investigate networked embedded systems. Notably, embedded systems are inherently self-adaptive, because they are embedded in an environment and are meant to observe and/or influence it.

5   Short and Long-Term Research Questions - A Roadmap

In the following, open research challenges for models@run.time will be discussed. We examine short-term research topics, followed by long-term research topics.

5.1   Short-Term Research Challenges

As short-term research challenges, we identified the application of MDE techniques, the optimization of reasoning and reconfiguration in terms of efficiency (i.e., optimal tradeoff between cost and utility), the management of uncertainty inherent to models@run.time, synchronization of reflexive models and safety assurance at runtime. In the following, we elaborate on each challenge.

Model-Driven Engineering. Modeling is a central constituent of models@run.time. Hence, in theory, models@run.time could directly benefit from tools and approaches developed by the Model-Driven Engineering (MDE) community: metamodels, editors, simulators, compilers, etc. In practice, however, it is difficult to embedded MDE tools at runtime, since these tools, usually thought for design-time usages in a rather standalone and controlled environment (IDE), come with important memory and performance (time) penalties. Thus, current MDE techniques should be investigated, extended, adjusted and/or directly be applied to models@run.time.

Efficiency @ Runtime. Dynamic adaptation of a software application is a process that might take some time, which–depending on the context–might or might not be an issue. For example doing some reconfiguration to better balance load and energy consumption in a cloud might afford a reconfiguration delay of several seconds, while an interactive system should be able to handle the overall reconfiguration in less than 200 ms. Even worse, if we want to push these system towards safety critical, real-time embedded systems, the constraints might be much harsher.

In our experience, the two main limiting factors in reconfiguring an application are (1) the time and resources taken for the reasoning itself (compute which configuration is to be chosen) and the (2) the adaptation itself (e.g., stopping and starting components, loading new code, transferring state, etc.).

On the first account, one challenge is of course to leverage reasoning techniques that might be able to make the right tradeoff between time and intelligence. New advances in incremental reasoning, or time constrained reasoners might also be needed. The layering ability of models@run.time (i.e., the ability to manage models@run.time systems by models@run.time systems themselves) allows to adapt or optimize the reasoning and reconfiguration itself. The key challenge to be addressed here are (a) the assessment of reasoners and reconfigurations in terms of their costs (time, energy, etc.) and resulting utility and (b) the determination of cost budgets, which most not be exceeded by reasoning and reconfiguration. For example, if a system can perform a task either in one minute or, if reconfigured, in half a minute, the time budget for reasoning and reconfiguration is less than half a minute. If reasoning and reconfiguration take more than half a minute, the gain of running the task on the reconfigured system is lost.

Additionally, on the adaptation process itself, a few points are subject to possible optimizations, combining system issues (such as maintaining caches for frequently used configurations, efficient code loading, light component models etc.) with optimizations in the reconfiguration planning algorithms taking into account the specificity of the underlying platforms.

Managing Uncertainty. Systems adhering to the models@run.time paradigm have to cope with the uncertainty of the systems they manage or, in other words, uncertainty is inherent to models@run.time systems. This is because the managed systems environment is uncertain by nature. Hence, novel approaches, which enable reasoning in the presence of uncertainty are required.

Handling Reflexive Models of Distributed Systems. Handling reflexive models of distributed systems is a well-known issue in the distributed systems community. Having a centralized reasoner working on a centralized model of a distributed system makes little sense for reliability and robustness reasons, but managing a distributed model implies that the reasoner has to also handle consensus and synchronization issues. Several works already go into that direction [ECBP11], but more is to be done to also deal with performance issues and real-time constraints.

Realizing Safety Assurance at Runtime. Most of the safety-critical business nowadays follows very stringent procedures that are statically checked, most often under strict legal regulation as it is the case in the aerospace domain. Such systems can still be somehow adaptive within well defined boundaries (often called *modes*). There are typically very few modes (such as *normal mode, recovery mode, survival mode, panic mode*, etc.). They are well identified and individually checked for safety. All possible transitions between modes are also checked.

Providing the same level of safety for systems having modes only computed at runtime would imply having the same level of safety checking done on the fly at runtime. While using verification technologies such as *Model Checking* at runtime (using, e.g., the power of the cloud) is no longer considered as science-fiction, it is clear that this is still a challenge, and the proof that models@run.time can be safe and adaptive concurrently even in principle remains to be made.

5.2   Longer-Term Research Challenges

Several challenges of models@run.time, which demand for long-term investigation, can be identified. This includes the handling of quality interferences, the handling of interconnected control loops and the attainment of predictability by top-level feedback loops.

Quality Interferences. As has been pointed out by Salehie and Tahvildari [ST09], most of the current approaches to self-adaptive software exploit only a single quality. The exclusive focus on either reliability or energy or performance or security hides the problem of interferences and general dependencies between qualities. To consider multiple qualities simultaneously, their interdependent behavior needs to be determined and considered in the reasoning approaches. Thus, the monitoring and analysis phase need to be aware of the dependencies between qualities, which leads to a combinatorial explosion of cases to be considered in these two phases (i.e., all situations need to be investigated for all combinations of qualities). In addition, the reasoning approaches for the decision or planning phase need to support multi-objective decision-making, which is known to be an NP-hard problem. Finally, approaches for the act or execute phase need to consider quality interferences too, because their actions might imply a chain of reactions w.r.t. the quality assurance of the system. Thus, all phases of the feedback loop need to be investigated w.r.t. dependencies and interferences between qualities.

Interconnection of Multiple Feedback Loops. The need for multiple, interconnected feedback loops arises from the need for seamless system integration as envisioned by the CPS or Systems-of-Systems community. If multiple models@run.time systems are meant to cooperate, their feedback loops need to be capable of cooperation too. But, the interconnection of multiple feedback loops (e.g., in terms of layers as has been shown in CRC 614 [ADG+09]) opens further research questions, which affect all aspects of self-adaptive systems. The monitoring and analysis phase need to be aware that the system under investigation might not be a (continuous) physical system, but is itself a (discrete) models@run.time system. The same holds for the decision-making or planning and the act or execute phase, which, for example, need to differentiate between continuous and discrete systems. Clear interfaces between models@run.time systems, which are subject to integration, are required. Besides differentiating between continuous and discrete systems, the architecture or architectural style of a models@run.time system is a key characteristic, which needs to be considered throughout the complete feedback loop of a dependent models@run.time system.

Predictability. Maybe the central challenge of models@run.time system is to reach full predictability of their behavior. The underlying problem is the dichotomy of adaptivity and predictability. Models@run.time systems are highly adaptive systems, but demand for precise predictability to enable more intelligent reasoning approaches. Precise predictability is a key enabler for several technologies as explained in section 2.

6 Conclusion

As highlighted by important roadmaps in research and industry, cyber-physical systems [Lee08] are considered to be the next generation of embedded systems. For example, in the agricultural domain already today it is possible to connect a tractor with another autonomously driving tractor [Fen11]. In the near future, this kind of interconnection of different systems is expected to increase rapidly throughout a broad range of further application domains such as automotive and healthcare. In the former, cars will dynamically connect to each other to implement functionalities like automated cross roads assistants [Con11]. In the latter, medical devices, telecommunication infrastructure and IT-based service systems will build dynamic ecosystems leading to a new generation of health care systems [All11].

All of these examples share the commonality that different devices, machines, and vehicles are integrated at runtime and that they have to adapt to dynamically changing environment contexts. In consequence, neither the structure nor the behavior of the cyber-physical systems can entirely be predicted at design time. This greatly complicates the assurance of important functional and nonfunctional properties - up to the point of impossibility for some cases. One of these particularly difficult cases is the assurance of safety, which is nevertheless mandatory since many of these cyber-physical systems are inherently safety-critical. As of today, only proprietary approaches are used to ensure safety of strictly predefined machine combinations. This obviously requires an immense effort and strongly limits the desired flexibility. Since traditional approaches are not expected to scale to adequately address cyber-physical systems, safety is a bottle neck preventing the transition from a promising idea to a real business success. Thus, there is an inescapable need for new approaches enabling the development of dynamically adaptive yet safe cyber-physical systems.

Solving this challenge can be a killer application for models@run.time. Regarding the examples mentioned above, it is not any longer the question whether dynamic adaptation is necessary or not. It is the question how important properties such as safety can be assured in the context of open adaptive cyber-physical systems. A general solution approach is to shift parts of the required assurance measures into runtime by means of adequate models@run.time. As opposed to other approaches, models@run.time explicitly define all facets of the dynamic adaptation behavior of a system. Moreover, models@run.time enable a system to systematically reason at runtime about its current quality state, to predict the impact of possible system modifications on system quality, and, therefore, to select safe adaptation strategies following predictable and traceable rationales.

Particularly safety, as a bottleneck to business success, can be an important factor to create the pressure necessary to introduce a new technology. So the idea of using models@run.time for assuring safety in cyber-physical system can be a door opening killer application for models@run.time. Once the door is opened, the application can easily be extended to any other quality properties.

In summary, models@run.time advance over reflective systems in that they offer abstract, tractable and predictive reflection as shown by the reference architecture presented in section 3. This enables improvements to existing application domains, which already make use of reflection, and–in particular–enables the realization of safety-critical, cyber-physical systems.

References

[ADG+09]   Adelt, P., Donoth, J., Gausemeier, J., Geisler, J., Henkler, S., Kahl, S., Klöpper, B., Krupp, A., Münch, E., Oberthür, S., Paiz, C., Podlogar, H., Porrmann, M., Radkowski, R., Romaus, C., Schmidt, A., Schulz, B., Vöcking, H., Witkowski, U., Witting, K., Znamenshchykov, O.: Selbstoptimierende Systeme des Maschinenbaus - Definitionen, Anwendungen, Konzepte. HNI-Verlagsschriftenreihe (2009)

[AG93]   Atlee, J.M., Gannon, J.: State-based model checking of event-driven system requirements. IEEE Transactions on Software Engineering 19, 24–40 (1993)

[All11]   The Continua Alliance. The continua alliance webpage, http://www.continuaalliance.org (visited on December 14, 2011)

[BBF09]   Blair, G., Bencomo, N., France, R.B.: Models@run.time. IEEE Computer 42(10), 22–27 (2009)

[BCL+03]   Bruneton, E., Coupaye, T., Leclercq, M., Quéma, V., Stefani, J.-B.: The fractal component model and its support in java. Software Practice and Experience 36(11-12), 1257–1284 (2003)

[BGW93]   Bobrow, D., Gabriel, R., White, J.: Clos in context—the shape of the design. In: Paepcke, A. (ed.) Object-Oriented Programming: The CLOS Perspective, pp. 29–61. MIT Press (1993)

[CBG+08]   Coulson, G., Blair, G., Grace, P., Taiani, F., Joolia, A., Lee, K., Ueyama, J., Sivaharan, T.: A generic component model for building systems software. ACM Transactions on Computer Systems 26, 1:1–1:42 (2008)

[CCOR06]   Chang, H., Collet, P., Ozanne, A., Rivierre, N.: From Components to Autonomic Elements Using Negotiable Contracts. In: Yang, L.T., Jin, H., Ma, J., Ungerer, T. (eds.) ATC 2006. LNCS, vol. 4158, pp. 78–89. Springer, Heidelberg (2006)

[CGK+11]   Calinescu, R., Grunske, L., Kwiatkowska, M., Mirandola, R., Tamburrelli, G.: Dynamic QoS Management and Optimization in Service-Based Systems. IEEE Transactions on Software Engineering 37(3), 387–409 (2011)

[Con11]   Car2Car Communication Consortium. Car2car communication consor-
            tium webpage, http://www.car2car.org (visited on December 14, 2011)
[Dij82]   Dijkstra, E.W.: On the role of scientific thought. In: Selected Writings
            on Computing: A Personal Perspective, pp. 60–66. Springer (1982)
[ECBP11]   Etchevers, X., Coupaye, T., Boyer, F., De Palma, N.: Self-configuration
            of distributed applications in the cloud. In: IEEE CLOUD, pp. 668–675
            (2011)
[ELLSV02]   Edwards, S., Lavagno, L., Lee, E.A., Sangiovanni-Vincentelli, A.: Design
            of embedded systems: formal models, validation, and synthesis. In: Read-
            ings in Hardware/software Co-Design, pp. 86–107. Kluwer Academic
            Publishers, Norwell (2002)
[Fen11]   AGCO Fendt. Fendt guideconnect: Two tractors - one driver. Website
            (2011)
[FMS11]   Fleurey, F., Morin, B., Solberg, A.: A model-driven approach to develop
            adaptive firmwares. In: SEAMS 2011: ICSE Symposium on Software
            Engineering for Adaptive and Self-Managing Systems, SEAMS 2011,
            Waikiki, Honolulu, USA, May 23-24, pp. 168–177 (2011)
[FS09]   Fleurey, F., Solberg, A.: A Domain Specific Modeling Language Support-
            ing Specification, Simulation and Execution of Dynamic Adaptive Sys-
            tems. In: Schürr, A., Selic, B. (eds.) MODELS 2009. LNCS, vol. 5795,
            pp. 606–621. Springer, Heidelberg (2009)
[GHJV95]   Gamma, E., Helm, R., Johnson, R., Vlissides, J.: Design Patterns: El-
            ements of reusable Object-Oriented Software. Addison-Wesley Profes-
            sional (1995)
[GWCA11]   Götz, S., Wilke, C., Cech, S., Aßmann, U.: Runtime variability manage-
            ment for energy-efficient software by contract negotiation. In: Proceed-
            ings of the 6th International Workshop Models@run.time, MRT 2011
            (2011)
[GWCA12]   Götz, S., Wilke, C., Cech, S., Aßmann, U.: Architecture and Mechanisms
            for Energy Auto Tuning. In: Sustainable ICTs and Management Systems
            for Green Computing. IGI Global (June 2012)
[KM09]   Kramer, J., Magee, J.: A rigorous architectural approach to adaptive
            software engineering. Journal of Computer Science and Technology 24(2),
            183–188 (2009)
[Lee08]   Lee, E.A.: Cyber physical systems: Design challenges. In: 2008 11th IEEE
            International Symposium on Object Oriented Real-Time Distributed
            Computing (ISORC), pp. 363–369 (May 2008)
[MBJ+09]   Morin, B., Barais, O., Jezequel, J.-M., Fleurey, F., Solberg, A.: Models@
            run.time to support dynamic adaptation. IEEE Computer 42(10), 44–51
            (2009)
[MBNJ09]   Morin, B., Barais, O., Nain, G., Jézéquel, J.-M.: Taming Dynamically
            Adaptive Systems Using Models and Aspects. In: International Confer-
            ence on Software Engineering (ICSE2009). IEEE, Los Alamitos (2009)
[OSG12]   OSGi Alliance. Osgi core release 5 (March 2012)
[RWLN89]   Rothenberg, J., Widman, L.E., Loparo, K.A., Nielsen, N.R.: The Nature of
            Modeling. In: Artificial Intelligence, Simulation and Modeling, pp. 75–92.
            John Wiley & Sons (1989)
[SCG+12]   Schroeter, J., Cech, S., Götz, S., Wilke, C., Assmann, U.: Towards mod-
            eling a variable architecture for multi-tenant saas-applications. In: Pro-
            ceedings of Sixth International Workshop on Variability Modelling of
            Software-Intensive Systems, VaMoS 2012 (2012)

[ST09]   Salehie, M., Tahvildari, L.: Self-adaptive software: Landscape and re-
          search challenges. ACM Transactions on Autonomous and Adaptive Sys-
          tems 14, 14:1–14:42 (2009)
[ST11]   Schneider, D., Trapp, M.: A safety engineering framework for open adap-
          tive systems. In: Proceedings of Fifth IEEE International Conference
          on Self-Adaptive and Self-Organizing Systems (SASO 2011), pp. 89–98.
          IEEE (2011)

Mechanisms for Leveraging Models at Runtime in Self-adaptive Software

Amel Bennaceur[1], Robert France[2], Giordano Tamburrelli[3], Thomas Vogel[4],
Pieter J. Mosterman[5], Walter Cazzola[6], Fabio M. Costa[7],
Alfonso Pierantonio[8], Matthias Tichy[9], Mehmet Akşit[10], Pär Emmanuelson[11],
Huang Gang[12], Nikolaos Georgantas[1], and David Redlich[13]

[1] Inria, France
[2] Colorado State University, US
[3] Università della Svizzera Italiana, Switzerland
[4] Hasso Plattner Institute at the University of Potsdam, Germany
[5] MathWorks, US
[6] Università degli Studi di Milano, Italy
[7] Universidade Federal de Goiás, Brazil
[8] Univ. degli Studi di L'Aquila, Italy
[9] Chalmers, University of Gothenburg, Sweden
[10] University of Twente, Netherlands
[11] Ericsson AB, Sweden
[12] Peking University, China
[13] Lancaster University, UK

Abstract. Modern software systems are often required to adapt their behavior at runtime in order to maintain or enhance their utility in dynamic environments. Models at runtime research aims to provide suitable abstractions, techniques, and tools to manage the complexity of adapting software systems at runtime. In this chapter, we discuss challenges associated with developing mechanisms that leverage models at runtime to support runtime software adaptation. Specifically, we discuss challenges associated with developing effective mechanisms for supervising running systems, reasoning about and planning adaptations, maintaining consistency among multiple runtime models, and maintaining fidelity of runtime models with respect to the running system and its environment. We discuss related problems and state-of-the-art mechanisms, and identify open research challenges.

1 Introduction

Many modern distributed and open software-based systems are required to adapt their behavior at runtime in order to maintain or enhance their utility [19, 58]. *Models at runtime* (M@RT) research focuses on how models describing different aspects of a software system and its environment (e.g., requirements, design, runtime configuration) can be used to manage the complexity of effectively adapting software systems at runtime [11, 40]. This chapter is a distillation of discus-

N. Bencomo et al. (Eds.): Models@run.time, LNCS 8378, pp. 19–46, 2014.

sions held in a working group at the *Dagstuhl Seminar on Models@run.time*[1]. The working group discussions focused on challenges associated with developing M@RT mechanisms to support runtime software adaptation. Specifically, we discussed challenges associated with developing mechanisms for (1) creating runtime models, and updating them in response to changes in the system and its environment, (2) reasoning about changes in the system, its requirements, or the environment to select or produce appropriate adaptation strategies, (3) analyzing and maintaining multiple runtime models, which represent different aspects of the running system or its environment, and (4) establishing and maintaining fidelity of the runtime models with respect to the running system, its requirements, and its environment.

It is important to notice that M@RT can support a plethora of tasks other than software adaptation, such as for example software auditing and monitoring. However, software adaptation is by far the most challenging application of M@RT mechanisms and thus represents the focus of our discussions. Analogously, it also important to mention that M@RT is not the only way to implement self-adaptive systems even if it represents a common approach.

We developed a *conceptual M@RT reference model* to provide a framework for our discussions. The reference model is based on what we considered to be core M@RT concepts and terminology, and it was used to situate the mechanisms we discussed. For each mechanism we identified challenges associated with its development and use in the context of the reference model. In addition, we reviewed the state of the art and formulated open research challenges for the mechanisms. The discussions raised a number of challenging research questions, for example, *What are the key abstractions needed to support effective M@RT adaptation?* and *How can these abstractions be used to create appropriate adaptation mechanisms in open settings, e.g., in Internet of Things and Cyber-Physical Systems?*

In contrast to other work that discusses the state of the art and research challenges for self-adaptive software systems [19, 58, 75, 79], our discussions focused on adaptive systems based on M@RT.

The chapter is structured as follows. Section 2 presents the terminology and the conceptual reference model we used to frame our discussions. Section 3 discusses the challenges associated with developing appropriate M@RT mechanisms. Section 4 reviews the state of the art and discuss open research challenges. Finally, Section 5 concludes with an overview of the major contributions of this chapter.

2   Terminology and Reference Model for M@RT

In this section, we define the terminology underlying the conceptual reference model for M@RT that will be presented afterwards and used to frame our discussions in the rest of the paper. The terminology and the conceptual reference model presented here are generic so that they can be applied to a wide variety

---

[1] Dagstuhl Seminar 11481: http://www.dagstuhl.de/11481

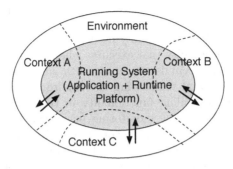

Fig. 1. A Terminological Framework for M@RT

of adaptive software systems driven by M@RT, including open, distributed, and embedded systems (e.g., cyber-physical systems) and cloud-based systems.

2.1 Terminology

One of the key questions we attempted to answer was the following: *What constitutes a M@RT system?*, i.e., *What are the major parts of an adaptive software system in which adaptation is driven by models?* The terminological framework we converged on during the discussion is shown in Figure 1. The *Running System* shown in the framework represents the executing software system. The *Environment* represents the external elements that the Running System interacts with to fulfill its requirements. The Environment corresponds to the concept of *World* that interacts with the *Machine* (i.e., the Running System) in the seminal work by Jackson and Zave [51, 101].

The usage and operation of a M@RT system can be influenced by one or more *Contexts*, that is, a context can determine how a M@RT system adapts itself to changes in its environment. For example, the types of adaptations that software on a mobile device can undergo may vary based on the device's location and time at which the change occurred; both time and location define the context. Context elements may include elements from the Running System, including hardware resources and network elements, and elements from the environment, for example, the location and time. Moreover, it is important to note that different contexts may also overlap.

A *Running System* consists of two major parts:

The Application: This part of the system is concerned with delivering the desired functionality and with adapting how the desired functionality is delivered to users or other systems.

The Runtime Platform: This part of the system provides the infrastructure on top of which the *Application* runs. For example, it can consist of middleware, a language runtime environment, an operating system, a virtualization system, and hardware resources.

The *Application* may be further broken down into the following parts:

Core: This is the "default" functionality used to meet users' functional requirements. It is the functionality that executes when the system is first started.

Supervision: This component is concerned with supervising the behavior of
the Running System and monitoring the Environment. It triggers appropriate adaptations by calling functionality in the Adaptation part of the
Application (see below). The monitoring performed by this component is
model-driven, that is, monitoring involves providing and maintaining runtime models of the running system and its environment. Note that this
component is responsible for the monitoring aspect of the MAPE-K (Monitor, Analyse, Plan, Execute, Knowledge) model [50] proposed for autonomic
control systems.

Adaptation: This component is in charge of reasoning, planning, and enforcing
adaptations on parts of the Running System. The adaptation functionality is
triggered by the Supervision component. In a M@RT system, the adaptation
functionality is driven by models. Note that this component is responsible
for the analysis, planning, and execution aspects of the MAPE-K model.

It is important to understand what can and cannot be adapted by a M@RT
system. Therefore, the concepts in the terminological framework are classified as
adaptable, non-adaptable, or *semi-adaptable.* Adaptable entities are those whose
behaviors can be modified at runtime by the system. The Core part of an Application is an adaptable entity because it has been designed for adaptability by
software developers. The Supervision and Adaptation parts can conceivably be
designed for adaptation, for example, it may be possible to use what the system
"learned" from past applications of adaptation rules to improve the adaptation
mechanisms. On the other hand, the environment is typically a non-adaptable
entity since it consists of entities external to the system (e.g., users) that cannot
be controlled by the system[2] Some elements in the Runtime Platform may be
semi-adaptable, that is, it may be possible to partially modify or configure them
at runtime (e.g., by tuning certain parameters of the operating system, or setting
the configuration of hardware devices).

The conceptual reference model for M@RT presented in the following subsection is based on the above terminological framework.

2.2   A Conceptual Reference Model for M@RT

The conceptual reference model we propose is structured into four levels ($M0$,
$M1$, $M2$, and $M3$) as illustrated in Figure 2. The $M0$ level consists of the Running System that observes and interacts with the Environment. A detailed view
of this level is depicted in Figure 3. The view refines the Running System and its
relationship to the Environment. The Supervision and Adaptation components
provide the means to effect adaptations on the Core functionality and on the

---

[2] Notice that, in some particular domains, the environment may be partially controllable as for cyber-physical systems.

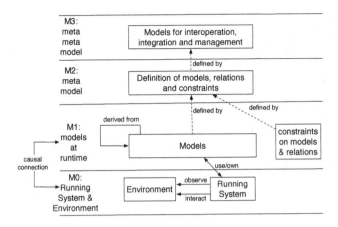

Fig. 2. A Conceptual Reference Model for M@RT

Runtime Platform, based on observations made on the Environment, the Core, and the Runtime Platform. The Supervision component triggers the Adaptation component to reason and plan an adaptation based on observations of the Environment, Core, or Runtime Platform. An adaptation, performed by the Adaptation component, adjusts the Core or the Runtime Platform. The Adaptation component may request more detailed information from the Supervision component that triggered its behavior. The Supervision component, on receiving such a request, monitors the Environment, Core, or Runtime Platform at a more fine-grained level in order to provide this information. The Core functionality interacts with the Environment (as is typical of software applications), and with the Runtime Platform (e.g., to use middleware services). The Runtime

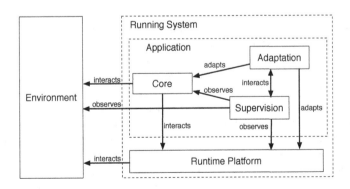

Fig. 3. *M*0 Level

Platform also interacts with the Environment (e.g., to establish communication with external devices or services).

While level $M0$ includes adaptation mechanisms, it does not restrict the forms of information used to drive the adaptation and thus, it is applicable to many types of adaptive systems, including those that do not use models. Level $M1$ and above specialize the form of adaptive systems to M@RT systems because they make models the primary drivers of the adaptation.

Level $M1$ includes the runtime models, relations between these models, and constraints on these models and relations. The models are used to drive the adaptation mechanisms at level $M0$. This level may have a variety of diverse models, for example, Queuing Networks, Simulink models, and UML Diagrams. The models may be derived from other models or may be composed of other models defined in the level.

$M1$ models are causally connected with (1) events and phenomena occurring in $M0$, specifically, those observed and handled by the Supervision component, and (2) change actions enacted by the Adaptation component. The Supervision component uses the $M1$ models in its event-handling processes. The processing of these events updates $M1$ models such that the models properly reflect the Running System and Environment. Event processing can lead to the invocation of adaptation functionality in the Adaptation component. Adaptations are performed by changing the models and propagating the changes to the Running System through causal connections between the models and the Running System.

Conceptually, this part of the reference model describes a *feedback control loop* between the models in level $M1$ and the Running System at $M0$, and it is based on the autonomic control loop discussed in [13, 54]. At runtime, the Running System provides data (feedback) used to attain a desired level of fidelity between the models and the system and between the models and the environment. Adaptations produced by the adaptation reasoning and planning mechanisms in the Supervision and Adaptation components are performed on the models and changes in the models are propagated to the Running System.

It is important to note that $M1$ may consist of several models representing different aspect of the Running System and Environment. These models may overlap and, as a consequence, may be in conflict in terms of actions to be triggered in the adaptation step. Inter-model conflicts and dependencies within one level are discussed later in this chapter.

The languages used to create $M1$ models are defined by metamodels. Such metamodels are located in the $M2$ level. Examples of languages defined by metamodels are UML, SysML, SPEM, BPMN, or ADLs. Likewise, languages for specifying constraints on $M1$ models are part of the $M2$ level, for instance, OCL [72] can be used as a language defined at the $M2$ level to describe constraints for $M1$ models created with UML. In addition, the types of relationships that can be defined among the different $M1$ models are defined at the $M2$ level.

The $M2$ level is relevant since it determines the languages that are used to create $M1$ models and thus, it determines the syntax and semantics of these models. Proper syntax and semantic definitions are required for automated processing of models. For instance, model transformation techniques transform a source model to a target model at the $M1$ level and such a transformation is typically specified by referring to the abstract syntax (i.e., the metamodel) of the source and target $M1$ models [82]. Specifying a transformation using metamodels makes use of the syntax and semantic definitions and it supports the application and reuse of the transformation for all possible models that are instances of these metamodels. Such reuse eases the engineering of mechanisms. In contrast, without an $M2$ level, each individual model in the $M1$ would require a specific transformation.

Finally, the top level in the conceptual reference architecture is $M3$ which is the meta-metamodeling level. This level defines models for interoperation, integration, and management of the modeling stack and, thus, it is used to define the metamodels contained in $M2$. An example for a meta-metamodel model at the $M3$ level is the *Meta Object Facility* (MOF) [71] that is used to define the UML and other languages such as SPEM [69]. In this case, having a common meta-metamodel eases the integration of the UML and SPEM languages at the $M2$ level, which in turn, enables interoperability between UML and SPEM model processing activities.

3   M@RT Engineering Challenges

In this section we present the challenges associated with engineering adaptive systems that follow the M@RT reference model described in the previous section. Specifically, we consider (1) the development and evolution of runtime models for supervision, (2) the reasoning and planning of adaptation based on runtime models, (3) the maintenance of multiple and different runtime models, and (4) the maintenance of fidelity of runtime models with respect to the running system and its environment. Mechanisms that realize the reference model can be used to tackle these challenges.

3.1   Developing and Updating Runtime Models for Supervision

Supervision is concerned with observing the running system and its environment in order to trigger the necessary adaptation. These observations may relate to functional and non-functional concerns, which should be explicitly captured in runtime models. Realizing the conceptual M@RT reference model requires one to tackle issues related to how the runtime models at levels $M1$, $M2$, and $M3$ (cf. Figure 2) are created and updated at runtime. For $M3$, a meta-metamodel can be developed or an existing one such as the *Meta Object Facility* (MOF) [71], can be used. This meta-metamodel is used to define $M2$ metamodels. The $M2$ metamodels define the languages used to express $M1$ models.

Runtime models describe entities in a *running* software system and in its environment. Unlike development models, they capture dynamic runtime behavior. For this reason, meta-metamodels and metamodels that capture runtime aspects are required at the $M3$ and $M2$ levels, in addition to the meta-metamodels and metamodels used at development. Runtime and development meta-metamodels and metamodels must be integrated in a M@RT system, and thus it is important to seamlessly connect model-driven development processes with the processes for creating and evolving runtime models.

The state of a runtime model should correspond as closely as possible/needed with the current state of the running system and its environment. Timely information on a running system and its environment provided by sensors can be used by a Supervision component (cf. Section 2) to update the runtime models. This requires instrumentation mechanisms that allow the Supervision component to connect runtime models with running systems and their environments. These mechanisms causally connect levels $M1$ to $M0$. It is a challenge to maintain this causal connection such that the models and the running system with its environment do not drift.

3.2   Reasoning and Planning Adaptation Based on Runtime Models

Runtime models reflecting the running system and its environment are also utilized by the adaptation process. Reasoning about the system and its environment to identify the need for adaptation involves manipulating these models. The need to adapt can be raised through actual or predicted violations of functional or non-functional properties. If reasoning determines the need to adapt, changes are planned and analyzed using the runtime models before they are propagated to the running system. Such model-driven adaptations require automatic reasoning and planning mechanisms that work on-line and on top of runtime models.

Reasoning and planning mechanisms themselves can be adapted, as in adaptive or reconfigurable control architectures [55]. Such adaptations can be supported by explicitly describing these mechanisms in runtime models. The most popular adaptation models are rule-based or goal-based models.

3.3   Maintaining Multiple and Different Runtime Models

As discussed in Section 2, many different runtime models may have to be maintained in a M@RT-based adaptive system. This necessity arises because of the need to manage multiple concerns, for example, performance, reliability, and functional concerns. Each concern typically requires specific models that are able to capture the individual concern and to provide a basis for reasoning about it.

However, dealing with multiple concerns raises issues of maintaining multiple models at runtime and keeping them consistent with each other. The first issue can be handled by mechanisms that architect the runtime environment by organizing and structuring multiple runtime models in a system. In terms of the reference model, handling this issue involves refining the concepts of the Supervision and Adaptation components to realize concrete model architectures and component implementations. The second issue is concerned with defining dependency and other relationships between runtime models. Models describing a running system and its environment from different viewpoints are likely dependent on each other; they all need to provide views that are consistent with each other. Moreover, when separating concerns in different models for reasoning, these concerns must be integrated at a certain point in time, at the latest when it comes to planning adaptations. Thus, relationships across models reify dependencies among concerns. This requires mechanisms to manage such relationships between models, especially consistency relationships among models.

3.4 Establishing and Maintaining Fidelity of the Runtime Models with the Running System and Its Environment

Runtime models also provide the basis for propagating changes to the running system. Thus, planned adaptations are performed on runtime models and then enacted on the running system. This requires mechanisms to map changes at the model level to changes at the system level. For this mapping mechanism, the typically significant abstraction gap between a running system and the runtime models imposes the need for refining changes on the models. For example, removing a model element that represents a component from a runtime model in order to uninstall the component might result in several system-level changes, including identifying, stopping, and uninstalling the component and to perform further clean-up activities.

Moreover, mechanisms enabling *safe* adaptations of the running system are required. This includes establishing and maintaining fidelity of runtime models with the running system and its environment. This is especially relevant in situations when adaptation fails. If the enactment of planned model changes to the running system fails, the runtime models and the running system may drift and therefore the fidelity decreases. Mechanisms that ensure fidelity, at least to a certain degree, in the face of dynamic environments and failing adaptations are needed in M@RT-based adaptive software systems.

4 M@RT Mechanisms: State of the Art and Research Challenges

This section discusses the state of the art and research challenges for M@RT mechanisms in adaptive software systems. The discussion is structured around the engineering challenges we identified in the previous section. For each of them, we discuss existing approaches based on a literature review and we identify open research challenges for the mechanisms. Finally, we present a research challenge that cross-cuts many of the challenges we discuss.

4.1 Developing and Updating Runtime Models for Supervision

State of the Art

There is currently no systematic way to develop runtime models and especially their metamodels. There are some initial ideas on how to manually move from design-time metamodels to runtime metamodels by following an abstract metamodeling process [57]. To increase the level of automation of such a process, approaches aim at providing support for inferring metamodels for runtime models by statically analyzing the source code of client programs that use system management APIs [84]. However, these inferred metamodels are preliminary and have to be revised by engineers. Thus, there is a lack of means to systematically, seamlessly, and automatically generate or transform runtime metamodels/models from design-time metamodels/models. Moreover, most M@RT approaches [57, 84, 85, 94, 98] typically use a subset of MOF as a meta-metamodel, but the suitability of MOF as a runtime meta-metamodel has not been analyzed or even assessed so far. The use of MOF is motivated by relying on existing MDE frameworks, like the *Eclipse Modeling Framework Project* (EMF)[3] that provides an implementation of a subset of MOF, which is similar to *Essential MOF* (EMOF) [71].

Besides such MDE frameworks, earlier work originating from the software architecture field employs architecture description languages (ADLs) [61] to describe a running system from an architectural viewpoint. Examples are the work by Oreizy et al. [74] and Garlan et al. [41]. Both approaches connect an architectural model to a running system. Such a connection is the key to M@RT-based systems since it allows one to maintain a runtime model for a running system.

The most direct manner to achieve a causal connection between a model and a running system is to require the running system to be organized in a pre-defined form that is directly linked with the model. For example, Oreizy et al. [74] prescribe an architectural style for the running system. Concepts of this style are first class elements in the system implementation and in the runtime model, and there is a direct one-to-one mapping between the system and model elements. This eases developing the causal connection since there is no abstraction gap between the model and the system. Others, like Garlan et al. [41], take a framework perspective and specifically consider probes and executors as part of a framework. Probes and executors instrument the running system and they realize the mapping and connection between the system and its runtime model. In contrast, recent work [83, 85, 94, 98] relies on management capabilities already offered by Runtime Platforms (cf. Section 2), like the management APIs provided by a middleware or application servers. On top of such APIs, a causal connection is often manually implemented while there exists preliminary work to simplify the development by increasing the level of automation using code generation techniques [85]. Similar to developing runtime models and metamodels, there is no systematic way to develop a causal connection when engineering a system that should provide M@RT-based reflection capabilities, that is, models at higher-levels of abstraction than those known from computational reflection [11].

Another relevant stream of research that considers models of running systems is the field of reverse engineering. The goal is to extract models from an existing system to obtain a high-level view of it. Besides creating models statically from the source code, they can also be extracted by tracing a running system. One approach is to leverage features provided by reflective programming languages to extract runtime models [52], which, however, requires that the (legacy) system

---

[3] http://www.eclipse.org/modeling/emf/ (last visited on July 2nd, 2012).

is implemented in such a language. Another reverse engineering approach is MoDisco [14]. This project provides a library for a number of widely-used systems to assist the development of so called *model discoverers*, which represent the implicit system state in models.

A key task for developers constructing runtime models/metamodels and causal connections is to understand what kinds of data can be obtained from the running system and how to obtain them. Some existing approaches to inferring system data and management APIs may be helpful for this task. Garofalakis et al. [42] provide an automated approach to infer the schema of XML files, and Fisher et al. [36] provide tools to extract types from the plain-text files and to automatically generate the text processing tools from the extracted types. Antkiewicz [2] provides a code analysis approach to infer how to use the system APIs provided by different frameworks. All these approaches may help in systematically developing runtime models and metamodels and, as discussed above, similar ideas for M@RT have already been proposed [84].

Research Challenges

Finding the right abstractions: A key research challenge is identifying the abstractions that models need to represent in order to support effective adaptation. Once identified, further research is needed to determine the most effective representations for the abstractions. These representations should precisely capture the information needed to describe the phenomena and should do so in a manner that allows the M@RT-based system to efficiently process the representation as it steers the behavior of the system. Finding and describing the right abstractions is key to building effective M@RT systems. Abstractions that are fine-grained may be able to deal with a variety of adaptations, but can lead to the production and manipulation of large amounts of data that are difficult to manage and costly to process. Higher-level abstractions can have representations that can be more efficiently processed, but can also ignore details that may be the actual causes of behaviors that require adaptation. Determining the right abstractions is typically a trade-off between the effectiveness of the representations and the types of adaptations that can be effectively supported.

Creating and maintaining models at runtime: In a M@RT-based system, the models should be faithful representations of the system and environment they abstract over. Techniques for creating faithful models and for maintaining the fidelity of the models as the system and its environment change are critical for the successful use and operation of M@RT systems. Maintaining fidelity involves monitoring (observing) runtime phenomena to be represented by models and updating the models in a timely manner when monitoring detects the phenomena.

To support effective monitoring we need to develop guidelines for determining what to monitor as well as how often and at which level of precision to monitor. These issues can dramatically impact the system performance and fidelity of the models. In addition, M@RT-based systems may also need to transform, summarize, and correlate the observations collected into pieces of information that meaningfully correspond to abstractions supported by the models at runtime. Techniques for transforming and aggregating information in an efficient manner are therefore needed. Inefficient techniques can lead to significant drift in model fidelity or less powerful adaptation opportunities.

Distribution of resources also adds to the complexity of aggregating information. For many kinds of modern systems, such as Internet of Things and Cloud Computing systems, components are often distributed across different nodes or devices. In order to maintain a global model at runtime, we need to integrate the local information from different nodes. The challenges here include when to perform the integration, what local information to retrieve and integrate, how to ensure the temporal correctness and timeliness of the global model, and how to achieve a better performance by reducing the communication between different nodes as well as the information exchanged during the communication.

4.2   Reasoning and Planning Adaptation Based on Runtime Models

State of the Art

Runtime models reflecting the running system and its environment are the basis for reasoning and planning adaptations of the system. Different techniques for reasoning and planning have been proposed and according to Fleurey and Solberg [38], they can be generally classified into two types of adaptation models.

First, rule-based approaches specify the adaptation by some form of event-condition-action (ECA) rules or policies [18, 27, 37, 41, 43, 45, 64]. An event triggers the adaptation process and conditions determine which reconfiguration action should be performed. According to Fleurey and Solberg [38], such approaches can be efficiently implemented with respect to runtime performance, and they can be simulated and verified early in the development process. However, if the number of rules grows, the approach suffers from scalability issues concerning the management and validation of the rules. The variability space of a system may be too large to enumerate all possible configurations, which is, however, required to some extent for rule-based approaches that explicitly specify the adaptation.

Therefore, the second type of adaptation models has emerged, which avoids the explicit specification of the adaptation. These search-based approaches prescribe goals that the running system should achieve, and guided by utility functions they try to find the best or at least a suitable system configuration fulfilling these goals [21, 22, 39, 76]. Other search-based mechanisms are based on model checking techniques to find plans on how to adapt the running system [90]. In general, search-based approaches solve the scalability problem of rule-based approaches, but they suffer from costly reasoning and planning processes, and weaker support for validation (cf. [38]). Since these processes have to be carried out at runtime, the runtime performance is crucial for any reasoning and planning mechanism.

Based on the different characteristics of rule-based and search-based approaches, Fleurey and Solberg [38] propose a mixture of them to balance their advantages and disadvantages. Their general idea is to use rules to reduce the variability space of the system and environment that subsequently has to be searched for suitable configurations.

Overall, more work needs to be done to understand different reasoning and planning techniques or mechanisms and their characteristics. This is a prerequisite for selecting and tuning existing techniques or developing new techniques for a specific system. Moreover, the impact of M@RT and the benefits offered by M@RT on reasoning and planning mechanisms have to be more thoroughly investigated. Therefore, requirements for adaptation models, that is, for reasoning and planning mechanisms operating on runtime models, have been proposed in [96]. Such requirements are helpful to evaluate existing adaptation models and to systematically develop new ones.

Research Challenges

Reasoning about adaptations: Research is needed to produce efficient and effective analysis techniques for reasoning about adaptations in environments that are highly dynamic and that offer limited computational resources. The limited computational resources and time constraints make design-time formal analysis techniques too costly to apply at runtime. The identification of appropriate heuristics can dramatically improve model analysis at runtime. The language used to express the models has a direct bearing on analysis efficiency and thus should be considered when developing the metamodels to be used for runtime models. Another consideration related to model analysis concerns the exploitation of structural deltas between model changes. Techniques that allow analysis to focus only on the parts of the model that have changed can significantly reduce the time for analysis when the deltas affect small parts of the models.

Performance and reliability analysis: We identified the following key technologies to analyze the performance and reliability of a running system: Probabilistic model checkers, for example, PRISM [49, 56], and Queueing Network solvers, for example, MT [7, 8]. These technologies support efficient and effective model checking of complex performance and reliability models against required properties described in appropriate formalisms. Their adoption at runtime may require specific forms of optimization [15, 32, 33, 44], and thus investigating their applicability may lead to other research challenges. In the specific context of cloud computing, auto scaling technologies, which provide the means to automatically scale up or scale out a given architecture, may be used to implement automatic performance adaptation in the cloud [59].

User-centric models: During the Dagstuhl seminar, it was largely acknowledged that human users will inevitably be part of the process of system evolution through adaptation. To the extent that models are appropriate artifacts to communicate system requirements and functionality at a high level of abstraction, it makes sense to use them as handles for the end-user to exert some form of control over how the system behaves at runtime. The exercise remains in terms of how to enable such high-level models to be causally connected with the system in meaningful ways and in particular how to fill the gap between the model and implementation in order to render effectively the provided control.

An example in this direction is the Communication Virtual Machine technology [25]. It enables non-expert end-users to input high-level communication models that are then interpreted to configure the desired communication sessions out of a selection of underlying communication providers. It also allows users to dynamically update the communication session by changing the model at runtime. The interpretation of such high-level, user-defined models is made possible by the adoption of a layered architecture, which contributes bridging the abstraction gap between the model and the underlying basic services in an incremental way, as well as by focusing on a specific domain, which limits the scope of choices in the interpretation process. While this approach is currently limited to the communication domain, generalizations for other domains, as well as to aspects of the middleware itself can be the subject for further research.

Analysis and Planning based on M@RT: Analysis and planning is concerned with reasoning about the running system and its environment and, if needed, with planning an adaptation of the system. Therefore, reasoning mechanisms are employed that operate on runtime models.

Different reasoning mechanisms have been proposed such as rule-based or search-based techniques as discussed previously. Such techniques have different effectiveness and efficiency characteristics. To systematically select or develop appropriate reasoning techniques when engineering adaptive systems requires an understanding of these characteristics. For example, the results of reasoning may differ between the techniques. A technique may provide one optimal solution at the end of the reasoning, while another technique may provide a list of all possible solutions. Considering efficiency, a technique may incrementally return solutions as soon as they are found. Moreover, techniques need not be deterministic in the sense that repeated runs of reasoning may result in different solutions for the same problem. Thus, it is important to identify and understand these characteristics when applying reasoning techniques in different application contexts. This leads to a major challenge in understanding which specific reasoning technique is best for which problems, adaptation models, or domains of adaptive systems.

In this context, influential factors, like the exponential growth of the problem size (number of environment conditions, constraints, or adaptation options), the time and resource limitations for reasoning, the accuracy or in general the quality of the resulting solution, or assurance for the resulting solution, are critical. This likely requires trade-offs between these factors, for example, between the quality of a solution and the acceptable time in which a solution has to be found.

Considering these different influential factors as well as the different reasoning techniques, it is a challenge to identify the most suitable technique and acceptable trade-offs for a certain system or problem. On the one hand, this is additionally impeded by a lack of traceability between the reasoning results and the reasoning goals or problems. Thus, it is often difficult to understand why a certain solution has been chosen by a reasoning technique for a given problem. This is even more complicated for adaptive systems with their inherent uncertainty related to the systems' functional and non-functional goals and actual behavior as well as to the systems' operational environments. Thus, incomplete and insufficient knowledge about a system and its environment makes the development or even the selection of suitable reasoning techniques challenging. Furthermore, it impedes the software engineer's understandability and traceability of the reasoning decisions.

All these issues motivate the need for smart reasoning techniques that leverage, among others, learning techniques, incremental techniques, abstraction, problem partitioning, and decentralized reasoning to enable acceptable trade-offs considering effectiveness and efficiency of the reasoning results. Thereby, each individual system and even each situation of a running system may need different trade-offs, which requires reasoning techniques to be adaptive. Systematically engineering or employing such techniques is challenging since it requires one to grasp the influential factors for reasoning, the uncertainty in adaptive systems, and the traceability between all of the constituent parts in reasoning.

4.3 Maintaining Multiple and Different Runtime Models in an Adaptive System

State of the Art

M@RT-based systems are likely to use several runtime models for different aspects of the system and at different abstraction levels (cf. Figure 2 or [99]). This calls for mechanisms to structure and operationalize multiple runtime models and the relationships among those models. A similar problem exists in model-driven software development where a plethora of interdependent models are employed to describe the requirements, design, implementation, and deployment of a software system. The field of *Multiparadigm Modeling* has made much progress in defining, relating, transforming, and analyzing models of potentially different paradigms [65–67] based on the premise that out of a set of issues to tackle, each problem is best solved by employing the most appropriate abstractions using the most appropriate formalisms. This generally leads to a complex overall organization of a large set of models. Therefore, the concept of *megamodels*, which are models that contain other models and relationships between those models, has emerged in the model management research field [4, 9, 10, 31]. The goal is to capture the different development models and their dependencies to address traceability and consistency in the development process.

Recently, such megamodel concepts have been proposed for runtime models employed in self-adaptive software [99]. In this context, megamodels are used to specify and execute adaptation processes by means of feedback loops. Besides structuring runtime models, megamodels describe the activities of a feedback loop as a flow of model operations working on runtime models. Additionally, such megamodels are kept alive at runtime to actually maintain runtime models and to directly execute a feedback loop using a megamodel interpreter. Overall, megamodels together with an interpreter support the explicit specification and execution of feedback loops, while the flexibility provided by interpreted models also leverages the adaptation and composition of feedback loops [95, 97].

While megamodels help in structuring the interplay of runtime models, mechanisms are required that substantiate the megamodel's model operations, that is, the relationships between runtime models. Such operations are, for example, reasoning and planning mechanisms discussed previously. A particular relationship between runtime models is concerned with consistency among models describing the same running system from different viewpoints.

Consistency can be tackled by model transformation and synchronization mechanisms. Transformations are suitable for initially deriving runtime models from other models, while synchronizations support the continuous consistency by propagating changes between models. A lot of research has gone into the development of model transformation and synchronizations languages (cf. [23, 24, 63, 86]). Many such languages are based on graphs and graph transformations [29, 45, 78] that have a sound formal basis in category theory. Thus, they enable formal reasoning [5, 77] in addition to their execution. Prominent approaches are Progress [81], Story Diagrams [35], AGG [88], and Henshin [3]. A graph transformation contains a left hand side and a right hand side which are both specified as graphs. If an occurrence of the left hand side is found in the host graph, that is, in the model, it is replaced by the right hand side. Several approaches have been developed to ensure structural constraints [5, 48] which can be used to ensure consistency.

The aforementioned transformation languages mainly address the transformation of single models. Triple Graph Grammars (TGGs) [47, 80] are an approach to handle two models (with extensions to an arbitrary number of models) potentially conforming to different metamodels. TGGs specify how a subgraph in one model corresponds to a subgraph in another model. They can be used for a forward transformation from a source model to a target model, a backward transformation from a target model to a source model as well as for keeping models synchronized [46]. By construction, TGGs ensure that the specified correspondence relations exist, which can be used for consistency purposes. However, TGGs are best suited for models whose metamodels share structural similarities. Query/View/Transformation (QVT) [70] is a set of standardized languages. While QVT-Operational enables the operational specification of model transformations, QVT-Relational targets a declarative specification of relations between models similar to TGGs. Further model transformation approaches are the Atlas Transformation Language (ATL) [53], PMT [93], and the Janus Transformation Language (JTL) [20]. The latter focuses on non-bijective bidirectional model transformations. In the context of M@RT, this also enables the handling of models that do not share structural similarities.

Several approaches have been developed that deal with inconsistencies by constructing repair actions [28, 34, 68]. They address the problem of consistency preservation in the context of user induced changes. Consequently, those approaches rely on the user to select the appropriate repair action. Thus, they are employable in the context of M@RT systems that incorporate the user in the adaptation process.

In general, model transformation and synchronization mechanisms are designed for off-line usage. They are employed in model-driven development processes but not on-line within a running M@RT system. Performing model transformations and synchronizations on-line requires light-weight and efficient mechanisms. For instance, Song et al. [83] apply a model transformation mechanism based on QVT-Relational [70] (QVT-R) on-line to support runtime software architectures. Vogel et al. [94, 98] employ on-line a model synchronization mechanism based on TGGs [45] to support self-adaptation. In particular, the efficiency of this synchronization mechanism for runtime models is shown in [98].

Overall, model transformation and synchronization mechanisms are promising for M@RT systems to maintain and keep multiple runtime models consistent to each other. However, more research is required to address scalability, efficiency, and especially assurances for such mechanisms.

Research Challenges

Maintaining model consistency: A M@RT system may require different types of models to support adaptation. In these cases, mechanisms for ensuring consistency between the models before, during, and after adaptations are needed. Short-term research in this area should focus on gaining a better understanding of what it means for models to be consistent in dynamically changing systems. This requires an understanding of the degrees of inconsistency that can be tolerated (if any) and when consistency must be established. The notion of consistency should also be applied to the cases where runtime models are organized in abstraction layers, that is, when the models are related by abstraction or refinement relationships. In these cases, it is important to understand when and how consistency is established across the abstraction layers.

Runtime model interoperability: The problem of model interoperability at runtime and its management present researchers with significant challenges. Any solution must include practical methods and techniques that are based on theoretical foundations. Keeping different models in a coherent and consistent state is an intrinsically difficult problem. In general, model interoperability can be pursued through *i)* consistency specification – describing not only the views but also the correspondences they have with one another, and *ii)* consistency assurance and enforcement – guaranteeing consistency before, during, and after adaptations. In essence, whenever a model describing an aspect of the Running System undergoes modifications (regardless of whether the change is performed manually or automatically), the overall consistency may be compromised. Any procedure to restore the consistency must propagate the changes and consistently adapt the other models.

Bidirectional model transformation languages seem the most adequate instrument for addressing this problem. For instance, QVT-Relational [70] (QVT-R) support the specification of correspondences as *relations* and the management of the consistency by means of the rule *check-only* and *check-then-enforce* semantics. Unfortunately, although non-bijectivity in bidirectional model transformation is recognized to be useful and natural (see [92]) the way it is supported and implemented in current languages is not always satisfactory: even the QVT-R specification is in this respect ambivalent [87]. The main difficulty is addressing non-determinism in change propagation. This occurs when model changes that are propagated through model correspondences give rise to more than one alternative adaptation of the linked models. As typically required in current bidirectional languages (e.g., QVT-R [70], TGGs [80]), the ambiguities among transformation solutions are solved programmatically by means of choices that a designer can make when writing the transformation. In other words, these solutions require the mapping to be bijective by adding additional constraints, which have to be known before the transformation is implemented. In this way, the problem of consistency enforcement among different models is reduced to the problem of model synchronization which is inherently difficult. However, in many cases the constraints to make the mapping bijective are unknown or cannot be formalized beforehand, thus it is important to deal with non-bijectivity by managing multiple solutions.

Existing work proposes mechanisms to deal with non-bijectivity in an explicit way. For instance, PROGRES [6] is a TGG solution to create integration tools capable of dealing with non-deterministic cases, that is, when multiple rules can be applied in the current direction of a transformation. A similar approach is proposed by JTL [20], a bidirectional model transformation language specifically designed to support non-bijective transformations and change propagation. In particular, the language propagates changes occurring in a model to one or more related models according to the specified transformation regardless of the transformation direction, that is, JTL transformations can generate all possible solutions at once. Both PROGRESS and JTL have the drawback of requiring human intervention: The former requires the designer to choose the rule to be applied among the candidate rules, whereas the latter requires the modeler to choose the correct model in the solution space. Adopting these approaches requires that the knowledge necessary to resolve the non-determinism at runtime is made accessible to the transformations. For example, this knowledge can take the form of heuristics. The overall problem is worsened by the fact that model adaptations reflect or drive adaptations on the Running System (regardless of the causal dependency). This is clearly a coupled evolution case, where adaptations written in a transformation language (at the $M1$ layer) must correspond to adaptation at the $M0$ layer which can be expressed, for instance, in terms of aspect-oriented programming techniques.

4.4 Establishing and Maintaining Fidelity of the Runtime Models with the Running System and Its Environment

State of the Art

An essential aspect of M@RT is the causal connection between runtime models and the running software system. On the one hand, this includes the Supervision (cf. Figure 3) to reflect changes of the running system or environment in the model as discussed in Section 4.1. On the other hand, this includes the Adaptation, that is, that planned changes are performed on the runtime models before they are executed to the system. Both Supervision and Adaptation realize the causal connection and must ensure the fidelity of the models with the running system and its environment.

While the Supervision has been discussed in Section 4.1, two general kinds of mechanisms are employed to enact changes of a runtime model to the running system. First, state-based approaches compare the runtime model before the change with the runtime model after the change. Thus, changes to the model are actually performed on a copy of the model or applying changes results in a copy. Mechanisms for comparing models are provided, for example, by EMF[4]. The resulting differences are the changes that have been performed and they serve as a basis to derive a reconfiguration script to be executed to the running system. Such an approach is followed by [64]. Second, operation-based approaches monitor a model to directly obtain the operations that constitute the changes, for example, setting attribute values or relationships. For example, EMF provides a notification mechanism that emits events representing these change operations. These events serve as a basis to obtain a reconfiguration script or to map the performed operations to system-level changes [94].

In this context, the problem of refining changes performed on abstract runtime models to system-level changes is discussed in [94]. The problem is tackled by model synchronization and graph transformation techniques between abstract runtime models used for reasoning and planning adaptation and a system-level runtime model at the same abstraction level as the system implementation. Thus, the changes are refined between models before they can be directly mapped to the management capabilities provided by the running system.

Such an abstraction gap between runtime models and the running system has to be addressed for M@RT-based systems. Developing a causal connection between a model that is at the same abstraction level as the system is simpler, which is the motivation to follow this approach in [74]. However, such a model does not provide problem-oriented views at appropriate abstractions, which is the goal of M@RT [11]. Providing runtime models that abstract from platform- or implementation-specific details, and thus from the solution space, must cope with an abstraction gap. This abstraction gap created by the Supervision through discarding system-level details may complicate the Adaptation when moving from abstract runtime models down to the concrete Running System (cf. [94]).

Besides realizing the Supervision and Adaptation components by connecting runtime models to the running system, these components have to cooperate to maintain fidelity of the models and the system. If the Adaptation part fails in executing model changes to the system, the models and the system drift, which has to be recognized by the Supervision part. Then, both parts have to cope with the failure to ensure again fidelity and consistency between the model and

---

[4] EMF Compare Project, http://www.eclipse.org/emf/compare/ (last visited on July 2nd, 2012).

the system. In general, the M@RT research field lacks work on assurances for the causal connection and for the co-evolution of the runtime models and the Running System over time. This is mandatory for safe adaptations and for coping with partially correct/valid runtime models in the face of uncertainty inherent to dynamically adaptive systems. Moreover, there is also a lack of work addressing the systematic engineering of causal connections, which has to be seamlessly integrated with work on engineering of the Application (cf. Section 2) and the runtime models/metamodels (cf. Section 4.1).

Research Challenges

Propagating model changes to the Runtime System: Several research issues need to be investigated for developing effective causal links between models and the running system. We obviously need to identify how to propagate changes from the model down to the system efficiently and effectively. This requires the identification of the points in the Running System where changes need to be applied, as well as constraints on when the changes can be applied. One possible approach to solve the problem of identifying the points of adaptation in the running system is to adopt a programming model that allows for changes at specific points in an execution of a program. Component-based and aspect-oriented programming models are typical examples. In addition, we need to develop mechanisms that support rollback of current operations when changes occur while the system is processing transactions.

Maintaining model fidelity: Middleware technologies can be used to facilitate the adaptation of applications in response to changes in the environment. In particular, reflective middleware technologies [60] use causally connected self-representations [16] to support the inspection and adaptation of the middleware system [89]. Components defined at the model level are directly mapped to specific artifacts that realize those components at the implementation level. From a software-quality perspective, this mapping is a form of traceability. In general, the term traceability can refer to any mechanism for connecting different software artifacts. In this context we specifically mean traceability from model to implementation elements, and vice-versa [91]. Maintaining the traceability link allows the model and implementation to co-evolve. Model evolution can be triggered by changes in, for example, (1) the requirements, (2) the environment, and (3) resource availability.

Keeping the model and the running system synchronized is a challenging problem, involving issues such as safety and consistency, especially when changes can be initiated in either the model or at the implementation level [17, 26, 62]. An interesting approach that has received a lot of attention over the years is generating (parts of) implementations directly from their designs using model-driven development technologies [73]. Such technologies can be used to generate (partial) implementations from detailed design models, and thus is an attractive strategy for maintaining the fidelity of models with respect to the running system they describe. For example, given a sufficiently detailed architectural specification, including structural, interface, and complete behavioral specifications, it is possible to generate a full implementation of a component, connector, or even an entire system [100]. In theory, architectural drift and erosion can be eliminated, by generating new implementation parts from the models as the models evolve [12]. For this to be practical, the description of the detailed models must require significantly less effort than writing the implementations in a programming language. This is often not the case, primarily because the abstractions supported by the modeling languages used to describe detailed behavior are often at a level that is close to the abstractions provided by programming languages. More research is needed for developing behavioral modeling languages that are based on abstractions that allow a developer to build a model that can be efficiently transformed to code using significantly less effort than that of directly writing the implementation in a programming language.

Another approach is to generate models from running code [17, 30, 62]. The challenge here is to generate models that are based on abstractions that are at a higher level than those found in the runtime environment of the programming languages. For example, it is relatively straightforward to obtain class diagram and sequence diagram descriptions of code, but it quickly becomes clear to anyone looking at the diagrams that they simply present views of the code with very little abstraction. Generating abstractions from code is a very difficult challenge. Some progress can be made in the context of domain-specific applications where known patterns and heuristics can be used to identify potentially useful abstract concepts.

4.5 A Cross-Cutting Research Challenge: Developing Development Processes for M@RT Systems

Research that focuses on producing effective processes, methods, and techniques for developing M@RT-based adaptive systems is needed in the short term to support systematic development and operation of these systems. Methods, techniques, and tools should be tied together to provide an end-to-end development approach that supports evolution before and after the M@RT-based system becomes operational. This problem has also been identified in [1] for self-adaptive software systems in general.

5   Conclusion

This chapter presents a summary of the Dagstuhl discussions on the mechanisms used to manage runtime software adaptation. The chapter is based on a conceptual model for M@RT developed at the seminar to provide a common concept and terminology framework for the discussions.

By relying on the reference model the chapter provides an analysis of the related open problems for each M@RT mechanism identified. We analyzed and classified them into four distinct areas: (1) developing and updating runtime models, (2) reasoning and planning for adaptation, (3) maintaining different runtime models, and (4) establishing fidelity and consistency among models and the running system.

The identified problems and their classification into such areas were also used to structure discussions on existing related work. By matching the identified problems with the existing work we formulate a set of open research challenges and goals classified in the same four areas. The identified research directions constitute an early roadmap which is the main contribution of the chapter. The roadmap's goal consists of stimulating, organizing, and driving the ongoing efforts of the research community on M@RT. Clearly, such a roadmap will be refined and extended as research that tackles the identified research goals uncovers further challenges.

References

1. Andersson, J., Baresi, L., Bencomo, N., de Lemos, R., Gorla, A., Inverardi, P., Vogel, T.: Software Engineering Processes for Self-Adaptive Systems. In: de Lemos, R., Giese, H., Müller, H.A., Shaw, M. (eds.) Self-Adaptive Systems. LNCS, vol. 7475, pp. 51–75. Springer, Heidelberg (2013)
2. Antkiewicz, M., Czarnecki, K., Stephan, M.: Engineering of framework-specific modeling languages. IEEE Transactions on Software Engineering 35(6), 795–824 (2009)
3. Arendt, T., Biermann, E., Jurack, S., Krause, C., Taentzer, G.: Henshin: Advanced concepts and tools for in-place EMF model transformations. In: Petriu, D.C., Rouquette, N., Haugen, Ø. (eds.) MODELS 2010, Part I. LNCS, vol. 6394, pp. 121–135. Springer, Heidelberg (2010)
4. Barbero, M., Fabro, M.D.D., Bézivin, J.: Traceability and Provenance Issues in Global Model Management. In: Proc. of 3rd ECMDA Traceability Workshop (ECMDA-TW), pp. 47–55 (2007)
5. Becker, B., Beyer, D., Giese, H., Klein, F., Schilling, D.: Symbolic invariant verification for systems with dynamic structural adaptation. In: Proceedings of the 28th International Conference on Software Engineering (ICSE), Shanghai, China. ACM (2006)
6. Becker, S.M., Herold, S., Lohmann, S., Westfechtel, B.: A graph-based algorithm for consistency maintenance in incremental and interactive integration tools. Software and System Modeling 6(3), 287–315 (2007)
7. Bertoli, M., Casale, G., Serazzi, G.: The jmt simulator for performance evaluation of non-product-form queueing networks. In: Annual Simulation Symposium, pp. 3–10. IEEE Computer Society, Norfolk (2007)
8. Bertoli, M., Casale, G., Serazzi, G.: An overview of the jmt queueing network simulator. Tech. Rep. TR 2007.2, Politecnico di Milano - DEI (2007)
9. Bézivin, J., Gérard, S., Muller, P.A., Rioux, L.: MDA components: Challenges and Opportunities. In: Proc. of the 1st Intl. Workshop on Metamodelling for MDA, pp. 23–41 (2003)
10. Bézivin, J., Jouault, F., Valduriez, P.: On the Need for Megamodels. In: Proc. of the OOPSLA/GPCE Workshop on Best Practices for Model-Driven Software Development (2004)
11. Blair, G., Bencomo, N., France, R.B.: Models@run.time: Guest Editors' Introduction. Computer 42(10), 22–27 (2009)

12. Blair, G.S., Blair, L., Issarny, V., Tůma, P., Zarras, A.: The role of software architecture in constraining adaptation in component-based middleware platforms. In: Coulson, G., Sventek, J. (eds.) Middleware 2000. LNCS, vol. 1795, pp. 164–184. Springer, Heidelberg (2000)

13. Brun, Y., Di Marzo Serugendo, G., Gacek, C., Giese, H., Kienle, H., Litoiu, M., Müller, H., Pezzè, M., Shaw, M.: Engineering Self-Adaptive Systems through Feedback Loops. In: Cheng, B.H.C., de Lemos, R., Giese, H., Inverardi, P., Magee, J. (eds.) Self-Adaptive Systems. LNCS, vol. 5525, pp. 48–70. Springer, Heidelberg (2009)

14. Bruneliere, H., Cabot, J., Jouault, F., Madiot, F.: Modisco: a generic and extensible framework for model driven reverse engineering. In: Proceedings of the IEEE/ACM International Conference on Automated Software Engineering, pp. 173–174. ACM (2010)

15. Calinescu, R., Grunske, L., Kwiatkowska, M.Z., Mirandola, R., Tamburrelli, G.: Dynamic qos management and optimization in service-based systems. IEEE Trans. Software Eng. 37(3), 387–409 (2011)

16. Cazzola, W.: Evolution as Reflections on the Design. In: Bencomo, N., Chang, B., France, R.B., Aßmann, U. (eds.) Models@Run-Time. LNCS, vol. 8378, pp. 259–278. Springer, Heidelberg (2014)

17. Cazzola, W., Pini, S., Ghoneim, A., Saake, G.: Co-Evolving Application Code and Design Models by Exploiting Meta-Data. In: Proceedings of the 12th Annual ACM Symposium on Applied Computing (SAC 2007), Seoul, South Korea, pp. 1275–1279. ACM Press (March 2007)

18. Chauvel, F., Barais, O.: Modelling Adaptation Policies for Self-Adaptive Component Architectures. In: Proceedings of the Workshop on Model-Driven Software Adaptation (M-ADAPT 2007) at the 21st European Conference on Object-Oriented Programming (ECOOP 2007), Berlin, Germany, pp. 61–68 (2007)

19. Cheng, B.H.C., et al.: Software Engineering for Self-Adaptive Systems: A Research Roadmap. In: Cheng, B.H.C., de Lemos, R., Giese, H., Inverardi, P., Magee, J. (eds.) Self-Adaptive Systems. LNCS, vol. 5525, pp. 1–26. Springer, Heidelberg (2009)

20. Cicchetti, A., Di Ruscio, D., Eramo, R., Pierantonio, A.: JTL: A bidirectional and change propagating transformation language. In: Malloy, B., Staab, S., van den Brand, M. (eds.) SLE 2010. LNCS, vol. 6563, pp. 183–202. Springer, Heidelberg (2011)

21. Cugola, G., Ghezzi, C., Pinto, L.S., Tamburrelli, G.: Adaptive service-oriented mobile applications: A declarative approach. In: Liu, C., Ludwig, H., Toumani, F., Yu, Q. (eds.) Service Oriented Computing. LNCS, vol. 7636, pp. 607–614. Springer, Heidelberg (2012)

22. Cugola, G., Ghezzi, C., Pinto, L.S., Tamburrelli, G.: Selfmotion: A declarative approach for adaptive service-oriented mobile applications. Journal of Systems and Software (2013),
http://www.sciencedirect.com/science/article/pii/S0164121213002653

23. Czarnecki, K., Helsen, S.: Feature-based survey of model transformation approaches. IBM Systems Journal – Model-Driven Software Development 45(3), 621–645 (2006)

24. Czarnecki, K., Foster, J.N., Hu, Z., Lämmel, R., Schürr, A., Terwilliger, J.F.: Bidirectional transformations: A cross-discipline perspective. In: Paige, R.F. (ed.) ICMT 2009. LNCS, vol. 5563, pp. 260–283. Springer, Heidelberg (2009)

25. Deng, Y., Sadjadi, S.M., Clarke, P.J., Zhang, C., Hristidis, V., Rangaswami, R., Prabakar, N.: A communication virtual machine. In: 30th Annual International on Computer Software and Applications Conference, COMPSAC 2006, vol. 1, pp. 521–531. IEEE (2006)
26. D'Hondt, T., De Volder, K., Mens, K., Wuyts, R.: Co-Evolution of Object-Oriented Software Design and Implementation. In: Akşit, M. (ed.) Proceedings of the International Symposium on Software Architectures and Component Technology, Twente, The Netherlands, pp. 207–224. Kluwer (January 2000)
27. Dubus, J., Merle, P.: Applying OMG D&C specification and ECA rules for autonomous distributed component-based systems. In: Kühne, T. (ed.) MoDELS 2006. LNCS, vol. 4364, pp. 242–251. Springer, Heidelberg (2007)
28. Egyed, A., Letier, E., Finkelstein, A.: Generating and evaluating choices for fixing inconsistencies in uml design models. In: 23rd IEEE/ACM International Conference on Automated Software Engineering (ASE 2008), L'Aquila, Italy, 15-19 September, pp. 99–108. IEEE (2008)
29. Engels, G., Lewerentz, C., Schäfer, W., Schürr, A., Westfechtel, B. (eds.): Nagl Festschrift. LNCS, vol. 5765. Springer, Heidelberg (2010)
30. Epifani, I., Ghezzi, C., Mirandola, R., Tamburrelli, G.: Model evolution by runtime parameter adaptation. In: ICSE, pp. 111–121. IEEE (2009)
31. Favre, J.M.: Foundations of Model (Driven) (Reverse) Engineering: Models – Episode I: Stories of The Fidus Papyrus and of The Solarus. In: Language Engineering for Model-Driven Software Development. No. 04101 in Dagstuhl Seminar Proceedings, IBFI, Schloss Dagstuhl (2005)
32. Filieri, A., Ghezzi, C., Tamburrelli, G.: Run-time efficient probabilistic model checking. In: 2011 33rd International Conference on Software Engineering (ICSE), pp. 341–350 (2011)
33. Filieri, A., Ghezzi, C., Tamburrelli, G.: A formal approach to adaptive software: continuous assurance of non-functional requirements. Formal Asp. Comput. 24(2), 163–186 (2012)
34. Finkelstein, A.C.W., Gabbay, D., Hunter, A., Kramer, J., Nuseibeh, B.: Inconsistency handling in multiperspective specifications. IEEE Transactions on Software Engineering 20(8), 569 (1994)
35. Fischer, T., Niere, J., Torunski, L., Zündorf, A.: Story diagrams: A new graph rewrite language based on the unified modeling language and java. In: Ehrig, H., Engels, G., Kreowski, H.-J., Rozenberg, G. (eds.) TAGT 1998. LNCS, vol. 1764, pp. 296–309. Springer, Heidelberg (2000)
36. Fisher, K., Gruber, R.: Pads: a domain-specific language for processing ad hoc data. In: ACM SIGPLAN Notices, vol. 40, pp. 295–304. ACM (2005)
37. Fleurey, F., Dehlen, V., Bencomo, N., Morin, B., Jézéquel, J.-M.: Modeling and Validating Dynamic Adaptation. In: Chaudron, M.R.V. (ed.) MODELS 2008. LNCS, vol. 5421, pp. 97–108. Springer, Heidelberg (2009)
38. Fleurey, F., Solberg, A.: A Domain Specific Modeling Language Supporting Specification, Simulation and Execution of Dynamic Adaptive Systems. In: Schürr, A., Selic, B. (eds.) MODELS 2009. LNCS, vol. 5795, pp. 606–621. Springer, Heidelberg (2009)
39. Floch, J., Hallsteinsen, S., Stav, E., Eliassen, F., Lund, K., Gjorven, E.: Using Architecture Models for Runtime Adaptability. IEEE Software 23(2), 62–70 (2006)
40. France, R., Rumpe, B.: Model-driven Development of Complex Software: A Research Roadmap. In: FOSE 2007: 2007 Future of Software Engineering, pp. 37–54. IEEE Computer Society, Washington, DC (2007)

41. Garlan, D., Cheng, S.-W., Huang, A.-C., Schmerl, B., Steenkiste, P.: Rainbow: Architecture-Based Self-Adaptation with Reusable Infrastructure. Computer 37(10), 46–54 (2004)
42. Garofalakis, M., Gionis, A., Rastogi, R., Seshadri, S., Shim, K.: Xtract: A system for extracting document type descriptors from xml documents. In: ACM SIGMOD Record, vol. 29, pp. 165–176. ACM (2000)
43. Georgas, J.C., Hoek, A., Taylor, R.N.: Using Architectural Models to Manage and Visualize Runtime Adaptation. Computer 42(10), 52–60 (2009)
44. Ghezzi, C., Pinto, L.S., Spoletini, P., Tamburrelli, G.: Managing non-functional uncertainty via model-driven adaptivity. In: Notkin, D., Cheng, B.H.C., Pohl, K. (eds.) ICSE, pp. 33–42. IEEE/ACM (2013)
45. Giese, H., Lambers, L., Becker, B., Hildebrandt, S., Neumann, S., Vogel, T., Wätzoldt, S.: Graph Transformations for MDE, Adaptation, and Models at Runtime. In: Bernardo, M., Cortellessa, V., Pierantonio, A. (eds.) SFM 2012. LNCS, vol. 7320, pp. 137–191. Springer, Heidelberg (2012)
46. Giese, H., Wagner, R.: From model transformation to incremental bidirectional model synchronization. Software and Systems Modeling (SoSyM) 8(1) (2009)
47. Greenyer, J., Kindler, E.: Comparing relational model transformation technologies: implementing query/view/transformation with triple graph grammars. Software and System Modeling 9(1), 21–46 (2010)
48. Heckel, R., Wagner, A.: Ensuring consistency of conditional graph rewriting - a constructive approach. Electr. Notes Theor. Comput. Sci. 2, 118–126 (1995)
49. Hinton, A., Kwiatkowska, M., Norman, G., Parker, D.: PRISM: A tool for automatic verification of probabilistic systems. In: Hermanns, H., Palsberg, J. (eds.) TACAS 2006. LNCS, vol. 3920, pp. 441–444. Springer, Heidelberg (2006)
50. IBM: An architectural blueprint for autonomic computing. Tech. rep., IBM (2003)
51. Jackson, M., Zave, P.: Deriving specifications from requirements: an example. In: ICSE 1995: Proceedings of the 17th International Conference on Software Engineering, pp. 15–24. ACM, New York (1995)
52. Jouault, F., Bézivin, J., Chevrel, R., Gray, J.: Experiments in Run-Time Model Extraction. In: Proceedings of 1st International Workshop on Models@run.time (2006)
53. Jouault, F., Kurtev, I.: Transforming models with ATL. In: Bruel, J.-M. (ed.) MoDELS 2005. LNCS, vol. 3844, pp. 128–138. Springer, Heidelberg (2006)
54. Kephart, J.O., Chess, D.M.: The vision of autonomic computing. Computer 36(1), 41–50 (2003)
55. Kokar, M.M., Baclawski, K., Eracar, Y.A.: Control Theory-Based Foundations of Self-Controlling Software. Intelligent Systems and their Applications 14(3), 37–45 (1999)
56. Kwiatkowska, M., Norman, G., Parker, D.: PRISM: Probabilistic symbolic model checker. In: Field, T., Harrison, P.G., Bradley, J., Harder, U. (eds.) TOOLS 2002. LNCS, vol. 2324, pp. 200–204. Springer, Heidelberg (2002)
57. Lehmann, G., Blumendorf, M., Trollmann, F., Albayrak, S.: Meta-modeling Runtime Models. In: Dingel, J., Solberg, A. (eds.) MODELS 2010. LNCS, vol. 6627, pp. 209–223. Springer, Heidelberg (2011)
58. de Lemos, R., et al.: Software Engineering for Self-Adaptive Systems: A Second Research Roadmap. In: de Lemos, R., Giese, H., Müller, H.A., Shaw, M. (eds.) Self-Adaptive Systems. LNCS, vol. 7475, pp. 1–32. Springer, Heidelberg (2013)
59. Mao, M., Li, J., Humphrey, M.: Cloud auto-scaling with deadline and budget constraints. In: 2010 11th IEEE/ACM International Conference on Grid Computing (GRID), pp. 41–48. IEEE (2010)

60. McKinley, P.K., Cheng, B.H.C., Ramirez, A.J., Jensen, A.C.: Applying evolutionary computation to mitigate uncertainty in dynamically-adaptive, high-assurance middleware. Journal of Internet Services and Applications, 1–8 (2011)
61. Medvidovic, N., Taylor, R.: A Classification and Comparison Framework for Software Architecture Description Languages. IEEE Transactions on Software Engineering 26(1), 70–93 (2000)
62. Mens, K., Kellens, A., Pluquet, F., Wuyts, R.: Co-evolving Code and Design Using Intensional Views - A Case Study. Journal of Computer Languages, Systems and Structures 32(2), 140–156 (2006)
63. Mens, T., Van Gorp, P.: A taxonomy of model transformation. Electronic Notes in Theoretical Computer Science 152, 125–142 (2006)
64. Morin, B., Fleurey, F., Bencomo, N., Jézéquel, J.-M., Solberg, A., Dehlen, V., Blair, G.S.: An Aspect-Oriented and Model-Driven Approach for Managing Dynamic Variability. In: Czarnecki, K., Ober, I., Bruel, J.-M., Uhl, A., Völter, M. (eds.) MODELS 2008. LNCS, vol. 5301, pp. 782–796. Springer, Heidelberg (2008)
65. Mosterman, P.J., Sztipanovits, J., Engell, S.: Computer-automated multi-paradigm modeling in control systems technology. IEEE Trans. Contr. Sys. Techn. – special issue on Computer Automated Multiparadigm Modeling 12(2), 223–234 (2004)
66. Mosterman, P.J., Vangheluwe, H.: Computer automated multi-paradigm modeling in control system design. In: Proceedings of the IEEE International Symposium on Computer-Aided Control Systems Design (CACSD 2000), pp. 65–70 (2000)
67. Mosterman, P.J., Vangheluwe, H.: Guest editorial: Special issue on computer automated multi-paradigm modeling. ACM Trans. Model. Comput. Simul. 12(4), 249–255 (2002)
68. Nentwich, C., Emmerich, W., Finkelstein, A.: Consistency management with repair actions. In: Proceedings of the 25th International Conference on Software Engineering, Portland, Oregon, USA, May 3-10, pp. 455–464. IEEE Computer Society (2003)
69. Object Management Group (OMG): Software & Systems Process Engineering Metamodel specification (SPEM) Version 2.0 (2008), OMG Adopted Specification formal/2008-04-01
70. Object Management Group (OMG): MOF 2.0 QVT Final Adopted Specification v1.1 (2011), OMG Adopted Specification formal/2011-01-01
71. Object Management Group (OMG): OMG Meta Object Facility (MOF) Core Specification, Version 2.4.1, OMG Adopted Specification formal/2011-08-07 (2011)
72. Object Management Group (OMG): OMG Object Constraint Language (OCL) Version 2.3.1, OMG Adopted Specification formal/2012-01-01 (2012)
73. OMG: Model Driven Architecture (MDA). Technical Report ORMSC/2001-07-01, OMG (July 2001)
74. Oreizy, P., Medvidovic, N., Taylor, R.N.: Architecture-based runtime software evolution. In: ICSE 1998: Proceedings of the 20th International Conference on Software Engineering, pp. 177–186. IEEE Computer Society, Washington, DC (1998)
75. Oreizy, P., Medvidovic, N., Taylor, R.N.: Runtime software adaptation: framework, approaches, and styles. In: ICSE Companion 2008: Companion of the 30th International Conference on Software Engineering, pp. 899–910. ACM, New York (2008)

76. Ramirez, A.J., Cheng, B.: Evolving Models at Run Time to Address Functional and Non-Functional Adaptation Requirements. In: Bencomo, N., Blair, G., France, R., Jeanneret, C., Munoz, F. (eds.) Proceedings of the 4th International Workshop on Models@run.time. CEUR Workshop Proceedings, vol. 509, pp. 31–40 (2009)
77. Rensink, A.: The GROOVE simulator: A tool for state space generation. In: Pfaltz, J.L., Nagl, M., Böhlen, B. (eds.) AGTIVE 2003. LNCS, vol. 3062, pp. 479–485. Springer, Heidelberg (2004)
78. Rozenberg, G.: Handbook of Graph Grammars and Computing by Grah Transformation, vol. 1. Foundations. World Scientific (1997)
79. Salehie, M., Tahvildari, L.: Self-adaptive software: Landscape and research challenges. ACM Trans. Auton. Adapt. Syst. 4(2), 1–42 (2009)
80. Schürr, A.: Specification of graph translators with triple graph grammars. In: Mayr, E.W., Schmidt, G., Tinhofer, G. (eds.) WG 1994. LNCS, vol. 903, pp. 151–163. Springer, Heidelberg (1995)
81. Schürr, A.: Programmed graph replacement systems. In: Handbook of graph grammars and computing by graph transformation: Foundations, vol. 1, pp. 479–546. World Scientific Publishing Co., Inc., River Edge (1997)
82. Sendall, S., Kozaczynski, W.: Model Transformation: The Heart and Soul of Model-Driven Software Development. IEEE Softw. 20(5), 42–45 (2003)
83. Song, H., Huang, G., Chauvel, F., Xiong, Y., Hu, Z., Sun, Y., Mei, H.: Supporting runtime software architecture: A bidirectional-transformation-based approach. Journal of Systems and Software 84(5), 711–723 (2011)
84. Song, H., Huang, G., Xiong, Y., Chauvel, F., Sun, Y., Mei, H.: Inferring Metamodels for Runtime System Data from the Clients of Management APIs. In: Petriu, D.C., Rouquette, N., Haugen, Ø. (eds.) MODELS 2010, Part II. LNCS, vol. 6395, pp. 168–182. Springer, Heidelberg (2010)
85. Song, H., Xiong, Y., Chauvel, F., Huang, G., Hu, Z., Mei, H.: Generating Synchronization Engines between Running Systems and Their Model-Based Views. In: Ghosh, S. (ed.) MODELS 2009. LNCS, vol. 6002, pp. 140–154. Springer, Heidelberg (2010)
86. Stevens, P.: A landscape of bidirectional model transformations. In: Lämmel, R., Visser, J., Saraiva, J. (eds.) Generative and Transformational Techniques in Software Engineering II. LNCS, vol. 5235, pp. 408–424. Springer, Heidelberg (2008)
87. Stevens, P.: Bidirectional model transformations in QVT: semantic issues and open questions. Software and Systems Modeling 8 (2009)
88. Taentzer, G.: AGG: A graph transformation environment for modeling and validation of software. In: Pfaltz, J.L., Nagl, M., Böhlen, B. (eds.) AGTIVE 2003. LNCS, vol. 3062, pp. 446–453. Springer, Heidelberg (2004)
89. Taïani, F., Grace, P., Coulson, G., Blair, G.S.: Past and future of reflective middleware: towards a corpus-based impact analysis. In: ARM, pp. 41–46 (2008)
90. Tajalli, H., Garcia, J., Edwards, G., Medvidovic, N.: PLASMA: a plan-based layered architecture for software model-driven adaptation. In: Proceedings of the IEEE/ACM International Conference on Automated Software Engineering (ASE 2010), pp. 467–476. ACM, New York (2010)
91. Taylor, R.N., Medvidovic, N., Dashofy, E.M.: Software Architecture: Foundations, Theory, and Practice. Wiley Publishing (2009)
92. Tratt, L.: Model transformations and tool integration. SOSYM 4(2), 112–122 (2005)
93. Tratt, L.: A change propagating model transformation language. Journal of Object Technology 7(3), 107–124 (2008)

94. Vogel, T., Giese, H.: Adaptation and Abstract Runtime Models. In: Proceedings of the 5th ICSE Workshop on Software Engineering for Adaptive and Self-Managing Systems (SEAMS 2010), pp. 39–48. ACM (2010)

95. Vogel, T., Giese, H.: A Language for Feedback Loops in Self-Adaptive Systems: Executable Runtime Megamodels. In: Proceedings of the 7th International Symposium on Software Engineering for Adaptive and Self-Managing Systems (SEAMS 2012), pp. 129–138. IEEE Computer Society (2012)

96. Vogel, T., Giese, H.: Requirements and Assessment of Languages and Frameworks for Adaptation Models. In: Kienzle, J. (ed.) MODELS 2011 Workshops. LNCS, vol. 7167, pp. 167–182. Springer, Heidelberg (2012)

97. Vogel, T., Giese, H.: Model-driven engineering of self-adaptive software with eurema. ACM Trans. Auton. Adapt. Syst. 8(4), 1–18 (2014)

98. Vogel, T., Neumann, S., Hildebrandt, S., Giese, H., Becker, B.: Incremental Model Synchronization for Efficient Run-Time Monitoring. In: Ghosh, S. (ed.) MODELS 2009. LNCS, vol. 6002, pp. 124–139. Springer, Heidelberg (2010)

99. Vogel, T., Seibel, A., Giese, H.: The Role of Models and Megamodels at Runtime. In: Dingel, J., Solberg, A. (eds.) MODELS 2010. LNCS, vol. 6627, pp. 224–238. Springer, Heidelberg (2011)

100. Zarras, A.: Applying model-driven architecture to achieve distribution transparencies. Information & Software Technology (2006)

101. Zave, P., Jackson, M.: Four dark corners of requirements engineering. ACM Trans. Softw. Eng. Methodol. 6(1), 1–30 (1997)

Living with Uncertainty
in the Age of Runtime Models

Holger Giese[1], Nelly Bencomo[2], Liliana Pasquale[3], Andres J. Ramirez[4],
Paola Inverardi[5], Sebastian Wätzoldt[1], and Siobhán Clarke[6]

[1] Hasso Plattner Institute at the University of Potsdam, Germany
{Holger.Giese,Sebastian.Waetzoldt}@hpi.uni-potsdam.de
[2] Aston University, UK
nelly@acm.org
[3] Lero - Irish Software Engineering Research Centre, Ireland
liliana.pasquale@lero.ie
[4] Michigan State University, USA
ramir105@cse.msu.edu
[5] University of L'Aquila, Italy
paola.inverardi@di.univaq.it
[6] Trinity College Dublin, Ireland
siobhan.clarke@scss.tcd.ie

Abstract. Uncertainty can be defined as the difference between information that is represented in an executing system and the information
that is both measurable and available about the system at a certain point
in its life-time. A software system can be exposed to multiple sources
of uncertainty produced by, for example, ambiguous requirements and
unpredictable execution environments. A runtime model is a dynamic
knowledge base that abstracts useful information about the system, its
operational context and the extent to which the system meets its stakeholders' needs. A software system can successfully operate in multiple
dynamic contexts by using runtime models that augment information
available at design-time with information monitored at runtime. This
chapter explores the role of runtime models as a means to cope with
uncertainty. To this end, we introduce a well-suited terminology about
models, runtime models and uncertainty and present a state-of-the-art
summary on model-based techniques for addressing uncertainty both at
development- and runtime. Using a case study about robot systems we
discuss how current techniques and the MAPE-K loop can be used together to tackle uncertainty. Furthermore, we propose possible extensions
of the MAPE-K loop architecture with runtime models to further handle
uncertainty at runtime. The chapter concludes by identifying key challenges, and enabling technologies for using runtime models to address
uncertainty, and also identifies closely related research communities that
can foster ideas for resolving the challenges raised.

N. Bencomo et al. (Eds.): Models@run.time, LNCS 8378, pp. 47–100, 2014.

1 Introduction

Uncertainty can be defined as the difference between information that exists in an executing system and the information that is both measurable and available at a certain point in time [1]. Within the context of software systems, uncertainty can arise from ambiguous stakeholders' needs, the system itself, or its operational or execution environment. For example, a stakeholder can introduce uncertainty by formulating an ambiguous specification [2], the system itself can introduce uncertainty by gathering monitoring information that may be inaccurate and/or imprecise [3], and the surrounding environment can introduce uncertainty by generating inputs that the system cannot interpret [4]. Unfortunately, these sources of uncertainty rarely occur independently of each other. Instead, the effects produced by these sources of uncertainty tend to compound and thereby inhibit the system from fully satisfying its requirements.

Traditional software design approaches tend to address these forms of uncertainty by identifying *robust* solutions at development-time that can continuously exhibit good performance at runtime. Nevertheless, identifying these robust solutions is a challenging task that requires identifying the set of operational contexts that the system might have to support. For systems that will be deployed in highly dynamic environments, identifying a robust solution might be infeasible since it is often impractical to anticipate or enumerate all environmental conditions a software system will encounter throughout its lifetime. Increasingly, software systems, such as context-aware systems and self-adaptive systems (SAS), use runtime models to cope with uncertainty [5,6] by either partially or, if possible, fully resolving sources of uncertainty at runtime. These models, when fed with data monitored at runtime, allow for the dynamic computation of a predictable behaviour of the system.

A runtime model is a knowledge base that abstracts useful information about the executing system, its environment, and the stakeholders' needs and that can be updated during the system's life time. It can be used by either the system itself, humans or other systems. Different types of development-time models and abstractions can be used to this end, including requirements, architectural, and behavioural models. Furthermore, we envision that other kinds of models (e.g., [7]), linking different development models and abstractions, can be used as well. Runtime models can support resolution of some forms of uncertainty, which can manifest, for example, when information that was previously unavailable becomes available during execution. In some cases, however, uncertainty remains present in one form or another, such as when physical limitations in monitoring devices result in monitoring data that is insufficiently accurate and precise for assessing the task at hand. In both cases, model-based techniques can be applied at either development- and runtime to address uncertainty. While development-time techniques focus on the explicit representation of sources of uncertainty that can affect a software system, runtime techniques focus on refining and augmenting runtime models with monitoring information collected as the system executes.

Research communities are increasingly exploring the concept of uncertainty and how it impacts their respective fields. Some of these research communities include economics [8], artificial intelligence [9], robotics [10], and software engineering [11]. While uncertainty has been studied in parallel by different research communities, a definitive solution for engineering systems that are able to handle uncertainty has not been provided yet. Within software engineering in particular, a key step forward in this direction is to first explicitly represent sources of uncertainty in models of the software system. Current modeling techniques such as variation point modeling [12,13], however, cannot be directly applied as uncertainty cannot be represented by enumerating all possible behavioural alternatives [4]. Thus, new abstractions must be provided to declaratively specify sources of uncertainty in a model at development-time, and then partially resolve such uncertainty at runtime as more information is gathered by the system.

This chapter first elaborates the relation between uncertainty and models - runtime models in particular. Furthermore, it reviews the fundamentals of handling uncertainties such as the relevant forms of uncertainty, the specific relation between time and uncertainty and the current approaches for development-time and runtime. In particular, it explores the role of feedback loops and the typical types of systems with runtime models. It also explores how runtime models can be leveraged to handle and reduce the level of uncertainty in an executing system. Ideally, if uncertainty is viewed as a function over the life-time of the system, then the level of uncertainty should monotonically decrease as design decisions are made and new information becomes available. In practice, however, the level of uncertainty in a software system might increase as new events emerge that were not anticipated previously. Thus, the vision of this roadmap chapter is to use development-time models to identify and represent sources and impacts of uncertainty. If possible, uncertainty should be resolved at development time. Furthermore, once monitoring information provides new insights about the system's behaviour and its surrounding execution environment, the running system should resolve and manage the remaining sources of uncertainty during execution by using runtime models.

This chapter is organized as follows. Section 2 presents a robotic system that will be used throughout the remainder of the chapter as an example of how to address uncertainty through runtime models. Section 3 discusses the general relationships between models and uncertainty. Model-based techniques for addressing uncertainty at development- and runtime are presented and discussed in Section 4. Emerging techniques to handle uncertainty in the context of epistemic, linguistic and randomized uncertainty are discussed in Section 5. Finally, Section 6 summarizes findings, presents research challenges, and future directions.

2   Case Study

In this section, we describe a simplified version of a real robot system. This case study simulates a distributed factory automation scenario[1]. It is used as a running example in this paper to discuss how development-time models and runtime models can be employed to cope with uncertainty. An extended description of our toolchain and development environment can be found in [10]. In the next Section we explain the possible types of uncertainty present in the case study. We also provide a goal, an environmental and an initial behavioural model to illustrate the requirements and the behaviour of the case study.

Fig. 1. Case Study: Factory automation robot scenario

In the factory automation scenario depicted in Figure 1, three autonomous robots have to fulfill different tasks to reach overall goals in an uncertain environment. The regular behaviour of one robot is to move around, transport pucks, or charge the batteries. Sensors and actuators are used to monitor the current situation and to navigate through different rooms along changing paths. Each robot is able to communicate with other robots inside the scenario and computational nodes (e.g., servers, mobile phones) outside the scenario. Strict behavioural constraints ensure safety as well as reliability requirements, such as avoiding battery exhaustion and collisions. Beside the transportation of pucks, which is a functional goal, the robots should also satisfy other goals related to the quality of how the functional goals are met (called softgoals). Examples of softgoals are minimization of energy consumption and maximization of throughput. Note that in this scenario throughput is estimated in terms of number of

---

[1] For more information about our related lab see: http://www.cpslab.de

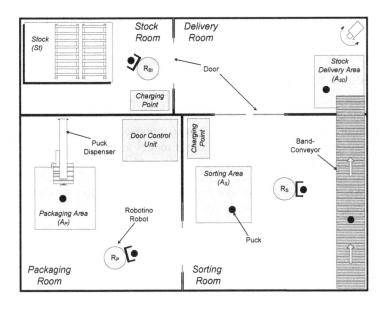

Fig. 2. Structural sketch of the robotic system including three autonomous robots. R_P is a robot that transports pucks from the packaging to the sorting room. Robot R_S (sorting) decides whether the puck is for a customer or the stock. Robot R_{St} transports the puck to the stock.

pucks transported to their final destination within a specific time unit (e.g., a day).

Figure 2 depicts a structural overview of the robot system. The whole simulation scenario is separated into four different rooms (Stock Room S_t, Delivery Room A_{SD}, Door Control Unit A_P and the Sorting Area R_S). In the room lower left of Figure 2, the pucks are packed and dropped for transportation in area A_P by a puck dispenser. The robot R_P transports the pucks from the packaging room to a second room (lower right) and drops it within the sorting area A_S. To maximize the throughput of puck transportation, another robot R_S picks up the puck from the sorting area and drops it on a band-conveyor. Depending on the current goals, the conveyor transports the puck to a customer delivery area outside the scenario (not shown in the picture) or to the stock delivery area A_{SD} (upper right room in the figure). A third robot R_{St} transfers the puck to the stock St. Each robot acts as an autonomous unit. Therefore, the tasks transportation, sorting and stocking are independent from each other. Within this scenario the execution conditions can be changed over time to handle certain loads, optimizing the puck transportation routes or cope with robot failures. As a result, the doors can be opened or closed dynamically. For example, robots can recalculate routes or take over additional transportation tasks. Furthermore, a robot can charge its battery at one of the two charging points if necessary. In the following sections we will use this scenario to illustrate possible types of uncertainty.

3 Models and Uncertainty

To set the stage for our chapter in this section we first introduce the meaning of fundamental terms such as models, runtime models and uncertainty by using an exemplary goal, context and behavioural model for one robot of the factory automation example. Furthermore, we identify which kinds of runtime models are employed and outline the most common types of systems using such runtime models. Furthermore, we discuss the role that runtime models can play for the different types of systems.

3.1 Models

The definition of a model can vary depending on its purpose of usage. In this chapter, we define a model as follows [14].

Definition 1. *A* model *is characterized by the following three elements: an (factual or envisioned)* original *the model refers to, a* purpose *that defines what the model should be used for, and an* abstraction function *that maps only purposeful and relevant characteristics of the original to the model.*

It is important to note that a model always refers to an *original*. This original can be factual, and either it may exist already or, it may be an envisioned system which does not exist yet. In both cases, the model is used as a representation of the original to ease development or runtime activities.

Models may differ in their *purpose*. For instance, the purpose of a goal-based model [15] is to capture the requirements of a system, while the purpose of a finite-state machine (FSM) is to capture the possible behaviours of the system.

In this paper, we use three different kinds of models for the robotic example. First, a goal model represents the requirements of our scenario. Second, a representation of the structure of the physical space (map) including the location of agents and objects in the physical space is adopted as an exemplary model to specify context information about the system operational environmnet, which may change at runtime. Third, we use a model based on state machines to describe the behaviour of the system with respect to the current goals and the context.

To start, we cover different requirements and constraints in the goal model of our robotic scenario shown in Figure 3. We use the KAOS notation [16] to represent the goal model. This model has a hierarchical structure, since goals can be refined into conjoined subgoals (AND-refinement) or into alternative combinations of subgoals (OR-refinement). When a goal cannot be decomposed anymore, (i.e. it is a leaf goal), it corresponds to a functional or non-functional requirement of the system [16] . In Figure 3, the main goal of the robot system is to

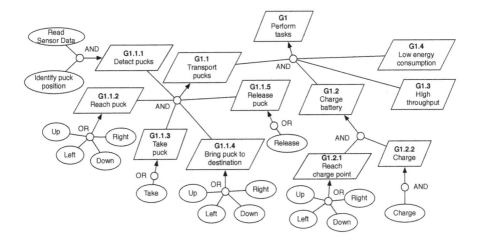

Fig. 3. The KAOS goal model of the Robot System

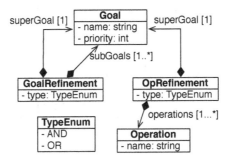

Fig. 4. An excerpt of the KAOS goal metamodel

perform its standard tasks, such as transport pucks ($G1.1$) and charge its battery ($G1.2$). To achieve the goal $G1.1$, the robot has to achieve the following functional requirements: detect a puck ($G1.1.1$), reach the puck ($G1.1.2$), take the puck ($G1.1.3$), bring the puck to its destination ($G1.1.4$) and finally release the puck ($G1.1.5$). A leaf goal that corresponds to a functional requirement can be "operationalized", that is, it can be decomposed into a set of conjoined or disjoined operations that should be executed to meet it [16]. For example, goal $G1.1.2$ is operationalized by operations Up, $Left$, $Down$, and $Right$, since the robot can move up, left, down, and right to reach the puck location. Note that the robot must also perform its standard tasks while satisfying the following non-functional requirements: high throughput ($G1.3$) and low energy consumption ($G1.4$).

In the robot system, we represent these goals according to a simplified KAOS metamodel as depicted in Figure 4. Note that each goal is associated with a

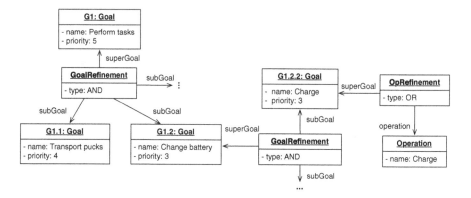

Fig. 5. An instance situation of the goal model shown in Fig. 3 of our robot system

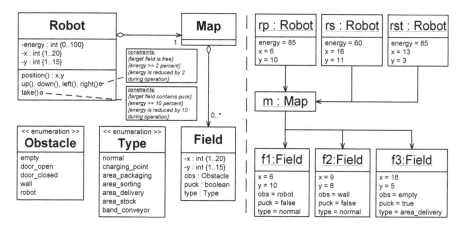

Fig. 6. On the left, the context metamodel of the robot as well as the internal map representation. On the right, an example snapshot of possible instance objects.

name and a priority. Context changes can affect goal priorities and therefore the tasks execution by the robots at runtime. Depending on the priority and the relation among the goals, the robot system weights the requirements during task execution and selects a set of tasks to be performed. Figure 5 presents an excerpt of an instance situation of the goal model shown in Figure 3. Because of the higher priority of the transportation task we have supposed, the robot will prefer this goal until it is necessary to charge the battery. Further constraints can also restrict the robot behaviour charging the battery only in adequate given situations (e.g. the power supply reaches a critical low level).

The second type of model is a structural context model of the robots. With this model we can represent the internal state of the robot, its internal representation of the environment (*Map*) as well as the possible relations between them according to the metamodel on the left in Figure 6. Each robot has an overall

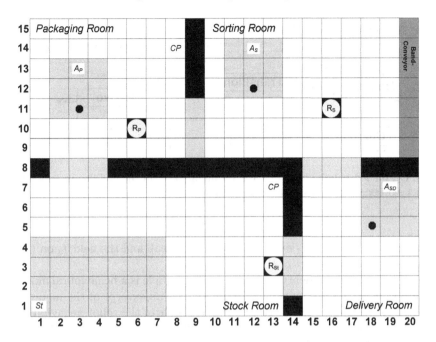

Fig. 7. Discrete grid map representation of the robot laboratory (cf. Fig. 2)

battery power supply with an energy level comprised between 0 and 100 percent. Additionally, its position is given by a x and y coordinate of the map associated with the laboratory. Furthermore, it can perform operations *up()*, *down()*, *left()*, and *right()* moving through the laboratory. Executing an operation consumes power as robots have to read sensor data necessary to detect pucks, and move inside the building. Therefore, each operation reduces the overall energy level of the battery. If the robot detects a puck, it can take it for transportation. Each robot maintains an environmental representation for navigation and localization issues.

The environment is represented as a discrete grid (*Map*) as shown in Figure 7. The smallest area in this map grid is a field (cell) with an unique position on the grid. It can contain obstacles as closed doors, walls, or other robots. Furthermore, a puck may lie on a field. Each cell has a type information that indicates special positions in the laboratory as charging points for the robot or the band conveyor (cf. Figure 2).

We assume that a robot is positioned on exactly one field at any time during its movement through the laboratory. Therefore, the operations up, down, left and right can be seen as atomic behaviours. There are no intermediate positions of objects (pucks) and a robot must be on the same field as a puck to grip it.

On the right in Figure 6, three robot instances with different positions and three field objects are shown. The battery of robot R_P contains 85 percent of the overall possible energy and the robot is on the position $x = 6$ and $y = 10$ in

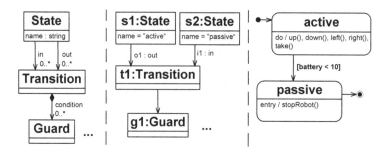

Fig. 8. On the left side: excerpt of the FSM metamodel; in the middle: initial example abstract syntax; on the right side: concrete syntax

the laboratory. The field f_2 on position $(9, 8)$ is a wall and the field f_3 on $(18, 5)$ contains a puck and is part of the delivery area.

The third and last model type for our robot example is a behavioural model in the form of a finite-state machine. Figure 8 shows an excerpt of the metamodel on the left as well as a very abstract initial example of the robot behaviour that is extended later (abstract syntax in the middle, concrete syntax on the right). In this version, the robot has two states. After an activation signal, the robot starts processing its tasks in the *active* state according to the goal model (cf. Fig. 3) until the battery is lower than a threshold of 10 percent. In this case, it will enter the *passive* state and stops all sensors, processing steps and actuators. Consequently, charging the battery automatically is not considered in this first version of our example.

Each model presented focuses on a specific concern of the robot scenario. The definition of a model explicitly states that the *abstraction function* is to eliminate characteristics of the original that are irrelevant as far as the purpose of the model is concerned. At the same time, the model abstraction should preserve the intent and semantics of those details that are relevant to the task at hand.

The same type of models can be used to represent different levels of abstraction. Several types of models and abstractions are often combined in a Hierarchical State Machine (HSM) [17] to provide a unique and comprehensive view of the same software system. In our robotic example, while one FSM can capture only the most abstract states of the robot, such as "the robot is stopped", another FSM can map those abstract states to finer-grained behaviours and state transitions.

If we consider the KAOS goal model (cf. Fig. 3) of our robot example, the original would be the real requirements that are in the stakeholders' minds and the purpose would be to represent the requirements of the system. Note that, for reasons of time and costs, some requirements may not be included in the system implementation, but only those that are relevant to the stakeholders. For this reason, the goal model abstracts the irrelevant goals and requirements and only focuses on the ones that will be implemented in the robotic system.

Moreover, if we consider the map representation, the difference between the real simulation area in the real world and the simplified field representation maintained by the robot is obvious. However, the map model abstraction covers all important aspects that are needed for the robot system offering special functionality, e.g., path planning as well as obstacle detection and avoidance.

In the case of the FSM (see Fig. 8), the original would be the robot and the purpose would be to capture the possible behaviours of the robot. Another case of abstraction is that only the relevant abstract states (modes) of the robot, like moving (*active*) or stopped (*passive*) as well as possible transitions between relevant abstract states, are captured.

A fundamental property of a model is its *validity*. This means that the model must correctly reflect the characteristics (i.e., goals, requirements, behaviours, and components) observed on the original. For example, in a goal model this property would imply that a set of goal operationalizations lead to the satisfaction of the requirements they are associated with. Likewise, given an appropriate input sequence for the FSM presented in Figure 8, a certain sequence of abstract states must be traversed. These states should correspond to the observable behaviour of the robot.

Even if a model is valid, it might not exactly predict the same behaviour of the original as this correlation depends on the model abstraction. Furthermore, it may be difficult to capture and interpret the non-determinism associated with unpredictable events and conditions in a model. In general, it is expected for a model to provide an acceptable degree of accuracy and precision. *Accuracy* measures how correct the model is at representing observable characteristics of the original. That is, accuracy measures the error between a predicted value and the value observed in the original. In contrast, *precision* measures how small the variation is in the prediction made by the model, as compared to the original.

With *over-approximation*, a model is guaranteed to include all possible behaviour of the original, but may also include behaviour that cannot be observed in the original. Therefore, over-approximation can result in false negatives, when a behaviour present in the model results in a failure that is never observed for the original. In contrast, with *under-approximation*, all behaviour captured in the model must also be possible for the original, but not necessarily vice versa. As such, under-approximation can prevent false negatives by ensuring that the characteristics represented in the model are also observable in the original. Note that under-approximation does not preclude the possibility of introducing false positives that take place when the model does not represent all behaviour that the original can exhibit. See for example [18] for a discussion about over- and under-approximation in the specific context of model checking.

3.2   Uncertainty and Uncertainty in Models

The definition of uncertainty depends on its context, origin, and effects upon the system. For the purposes of this chapter, we adopt and modify the definition proposed in [1,19] as follows:

Definition 2. *Uncertainty can be defined as the difference between the amount of information required to perform a task and the amount of information already possessed.*

This concept of uncertainty can be better understood by distinguishing between three main non-mutually exclusive forms of uncertainty: *epistemic, randomized,* and *linguistic.*

Epistemic uncertainty is a result of incomplete knowledge. For instance, the operationalization of requirements might be incomplete during system specification, and it can happen as the system designer might not know in advance what operations the system will provide.

Randomized uncertainty can occur due to system and environmental conditions that are either inherently random or cannot be predicted reliably. For instance, a sensor might introduce noise unpredictably into gathered values, thereby preventing a software system from accurately measuring the value of a property.

Lastly, *linguistic* uncertainty can result from a lack of precision or formality in linguistic concepts. For example, the satisfaction of requirements G1.3 and G1.4 in Figure 3 is vague because there is no precise way to express the notion of "high" throughput and "low" energy consumption.

The concept of uncertainty within a model can then be defined by extending Definition 2 as follows:

Definition 3. *Uncertainty is the difference between the information that a model represents about the original - that is relevant to its purpose - and the information that the model could, in theory, represent about the original that would be relevant for its purpose at a certain instant in the system lifetime.*

Uncertainty within a model can affect both the accuracy and precision of a model. Accuracy of a model refers to its the degree of closeness to the original, while precision refers to the degree to which the model is consistent (e.g., lead the system to the same behaviour under the same conditions). Although uncertainty may uniformly affect the entire model, its effects might be irrelevant if they are constrained within attributes that are never queried or evaluated. Thus, the relevance of uncertainty depends upon the criticality of the element that is affected with respect to the purpose of the model.

Dynamic models tend to increase the level of uncertainty over time because of the (possible) continuous updates which are performed to reflect changes in the original. A good example is our context model of the environment. It would be very hard for a robot to maintain a highly accurate model if humans or other moving obstacles frequently appear and disappear in the scenario. These observations can affect the behaviour of a single robot (e.g., path planning and route recalculation) as well as the overall scenario (e.g., new task distribution). As a consequence, this can also render the model imprecise, since the robots' behaviour might not be consistent with respect to previous and equivalent environmental situations. However, this phenomenon is not observable in static models.

In general, uncertainty in a model can be addressed by using internal or external techniques. Internal techniques address uncertainty by increasing the accuracy of the model at the expense of decreasing its precision. Thus, although the outcome of a model prediction might be inconsistent, it is closer to the possible outcomes of the original. External techniques, on the other hand, tend to under-approximate the original by increasing the precision of the model at the expense of decreasing its accuracy. For this reason, post-processing is usually required to ensure the outcome of a model prediction does not exceed certain bounds or thresholds of what the original can exhibit.

For the remainder of this chapter we focus on addressing uncertainty with internal techniques. We consider the predictions of a model, whether it is a requirements, structural or behavioural model, and its post-processing analysis as a *combined* prediction of an extended model. Furthermore, we also acknowledge that a model prediction might be correct while not being fully accurate, and that upper bounds on the prediction error might not necessarily be accounted for in such predictions.

3.3   Runtime Models

Definition 4. *A runtime model is a model that complies with Definition 1 and, in addition, is characterized as follows: part of its purpose is to be employed at runtime in a system and its encoding enables its processing at runtime. The runtime model is causally-connected to the original (running system), meaning that a change in the runtime model triggers a corresponding change in the running system and/or vice versa (extended from [20]).*

As outlined in the definition, runtime models differ from other types of models in both their purpose and encoding. Specifically, while development-time models, such as state machines, primarily support the specification, design, implementation, and testing, of a software system, a runtime model captures relevant information of the running system for different purposes, which either are part of the system functional features or are subject to assurance and analysis (non-functional features). Due to the encoding that enables its processing at runtime, other running systems, stakeholders (e.g., final users) and the system itself can alter these models at runtime.

A runtime model can span different types of models (e.g., structural or behavioural models), and can have different degrees of accuracy and precision. Independently on whether changes are automatically included or are externally applied on the model, a runtime model can be used for different purposes. It can be used as a knowledge repository about the system, its requirements, or its execution environment. It can also support adaptation of the system and/or its execution environment, as new information about the original becomes available. An overview about different runtime model categories and the relations between runtime models are described in [21].

In the following sections, we discuss a feedback-loop-based approach that enables handling of runtime models during system operation. Afterwards, we discuss some most common types of system that typically employ runtime models.

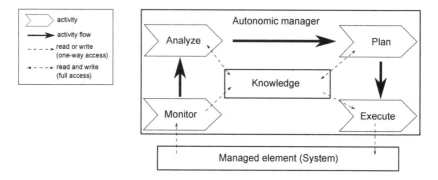

Fig. 9. MAPE-K feedback loop architecture according to [22]

3.3.1   The Feedback Loop in Systems with Runtime Models

Different types of software systems already adopt runtime models to control several aspects of their execution. In some cases, runtime models can be simply used to reconfigure system properties. In other cases, these models can be dynamically updated to reflect changes in the system and its context (the observable part of the surrounding environment).

The MAPE-K feedback loop [22], shown in Figure 9, emphasizes the role of feedback for autonomic computing. At first, it splits the system into a managed element (core system) and an autonomic manager (adaptation engine). It then defines four key activities that operate on the basis of a common knowledge base: *Monitoring, Analysis, Planning*, and *Execution. Monitoring* is primarily responsible for gathering raw data, such as measurements and events, about the state of the managed system. Analysis is used to interpret data collected by the monitoring activity and detects changes in the managed system that might warrant adaptation. Both monitored and analyzed data are used to update the knowledge base of the MAPE loop. Planning reasons over the knowledge base to identify how the managed system should adapt in response to their mutual changes. Execution applies the adaptations selected by the planning activity on the system.

The explicit consideration of runtime models leads to an extended MAPE-K architecture as depicted in Figure 10. A first major refinement is that now the adaptation engine also takes into account - in addition to the core system - its context and requirements as a knowledge base.

In this more refined view Monitoring is gathering raw data, such as measurements and events, about the state of the system and its context. Additionally, monitoring may recognize updates of the requirements. In any case, the accumulated knowledge is stored in the runtime models (M@RT). The Analysis interprets the collected data and detects changes to the system, context and/or requirements that might warrant adaptation. Then it updates the runtime models accordingly. The Planning employs the runtime models to reason about how the running system should adapt in response to changes. The Execution uses the runtime models as basis to realize planned adaptations.

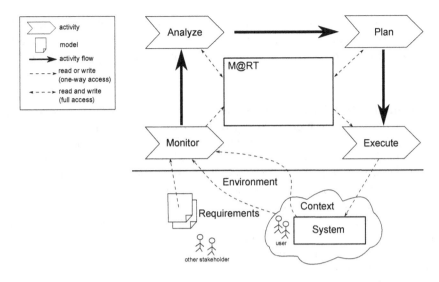

Fig. 10. Runtime Models in an extended MAPE-K architecture

3.3.2 Kinds of Runtime Models

As depicted in Figure 10, we can distinguish different kinds of runtime models depending on their possible original (i.e. subject):

System Models. The first and most common subject of a runtime model is the *system* itself. On the one hand, a runtime model provides an abstract view on the running system. Consequently, to maintain the causal relation, the runtime model has to be adjusted when a represented characteristics of its original changes [23,24]. On the other hand, the runtime model can be used to describe possible future configurations of the running system. Then, to realize the causal relation a related update of the running system has to be triggered. What can be controlled and observed via the runtime model is the system behaviour, as required sensors and actuators can be incorporated into the system if they minimally impact the system non-functional requirements.

Context Models. The *context* of the system – the part of the environment that can be observed by the system – can be a subject of a runtime model. Then, the runtime model represents some characteristics of the context observable via some sensors and the causal connection implies that the runtime model is accordingly updated when the context changes as indicated by changing measurements of the sensors. The case in which the runtime model is used to describe how the context should be changed is more subtle. Here only those changes that are under the indirect control of related actuators can be triggered via a runtime model and its causal connection. Often, only a small fraction of the context can be indirectly controlled via the actuators and sensors. Therefore, while only a few characteristics are controllable, more characteristics are usually observable via sensors. However, sometimes relevant characteristics cannot be observed directly and then a dedicated analysis is required to derive them indirectly from other observations.

Requirement Models. Last but not least the *requirements* of the system may be subject of a runtime model [25,26]. In this case, either some form of online representation of the requirements exists that is linked to the runtime model by a causal connection or changes of the requirements have to be manually reflected on to the runtime model. In both cases the runtime model carries information about the currently relevant requirements within the system and therefore the system can, for example, check whether the current requirements are fulfilled or try to adjust its behaviour such that the fulfillment of the requirements increases. However, a bidirectional causal relation between the requirements and the runtime model has not been usually considered. This relation would trigger modification of the system requirements from changes in the runtime model. However, if the requirements define a whole set of possible goals for the system, the runtime model can be used to capture which goals are currently selected.

Besides these typical kinds of runtime models, in practice it is also possible to find cases where a single runtime model has multiple subjects. For example, a single model may reflect knowledge about a fraction of the system and the context at once in order to allow analyzing their interplay.

3.3.3   Types of Systems with Runtime Models

Different kinds of systems leverage activities of the MAPE loop to control some aspects of their execution. The rest of this section provides a non exhaustive list of the most common types of systems leveraging runtime models. Note also that these categories may overlap.

Configurable Systems. *Configurable systems* [27] are perhaps the simplest type of software systems that leverage runtime models. Such systems often use runtime models in form of configuration files to determine the concrete configuration and the values of operational parameters that control the behaviour of the overall system. For this reason, no monitoring and analysis process is performed to automatically update the runtime model. Instead, planning and execution processes respectively read the configuration and parameters stored in the runtime model and reconfigure the system accordingly.

Context-Awareness w.r.t. Pervasive Systems. *Context-awareness* [28] describes that a system is able to monitor its context. Context-awareness is regarded as an enabling feature for *pervasive systems* [29,30] that offers "anytime, anywhere, anyone" computing by integrating devices and appliances in the everyday lives of its users. Pervasive systems select and apply suitable adaptations depending on their context. As the user's activity and location are crucial for many applications, context-awareness has been focused on location awareness and activity recognition. Pervasive systems can leverage runtime models to represent the context and cover all processes of the MAPE loop to foster adaptation. Monitoring acquires the necessary information about the context (e.g. using sensors to perceive a situation). Analysis abstracts and understands the context (e.g. matching a perceived sensory stimulus to a context) and updates the runtime models accordingly. Planning identifies the actions that the system should perform based on the recognized context and execution applies these actions at runtime.

Requirements-Aware Systems. *Requirement-awareness* is the capability of a system to identify changes to its own requirements. *Requirements-aware adaptive systems* [26,31] use runtime models to represent their requirements [32,33], track their changes [25,34] and trigger adaptation in the system behaviour in order to increase requirements satisfaction [35]. Other work [36] proposes to explicitly collect users' feedback during the lifetime of a system to assess the validity and the quality of a system behaviour as a means to meet the requirements. In these systems, requirements are conceived as first-class runtime entities that can be revised and reappraised over short periods of time. Modifications of requirements can be triggered due to different reasons, for example, by their varying satisfaction, or new/changing market needs and final users preferences.

These systems also leverage the activities of the MAPE loop to support requirements-awareness and adaptation. Monitoring collects the necessary data from the system and the context. In addition, if the system is *requirements-aware*, changes in the requirements are taken into consideration. Analysis uses the data about the system and context to update the requirements model or recompute the requirements satisfaction. Planning computes the adaptations to be performed by taking into account the current requirements and assumptions as captured by the runtime models. As a special case, this includes that a requirements changes may result in changes to the system itself (e.g., architectural or behavioural changes). Execution applies selected adaptations on the system.

It has to be emphasized that the use of requirements models at runtime during analysis and planning is conceptually independent of their monitoring (requirements-awareness).

Self-adaptive Systems. *Self-awareness* [37] is the capability of a system to monitor itself. The system can thus detect and reason on its internal changes (e.g., system behaviour, components, failures). *Self-adaptive systems* can in addition to self-awareness also react to observed changes by applying proper adaptations to themselves.

Nowadays, the term self-adaptive systems is used in a very broad sense and it can include self-awareness, context-awareness as well as requirements-awareness. Such systems manage different runtime models that represent the system itself, its context, and its requirements, respectively.

The next section explains how runtime models can be used to handle uncertainty. In particular, Section 4.3 provides further discussion of self-adaptive systems and the use of runtime models in the context of the case study and the MAPE-K loop.

4   Handling of Uncertainty

Nowadays, we can observe the trend to handle uncertainty later at runtime and not already at development-time, as discussed in Section 4.1. To better understand the benefits and drawbacks of using runtime models to handle uncertainty, we first discuss the classical approach to handle uncertainty using development-time models in Section 4.2. In Section 4.3 we explain more advanced solutions to handle uncertainty at runtime and outline how these solutions can benefit from runtime models. The case study has been used to provide specific examples.

4.1   Trend of Handling Uncertainty Later

In classical engineering, uncertainty in the available information about the system and its environment is a major problem. In particular, for models that capture characteristics of the environment it is frequently the case that the exact characteristics are not known at development-time. External techniques for uncertainty for a model such as safety-margins and robustness with respect to these known margins are then often employed to ensure that the developed solutions satisfy the system goals for all expected circumstances (cf. [38]).

Consequently, also in software engineering the classical approach is to build systems that work under all expected circumstances. This is achieved by using models at development-time, which capture the uncertainty internally. Alternatively external techniques can be employed to handle the uncertainty, such that the developed systems work under all circumstances predicted by these development-time models.

However, nowadays it has been recognized that we can achieve smarter and more efficient solutions, when we build systems that are context-aware [28] and/or self-aware [37]. Due to the self-awareness, context-awareness and requirement-awareness, self-adaptive systems become capable of adjusting their structure and behaviour to the specific needs of the current system state, context, and/or requirements. This results in a number of benefits: (1) achievement of better performance and less resource consumption at the same time, (2) minimization of manual adjustments required to the administrators or users, and (3) provisioning of functionality that would be infeasible without the information about the context.

In contrast to the classical software engineering approach, in self-adaptive systems uncertainty concerning the system or context can be handled - to some extent - at runtime and not just at development-time. The classical software engineering approach can only cope with uncertainty that can be handled based on reasonably complex development-time models. A self-adaptive system can in contrast employ runtime measurements to reduce the uncertainty and adjust its behaviour accordingly. Consequently, self-adaptive systems can handle more situations than classical solutions and their ability to address uncertainty more actively is one of their major advantages. In [39] it is therefore argued that uncertainty should be considered as a first class element when designing self-adaptive systems.

4.2   Handling Uncertainty at Development-Time

This section discusses how models can be used to address uncertainty during development-time. We describe the classical approach, through our case study and then explain the various forms of uncertainty that can arise.

The classical approach tries to exclude uncertainty at the level of requirements in order to have a solid basis for the later development activities. However, it has been observed that stable requirements rarely exist on the long run (cf. [40,41,42]). Watts Humphrey observed that one of the principles of software engineering is that requirements are inherently uncertain [40]: "This creative design process is complicated by the generally poor status of most requirements descriptions. This is not because the users or the system's designers are incompetent but because of what I call the requirements uncertainty principle: For a new software system, the requirements will not be completely known until after the users have used it." Also Lehman's Software Uncertainty Principle [41] states that for a variable-type program, despite many past satisfactory executions, a new execution may yield unsatisfactory results. This is based on the observation that software inevitably reflects assumptions about the real world [43].

During design and implementation, the uncertainty in environment models is usually handled by building robust solutions that simply work for all possible cases. Therefore, the development-time model employed for the environment has to capture all relevant and possible future environments the system will face. In this way, a system designed according to a development-time model should guarantee that in any relevant and possible future environment the required goals and constraints can be satisfied.

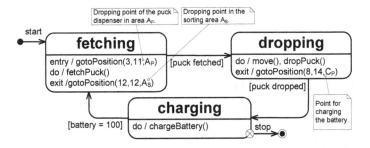

Fig. 11. Behaviour development model of the robot system

Example 1 (Robot Design with Development-Time Models Only). For our case study, the developer must make several design decisions. If we assume that each of our three robots has a clear task and that their overall behaviour fulfills the given goals, a possible solution is the fixed encoding of the different tasks.

According to Figure 2 on page 51, robot R_P must transport pucks from the Packaging Room to the Sorting Room in the specific Areas A_P and A_S respectively. We can model at development-time a state machine that representes the states and transitions necessary for the robot to solve this task. The behaviour model depicted in Figure 11 has three states. First, the robot fetches the puck in the Packaging Room (cf. Fig. 2) and transports it according to the sorting position. Due to our discrete grid map model of the laboratory, we can pinpoint the target locations for the robot navigation. The developer knows the maximal distance and whether the robot has enough power for puck transportation. Afterwards, the robot always loads its battery at a fixed charging point avoiding to exhaust its power supply, which is one of the constraints of the system. Furthermore, one can stop the puck transportation while the robot loads the battery or it will fetch and transport the next puck.

There are many restrictions to the environment, e.g., pucks must always be at the same position, the environment must be very static without relevant disturbances, and goals should not change at runtime ensuring that such a fixed transportation scenario works. This is the case for many systems, such as an assembly line with static working steps in a fixed area. In practice the robot will increasingly diverge over time from the planned trajectory as the move commands are inherently imprecise. In fact only in more restricted cases for embedded systems, such as automation systems with a fixed track layout where the errors of the vehicle movements do not accumulate over time, a solution that is not context-aware really works.

In our specific system design, the handling of the battery loading is one example of resolving uncertainty during development-time. It does not matter how much the power level of the battery is decreased during the task as long as the robot reaches the charging point. Furthermore, the amount can be estimated or measured upfront and results in a simple, not context-aware system solution. Additionally, the fixed encoding of the task further reduces uncertainty due to the fact that no communication between robots and runtime task distribution capabilities are needed.

All the development models are only used for code generation or system implementation. The running system does not reflect or use these models but simply complies with them.

4.2.1   Forms of Uncertainty

The problems of uncertain requirements according to [40,41,42] relate to *epistemic uncertainty* where the requirements captured at development-time may not precisely and accurately reflect the real needs when the system is operating. In the case of the Example 1, the designed behaviour is not able to handle a shift in the priorities of the goals by the operating organization that may occur over time. Thus, in this case the performance will not be rated as good as in the beginning when the shift in the prioritization of the goals by the operating organization has occurred, as expectations have evolved while the system behaviour stays the same. As a result, a new state machine model must be developed and deployed to the robot. Another related reason for *epistemic uncertainty* is that stakeholders may formulate ambiguous requirements specifications [2], or they may have conflicting interests or uncertain expectations on the resulting software quality. The changes that will occur for the system and environment in between the development-time and when the system is executing may also result in *epistemic uncertainty*. The development-time model of the system or context cannot precisely and accurately reflect the real system and its environment as it is characterized later when the system is under operation.

Also, practical limitations in development and measurement tools can, in principle, cause *epistemic uncertainty* where a development-time model of the system or context cannot precisely and accurately reflect the real system and its execution environment as it is known at development-time. For instance, in the Example 1, it is only possible to measure the initial characteristics of the floor plan with a certain precision and accuracy and at certain points in time. As a result, a development-time model of the floor plan may perhaps never truly reflect the real environment unless, due to abstraction, neither the measurement precision or changes matter after the measurement are relevant.

Furthermore, *randomization* plays a role that may be covered appropriately by probabilistic models such as probabilistic automatas [44]. In our Example 1 the known likelihood of failed operations can be described by probabilistic transitions and still we can determine upper bounds for related unsafe behaviour using probabilistic reachability analysis. If no exact probabilities but rather only probability intervals are known due to epistemic uncertainty, interval probabilistic automata and related analysis techniques (cf. [45]) could still be used.

4.2.2   Time and Uncertainty

For a development-time model, we can observe that the uncertainty may change over time. It may stay stable, increase or even, in rare cases, decrease over time. If the energy level maintained by the robot in our Example 1 changes over time and a design-time model is used, the three cases mentioned above can result in the following situations:

The uncertainty is *increasing over time* as outlined before, which may happen if the set of possible reached states grows over time. If for all activities of the robot only rough upper and lower bounds for the energy consumption are known, after a number of operations, the uncertainty concerning the consumed energy will be quite large. In this case, the model still provides enough information about the system at development-time to build a sufficiently robust design for the system by simply calculating the worst-case and therefore act accordingly. However, the resulting behaviour will be rather sub-optimal as the robot will recharge the battery very early.

The uncertainty *remains constant over time* if the set of possible reached states remains the same size over time. In the case of the robot and the energy consumption this would require that the energy consumption of each operation is exactly known such that the initial uncertainty concerning the state of the battery is neither increasing nor reduced. In this unrealistic case this knowledge can be exploited to build a robust design where the initial worst-case plus the exactly known consumption is employed to determine when to recharge the battery.

The uncertainty is *reduced over time* when after a certain time the state is exactly known as the set of possible reached set of states has collapsed into a smaller set or even a single state. In our example, if loading the battery is blocked we could be certain that after a while the battery will be empty. However, it is rarely the case that such a decrease of the uncertainty in a model can be guaranteed.

While all three cases are possible, we can conclude that unless actively tackled, the uncertainty will increase over time. Consequently, identifying means to counteract this growth in uncertainty is crucial for handling uncertainty properly.

4.2.3   Maintenance and Reengineering for Handling Uncertainty

The standard approach to tackle the aging problem for software is *maintenance*, where required adjustments to changes in the context or requirements are taken into account by a dedicated additional development step. Since the development of the original system has been stopped, in this step the changes in the context and requirements should be identified such that the related uncertainties are reduced. However, often the time for a maintenance step is rather limited and therefore the related analysis is superficial and potentially incomplete. Also, maintenance teams might differ from design and implementation teams, possibly leading to more uncertainty in the form of incomplete understanding.

If the internal quality of the software deteriorates considerably, maintenance is no longer feasible and, instead, dedicated reengineering activities with a reverse-engineering part that recovers lost information about the software and a forward engineering phase are required. Here, reengineering addresses the uncertainty that results from the loss of information concerning the system. Usually, reengineering also has to address changes in the context and requirements since the development of the original system has been stopped to minimize related uncertainties.

4.3   Handling Uncertainty at Runtime

Using runtime models during system operation, as for example it is done for self-adaptive systems, brings up different forms of uncertainty that must be handled. In contrast to the classical software engineering approach, these forms of uncertainty are tackled at runtime and not at development-time.

Before discussing the different forms of uncertainty at runtime, we illustrate in the following example the use of runtime models for the planning step of the MAPE-K feedback loop for our robot case study.

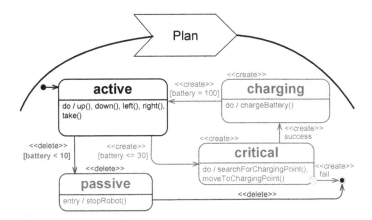

Fig. 12. The planning step of the MAPE-K loop creates a new version of the state machine runtime model

Example 2 (Robot Scenario with Runtime Models). We use the following runtime models in our case study scenario: First, we have an environment model that captures the current position in the floor plan represented by discrete fields in an overall map with current puck positions, obstacles and charging points (cf. Fig. 6 in Section 3) and available puck transportation requests. Second, a goal runtime model exists that includes priorities and constraints of our system and reflects the requirements of the overall system behaviour. Furthermore, the behaviour of the robot should fulfill those constraints and performs according to the given goals and priorities. The abstract syntax as well as a concrete instance situation are depicted in Fig. 3 and 4. The current state information of a robot during operation is represented by a finite state machine runtime model (cf. Fig. 8).

These runtime models can be used and changed within the different activities of the MAPE-K loop. In the following, we assume that the robot system has at least self-awareness capabilities concerning its battery functionality including the current battery level and is context-aware for its current goals. We consider the following exemplary execution steps inside one robot: the monitor activity retrieves information about the current map situation, the possible available pool of operations, the current behaviour specification in the form of a state machine as well as a goal model. It updates this information in the runtime model representation of the robot.

In a next step, the analyze activity is aware of the goals and constraints and it is able to conclude that the battery should not be exhausted. Furthermore, it detects in the possible operation pool of the robot the battery charging capability. As

a result of applying strategies to fulfill the goals, it decides to include a charging mechanism into the robot behaviour. The following third activity of the MAPE approach is the planning step according to the decision of the analyze step before. For example, the planner can adapt the retrieved simple state machine (representing the robot behaviour) depicted in Figure 8. It comes up with a detailed plan to adapt the behaviour from the current state to the envisioned one. An excerpt of the new adapted state machine is shown in Fig. 12. The passive state as well as ingoing and outgoing transitions are marked as to be deleted and two states charging and critical (with underlying behaviour) must be created. New transitions reflect the constraints from the goal model. In this case, the robot processes incoming puck transportation tasks in the active state. If the battery power level drops below 30 percent, the robot behaviour changes by entering the critical state. There, it searches for a charging point nearby and tries to reach it. If the robot successfully reaches one, it charges the battery until it is full in the charging state and returns to normal execution behaviour. Otherwise, the battery is exhausted and the robot stops the execution of the task.

Afterwards, the last activity in the MAPE-K loop takes the plan and applies the planned changes to the real system (it synchronizes the updated runtime model with the real system). After a successful update, the behaviour of the real robot is adapted according to the current goals and constraints.

4.3.1 Forms of Uncertainty

For the case of runtime models *epistemic uncertainty* can arise from multiple sources that include sensing - when building or updating the models - and the passing of time. If the original of a runtime model is monitored at runtime, the resulting update of the corresponding runtime model should, in principle, lead to less uncertainty. This effect may be limited because the measurements at runtime usually include randomized errors and they are limited concerning the *when* and *what*. Looking at *epistemic uncertainty* in our Example 2, retrieval of environment information and subsequent update of the runtime model with information about which fields are blocked as well as the positions of the charging points based on measurements by the robot, would help reduce the level of uncertainty. However, there are details we should take into account as, for example, if the blocked fields change frequently, the effect of reducing the uncertainty would only be temporary. In contrast, if we continuously update the information concerning the location of permanent obstacles (e.g., walls) in the robot of Example 2, the robot will - on the long run, after it has explored the whole area - derive a sufficient floor plan of those permanent obstacles. This will contain only the unavoidable uncertainty due to measurement errors.

If a runtime model is also employed to store the planned changes, its state is somehow permanently evaluated against the original. This should, in principle, lead to a high consistency between the two and therefore a lower level of uncertainty. However, this effect may be limited as also changing the original may include a randomized error due to actuator errors.

When we are able to learn what can happen in the environment, we may be even able to improve the prediction of behaviour for the case of uncertainty associated with *randomization*. For example, in the case of the robot scenario, we may learn how likely temporal blocks occur for certain fields. If a certain transition relates to an activity such as a measurement that fails with a given probability, we may be able to learn the probability for a longer sequence of measurements, as it will be very likely that the number of failed attempts to take the transition divided by the total number of tries converges towards the failure probability. However, there may be problems while using this kind of assumptions. For example, if the assumption that the observed phenomena is related to a probability is not correct, we will likely see no convergence and thus the learning will fail.

The case of *linguistic ambiguities* is slightly different since it covers the cases when the concepts in the model are not known in a precise way. Approaches such as fuzzy automata can be used to deal with this issue. They include a fuzzification and de-fuzzification of the linguistic concepts which allows them to handle this form of uncertainty, while complicating the analysis considerably [46]. If we consider the soft goals in Figure 3 that describe a *low energy consumption* and *high throughput*, these constraints could be good candidates to be specified in a fuzzy automata. Note that the translation of those goals from a linguistic concept to a manageable runtime model may introduce additional uncertainty.

Unfortunately, the sources of uncertainty described above rarely occur independently from each other. Instead, the effects produced by these sources of uncertainty can compound and thereby inhibit the system from clearly assessing the extent to which it satisfies its requirements. Therefore, solutions to tackle composed sources of uncertainty are required. For example, having temporary blocks of certain fields arising in the robot scenario can be related to *randomization* as well as *epistemic uncertainty* and therefore, tackling this issue by only learning probability values would not be enough. Instead, intervals for the probabilities as provided by interval probabilistic automata would be required.

4.3.2   Time and Uncertainty

Furthermore, as in the case of development-time models, for runtime models we can also observe that uncertainty may stay stable, decrease or even increase over time. In case of the energy level maintained by the robot that changes over time, the three cases can result in the following situations:

Even if certain parameters are measured, the uncertainty *increases over time* as the parameters that are not updated over time may also be uncertain. In this case the runtime model represents a partial view that may not provide enough information of the system at runtime to be able to support a solution to cope with the situation. As an example, currently we have not considered in a runtime model that hardware parts of the robot can be worn out. Therefore, the uncertainty about the status of those parts is not handled in any activity of the MAPE-K loop. We can only assume that the quality of the hardware parts decreases over time but as long as those parts are not broken or fail, we cannot reason about the impact on the robot's behaviour.

The uncertainty remains *constant over time* if the measurements are sufficient to keep the uncertainty within certain bounds. In this case the runtime model can be exploited to chose a proper behaviour that works with the captured circumstances. In the Example 2, the battery level is measured periodically to decide when it is time to load it. We can cope with two constant uncertainty issues in this example. First, if we know the period of the measurement, we can estimate lower and upper bounds of energy decreasing for that specific time slot. Secondly, the used hardware sensor and the runtime model representation has a certain precision that is known upfront and stay in a bound too (assuming that the sensor works correctly).

The uncertainty is *reduced over time* if measurements collect information about the system status and step-by-step increase the accuracy of the corresponding model representation of the system. As an effect, this will reduce the uncertainty over time. Usually, there is saturation of this effect after a while and a certain level of the uncertainty remains (see former case). Otherwise, after a certain time the uncertainty would have been completely eliminated and the characteristics of the original as far as covered by the model are exactly known. A very simple example is the exhaustion of the battery. In that specific case, there is no uncertainty and we exactly know that the battery is empty (even if this is not very helpful).

4.3.3   Feedback Loops and Uncertainty

In classical engineering feedback loops are a well known solution to address uncertainty concerning the environment [47]. Consequently, feedback loops have also been identified as the core element for engineering self-adaptive systems [48]. See also [49] for a discussion of uncertainty in autonomic systems with feedback loops. Therefore, the role of uncertainty in systems with runtime models and related concepts such as self-awareness, context-awareness, and requirement-awareness is best discussed referring to the extended architecture of a feedback loop as outlined in Figure 9.

As explained earlier, the more detailed view of the architecture comprises four key activities which are Monitoring, Analysis, Planning, and Execution (see Figure 13). Each of these activities can be seen as relying on the use of runtime models that serve as a knowledge-base. The runtime models of the system, context, and requirements plus additional strategic knowledge can then be seen as driving the feedback loop.

The basic MAPE-K architecture can be extended to leverage models that can evolve, thereby enabling a software system to cope with uncertainty by learning new properties about itself and its execution environment based on monitoring information that can only be collected at runtime. Specifically, to gradually reduce the level of uncertainty in the system, the four key processes in the MAPE-K architecture can analyze system and environmental data in order

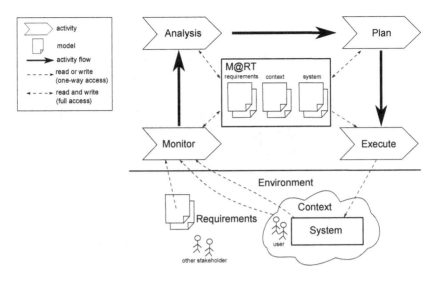

Fig. 13. Resolving uncertainty at run time with an extended MAPE-K architecture

to refine, augment, and revise the information stored in the runtime models, and then leverage that information to guide the adaptation process as necessary.

Next, we will review the objective of each of the four key activities and explore how uncertainty affects each of them. We will also review identified research questions associated with each phase of the MAPE-K loop that can potentially be tackled with the use of runtime models.

Monitor. In the detailed view on the architecture proposed in Figure 14, the monitoring process is primarily responsible for *measuring* raw data, about the current state and/or occurring events of the system, the context, and the requirements, and to *update* the runtime models representing the knowledge about the state, context and requirements.

The monitoring helps the software system to cope with uncertainty by continuously updating the information contained in a runtime model. Nevertheless, as explained above, the sensors used to obtain this monitoring information are limited by the precision and accuracy of their measurements. Moreover, sensors may fail at runtime or report values that the software system may simply be unable to interpret. As a result, even if monitoring reduces the level of uncertainty in a software system, it will depend on its accuracy, precision and frequency. The information it provides ultimately reflects an approximation that may contain some uncertainty.

Research questions associated with the *Monitoring* phase of the MAPE-K loop that can potentially be tackled with the use of runtime models and related to the fact that sensing and monitoring can be imprecise and partial are: *How can we determine the imprecision caused by temporal constraints / delays? Does the monitor engine also need to adapt (i.e., monitoring periods)? How can runtime*

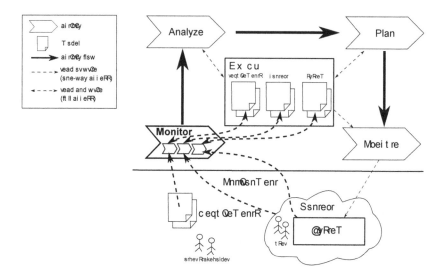

Fig. 14. Monitoring and resolving uncertainty with runtime models

models incorporate or learn new information using machine learning techniques and preserving at the same time the system under a reasonable behaviour? How does the runtime model represent what to monitor and how to do it?

Analyze. The architecture uses the analysis process to interpret data collected by the monitoring process and detect system and environmental changes that might warrant adaptation (see Figure 15).

In case more subtle updates are required, the analysis may, in addition to the monitoring, take as input the most recent data available as well as older data to obtain more accurate initial analysis models of the system and the environment. For example, techniques such as smoothening may allow better capturing of what is known about the system or environment than simply using the last measurement. In this context the complex update can be seen as a learning step that uses the observations made to provide a better runtime model. Accordingly, the employed learning/update strategy can have high impact on how successful the uncertainty is reduced. While more specific strategies may provide highly accurate runtime models, unless severe changes in the system or environment occur, more generic strategies may provide more robustness but solutions that performe worse.

In addition, the analysis activity verifies in a second step that monitoring information satisfies the requirements given, for example, in the form of relevant system and environmental goals and constraints. If necessary, this process also has to trigger an adaptation by the subsequent planning process if it detects that a requirement is, or could potentially become, unsatisfied. Moreover this analysis step concerning the goals and constraints is highly affected by the uncertainty in the runtime models. The analysis step can here only result in the

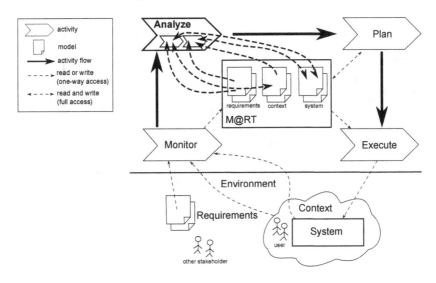

Fig. 15. Analysis and resolving uncertainty with runtime models

required precision and accuracy when the uncertainty present in the runtime model can be successfully handled and therefore, does not make an analysis infeasible. Depending on how the analysis results are presented as models, these runtime models can, due to a higher level of abstraction, contain considerable less uncertainty than what could have been observed for the monitoring.

As diagnosis and analysis can also be ambiguous and imprecise, the following research questions associated with the *Analysis* phase of the MAPE-K loop arise: *What is the effect of analysis techniques to resolve unknown uncertainty? Does the perspective on what is "relevant" for the runtime model need to adapt at run time? Should the criteria for decision-making adapt itself? How can we retain the ability of analysis even if we have incorporated newly learned information? How do the objectives of the analysis are represented and how can they be mapped onto a specific analysis technique?*

Plan. The Planning, if triggered, reads the runtime models enriched by the analysis and performs some reasoning to identify how the running system should be best adapted to changes of the system, context, and/or requirements. It may, for example, identify a plan to change the running system to also take into account a novel system goal.

The planning activity therefore reads the system, context and requirement runtime models and records the planned changes also in the form of a runtime model (see Figure 16). The identified changes can, for example, be captured by modifications of a runtime model of the system that we call *system'* (see the entity *system'* in Figure 16). Here, uncertainty only plays a role when identified changes cannot be safely planned as the related current state of the system is not available in the current runtime model of the system. The precision and

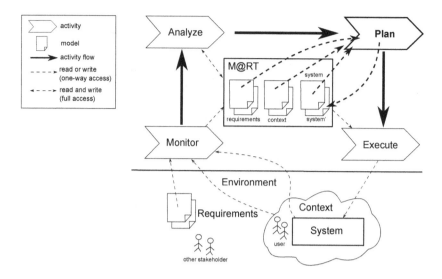

Fig. 16. Planning and resolving uncertainty with runtime models

accuracy of the planning is again determined by the uncertainty of the employed runtime models. For the case of the resulting prescriptive runtime model of the system, the runtime model usually captures only what should be changed and thus will not include any uncertainty at all.

For the *Planning* phase of the MAPE-K loop holds that the final outcome of an applied strategy cannot be accurately predicted and thus the following research questions result: *Should the planner take uncertainty into account? If so, how does it handles strategies when uncertainty exist or what kind of runtime models are more suitable? Furthermore, how can the planning activity be instrumented to achieve a specific objective (e.g., minimise the number of changes to be applied onto the system).*

Execute. The Execution activity directly applies a set of changes for the running system stored in some runtime models (see *system′* in Figure 17) by the planner. Even if these changes can have the direct consequences limited to the system itself, the changes may also indirectly affect the context in the longer run. The execute activity can be seen as the mechanism that support the causal connection which influences the running system according to the updated runtime models.

Assuming that applying the changes always works, the execute activity would guarantee that the employed runtime model of the system is now perfectly in sync with the system. However, in practice the execution activity cannot give such guarantees as its actuators provide only limited accuracy or may even completely fail. Furthermore, the system may have evolved in parallel to the feedback loop such that the planned updates become impossible or the changes do not result exactly in the planned outcome. Overcoming this problem, the

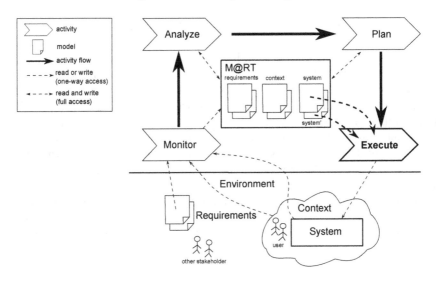

Fig. 17. Executing and resolving uncertainty with runtime models

next loop iteration should detect it and try to solve the inconsistencies again, or otherwise one can try to exclude it in such a way that changes occurring in the managed system can never result in inconsistencies with planned changes.

The effects of the *Execution* phase of the MAPE-K loop on the running system may not be as expected as also external influences as for example, disturbances from the environment or user interactions may exist which are not under control of the MAPE-K loop. Therefore, the following research questions have to be addressed: *Do temporal delays create an inconsistent view of the runtime model? How are the runtime models affected by external influences outside the MAPE-K loop?*

Summary. Uncertainty in self-adaptive systems can arise from multiple sources that include, but are not limited to, the system itself, its environment, and its stakeholders. For instance, the system itself uses its monitoring infrastructure, which may be inaccurate and imprecise, to measure properties about itself (self-awareness). Similarly, the surrounding context can introduce uncertainty because it is dynamic, unpredictable and ever changing, perhaps even leading to the violation of domain assumptions (context-awareness). Lastly, stakeholders can also introduce uncertainty by either modifying the current set of requirements that the system must satisfy, or by the emergence of new business needs or regulations that the system must comply with (requirement-awareness).

The uncertainty in the runtime models usually increases when time passes as the monitored information becomes outdated after a while as discussed in Section 4.3.2. A more frequent execution of the feedback loop can counteract this tendency and also guarantee faster adaptation reactions. However, the chosen frequency has to be cost-effective since it must balance a trade-off between the quality of the feedback loop and the overhead added to the execution of the system.

Also, a suitable trade-off decision has to be made concerning the accuracy of the runtime models. It is usually not cost-effective to monitor frequently as this not only increases the monitoring costs but also the subsequent analysis and planning activities. Therefore, enough monitoring to enable a suitable analysis and planning is necessary. Again, as in case of the updating/learning strategies, we have here also a trade-off between well-performing solutions within an envelope of expected likely changes and a robust solution. While for the former the required effort can be optimized, for the latter more overhead has to be accepted. Adjusting different activities such as monitoring, analysis and planning that are covered by the runtime models during system operation of higher-level adaptation loops (see Section 4.3.4) enables solutions where the overhead for robustness can be reduced by adjusting and intensifying the specific activities when necessary rather than always run them with a maximal overhead.

4.3.4   Types of Systems with Runtime Models

In the following, we will discuss the implications of using runtime models for different classes of systems ranging from configurable systems to those with full self-managing capabilities.

Configurable Systems. The simplest case of an adaptation loop (not a complete MAPE-K loop) is a runtime model, in which an externally initiated update triggers an adaptation of the system.

This kind of systems is neither self-aware nor context-aware and does not monitor the system itself or the environment. A requirement of self-awareness is that the system must consider itself at a higher level of abstraction. Instead, configurable systems do not actively change themselves and thus the required adaptation triggered by the external update can simply be enforced from outside the running system.

As a typical case, the user configures or changes requirements at runtime. A very simple configurable system takes the potentially updated runtime requirements model and checks it during operation. If constraints are not fulfilled an exception is thrown. Otherwise, the system will perform according to the given configuration parameters. A more elaborated version is that the updated runtime requirement model is used to derive the required behaviour. For example, the system selects a strategy with a good/optimal expected revenue by evaluating possible alternative behaviours and chooses the best performing one according to the actual requirements.

Example 3 (Configurable Robot Scenario with Runtime Models).

In this system scenario, the robot is neither self-aware nor context-aware. For this reason it cannot sense the environment. In this case, the runtime model is a valid map configuration that informs the robot about the actual position of pucks and obstacles. The robot gets an initial model of the environment according to

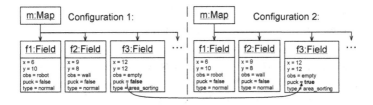

Fig. 18. Static map and instance situation with two possible configuration for the Example 3

the metamodel in Fig. 6 in Sec. 3, maintains all fields in this map and uses the given instance situation for navigation as well as fulfilling its goals. A snapshot of two (partial) environment configurations is depicted in Fig. 18. In this case, a puck is placed on field f_3.

The robot behaves according to the simple state machine in Fig. 19. Each time the robot enters the active *state, it checks the current map configuration data (*loadCurrentMap()*), searches for pucks to transport and calculates routes accordingly. We assume that the parameters in the configuration are valid and triggered from outside. In the* critical *and* charging *states, no adaptation is possible in this example.*

Each change in the map influences the behaviour of the robot because each one must reschedule the transportation tasks or recalculate routes. We have three robots in our scenario (cf. Fig. 2). The R_P robot transports pucks from the packaging room to the sorting room and this causes a change in the map of the example. The second robot R_S is affected by the map change because of a new incoming transportation task. The third robot, which transports pucks to the stock, can simply ignore the change of the map or the overall system does not update the local map of this robot.

The configuration of the system can easily be extended to other runtime models. However, if the system has to deal with very frequent changes, which causes, for example, a map update, the robots have to read the configuration file and possibly change their behaviour too often. Consequently, this solution is only applicable to rather static environments such as assembly lines with fixed mounted

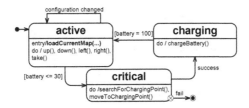

Fig. 19. State machine of a configurable robotic system

robot arms or runtime data that does not change often over time (e.g., the soft-goals throughput and low energy consumption).

Context-Awareness and/or Pervasive Systems. According to our definition of context-awareness provided in Section 3.3.3, a context-aware system that is not self-aware does not monitor the system itself but only the environment. Therefore, it usually requires that the system characteristics of interest do not change and thus the required adaptation according to the observed changes in the environment can be simply enforced without taking any changes of the system itself into account.

Example 4 (Context-Aware Robot Scenario with Runtime Models). A context-aware version of the Example 3 has additional sensing capabilities for monitoring the environment. As a result, it continuously corrects the internal environment model according to the measurements and needs no external trigger for updating the map. Additionally to the error correction of the map, the robot corrects its position over time to reduce the error introduced by the wheel actuators.

At deployment time, the robot system gets the same static map instance situation as in Example 3 (cf. Fig. 18). But now, it searches for pucks and reschedule the transportation tasks by itself. The context-aware state machine is shown in Fig. 20. The new sensing, updateMap, searchPuck() *and* correctPositionInMap() *functions are the context-aware parts of the robot and influence the behaviour, e.g., by updating the internal map and a better path planning with less uncertainty over time due to the better environment sensing capabilities.*

Requirement-Aware Systems. These kind of systems conceive requirements as first class entities in the runtime models (c.f. Section 3.3.3). They take care of changes of their own requirements as well as track them over time. According to current constraints or varying needs, the systems adapt the behaviour to fulfill current requirements.

Example 5 (Requirement-Aware Robot Scenario with Runtime Models). In the previous Examples 3 and 4, we have the implicit assumption that the behaviour of the robot system always conforms to the given goals. In a requirement-aware adaptive system, these goals can be considered explicitly. In this example, the runtime model is a valid goal configuration that influences the behaviour of the

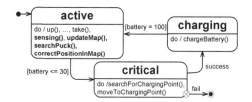

Fig. 20. State machine of a context-aware robotic system

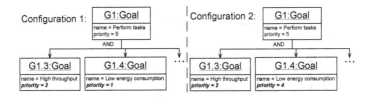

Fig. 21. Two goal configurations for the requirement-aware robotic system

robot. A snapshot of the partial goal configurations is depicted in Fig. 21. The difference between the left and right configuration in the picture is the priority of saving energy during task execution. The robot behaves according to the state machine in Fig. 22. Each time the robot enters the active *state, it checks the current configuration data and calculates the normal drive speed accordingly (*calculateSpeed(config)*). We assume that the parameters in the configuration are valid and triggered from outside. In the* critical *and* charging *states, no adaptation is possible in this example.*

For the two configurations in Fig. 21, the speed of the robot might be much higher for configuration 1 *than for the second one, because of the different priorities of the goals. Saving energy has a higher priority in the second goal configuration, which implies (among other changes) a reduction of the movement speed to an optimal power saving level.*

Self-adaptive Systems. Self-adaptive systems as introduced in Sec. 3.3.3 use the feedback loop to identify and compensate several changes in the system or environment. In essence, it provides the capability to live with the uncertainty related to the changes in the system or environment. They adjust to specific current needs of the different situations that can be identified at runtime.

Example 6 (Self-Adaptive Robot Scenario with Runtime Models).

A self-adaptive version of our robotic scenario extends the monitor activity from the context-aware system in Example 4. The analysis and planning steps are also extended. More precisely, the system runtime models are now an environment model (the first version is initially loaded), a goal model with constraints,

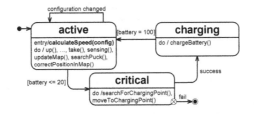

Fig. 22. State machine of a requirement-aware robotic system

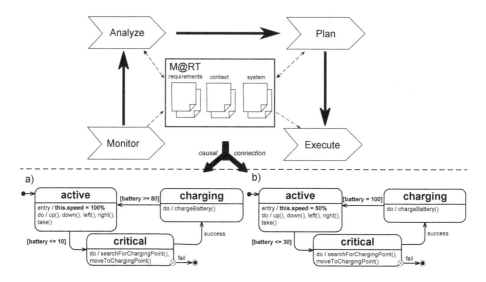

Fig. 23. Self-Adaptive robotic system scenario. The MAPE-K loop has a casual connection to the runtime model in form of a state machine. This state machine is adapted over time from variant a) to b).

and an initial behaviour model in form of a finite state machine. The runtime models are not static in this scenario, which is different from Examples 3 and 4.

Due to the sensing capabilities, the robot system can update its position in the map during runtime observations. Furthermore, it is aware of its requirements and goals. During the analysis and planning step, the self-adaptive system generates a state machine according to the current instance situation and constraints as depicted in Fig. 23.

Let us assume, the analysis step is aware of the possible configuration space of the behaviour parameter in the robot. The first goal parameters can look like the right instance situation in Fig. 21. The subgoal High throughput has a higher priority than the subgoal Low energy consumption. Therefore the planning step can generate a new behaviour model or adapt the existing one as depicted on the lower left in Fig 23 (state machine (a)). Here, the driving speed is set to a maximum and the robot moves are risky because of the reduced battery safety margins (only if battery is lower than 10 percent, the critical behaviour state is entered). Additionally, loading takes a lot of time (especially the last 20 percent) so that this timing behaviour is optimized in a second step. The overall behaviour of the robot must still guarantee that other constraints, e.g., exhausting the battery, are fulfilled during the execution.

The robot can perform its task according to this specialized state machine until the goals change. Goals can be changed by the user or the system itself. For example, the system can adapt its strategy according to the monitored environment information.

Let us assume, the goals change to the situation as depicted in the second configuration of Fig. 21. Now, the energy saving subgoal has a much higher priority. This is sensed and updated in the runtime model by the monitor step. The analyze activity decides that a behaviour adaptation is necessary and the planning step tries to fulfill the new constraints. In this case, the MAPE-K loop will generate/ adapt the existing state machine as depicted on the right in Fig. 23 (state machine (b)). The new behaviour model (state machine) uses a fix drive speed of 50 percent, which is much more energy efficient than before. Additionally, the safety margin of the battery is much higher (30 percent) and the battery is loaded to the maximum.

Therefore, our adaptive robot system is able to change its behaviour model according to the runtime requirements, context as well as system models. The analysis step must decide whether the adaptation to a new behaviour model is necessary and convenient. Indeed, the planning step must find an acceptable solution in the configuration space and the execute step changes or generates a new behaviour model that is directly used by the robot and therefore forces an adaptation of the system behaviour.

Self-adaptive Systems with Multiple Layers. As advocated in [50] more sophisticated self-management capabilities do not result from a single adaptation feedback loop but from the combination of two loops in two layers. Similarly to adaptive control schemes and robot control architectures, multiple layers - where multiple adaptation loops operate on top of a regular feedback loop - have to be employed. It is outlined in [50] that adaptation related to context-awareness and self-awareness can be handled by a lower level change management layer if the core system stays within certain bounds. For changes of the requirements a higher level goal management layer that adjusts the change management layer is proposed.

Example 7 (2 Layered Self-Adaptive Robot Scenario with Runtime Models). An extended version of our self-adaptive Example 6 includes also adaptation behaviour that happens at the 2nd layer. There, we will determine error handling capabilities if necessary. Furthermore, we assume the same adaptation loop as before in Example 6 with the same change in the requirements.

Fig. 24 shows the influence of each loop to the outcome of the system behaviour (state machine) on two layers. On top, the error handling loop monitors upcoming failures of the system (e.g., the robot does not find a charging station and therefore fails during operation) and the adaptation rate of the underlying MAPE loop. In our example, the analyze step decides to add more robust robot behaviour to guarantee better task execution performance. The key idea for hierarchical loops is that the upper loop only changes the runtime models of the loop below. In our case, the planning activity of the error handling loop manipulates the knowledge base of our introduced MAPE loop in Example 6 by adding additional robot operations (functions) and better analyzing as well as planning capabilities for that loop.

Therefore, if the loop at the bottom is executed, it will detect those new capabilities and can come up with a more sophisticated state machine, which includes now the error handling extensions (or a subset according to the current needs). The bold parts in the state machine depicted in Fig. 24 (state machine (a)) as well as the new error state are the outcome of the indirect influence of the error handling MAPE loop. In another case, the robot can correct its position at runtime in the active *state and/or has more possibilities finding the charging station using the* advancedLaserScan() *operation. Additionally, the robot can now inform other robots about failures and tries to recover its own state in case of failure.*

Another scenario is that the error handling loop detects the decreasing capacity of the battery over time. An additional repairBattery() *function (state machine (b)) can solve this problem and can be removed afterwards in the next adaptation cycle if the full capacity is restored.*

At this point, it is important to mention that the different adaptation loops can influence or work against each other. For example, if the upper loop wants to compensate losses by recharging the battery but the lower loop must consider the High throughput *subgoal (cf. the first configuration in Fig. 18) it may decide to exclude the* repairBattery() *function as shown in the left state machine in Fig. 24 to reach this goal (because repairing the battery will take a lot of additional time). This is one example that the influences of several adaptation loops can be rather complex and has to be designed with care.*

Again, the required subset of all these changes is handled by the upper loop, which can influence the lower loop in each cycle by manipulating the corresponding runtime models accordingly. As an overall effect, the lower loop will generate an adapted state machine that integrates all these changes but still ensures the system goals.

5   Runtime Models for Handling Uncertainty

In this section, we focus on the state-of-the-art in the use of models to mitigate uncertainty. As discussed in earlier sections of this chapter, epistemic, randomized, and linguistic forms of uncertainty can affect the design and operation of a software system. Both epistemic and linguistic forms of uncertainty prevail during the requirements analysis and design, while randomized forms of uncertainty - for the most part - directly affect a software system during runtime.

Development-time uncertainty can compound the different forms of uncertainty explained above and can prevent a software system from delivering its functionality. Therefore, these consequent effects need to be treated during the system execution. During execution, uncertainty may appear in the form of environmental conditions that might have not been foreseen during development-time, because they may be unpredictable by nature. Other sources of uncertainty may be due to unreliable monitoring infrastructure.

We focus on the state-of-the-art of approaches that tackle uncertainty, due to the causes explained above, and which are or can be supported by runtime

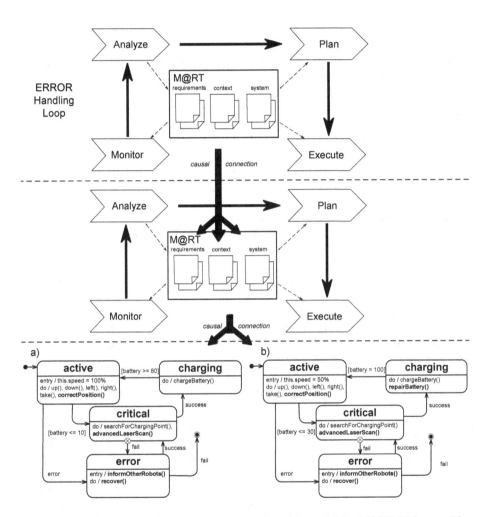

Fig. 24. Self-Adaptive robotic system scenario with multiple MAPE-K loops. The causal connection of the error handling loop influences the knowledge base of the MAPE-K loop below and therefore the outcome of the adapted state machines a) and b) indirectly.

models. The approaches described in the rest of this section are relevant in the context of the use of runtime models, although they focus on system's abstractions that characterize different stages and different qualities of the system life time.

5.1 Forms of Uncertainty

Next we provide a literature review of approaches that use runtime techniques to tackle epistemic, linguistic uncertainty as well as randomized uncertainty.

5.1.1 Epistemic Uncertainty

In [43] authors propose a technique to explicitly document the existence of uncertainty about how architectural decisions contribute towards satisfying nonfunctional properties (in the form of softgoals). The technique allows developers to deal with uncertainty during both development time and runtime [51]. A Claim can also be monitored at runtime to prove or disprove its validity [51]. *Claims* are particularly useful for ensuring that developers can revisit sources of uncertainty further along the development life cycle, including runtime, when new information may become available [52] tackling directly epistemic uncertainty.

In [53], probabilistic automatas are used to represent uncertainty for dynamically discovered and/or learned behavioural models and, as far as functional property validation is concerned, the uncertainty can be potentially tamed by using appropriate architectural models. Hidden Markov Models (HMM) [54] are typically used to model systems that have markovian characteristics in their behaviour, but they also have some states (and transitions) for which only limited knowledge is available. An example of an approach based on HMM that aims at evaluating the reliability of a software component with partial knowledge of its internal behaviour has been provided in [55]. Feature-based abstract models have been used to represent system's variability and configurations like in [56] to allow efficient symbolic model checking of product-line systems. Variability in the code is provided in context-oriented programming approach [57] as well as in the Chamaleon framework that supports a java extension to allow programming variability explicitly in the code [58]. Such variability is then solved by means of a resource-based analysis at deployment time when information about the execution context becomes available.

5.1.2 Linguistic Uncertainty

Fuzzy sets theory, which represents elements as partial members of a set, has been used in linguistics to deal with vagueness and ambiguity of the statements. In terms of self-adaptive systems, several techniques have been developed to deal with linguistic uncertainty.

An example of the use of Fuzzy theory RELAX [4], a specification language to express requirements that can be affected by uncertainty due to unanticipated system and environmental conditions. RELAX has been applied [59] to identify sources of uncertainty in the environment and monitor those conditions that pose uncertainty. Using RELAX and KAOS, Ramirez et al. [6] have tackled the fact that design assumptions can also be subject to uncertainty with potential negative consequences on the behaviour of the adaptive system. FLAGS [35] is an approach that distinguishes between crisp and fuzzy goals where goals are specified using linguistics constructors. FLAGS also defines the concept of an adaptive goal to express countermeasures that can be executed when goals are not satisfied.

Torres et al. [46] use Fuzzy sets to underpin an approach that encourages architects to specify the set of requirements of a system as an abstract specification model by using linguistic variables instead of numerical variables, as the latter are more prone to give allow the obsolescence of requirements. By doing so, the authors mitigate the obsolescence of the specification model of the system. The approach allows analysts to create specifications at design-time, while preserving the flexibility afforded by dynamic changes in the "meaning" of non-functional requirements as specific values, thus allowing to effectively assess runtime requirements compliance in non-stationary environments.

5.1.3   Randonmized Uncertainty

Randomized uncertainty is caused both by system and environmental conditions that are either inherently random or cannot be predicted reliably. Therefore, runtime techniques that help provide reliable reasoning and prediction have been developed. This kind of uncertainty has been traditionally expressed in approaches that consider system non functional properties, like performance and reliability. The uncertainty can therefore be accounted for by the use of stochastic models as non functional models. In [60] several techniques have been proposed to take into account non-functional attributes of software under uncertainty. In [61], parametric queuing network models of the performance of different system's configurations are managed at runtime in order to support dynamic reconfigurations of the system in response to unpredictable context variations. Probabilistic automatas [53] discussed earlier also consider dealing with uncertainty about non-functional properties as reliability on the behaviour of components to meet a goal and its costs during runtime.

Feature-based systems representation has been used to support predictive and non predictive system evolution [62], where the feature model can be dynamically evolved to support consistent configuration building. Bayesian models (such as Bayesian Networks [63]) provide a way to express in the non functional setting approaches a la assume-guarantee, typically adopted in the functional world and that we will briefly recall in the following. Bayesian probabilities enable stochastic models to be 'conditioned' to specific events that, in turn, have their own probability distributions. Other sophisticated stochastic models can be used to take into account uncertainty in non-functional validation processes. Discrete-Time Markov Chains (DTMCs) and Continuous-Time Markov Chains (CTMCs) have been used both at development and runtime, in [64] to reason about the reliability and performance of adaptable service-based application. In particular, the authors have started to study probability-based approaches to tackle the impact of the changes in the environment on the compositions of services and therefore the quality properties or QoS of the the service-based applications [64]. Their focus is on verification and dependability and in particular, on reliability and performance properties. In [7], the authors also focus on non-functional properties that can be specified quantitatively in a probabilistic way and target the challenge of making adaptation decisions under uncertainty. Given a decision that requires a certain configuration, the satisficement of a non-functional property can be modeled using probability distributions. However, differently from [64] they use Dynamic Decision Networks and focus on any non-functional property. Both [7] and [64] use Bayesian machine learning techniques to obtain information and support decision-making for self-adaptation during runtime.

5.2   Kinds of Runtime Models

The techniques described in this section recognize the need to produce, manage and maintain software models all along the softwares life time to support the realization and validation of systems adaptations while the system is already executing. In this section we describe more in depth the different techniques illustrated in the previous section and crucially focus on the runtime models they may involve. Furthermore, examples of the application of some of these techniques have already been introduced in Section 4.3. Additional information about model operations and a categorization of runtime models are further described in [21].

Furthermore, the purpose of this section is to show how to deal with uncertainty by focusing on system's abstractions (i.e. models) that characterize different stages and different relevant qualities of the system's life time. We consider two dimensions: the abstractions' dimension - and its corresponding software artifacts - that are used to explicitly represent uncertainty and system properties, and the properties' dimension. In particular, a system's abstractions have been considered that concern the following: systems models (e.g. architectural and behavioural system models, and coarse grain and fine grain system models), context models, and requirements models. On the properties' dimension, both the functional and non functional properties have been considered. The models described here represent uncertainty explicitly. More precisely, all these models are "loose" representations of the final system, i.e. the system that is actually running. All the approaches reviewed propose techniques to asses either functional or non functional properties on the system's artifact of reference. These models "contain" uncertainty but nevertheless are informative enough to allow assessment of some kinds of properties on the final system. The assessment allows the resolution of uncertainty at runtime.

5.2.1   Systems Models

In [65], runtime models of a system are used to reduce the number of configuration and reconfigurations that should be considered when planning the adaptations. In [66] variability models are reused during runtime to support self-reconfiguration of systems when triggered by changes monitored in the environment. In [67] architectural models (i.e. configuration graphs) are studied as a means for monitoring, visualizing and recording information about the system adaptations.

In [68] the authors tackle a key issue to support runtime software architectures. First, in their approach it is important to maintain a causal connection between the architecture and the running system to therefore ensure that (i) the architecture model represents the current system, and (ii) the modifications on the architecture model cause the corresponding system changes.

In [69] the authors present a model-driven approach to maintain and update several architectural runtime models using model-driven engineering techniques. The causal connection to the running system is realized by triple graph grammar transformation rules. The approach is implemented and evaluated for the Enterprise Java Beans component standard.

So far, researchers have focused on the use of runtime models for the representation of the architecture of the system with no much advance in the area of the use of runtime models to control and generate system behaviour. In [70] the authors focus on the novel use of runtime models to support the dynamic synthesis of software, and specifically the synthesis of mediators to translate actions of one system to the actions of another system developed with no prior knowledge of the former in order to achieve interoperability. Using discovery and learning methods, the required knowledge of the context and environment. is captured and refined. The knowledge is explicitly formulated and made available to computational manipulation in the form of a runtime model. This runtime model is based on labelled transition systems (LTSs) which offer the behavioural semantics needed to model the interaction protocols to enable the interoperability between the systems. A similar solution to enable components interoperability is presented in [71] . Specifically, the authors present a model-driven approach that integrates an automated technique for runtime identification of message mismatches and the generation of behavioural mediators and their deployment supported by runtime models. However, further research efforts are needed in the area.

5.2.2   Context Models

Beside modeling the system, in order to carry out V&V activities it is also necessary to use a model of the context or the environment. In [72] a probabilistic model of the context evolution is provided in order to allow the dynamic adaptation of a system's configuration by achieving an optimal trade-off between user benefits and reconfiguration cost. Other approaches provide either explicit or implicit representation of the context and of its possible evolutions [73] via context assumptions. Notably in this class we can recall the whole approach to validation that goes under the name of assume-guarantee techniques. Although the original motivation for this approach was to provide compositional means to validate large systems, this approach can also be characterized as what can be proved in terms of the inner knowledge of a component (the known) and what needs to be provided by the environment in which the component is executed (the unknown). Many approaches exist in the literature that range from the automatic synthesis of assumptions [74] for traditional behavioural models to the extension to probabilistic models [75].

Many other research efforts are devoted to support consistent adaptation of specific type of systems, notably in the service research arena [76]. These attempts, with reference to the MAPE cycle invest the planning activities, and provide solutions that can allow the evolution of the system in response to dynamic unplanned events. Other work handling uncertainty with the system itself is based on monitoring the values of properties over time and using statistical modeling techniques to predict likely future values [77]. For example, estimating the execution time reliably and precisely provides assurances about the suitability of the dynamically-adaptable software within its current operating environment, and may result in a requirement to trigger re-adaptation. Using a dynamically generated predictive model, forecasts are made about the values of any properties that may be analyzed from a series of values monitored over time. Such predictions can be used in the decision-making process of the MAPE feedback loops of self-adaptive systems described earlier.

5.2.3 Requirements Models

As previously discussed, design-time uncertainty can arise due to an imperfect requirements specification where requirements are missing or ambiguous [2,78,79]. Such uncertainty can often lead to a misalignment between the system's design and its original intent. Several techniques have been proposed for dealing with uncertainty at the requirements level, usually focusing either on documenting the existence of uncertainty or facilitating the analysis of how that uncertainty can affect the behaviour of the software system. In [52], the authors argue that requirements for self-adaptive systems need to be runtime entities (i.e. runtime models) that can be reasoned over at runtime.

Welsh et al. [43] have proposed REAssuRE that allows developers to deal with uncertainty during both development-time and runtime. Specifically, the authors used a *Claim* as a marker of uncertainty that explicitly documents the existence of uncertainty about how a system's goal operationalizations contribute towards the satisficement of soft goals. Techniques such as *Claims* are particularly useful for allowing developers to revisit sources of uncertainty further along the development life cycle when new information becomes available [52]. In that context, a Claim can also be monitored at runtime to prove or disprove its validity [51], thereby triggering an adaptation to reconfigure the system if necessary. Furthermore, in [51], the authors have demonstrated how goal-based runtime models can be held in memory in a form that allows the running system itself to evaluate goal satisfaction during execution and to propagate the effects of falsified Claims.

Fuzzy set theory, has been applied to represent and evaluate the satisfaction of functional [80] and non-functional requirements [81]. Ramirez et al. [6], recognize how Claims are also subject to uncertainty, in the form of unanticipated environmental conditions and unreliable monitoring information, that can adversely affect the behaviour of the adaptive system if it mistakenly falsifies a Claim. Therefore, the authors of [6] integrate Claims and RELAX, explained earlier, in order to assess the validity of Claims at runtime while tolerating minor and unanticipated environmental conditions that can trigger unnecessary adaptations and overhead.

Sutcliffe et al. [82] with their PC-RE method allow requirements to change over time in the face of contextual uncertainty. Epifani et al. [83] proposed to use a feedback control loop between models of non-functional properties and their implementations. During runtime, the system makes available information as feedback that is used to update the model to increase its correspondence with reality (hopefully decreasing uncertainty). Analysis of the updated model at runtime makes it possible to detect if a desired property (e.g. reliability or performance) is violated, causing automatic reconfigurations or self-healing actions to therefore meet the desired goals.

6   Research Challenges and Concluding Remarks

In this paper we have studied definitions and different types of uncertainty in the context of model-driven engineering putting emphasis on the use of models@run.time. We have revisited the concept of runtime models and have studied their impact and potential benefits in the management of uncertainty during execution. We have used a simple but illustrative example to discuss how development-time techniques together with runtime models can be used to cope with uncertainty. Also, we have discussed how runtime models can be used to extend the architecture of the MAPE-K loop to better manage uncertainty making use of abstractions (in the form of runtime models) to treat uncertainty as a first class entity during the system life cycle.

Based on the above, we summarize what we consider the most important research challenges, which are mainly explained in the context of the MAPE-K loop. We also argue the need for formal models and tools to support runtime models. Finally, we present some concluding remarks.

6.1   Runtime Models and the Feedback Adaptation Loop

The following are research challenges that have been identified and presented in the context of the MAPE-K loop.

6.1.1   Monitor

Sensing and monitoring can be imprecise and can provide just partial information. Runtime models should be able to make explicit this incompleteness of information during monitoring through the use of the right abstractions; to therefore make it amenable to subsequent phases and specially the Analysis phase. Finding the right runtime abstractions to use to make available and measurable the uncertainty related to imprecision and partial information during monitoring is challenge that deserves research efforts.

Furthermore, better ways to explore how the system and the environment can interact are needed. We think runtime models can extend their application to represent not only concerns related to the running system but also the surrounding environment. Specifically, testing techniques need to be developed to explore how the software system interacts with its execution environment. These tests should measure whether the software system is capable of satisfying its requirements while facing uncertain conditions. Runtime models can be used to represent uncertainty through a shared boundary between the software system and its execution environment while more information is captured by the system while it is running.

6.1.2 Analyze

Currently, a *"marker of uncertainty"* [43] provides an estimate of a "known-unknown" [84] that identifies and describes parts of a model that are partially known. While markers of uncertainty narrow the scope of uncertainty and make it more manageable at run time, they should be specified in a proper way. Ideally, a marker of uncertainty should identify parts of a model that are partially known and, if possible, describe how they can vary. Regardless of whether a marker of uncertainty is explicit or implicit, techniques applicable at design-time and also runtime are required to facilitate the analysis of how different sources of uncertainty, and their severity, can affect the behaviour of a software system.

Moreover, little attention has been directed to techniques for the synthesis or generation of software using runtime models during execution. In order to design software systems that are able to tackle uncertainty, inferring the knowledge necessary to reason about system behaviour looks like an essential task. Such knowledge can be used to build runtime models during execution. An example is the work presented by the authors of [70] who present early results on how to conceive runtime models during execution, based on information about the running system and inferred using machine learning techniques during the execution of the system.

As new information is acquired, models should be refined. We argue the need of further research on how to include machine learning techniques to be able to incorporate new information while the system is running. Of course, the new acquired knowledge could solve uncertainty but also could incorporate more. In either case, what are the techniques to guarantee that some given properties of the system are preserved to maintain the desired system behaviour remains an open challenge. For example, while the model is fed with new information, the related notion of what is "relevant" to the runtime model may change.The ability of analysis based on the runtime model should be retained in any case.

6.1.3 Plan

In the planning step one has to deal with uncertainty and incompleteness of events in the decision-making process. To evaluate the decision-making process, uncertainty but also dynamicity should be taken into account. We believe that due to uncertainty, probabilistic reasoning and decision planning techniques are required in decision making. Few researchers have already worked using those techniques to tackle uncertainty. For example, Markov Decision Process (MDP) and Bayesian networks have been applied for diagnosis and self-recovery in [85,86]. The authors of [87] use a stochastic Petri net for decision-making in fault-tolerance. In [88] a stochastic Petri net is used as a model to compute the optimal monitoring frequency for crashing failures of a service-oriented system. Bayesian Dynamic Decision Networks have been used to enhance decision-making in self-adaptive systems [7].

The research initiatives named above are novel and represent research progress. However, the runtime models they would require to be applied at runtime would demand considerable amounts of resources (e.g. memory, and CPU) to be done during runtime. Therefore, the application of those techniques still remain a big challenge.

6.1.4 Execute

The use of runtime models imply a causal connection with the running system. Temporal delays in the MAPE-K loop can create an inconsistent view of the runtime model with respect to the running systems. The latter remains a big research challenge.

6.2 The Need for New Forms of Abstractions and Tools

Suitable mathematical abstractions should be applied to formally describe and analyze uncertainty. We believe probability theory, fuzzy set theory, and machine learning techniques should be further investigated for this purpose. Probability theory can be used to describe situations where previous historical data is available and can provide insights about the current design of a software system. For instance, developers can analyze execution data gathered from a previous version of a system to identify which goals and requirements are less likely to be satisfied at runtime. Similarly, fuzzy set theory can be applied to describe types of uncertainty where it is not possible to categorically prove or disprove the validity of a statement. In this manner, fuzzy set theory can be applied to initially produce a more flexible system design that can be progressively tightened as more information about the system and its environment becomes known during the design phase. Fuzzy probability theory extends probability theory with the possibility of expressing uncertainty in the parameters of the probability density function. Lastly, further work is required to develop machine learning techniques to be able to manipulate values of probabilities or parameters of utility functions that change over time and therefore, to be able to quantify the impact of these values on the evaluation of alternative choices during the decision making process.

6.3 Concluding Remarks

Uncertainty about the running environments of software systems poses issues that software engineers need to face. Therefore, it is becoming increasingly important to come up with new methods and techniques to develop software systems able to deal with uncertainty at runtime. In this chapter we have discussed how runtime models are relevant in a reconceptualization of the development of software systems, which we assert is required to deal with uncertainty at runtime.

To establish a common ground for further discussions, we first introduced fundamental terms such as models, runtime models and uncertainty by using an exemplary goal, context and behavioural model for one robot of the factory automation example introduced earlier in the chapter. We also identified which kinds of runtime models are employed and outlined the most common types of systems using such runtime models. Furthermore, we discussed the role that runtime models can play for the different types of systems described.

Nowadays, we can observe the trend to delay decisions to handle uncertainty at runtime instead of doing it during development-time. To better understand the benefits and drawbacks of handling uncertainty at runtime by using runtime models, first we discussed classical approaches to handle uncertainty using development-time models and followed on considering how more advanced solutions to handle uncertainty at runtime can be used and how they can benefit from runtime models.

Specifically, we have discussed how the concepts of the MAPE-K loop can rely on runtime model techniques updating the knowledge data of the loop to tackle uncertainty during both development and runtime. We have argued how the above allows the management of uncertainty as a first class entity during the system life cycle. The envisioned framework includes a perpetual phase in which the runtime models can evolve, thereby allow the software system to cope with uncertainty by learning new information about itself and its execution environment based on monitored information that can only be collected during execution. We believe that in order to be able to support the extension of the MAPE-K loop proposed in this paper, several key challenges and enabling technologies need to be addressed. Crucially, synthesis of software during execution using runtime models has been identified as key challenge. Furthermore, such a capability requires inference of new knowledge during runtime. Therefore, we believe that machine learning techniques should be further studied to enable the incorporation of new information during the execution of the system while guaranteeing that the behaviour of the system is kept in the required behavioural envelop. Finally, to make this vision feasible new suitable and more efficient mathematical formalisms are also needed.

References

1. Galbraith, J.: Designing Complex Organizations. Organization development. Addison-Wesley (1973)
2. Noppen, J.: Imperfect Information in Software Design Processes. PhD thesis, University of Twente (2007)
3. Ramirez, A., Jensen, A., Cheng, B.H.C., Knoester, D.: Automatically exploring how uncertainty impacts behavior of dynamically adaptive systems. In: 2011 26th IEEE/ACM International Conference on Automated Software Engineering (ASE), pp. 568–571 (2011)
4. Whittle, J., Sawyer, P., Bencomo, N., Chen, B.H.C., Bruel, J.M.: RELAX: Incorporating uncertainty into the specification of self-adaptive systems. In: The Proceedings of the 17th International Requirements Engineering Conference (RE 2009), Atlanta, Georgia, USA, pp. 79–88. IEEE Computer Society (September 2009)
5. Welsh, K., Sawyer, P., Bencomo, N.: Towards Requirements Aware Systems: Run-time Resolution of Design-time Assumptions. In: Proceedings of the 26th IEEE/ACM International Conference on Automated Software Engineering, ASE 2011, Kansas, USA, November 6-10. ACM (2011) (to appear)
6. Ramirez, A.J., Cheng, B.H.C., Bencomo, N., Sawyer, P.: Relaxing claims: Coping with uncertainty while evaluating assumptions at run time. In: France, R.B., Kazmeier, J., Breu, R., Atkinson, C. (eds.) MODELS 2012. LNCS, vol. 7590, pp. 53–69. Springer, Heidelberg (2012)
7. Bencomo, N., Belaggoun, A., Issarny, V.: Dynamic decision networks for decision-making in self-adaptive systems: A case study. In: Software Engineering for Adaptive and Self-Managing Systems, SEAMS (2013)
8. Laffont, J.J.: The Economics of Uncertainty and Information. The MIT Press (1989)
9. Uncertainty in Artificial Intelligence, http://www.auai.org/
10. Wätzoldt, S., Neumann, S., Benke, F., Giese, H.: Integrated Software Development for Embedded Robotic Systems. In: Noda, I., Ando, N., Brugali, D., Kuffner, J.J. (eds.) SIMPAR 2012. LNCS, vol. 7628, pp. 335–348. Springer, Heidelberg (2012)
11. Cheng, S.W., Garlan, D.: Handling Uncertainty in Autonomic Systems. In: Proceedings of the International Workshop on Living with Uncertainties (IWLU 2007), Co-located with the 22nd International Conference on Automated Software Engineering (ASE 2007), Atlanta, GA, USA, November 5 (2007)
12. Ali, R., Dalpiaz, F., Giorgini, P.: A Goal Modeling Framework for Self-Contextualizable Software. In: Proceedings of the Fourteenth International Conference on Exploring Modeling Methods in Systems Analysis and Design, pp. 326–338. Springer-Verlag (2009)
13. Lapouchnian, A., Mylopoulos, J.: Modeling Domain Variability in Requirements Engineering with Contexts. In: Laender, A.H.F., Castano, S., Dayal, U., Casati, F., de Oliveira, J.P.M. (eds.) ER 2009. LNCS, vol. 5829, pp. 115–130. Springer, Heidelberg (2009)
14. Stachowiak, H.: Allgemeine Modelltheorie. Springer-Verlag (1973)
15. Chung, L., Cesar, J., Leite, S.P.: Non-functional requirements in software engineering (1999)
16. van Lamsweerde, A.: Requirements Engineering: From System Goals to UML Models to Software Specifications. John Wiley (2009)
17. Harel, D.: Statecharts: A Visual Formalism for Complex Systems. Sci. Comput. Program. 8(3), 231–274 (1987)

18. Albarghouthi, A., Gurfinkel, A., Chechik, M.: From Under-Approximations to Over-Approximations and Back. In: Flanagan, C., König, B. (eds.) TACAS 2012. LNCS, vol. 7214, pp. 157–172. Springer, Heidelberg (2012)
19. Mula, J., Poler, R., Garciasabater, J., Lario, F.: Models for production planning under uncertainty: A review. International Journal of Production Economics 103(1), 271–285 (2006)
20. Blair, G., Bencomo, N., France, R.B.: Models@run.time. Computer 42(10), 22–27 (2009)
21. Vogel, T., Seibel, A., Giese, H.: The Role of Models and Megamodels at Runtime. In: Dingel, J., Solberg, A. (eds.) MODELS 2010. LNCS, vol. 6627, pp. 224–238. Springer, Heidelberg (2011)
22. Kephart, J.O., Chess, D.M.: The vision of autonomic computing. IEEE Computer 36(1), 41–50 (2003)
23. Morin, B., Fleurey, F., Bencomo, N., Jézéquel, J.-M., Solberg, A., Dehlen, V., Blair, G.S.: An aspect-oriented and model-driven approach for managing dynamic variability. In: Czarnecki, K., Ober, I., Bruel, J.-M., Uhl, A., Völter, M. (eds.) MODELS 2008. LNCS, vol. 5301, pp. 782–796. Springer, Heidelberg (2008)
24. Morin, B., Barais, O., Nain, G., Jézéquel, J.M.: Taming dynamically adaptive systems using models and aspects. In: ICSE, pp. 122–132 (2009)
25. Bencomo, N., Whittle, J., Sawyer, P., Finkelstein, A., Letier, E.: Requirements reflection: Requirements as runtime entities. In: Proceedings of the 32nd ACM/IEEE International Conference on Software Engineering, Cape Town, South Africa, pp. 199–202. ACM (May 2010)
26. Sawyer, P., Bencomo, N., Letier, E., Finkelstein, A.: Requirements-aware systems: A research agenda for re self-adaptive systems. In: Proceedings of the 18th IEEE International Requirements Engineering Conference, Sydney, Australia, pp. 95–103 (September 2010)
27. Salehie, M., Tahvildari, L.: Self-adaptive software: Landscape and research challenges. ACM Trans. Auton. Adapt. Syst. 4(2) (2009)
28. Weiser, M.: The computer for the 21st century. SIGMOBILE Mobile Computing and Communications Review 3(3), 3–11 (1999)
29. Baldauf, M., Dustdar, S., Rosenberg, F.: A survey on context-aware systems. International Journal of Ad Hoc and Ubiquitous Computing 2(4), 263–277 (2007)
30. Bellavista, P., Corradi, A., Fanelli, M., Foschini, L.: A Survey on Context Data Distribution for Mobile Ubiquitous Systems. ACM Computing Surveys (2013) (to appear)
31. Souza, V.S., Lapouchnian, A., Robinson, W.N., Mylopoulos, J.: Awareness requirements for adaptive systems. In: Proceedings of the Sixth International Symposium on Software Engineering for Adaptive and Self-Managing Systems, Waikiki, Honolulu, HI, USA, pp. 60–69. ACM (2011)
32. Feather, M.S., Fickas, S., van Lamsweerde, A., Ponsard, C.: Reconciling system requirements and runtime behavior. In: Proceedings of the 8th International Workshop on Software Specification and Design, pp. 50–59. IEEE Computer Society (1998)
33. Fickas, S., Feather, M.S.: Requirements monitoring in dynamic environments. In: Proceedings of the Second IEEE International Symposium on Requirements Engineering, pp. 140–147. IEEE Computer Society (1995)
34. Silva Souza, V., Lapouchnian, A., Mylopoulos, J.: (Requirement) Evolution Requirements for Adaptive Systems. In: Proceedings of the 7th International Symposyum of Software Engineering for Adaptive and Self-Managing Systems. IEEE Computer Society (2012) (to appear)

35. Baresi, L., Pasquale, L., Spoletini, P.: Fuzzy goals for requirements-driven adaptation. In: Proceedings of the 18th IEEE International Requirements Engineering Conference, RE, Sydney, Australia, pp. 125–134. IEEE (2010)

36. Ali, R., Solís, C., Omoronyia, I., Salehie, M., Nuseibeh, B.: Social Adaptation - When Software Gives Users a Voice. In: Proceedings of the 7th International Conference on Evaluation of Novel Approaches to Software Engineering, pp. 75–84. SciTePress (2012)

37. Maes, P.: Concepts and Experiments in Computational Reflection. In: Proceedings of the 2nd International Conference on Object-oriented Programming Systems, Languages and Applications, OOPSLA 1987, pp. 147–155. ACM, New York (1987)

38. McManus, H., Hastings, D.: A Framework for Understanding Uncertainty and its Mitigation and Exploitation in Complex Systems. In: Proceedings of the Fifteenth Annual International Symposium of the International Council on Systems Engineering, INCOSE 2005, Rochester, NY (2005)

39. Garlan, D.: Software engineering in an uncertain world. In: Proceedings of the FSE/SDP Workshop on Future of Software Engineering Research, FoSER 2010, pp. 125–128. ACM, New York (2010)

40. Humphrey, W.: A Discipline for Software Engineering. SEI Series in Software Engineering Series. Addison Wesley Professional (1995)

41. Lehman, M.M., Belady, L.A.: Program evolution: Processes of software change. Academic Press Professional, Inc., San Diego (1985)

42. Parnas, D.L.: Software aging. In: Proceedings of the 16th International Conference on Software Engineering, ICSE 1994, Los Alamitos, CA, USA, pp. 279–287. IEEE Computer Society Press (1994)

43. Welsh, K., Sawyer, P.: Understanding the scope of uncertainty in dynamically adaptive systems. In: Wieringa, R., Persson, A. (eds.) REFSQ 2010. LNCS, vol. 6182, pp. 2–16. Springer, Heidelberg (2010)

44. Rabin, M.O.: Probabilistic automata. Information and Control 6(3), 230–245 (1963)

45. Piech, H., Siedlecka-Lamch, O.: Interval probabilities of state transitions in probabilistic automata. In: Rutkowski, L., Korytkowski, M., Scherer, R., Tadeusiewicz, R., Zadeh, L.A., Zurada, J.M. (eds.) ICAISC 2012, Part II. LNCS, vol. 7268, pp. 688–696. Springer, Heidelberg (2012)

46. Torres, R., Bencomo, N., Astudillo, H.: Mitigating the obsolescence of quality specifications models in service-based systems. In: MoDRE, pp. 68–76 (2012)

47. Xie, L.L., Guo, L.: How much uncertainty can be dealt with by feedback? IEEE Transactions on Automatic Control 45(12), 2203–2217 (2000)

48. Brun, Y., et al.: Engineering Self-Adaptive Systems through Feedback Loops. In: Cheng, B.H.C., de Lemos, R., Giese, H., Inverardi, P., Magee, J. (eds.) Self-Adaptive Systems. LNCS, vol. 5525, pp. 48–70. Springer, Heidelberg (2009)

49. Cheng, S.W., Garlan, D.: Handling Uncertainty in Autonomic Systems. In: Proceedings of the International Workshop on Living with Uncertainties (IWLU 2007), Co-located with the 22nd International Conference on Automated Software Engineering (ASE 2007), Atlanta, GA, USA, November 5 (2007), http://godzilla.cs.toronto.edu/IWLU/program.html

50. Kramer, J., Magee, J.: Self-Managed Systems: an Architectural Challenge. In: FOSE 2007: 2007 Future of Software Engineering, pp. 259–268. IEEE Computer Society, Washington, DC (2007)

51. Welsh, K., Sawyer, P., Bencomo, N.: Run-time Resolution of Uncertainty. In: Proceedings of the 19th IEEE International Requirements Engineering Conference, Trento, Italy, August 29-September 2, pp. 355–356 (2011)

52. Sawyer, P., Bencomo, N., Whittle, J., Letier, E., Finkelstein, A.: Requirements-Aware Systems: A Research Agenda for RE for Self-adaptive Systems. In: Proceedings of the 18th IEEE International Requirements Engineering Conference, Sydney, New South Wales, Australia, September 27-October 1, pp. 95–103 (2010)

53. Autili, M., Cortellessa, V., Di Ruscio, D., Inverardi, P., Pelliccione, P., Tivoli, M.: Integration architecture synthesis for taming uncertainty in the digital space. In: Calinescu, R., Garlan, D. (eds.) Monterey Workshop 2012. LNCS, vol. 7539, pp. 118–131. Springer, Heidelberg (2012)

54. Ephraim, Y., Merhav, N.: Hidden markov processes. IEEE Transactions on Information Theory 48(6), 1518–1569 (2002)

55. Cheung, L., Roshandel, R., Medvidovic, N., Golubchik, L.: Early prediction of software component reliability. In: Proceedings of the 30th International Conference on Software Engineering, ICSE 2008, pp. 111–120. ACM, New York (2008)

56. Cordy, M., Classen, A., Perrouin, G., Schobbens, P.Y., Heymans, P., Legay, A.: Simulation-based abstractions for software product-line model checking. In: ICSE, pp. 672–682. IEEE (2012)

57. Hirschfeld, R., Costanza, P., Nierstrasz, O.: Context-oriented Programming. Journal of Object Technology 7(3), 125–151 (2008)

58. Autili, M., Benedetto, P.D., Inverardi, P.: Hybrid approach for resource-based comparison of adaptable java applications. Science of Computer Programming (2012) (to appear)

59. Cheng, B.H.C., Sawyer, P., Bencomo, N., Whittle, J.: A goal-based modeling approach to develop requirements of an adaptive system with environmental uncertainty. In: Schürr, A., Selic, B. (eds.) MODELS 2009. LNCS, vol. 5795, pp. 468–483. Springer, Heidelberg (2009)

60. Mishra, K., Trivedi, K.S.: Uncertainty propagation through software dependability models. In: Dohi, T., Cukic, B. (eds.) ISSRE, pp. 80–89. IEEE (2011)

61. Caporuscio, M., Marco, A.D., Inverardi, P.: Model-based System Reconfiguration for Dynamic Performance Management. Journal of Systems and Software 80(4), 455–473 (2007)

62. Inverardi, P., Mori, M.: A Software Lifecycle Process to Support Consistent Evolutions. In: de Lemos, R., Giese, H., Müller, H.A., Shaw, M. (eds.) Self-Adaptive Systems. LNCS, vol. 7475, pp. 239–264. Springer, Heidelberg (2013)

63. Neil, M., Fenton, N., Tailor, M.: Using bayesian networks to model expected and unexpected operational losses. International Journal on Risk Analysis 25(4), 963–972 (2005)

64. Filieri, A., Ghezzi, C., Tamburrelli, G.: A formal approach to adaptive software: Continuous assurance of non-functional requirements. Formal Asp. Comput. 24(2), 163–186 (2012)

65. Morin, B., Barais, O., Jézéquel, J.M., Fleurey, F., Solberg, A.: Models@ Run.time to Support Dynamic Adaptation. IEEE Computer 42(10), 44–51 (2009)

66. Cetina, C., Giner, P., Fons, J., Pelechano, V.: Autonomic computing through reuse of variability models at runtime: The case of smart homes. Computer 42(10), 37–43 (2009)

67. Georgas, J., van der Hoek, A., Taylor, R.: Using architectural models to manage and visualize runtime adaptation. Computer 42(10), 52–60 (2009)

68. Song, H., Huang, G., Chauvel, F., Xiong, Y., Hu, Z., Sun, Y., Mei, H.: Supporting runtime software architecture: A bidirectional-transformation-based approach. Journal of Systems and Software 84(5), 711–723 (2011)
69. Vogel, T., Giese, H.: Adaptation and Abstract Runtime Models. In: Proceedings of the 5th Workshop on Software Engineering for Adaptive and Self-Managing Systems (SEAMS 2010) at the 32nd IEEE/ACM International Conference on Software Engineering (ICSE 2010), Cape Town, South Africa, pp. 39–48. ACM (May 2010)
70. Bencomo, N., Bennaceur, A., Grace, P., Blair, G., Issarny, V.: The role of models@run.time in supporting on-the-fly interoperability. Springer Computing (2013); special issue Models@runt.time
71. Hao, R., Morin, B., Berre, A.J.: A semi-automatic behavioral mediation approach based on models@runtime. In: Models@run.time, pp. 67–71 (2012)
72. Mori, M., Li, F., Dorn, C., Inverardi, P., Dustdar, S.: Leveraging State-Based User Preferences in Context-Aware Reconfigurations for Self-Adaptive Systems. In: Barthe, G., Pardo, A., Schneider, G. (eds.) SEFM 2011. LNCS, vol. 7041, pp. 286–301. Springer, Heidelberg (2011)
73. Hong, J., Suh, E., Kim, S.J.: Context-aware systems: A literature review and classification. Expert Syst. Appl. 36(4), 8509–8522 (2009)
74. Giannakopoulou, D., Pasareanu, C.S., Barringer, H.: Component verification with automatically generated assumptions. Autom. Softw. Eng. 12(3), 297–320 (2005)
75. Kwiatkowska, M., Norman, G., Parker, D., Qu, H.: Assume-guarantee verification for probabilistic systems. In: Esparza, J., Majumdar, R. (eds.) TACAS 2010. LNCS, vol. 6015, pp. 23–37. Springer, Heidelberg (2010)
76. Bucchiarone, A., Marconi, A., Pistore, M., Raik, H.: Dynamic Adaptation of Fragment-based and Context-aware Business Processes. In: Proc. of the 19th International Conference on Web Services. IEEE Computer Society (2012) (to appear)
77. Brennan, S., Cahill, V., Clarke, S.: Applying non-constant volatility analysis methods to software timeliness. In: Proceedings of the 21st Euromicro Conference on Real-Time Systems (ECRTS), WIP Track (2009)
78. Temponi, C., Yen, J., Tiao, W.A.: Assessment of customer's and technical requirements through a fuzzy logic-based method. In: Proceedings of the International Conference on Systems, Man and Cybernetics, vol. 2, pp. 1127–1132. IEEE Computer Society (1997)
79. Liu, X.F., Azmoodeh, M., Gerogalas, N.: Specification of non-functional requirements for contract specification in the ngoss framework for quality management and product evaluation. In: Proceedings of the Fifth International Workshop on Software Quality, pp. 36–41 (2007)
80. Liu, X.F.: Fuzzy requirements. IEEE Potentials, 24–26 (1998)
81. Glinz, M.: On non-functional requirements. In: IEEE International Requirements Engineering Conference, pp. 21–26 (2007)
82. Sutcliffe, A., Fickas, S., Sohlberg, M.M.: Pc-re: A method for personal and contextual requirements engineering with some experience. Requir. Eng. 11(3), 157–173 (2006)
83. Epifani, I., Ghezzi, C., Mirandola, R., Tamburrelli, G.: Model evolution by runtime parameter adaptation. In: Proceedings of the 31st International Conference on Software Engineering, ICSE 2009, pp. 111–121. IEEE Computer Society, Washington, DC (2009)
84. Cheng, B.H.C., et al.: Software Engineering for Self-Adaptive Systems: A Research Roadmap. In: Cheng, B.H.C., de Lemos, R., Giese, H., Inverardi, P., Magee, J. (eds.) Self-Adaptive Systems. LNCS, vol. 5525, pp. 1–26. Springer, Heidelberg (2009)

85. Robertson, P., Laddaga, R.: Model based diagnosis and contexts in self adaptive software. In: Babaoğlu, Ö., Jelasity, M., Montresor, A., Fetzer, C., Leonardi, S., van Moorsel, A., van Steen, M. (eds.) SELF-STAR 2004. LNCS, vol. 3460, pp. 112–127. Springer, Heidelberg (2005)
86. Robertson, P., Williams, B.: Automatic recovery from software failure. Commun. ACM 49, 41–47 (2006)
87. Porcarelli, S., Castaldi, M., Di Giandomenico, F., Bondavalli, A., Inverardi, P.: A framework for reconfiguration-based fault-tolerance in distributed systems. In: de Lemos, R., Gacek, C., Romanovsky, A. (eds.) Architecting Dependable Systems II. LNCS, vol. 3069, pp. 167–190. Springer, Heidelberg (2004)
88. Tichy, M., Giese, H.: A Self-Optimizing Run-Time Architecture for Configurable Dependability of Services. In: de Lemos, R., Gacek, C., Romanovsky, A. (eds.) Architecting Dependable Systems II. LNCS, vol. 3069, pp. 25–50. Springer, Heidelberg (2004)

Using Models at Runtime to Address Assurance for Self-Adaptive Systems

Betty H.C. Cheng[1], Kerstin I. Eder[2], Martin Gogolla[3], Lars Grunske[4], Marin Litoiu[5], Hausi A. Müller[6], Patrizio Pelliccione[7], Anna Perini[8], Nauman A. Qureshi[9], Bernhard Rumpe[10], Daniel Schneider[11], Frank Trollmann[12], and Norha M. Villegas[6,13]

[1] Michigan State University, US
chengb@cse.msu.edu
[2] University of Bristol, UK
Kerstin.Eder@bristol.ac.uk
[3] Universität Bremen, Germany
gogolla@informatik.uni-bremen.de
[4] TU Kaiserslautern, Germany
grunske@informatik.uni-kl.de
[5] York University, Canada
mlitoiu@yorku.ca
[6] University of Victoria, Canada
hausi@cs.uvic.ca
[7] Università degli Studi dell'Aquila, Italy
patrizio.pelliccione@univaq.it,
Chalmers University of Technology and University of Gothenburg, Sweden
patrizio.pelliccione@gu.se
[8] CIT - FBK - Povo Trento, Italy
perini@fbk.eu
[9] National University of Sciences and Technology (NUST), Pakistan
nauman.qureshi@seecs.edu.pk
[10] RWTH Aachen, Germany
rumpe@se-rwth.de
[11] Fraunhofer IESE - Kaiserslautern, Germany
daniel.schneider@iese.fraunhofer.de
[12] TU Berlin, Germany
Frank.Trollmann@dai-labor.de
[13] Icesi University, Colombia
nvillega@icesi.edu

Abstract. A self-adaptive software system modifies its behavior at runtime in response to changes within the system or in its execution environment. The fulfillment of the system requirements needs to be guaranteed even in the presence of adverse conditions and adaptations. Thus, a key challenge for self-adaptive software systems is assurance. Traditionally, confidence in the correctness of a system is gained through a variety of activities and processes performed at development time, such as design analysis and testing. In the presence of self-adaptation, however, some of the assurance tasks may need to be performed at runtime. This need calls for the development of techniques that enable continuous assurance throughout the software life cycle. Fundamental to the development of runtime assurance techniques is research into the use of models at runtime

N. Bencomo et al. (Eds.): Models@run.time, LNCS 8378, pp. 101–136, 2014.

(M@RT). This chapter explores the state of the art for using M@RT to address the assurance of self-adaptive software systems. It defines what information can be captured by M@RT, specifically for the purpose of assurance, and puts this definition into the context of existing work. We then outline key research challenges for assurance at runtime and characterize assurance methods. The chapter concludes with an exploration of selected application areas where M@RT could provide significant benefits beyond existing assurance techniques for adaptive systems.

1 Introduction

A self-adaptive system (SAS) modifies its behavior at runtime in response to changes in the system itself or in its environment.[1] An SAS generally comprises a component that delivers the basic function or service, often referred to as the *target* or *managed system*, and another component that controls or manages that target system through an *adaptation process*, often referred to as the *controller* [MAB+02] or *autonomic manager* [KC03]. The target system can be viewed as a steady-state program [ZC06a, GCZ08]. It is not adaptive and is applicable to a specific execution environment. The SAS controller can, via the invocation of an adaptation process that implements *adaptive logic* [ZC06a], transform this steady-state program to a different steady-state program—one that is suitable for a different set of environmental conditions [ZC06a]. As such, the steady-state program that delivers the basic function or service of an SAS is the target of the adaptation process that is managed by the controller. During the adaptation process, it is important to provide assurance that the system does not become inconsistent (e.g., no data is lost and transactions are not interrupted) [KM90, ZCYM05, ZC06b].

The IEEE Standard Glossary of Software Engineering Terminology defines *assurance* as "a planned and systematic pattern of all actions necessary to provide adequate confidence that an item or product conforms to established technical requirements" [IEE90].[2] For non-adaptive systems, assurance is typically performed at design and development time. In practice, assurance tasks comprise verification, validation, test, measurement, conformance to standards, and certification. Collectively, these tasks all contribute to gaining confidence that both the processes employed and the end product satisfy established technical requirements, standards, and procedures. In the presence of runtime adaptations in an SAS, the fulfillment of the system requirements need to be guaranteed at runtime, even during the adaptation process [ZC05, ZC06b, VMT+11b]. Thus, software assurance becomes a critical runtime concern, giving rise to the need for continuous assurance over the entire life cycle of a software system. Given the increasing use of SASs in safety-critical applications (e.g., power-grid management, transportation management systems, telecommunication systems, and health-monitoring), assurance for SASs is of paramount importance. The development of rigorous methods and techniques that extend

---

[1] This chapter uses the acronym SAS to refer to any software-based system that exposes self-* features.

[2] This chapter uses the term *software assurance* rather than the more specific term *software quality assurance* to not only include software quality concerns but also safety, reliability, and security concerns.

assurance from development time to runtime is therefore a high priority on the research agenda for the SAS research community.

Assurance is required for both functional properties (i.e., those describing specific functions of the system such as the result of a computation) and non-functional properties (i.e., those describing the operational qualities of the system such as availability, efficiency, performance, reliability, robustness, security, stability, and usability) [VMT+11b]. Guaranteeing these properties at runtime in SASs is particularly challenging due to the varying assurance needs posed by a changing system or execution environment, both fraught with uncertainty [RJC12, EM13]. Nevertheless, the properties specified in the system requirements need to hold *before*, *during*, and *after* adaptation [ZC06a, ZC06b, ZGC09].

Continuous assurance throughout the entire software life cycle provides unprecedented opportunities for monitoring, analyzing, guaranteeing, and predicting system properties throughout the operation of a software system. The fact that many variables that are free at development time are bound at runtime enables us to *tame* the state space explosion, thus enabling the exploration of states that could not have been considered at development time. This reduction in state space provides new opportunities for runtime verification and validation (V&V), leading to assurance of critical system properties at runtime [TVM+12]. Fundamental to the development of runtime assurance techniques is research into models that can be used at runtime.

This chapter presents models at runtime (M@RT) as a foundation for the assurance of SASs and discusses related research challenges. Section 2 reviews assurance criteria, both functional and non-functional, whose fulfillment depends on or can be affected by self-adaptation and therefore requires assurance at runtime. Section 3 classifies different types of models used for M@RT and discusses the application of M@RT to support a spectrum of assurance issues. Section 4 identifies research challenges in the area of M@RT for SAS assurance tasks. Section 5 characterizes existing methods used for assurance of SASs. Section 6 describes selected application areas that exhibit the type of assurance challenges that we consider amenable to the use of M@RT. Finally, Section 7 concludes the chapter.

2   Assurance Criteria for Self-Adaptive Software Systems

Assurance criteria for SASs include functional and non-functional requirements whose fulfillment depends on or can be affected by self-adaptation. It is important to distinguish between assurance criteria applicable to the *target system* (i.e., criteria that relate to properties of the current or a potential future state of that system), and assurance criteria applicable to the *adaptation process* itself. Sections 2.1 and 2.2 respectively discuss functional and non-functional requirements as fundamental assurance criteria for SASs.

2.1   Functional Requirements

A functional requirement specifies a function that a system or system component must be able to perform [IEE90]. Functional requirements are typically formulated as prescriptive statements to be satisfied by the system. While it is still a common practice to describe functional requirements using natural language, the potential for misinterpretation of such descriptions is considerable due to the inherent ambiguity of natural languages [Ber08, CNdRW06]. Formal languages with well-defined semantics provide a more rigorous and reliable means for specifying functional requirements in the context of system design. The following discussion is limited to formal descriptions.

Functional requirements decribe the behavioral objectives of the functions f of a system. They are typically defined in terms of relating the inputs I to the system with the outputs O of the system, with the expectation that $f : I \rightarrow O$. A function f may be some type of computation, data manipulation, or other specific functions that the system should execute. Accordingly, the input I may be data from a user, values from a sensor, such as a temperature value or a sequence of images. Similarly, the output O may be pictures, continuous video, a braking signal for a car, or the opening of a valve. It is important ot note that functional requirements describe the system behavior that is visible at the system boundaries (i.e., system interfaces) [ZJ97]. The boundaries can be at the human-computer interface, sensors, actuators, or even at the boundaries between interacting systems. As such, functional requirements describe "what" the system has to provide in terms of its functional behavior to meet the expectations of its users, leaving "how" this functionality will be achieved to the design and implementation of the system.

System adaptation may become necessary to handle changes in the requirements or in the environment that are visible at its boundaries and influence its behavior externally. These adaptations may lead to internal changes that manifest as changed behavior observable at the system boundary. While the former is a reaction to the system context and leads to retaining the functional behavior in the presence of external change, the latter is a reaction to changing user needs or system configuration needs and leads to behavioral adaptations to accommodate the new requirements.

Because an SAS tends to respond to changes in the environment, functional requirements should take into account the context of the system as well as explicit assumptions about its behavior. Adaptation provides a means to alter the way a system satisfies its functional requirements, including the use of machine learning techniques [KM07], agent-based techniques [SAS14], bio-inspired techniques [BSG+09, MV14], and selecting specific target configuration from a collection of different target configurations [GCH+04, ZC06a], each of which satisfies the functional requirements, but may be better suited for a specific context and/or set of environmental conditions. The functional requirements may be formalized in an "assume/guarantee" style [JT96]—assuming a set of conditions or restrictions holds, then the application of the function guarantees that the results satisfy a set of required properties. The definition of pre- and postconditions is an example of this style of functional requirements specification.

Common formalisms used to express functional requirements are Linear-Time Temporal Logic (LTL) [Pnu81] and Computational Tree Logic (CTL) [BAMP81], both of which are included in the logic CTL* [CE82]. Several languages have been proposed to facilitate the specification of functional properties; examples range from basic assertion languages such as PSL [Acc04], used in electronic system design, to scenario-based visual languages, such as Message Sequence Charts [HT04] or Property Sequence Charts [AIP07]. These languages are often less expressive than pure temporal logic, but are designed to be intuitive and user friendly.

Beyond property-based specification, various algebraic specification and system modeling techniques have been developed, including Statecharts [Har87]; set-theoretic approaches, such as VDM [BJ78] and Z [ASM80]; process or operational-oriented, including SDL [Uni99], the B Method [Abr88], Event-B[ABH+10]; object-oriented languages, such as UML and its numerous variants[3]; architectural description languages [Cle96]; and Matlab/Simulink[4] to name a few representative examples. Traditionally, these techniques are used during system design and development to achieve increased confidence in the functional correctness of the system. Several of the above listed techniques support automatic code generation from the system model as well as formal verification at varying levels of abstraction.

Several complementary approaches have been used to specify functional requirements of an SAS, where uncertainty of the execution environment is implicitly or explicitly acknowledged by allowing more flexibility in how requirements can be satisfied. The SAS determines at runtime how to realize the specified functionality when placed in its target environment. This flexibility can be achieved by describing functional requirements in terms of policies that encode high-level specifications of functional objectives together with a set of operational constraints. This implicit approach to acknowledging uncertainty in the execution environment can utilize utility functions and a rule-based approach in the context of a goal-oriented functional requirements specification. Another approach is to explicitly acknowledge specific system functionality affected by uncertainty and thus allow specific points of flexibility in satisfying the requirements, such as that provided by the RELAX [WSB+09, CSBW09, RFJB12, FDC14a] and FLAGS [BPS10, PS11] approaches. Section 5.1 provides further details on these approaches.

2.2 Non-functional Requirements

If we consider functional requirements of a software system to be a function f that directly maps input I to output O ($f : I \rightarrow O$), then non-functional requirements refer to properties about f, I, O or relationships between I and O [CPL09]. Non-functional requirements such as performance, dependability, safety, security, and their corresponding quality attributes such as latency, throughput, capacity, confidentiality, and integrity can include assurance concerns from the perspective of both the target system and the adaptation mechanism. Avižienis et al. [ALRL04] and Barbacci et al. [BKLW95] provide two comprehensive taxonomies of software quality attributes useful for the identification of assurance criteria in SASs.

It is necessary to validate and continually monitor non-functional requirements on both the target system and the adaptation process using techniques such as probabilistic monitoring [GZ09, Gru11], requirements monitoring [FF95], [FFvLP98], or utility function monitoring [GCH+04, RC11]. At runtime, the desired properties of the target system may no longer hold due to changes in the target system's context of use (e.g., user, platform, or environment context [SCF+06]), or side effects introduced by adaptations. In the latter case, it is possible to derive the impact of adaptations on properties of

---

[3] www.uml.org
[4] http://www.mathworks.com

the target system by analyzing adaptation properties such as stability, accuracy, settling time, small overshoot, and robustness. Specifically, it may be possible to take advantage of this relation to detect consequences of adaptations performed by controllers [KC03] or consequences of a changing environment (e.g., a failing component or a deficient Internet connection).

Several non-functional assurance criteria may be more easily guaranteed at runtime than at design time. For example, it is easier to assess latency when it is possible to measure and continually monitor delay times in the running system. Table 1 presents examples of non-functional assurance criteria with corresponding quality attributes (cf. Columns 1 and 2). Adaptation properties (cf. Column 3), defined as assurance criteria that concern the adaptation process [VMT+11b], can be mapped to quality attributes measurable at runtime for both the target system and the adaptation mechanism. Where to measure a given property, either in the adaptation process or in the target system, will depend on its definition and its assessment metric. For example, *settling time* defined as the time required for the adaptation process to take the target system to a desirable state, must be measured on the target system since the need for the adaptation and the conditions for a desired state can only be observed at this level. Moreover, settling time can be measured through different quality attributes, depending on the specific non-functional property that must be satisfied. For example, if the concern is performance, settling time can be observed in terms of the time the system takes to perform a particular process. When the accepted time limit for this process is exceeded, the adaptation process will be invoked. Once the process execution time is back within desired limits, the target system will have reached its desired state. As such, settling time is the time elapsed between the moment at which the need for adaptation was detected and the moment at which the system reaches the desired new state. Villegas *et al.* [VMT+11b] provide a comprehensive catalogue of adaptation properties and the corresponding quality attributes needed to identify the assurance criteria applicable to the adaptation process. This study also surveys definitions for the assurance criteria presented in Table 1.

Table 1. Examples of non-functional assurance criteria that are better guaranteed at runtime than at design time (including their mapping to quality attributes and adaptation properties) [VMT+11b]

Assurance Criteria	Quality Attribute	Adaptation Properties
Latency	Performance	Stability, accuracy, settling time, overshoot, scalability
Throughput	Performance	Stability, accuracy, settling time, overshoot, scalability
Capacity	Performance	Stability, accuracy, settling time, overshoot, scalability
Safety	Dependability	Stability
Availability	Dependability	Robustness, settling time
Reliability	Dependability	Robustness
Confidentiality	Security	Security

Assuring these criteria at runtime requires effective monitoring mechanisms and M@RT to analyze, guarantee, and predict the qualities of the target system and the adaptation process dynamically. Implementing these mechanisms effectively requires a thorough analysis of the interdependencies between non-functional assurance criteria, quality attributes, and adaptation properties as presented in Table 1. This mapping constitutes a valuable starting point to identify assurance criteria and adaptation properties. On the one hand, this mapping supports the identification of assurance criteria according to the target system's desired quality attributes. (For example, latency, throughput and capacity are relevant assurance criteria when performance is the negotiated quality attribute.) On the other hand, it is useful to identify adaptation properties, relevant to quality attributes, that are applicable to the adaptation mechanism. (For example, when performance is a key quality attribute for the target system, then stability, accuracy, settling time, small overshoot, and scalability constitute relevant properties to be guaranteed in the adaptation process.) Of course these mappings also depend on the actual target system, its technical implementation, and the performed adaptations.

3 Models at Runtime

SASs require rethinking the notion of the software life cycle for which the distinction between development time and execution time stages is no longer starkly apparent (e.g., PLASTIC,[5], SMScom[6]). Recent approaches recognize the need to produce, manage, and maintain software models all along the software's life time to assist the realization and validation of system adaptations while the system executes [Inv07, BBF09, BG10, ACR$^+$11, BDM$^+$11, VTM$^+$12, MV14] [CVM14].

Continuing with this line of reasoning, our objective is to explore models of different aspects of the application (e.g., requirements, specification, design, architecture, implementation, infrastructure, instrumentation, and context-of-use) and life cycle phases (e.g., design time, development time, configuration time, load time, and runtime) to deal with the inherent dynamics of self-adaptation in software systems. These abstractions, combined with suitable instrumentation, could provide effective techniques for monitoring, analyzing, guaranteeing, and predicting system properties throughout the operation of an SAS.

The kind of models used at runtime can be classified by (1) their purpose—predictive, prescriptive, constructive, or descriptive; (2) their underlying modeling languages—for example, the 14 UML 2.2 structural and behavioral diagrams, State-charts, Petri Nets, and logic based models (e.g., Temporal Logics); and (3) the aspects they describe—data structure, task or process state, I/O behavior, or interaction pattern.

One of the main principles of using M@RT for assurance is to exploit the causal connection [Mae87] between the model and the system under development at runtime. This connection determines synchronization between the model and the running system. For example, M@RT can be updated to reflect changes in the running system —we say that they are in *descriptive causal connection*. This type of modeling enables assurance techniques to analyze abstract models instead of the actual implementation of the application when collecting information for assurance. In contrast, the model can be changed to cause an adaptation of the application (i.e., *prescriptive causal connection*). This use of modeling can be used to implement adaptations of the running system that are required to assure system properties.

---

[5] FP6 IST EU PLASTIC project http://www.ist-plastic.org

[6] Carlo Ghezzi, Self-Managing Situated Computing Grant, ERC Advanced Investigator Grant N. 227977, European Union, 2008–2013

In the scope of assurance, M@RT can be used as a basis for assuring functional as well as non-functional properties of the system (cf. Section 2). From this perspective, models can play various roles. Depending on what the models describe, they can be used as a source of information about aspects of the running system. For instance, goal models can represent the requirements that need to be assured, the current state of the system, adaptations, or the context of use. M@RT can have several purposes for run-time assurance. Among others, they can be used as information sources for monitoring aspects of a running system, to influence the system via model manipulation, and as a basis for analysis methods, such as model-based verification and model-based simulation. For analysis methods, models are usually beneficial as they provide easy to use high-level knowledge about the system.

Development-time modeling approaches already exploit these advantages and enable the assertion of certain properties of a developed system. The use of M@RT has the advantage that some of the analysis constraints are relaxed as the current runtime state is available for reasoning, reaction, and regulation. At development time, full assurance is required to reason about all possible states. Several of these variables that are unknown at development time are bound at runtime and can allow for a more focused analysis of the current state and possibly several neighboring ones. This variable instantiation is especially useful for factors that can only be estimated at development time (e.g., network delay). A running system can continually monitor these aspects and react to them. The remainder of this section describes the dynamics of adaptive systems and the use of models during the adaptation process.

3.1   M@RT and the Dynamics of Self-Adaptive Software

The Software Engineering for Adaptive and Self-Managing Systems (SEAMS) community has identified three key subsystems needed for the design of effective context-driven self-adaptation: the control objectives manager, the adaptation controller, and the context monitoring system [VTM+12]. These subsystems represent three levels of dynamics in self-adaptation, each of which can be controlled through a corresponding feedback loop. Villegas *et al.* [VTM+12] provide a comprehensive characterization of these three levels of dynamics in SASs.

In general, assurance criteria drive the control objectives, adaptation, and monitoring feedback loops, as well as their interactions. As such, assurance governs the behavior of both the target system and the adaptation process. For example, system administrators can provide the control objectives manager with the required specifications. More specifically, the control objectives manager then sends the adaptation goals to the adaptation controller and monitoring requirements to the monitoring system. Thus, these specifications govern the behavior of the adaptation process and the behavior of the SAS throughout the adaptation process.

We argue that M@RT provide abstractions that are essential to support the feedback loops that control the three levels of dynamics identified in SASs. From this perspective, M@RT (cf. Figure 1) could be developed specifically for each level of dynamics to support the control objectives manager, adaptation controller, and the monitoring system. The figure also shows the interactions between these models and the respective subsystems in an SAS.

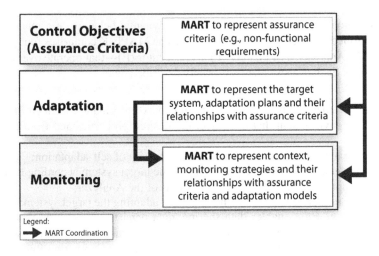

Fig. 1. The three levels of M@RT for the assurance of SASs

- At the *Control Objectives* level, M@RT represent requirements specifications subject to assurance in the form of functional and non-functional requirements.
- At the *Adaptation* level, M@RT represent states of the managed system, adaptation plans and their relationships with the assurance specifications.
- At the *Monitoring* level, M@RT represent context entities, monitoring requirements, as well as monitoring strategies and their relationships with assurance criteria and adaptation models.

Most importantly, M@RT at these levels must have efficient and effective methods of inter-level interaction since changes in requirement specifications may trigger changes at both the adaptation and the monitoring levels, as well as in the associated runtime models. Similarly, changes in adaptation models may imply changes in monitoring strategies or context entity models. In any case, M@RT at the adaptation and monitoring levels must maintain an explicit mapping to the models defined at the control objectives level that specify the requirements.

In summary, the architecture of SASs contains three interacting but functionally self-contained levels, each dedicated respectively to control objectives, adaptation, and monitoring of the SAS. Designing an SAS *for assurance*, as opposed to leaving assurance until after system design, requires the tight integration of assurance objectives into each level in the SAS architecture. We argue that this integration can most effectively be achieved by introducing dedicated M@RT that embody specific assurance criteria, focused either for the target system or the adaptation process.

3.2   Models at Runtime during the Adaptation Process

As a starting point for a research methodology we analyzed the MAPE-K loop in further detail. Kephart and Chess proposed this autonomic manager as a foundational component of IBM's autonomic computing initiative [KC03]. It constitutes a reference model for designing and implementing adaptation mechanisms in SASs. The MAPE-K loop is an abstraction of a feedback loop where the dynamic behavior of a managed system is controlled using an autonomic manager. The MAPE-K comprises four phases—Monitor (M), Analyzer (A), Planner (P) and Executor (E)—that operate over a knowledge base (K). Each of these phases is briefly described next.

1. *Monitors* gather and pre-process relevant context information from entities in the execution environment that can affect the desired properties and from the target system;
2. *Analyzers* support decision making on the necessity of self-adaptation;
3. *Planners* generate suitable actions to affect the target system according to the supported adaptation mechanisms and the results of the Analyzer;
4. *Executors* implement actions with the goal of adapting the target system; and
5. A *Knowledge Base* enables data sharing, data persistence, decision making, and communication among the components of the feedback loop, as well as arrangements of multiple feedback loops (e.g., the Autonomic Computing Reference Architecture (ACRA) [IBM06]).

In order to illustrate the role of M@RT as enablers of assurance mechanisms for self-adaptation, Figure 2 presents an extension of the MAPE-K loop, where assurance tasks complement each stage of the loop [TVM⁺12], and the knowledge base is replaced by M@RT. We aptly name the feedback loop depicted in this figure *MAPE-MART loop*.

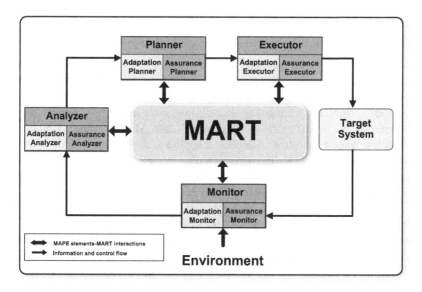

Fig. 2. MAPE-MART loop: The MAPE-K loop from autonomic computing extended with M@RT, and assurance instrumentation as foundational elements for the assessment of SASs

MAPE elements interact with M@RT along the adaptation process to either obtain or update information about system states, the environment, and assurance criteria. *Monitors* keep track of relevant context information according to monitoring conditions in the system itself (*assurance monitors*) and its adaptations (*adaptation monitors*). For example, monitors interact with M@RT in order to make monitored data available throughout the adaptation process, or to monitor the states of models or changes in assurance criteria. *Analyzers* will then use monitored context to identify whether desired conditions are being or could potentially be violated. Analyzers can also update models with identified symptoms. Again, we can distinguish between *assurance analyzers* that analyze the system and *adaptation analyzers* that analyze the adaptation process. *Adaptation planners* use the symptoms provided by analyzers to define a new adaptation plan. Adaptation plans can be defined in the form of models that are processable by executors to adapt the target system. Then *assurance planners* check whether the plan is correct with respect to the assurance criteria. Finally, *adaptation executors* perform the plan, after which point, *assurance executors* check whether both the system remains in a safe state and the desired properties are achieved. These verification tasks can be optimized using M@RT.

4   Research Challenges for Assurance at Runtime

This section overviews selected research avenues and research challenges for the assurance of SASs using M@RT.

4.1   Research Avenues

Software assurance is a large field with many subfields (e.g., software quality, V&V, safety, trust, and several 'ilities') that spans the realms of software engineering, systems engineering, control engineering, and many other engineering disciplines. From a software engineering perspective, assurance at *runtime* for SASs appears to be an emerging area of research [GCZ08, FDB+08, IPT09, TVM+12, FGT11, SBT11, FRC13a, FDC14b]. In contrast, runtime assurance in control engineering traces its roots to the industrial revolution, applied to devices such as the centrifugal governor. This device used a flyball mechanism to sense the rotational speed of a steam turbine and to adjust the flow of steam into the machine. By regulating the turbine's speed, it provided the safe, reliable, and consistent operation that enabled the proliferation of steam-powered factories [MAB+02].

In an instrumented, interconnected, and intelligent world, control and runtime assurance are core components in SASs, providing high performance, high confidence, and reconfigurable operation in the presence of uncertainties. The continuous integration of sensors, networks, cloud computing, and control presents significant opportunities for engineering in general and software engineering in particular. A key goal is to provide certifiable trust in resulting systems, which is a truly formidable challenge for researchers in the field of runtime software assurance.

Over the past 20 years, several research venues (i.e., journals, conferences, and workshops) have emerged in the broad software engineering research community to discuss the design and evolution as well as assurance of SASs.

Mining the rich histories, theories and experiences of fields such as biology, control engineering, and software engineering are worthwhile starting points for assurance at runtime research. In particular, we need survey papers that investigate models used for design time and runtime assurance techniques in these fields including research on the synergy between them. Moreover, it is useful to relate canonical practical applications to these findings. In a most stimulating 2002 control survey paper Murray *et al.* [MAB⁺02] posit that feedback is a central tool for uncertainty management in modern control. By measuring the operation of a system, comparing it to a *reference* at runtime, and adjusting available control variables, the controller can assure proper operation even in the presence of external disturbances or if its dynamic behavior is not fully known. In software, this reference can be realized with M@RT and evidence for assurance is gathered by checking conformance to the reference model. Murray *et al.* [MAB⁺02] argue that the challenge is to go from the traditional view of control systems as a single process with a single controller, to recognizing control systems as a heterogeneous collection of physical and information systems, with intricate interconnections and interactions [MAB⁺02]. One manifestation of this approach in software engineering is the three levels of runtime control models discussed in Section 3 [TVM⁺13].

The self-adaptive and self-managing systems community has produced a spectrum of runtime models [WMA10] [TVM⁺13] and patterns [RC10b, GH04] with control-centric models [KC03, HDPT04, IBM06, BSG⁺09] at one end and architecture-centric models [BCD97, OGT⁺, GCH⁺04, KM07] at the other end. These models come with different attributes and properties that can be exploited for runtime assurance. There is plenty of room for research to compare and evaluate the benefits and synergy of these different runtime model strategies [MKS09, TVM⁺13].

4.2 Selected Research Challenges

This section outlines selected open research problems and challenges aligned with the research avenues presented in the previous section. The focus is on the use of M@RT as a basis for developing runtime assurance techniques.

Runtime Assurance Criteria and Adaptation Properties. In Section 2.2 we related selected non-functional assurance criteria (e.g., latency) to adaptation properties (e.g., settling time) using quality attributes. One challenge is to extend this characterization of criteria and properties for the target system, controller, and adaptation process. While other approaches may be used to characterize and relate assurance criteria and adaptation properties, the properties are only meaningful if they can actually be measured. Monitoring infrastructure to measure properties is critical for runtime assurance methods. Over the past decade, the SAS community has published numerous papers on various aspects of monitoring. Many of these papers concentrate on the monitoring of raw measures in the managed system but only a limited number of approaches make the information amenable for runtime assurance assessment purposes, including functional requirements monitoring [FF95, FFvLP98, BWS⁺10, DDKM08, MPS08], assumptions monitoring [WSB11, RCBS12], and adaptive monitoring capabilities for changing environmental conditions [RC10a].

M@RT as a Foundation for Run-Time Assurance. While M@RT for SAS are increasingly being developed for complex SASs, including reference models [WMA10, VTM+12], few of these models are explicitly designed for runtime assurance. Thus, MART construction for runtime assurance is a key research challenge. The models introduced in Section 3 present good starting points for integrating assurance components into common SAS models. The central challenge for MART construction is to model uncertainty (e.g., environmental disturbances or evolving requirements). Understanding, managing, and leveraging uncertainty is important for delivering SASs with assurance guarantees such as reliability. Ramirez and Cheng [RJC12] have developed a taxonomy of uncertainty commonly faced by SAS, which could be used to facilitate uncertainty modeling and analysis efforts [EKM11, RCBS12]. Fields such as performance engineering and queuing theory have developed advanced models for many different applications. In particular, these fields have developed theories on how to transduce raw measures from a target system into meaningful measures for selected assurance criteria. However, performance constitutes just one dimension of the modeling and assurance problem. Many other quality criteria are applicable to SASs, such as trust, where quantification is rather difficult yet certifiable trust is one of the most important goals for an SAS [Dah10]. Moreover, models are needed to design trade-off analyses schemes for combinations of quality criteria. Models and quality criteria related to governance, compliance, and service-level agreements are of particular importance for service-oriented SASs [BHTV06, TVM+13]. Since M@RT form the foundation of many assurance tasks, the quality of these tasks directly depends on the quality of the models. Defining properties (e.g., accuracy, performance, or safety) for the evaluation of models at runtime is a significant research challenge [TVM+13].

To motivate researchers and practitioners to work on this subject we need compelling reasons for using M@RT for assurance [TVM+13]. A key goal for the SAS assurance research community is to develop exemplars that can be used to evaluate SAS runtime assurance techniques [TVM+13]. Most SAS conferences and workshops regularly call for exemplars but not usually explicitly targeted for SAS runtime assurance. An example of compelling motivation for work in this area is a 20-year science and technology research agenda and outlook for the US Air Force (USAF) [Dah10]. Approximately one third of this agenda is devoted to self-adaptive and autonomous systems with explicit calls for certifiable V&V techniques. V&V is also one of the most promising subfields of assurance where researchers can mine well-established design time models and transition them to runtime. The IBM autonomic computing initiative generated the highly acclaimed MAPE-K [KC03] and ACRA [IBM06] runtime models. The MAPE-K model separates four phases of the feedback loop and thus effectively decomposes the feedback loop assurance problem. The three-layer ACRA hierarchy facilitates integrated assurance reasoning from individually-managed resources at the lowest layer, to managing a collection of resources at the middle layer, to orchestrating an entire system by trading off resource managers at the top layer.

Run-Time Assurance Methods and Techniques. For SASs, the boundary between development time and runtime is rapidly disappearing [BG10]. As a result, we need to re-examine the distribution and effectiveness of assurance tasks over the entire life cycle of an SAS. At the same time, we need to determine which models are most appropriate as a foundation for assurance tasks for the different stages of the software life cycle. In particular, we need to investigate whether models that are used for design-time assurance can be effectively used at runtime. In particular, what properties can be guaranteed at development, configuration, or load time as opposed to runtime. While not all assurance tasks can be transitioned to runtime, there is significant opportunity to conduct assurance tasks at runtime thereby making the system more resilient, reliable, responsive, secure, and cost-effective. Regardless of how dynamic a system really is, a substantial part of its assurance will always be done at development time. What (lightweight) design-time techniques can be readily transitioned to runtime? What development-time assurance methods, models, and techniques (i.e., descriptive, prescriptive, constructive and predictive) readily extend to runtime? How do traditional assurance models and methods from domains such as performance, safety, and reliability extend to runtime?

As illustrated in Figure 2, MART play an important role as the abstraction mechanisms required to support every stage of the SAS adaptation process. A key question is what MART techniques are useful for supporting the relevance of runtime monitoring with respect to the assurance criteria. Moreover, to deal with the dynamic nature of functional and non-functional requirements, as well as the execution environment, every component of the adaptation process can also be an adaptive component. Thus, how can M@RT support changes in monitors, analyzers, planners and executors according to changes in functional and non-functional requirements? In the realm of control system engineering, changing the controller is referred to as *adaptive control* [AW94]. Another important avenue of research is how to characterize runtime assurance techniques according to the different levels of dynamics in SASs (i.e., changes in requirements, relevant context, adaptation mechanisms, and the target system itself).

Assurance obligations vary from one application domain to another. For example, the area of safety-critical systems has developed specialized assurance criteria and models—albeit mostly design-time techniques (e.g., ISO26262 for automotive subsystems,[7] and numerous safety standards set by the International Electrotechnical Commission).[8] The service-oriented architecture (SOA) community has developed SOA governance models—a combination of design time and runtime models—for assurance tasks for service-oriented systems on SOA platforms [SMB+09]. Thus, it is useful for researchers to classify runtime assurance criteria, models, and techniques according to their applicability to different domains and applications (e.g., application-independent, domain-dependent, mission-critical systems, embedded systems, real-time systems, etc.). Run-time assurance techniques can also be classified according to different types of runtime changes (e.g., dynamic context, changing requirements, or evolving models).

With the increasing use of computing-based systems for delivering critical societal services that demand long-running or even continuous operation (e.g., telecommunication, power grids, financial systems, etc.), even in the face of adversity, adaptation and runtime evolution [MV14] is a necessity, not a luxury. Even with meaningful reactions to changes, the triggered SAS adaptation should preserve selected core properties, thus posing a need for incremental and compositional assurance for SASs. An enabling

---

[7] http://www.iso.org/
[8] http://www.iec.ch/

step, in this direction, is to split functional and non-functional requirements into sub-requirements associated with single services and components of the system. The idea is to decompose the requirement specification into properties associated with the behavior of small parts of the system. Thus, it becomes possible to check these properties locally and to deduce from local checks whether the system satisfies the overall specification. By decomposing the assurance task in such a way, it may not be necessary to build a complete model of the system and thus the combinatorial state explosion problem is mitigated. The main challenge of this approach is that local properties are typically not preserved at the global level because of dependencies among the aggregate subparts of the system. Another approach to decomposing the assurance problem is to separate the verification of the functional properties from the verification of adaptation properties. Zhang *et al.* [ZGC09] developed AMOEBA, a modular verification approach for SASs where the functional properties are specified in terms of LTL and the adaptation properties are specified in terms of A-LTL [ZC06b]. With this separation of concerns, AMOEBA uses an assume/guarantee approach [JT96] to perform incremental model checking of both types of properties. AMOEBA-RT is an extension that monitors the adaptation properties at runtime based on state-based models of the adaptive logic [GCZ08].

As another example of assurance for the adaptation process, suppose *settling time* (i.e., the time required for the adaptation mechanism to take the target system to the desired state) has been defined as a performance-oriented assurance concern for a particular adaptive system. As such, the assurance mechanisms must keep track of the time the adaptation mechanism is taking to complete the adaptation process—generally goals must be reached within a suitable time interval. An extremely long adaptation process could render the system to be useless or even detrimental to the system's overall safety. The desired thresholds, monitoring conditions, and entities to be monitored can be specified using M@RT, such as goal-based models [WSB+09] or contextual RDF graphs [VMT11a, VMM+11].

5 Characterizing Assurance Methods

Researchers from communities related to the engineering of SASs have contributed a spectrum of approaches to the assessment of adaptive software. Rather than producing a comprehensive and systematic literature review of the state of the art, the goal of this section is to provide an overview of how M@RT have been used as runtime assurance enablers in selected domains. This characterization of assurance approaches provides a starting point upon which researchers can build to address the research challenges posed by model-based runtime assurance of SASs.

5.1 Classifying Assurance Methods According to Techniques

This section presents and classifies selected existing approaches for runtime assurance of SASs according to the techniques and methods used for their realization.

Goal-Oriented Approaches. A first step towards assuring software systems is the articulation of assurance criteria. This task can be complex for functional requirements because it requires a deep understanding of the application domain. Nguyen *et al.* [NPT+09] argue that goal-oriented techniques are effective for deriving assurance criteria from functional requirements specifications. At development time (or requirements negotiation time), goal models can be used to specify stakeholder expectations for SASs, and the decision criteria for acceptable system behavior can be derived from these models. Moreover, goals, and especially high-level goals, have been recognized as more stable (i.e., less volatile) than specific system requirements [vLDL98]. Thus, high-level goals provide suitable candidate assurance criteria in highly dynamic systems. Qureshi *et al.* [QJP11, QLP11, QP10] rely on this assumption in their work on continuous requirements engineering. They represent functional behavior in terms of high-level goals (i.e., functional goals) that are decomposed into sub-goals. Alternative decompositions are qualified by quality criteria, user preferences, and context that contribute positively or negatively to their ranking. To ensure the expected behavior, the system must select the most appropriate goal decomposition path.

The effectiveness of the assurance of SASs at runtime is highly dependent on the changing conditions of the execution environment that can affect not only the target system, but also the adaptation mechanism and monitoring infrastructure. Ramirez and Cheng proposed an approach to manage changes in monitoring conditions according to environmental situations at runtime [RC11]. They specify requirements goal models using the RELAX language [WSB+09]. Recently, AutoRELAX has been developed to automatically add RELAX operators to goal models to handle uncertainty in the environment while minimizing the number of reconfiguration adaptations [FDC14a]. In a similar approach, Pasquale *et al.* [BPS10, PS11] developed FLAGS, a KAOS goal modeling framework that introduces the concept of a fuzzy goal whose satisfaction can be evaluated through fuzzy logic functions. Both goal-modeling approaches use fuzzy logic-based functions to add flexibility to the satisfaction criteria of goals in a goal-oriented model. In contrast to RELAX, however, FLAGS does not focus on identifying sources of uncertainty, but focuses rather on evaluating the degree to which a goal is satisfied. Goal-based models can be transitioned from design time to runtime to track changes in SAS requirements at runtime. Morandini *et al.* have investigated the life-cycle of goals at runtime [MPP09]. Souza *et al.* [SSLRM11] have developed a system, *Zanshin*, a requirements monitoring framework based on multiple feedback loops to monitor awareness requirements and progress towards adaptation objectives at runtime [ASaP13].

Automatic Test Case Generation- Based Methods. The complexity of system structure and behavior is growing exponentially, coupled with the comparable volume of possible scenarios and combinations of environmental conditions to be handled by an SAS. As such, successful strategies for automatic test case generation used for non-SAS application areas are being leveraged and explored for SAS testing. For example, given that multi-agent based software systems expose high levels of runtime dynamism, applicable testing techniques for these types of systems can be leveraged to assess SASs using M@RT [NPB+09]. An important challenge in the validation of SASs at runtime using direct-testing techniques is the generation of test cases that are relevant to the system's current execution context and goals. As a means to evaluate system performance, Nguyen *et al.* [NPT$^+$09] use evolutionary testing techniques to automatically generate test cases based on quality functions. Quality functions are associated with stakeholder expectations of the behavior of an autonomous system which are expressed as goal-oriented requirements. (e.g., the quality function associated with the goal of a cleaning agent to maintain its battery can be a minimum battery level to be satisfied). This approach allows the automatic generation of test cases with increasing difficulty levels, guided by a fitness function associated to the quality of interest (e.g., a function inversely proportional to the total power consumption of the system throughout its lifetime). A complementary approach is taken by Fredericks *et al.* [FRC13b] where an SAS is exposed to a wide range of adverse environmental conditions that are used to generate SAS execution traces as the system adapts and reconfigures to handle the adverse conditions. These traces can then be analyzed for unexpected and/or unwanted behavior, both in the functional and in the adaptive logic. EvoSuite [FA11] is a framework that implements an evolutionary algorithm to generate test suites that consider a single coverage criterion, for instance the introduction of artificial defects into a program. Finally, a MAPE-T loop [FRC13a] has been proposed to provide a framework for monitoring the applicability and utility of test cases for an SAS as it undergoes environmental changes and reconfiguration. A set of research challenges were posed as part of the proposed framework, including explicit reference to the importance and use of M@RT. Veritas [FDC14b] is a recent realization of the MAPE-T loop that adapts test cases to ensure testing relevancy as an SAS reconfigures to handle changing environmental conditions.

Model Checking. Model checking [CGP01, PPS09] was proposed in the 1980s independently by Clarke and Emerson [CE82], and Quielle and Sifakis [QS82]. It assumes an available mathematical model of a system and a property to check against the model expressed in a formal logic, such as Linear Temporal Logic (LTL) [Pnu81] or Computational Tree Logic (CTL) [BAMP81]. The goal of model checking is to use an algorithmic approach to check the consistency between the given model and the property specification. Model checking has been used extensively to verify hardware [BLPV95] and software systems [CGP02] in many application domains to assure desired properties. Model checking at runtime is a key strategy to verify SASs based on runtime models. Weyns *et al.* surveyed formal methods in self-adaptive systems [WIdlIA12]. They showed that there are no standard tools for formal modeling and verification of self-adaptive systems. According to their survey, however, 40% of the surveyed studies use tools for formal modeling or verification, and 30% of those studies use model checking tools.

A number of model checking techniques have been used to analyze various properties of SASs. Baresi *et al.* used model checking to check whether an architecture is a refinement of another one [BHTV06]. Specifically, they defined refinement relationships between abstract and concrete styles. The defined refinement criteria guarantee both semantic correctness and platform consistency. In another approach, Abeywickrama and Zambonelli proposed to model check goal-oriented requirements for SASs [AZ12].

Cámara and de Lemos used probabilistic model checking to verify resilience properties of SASs, with the goal of verifying whether the self-adaptive system is able to maintain trustworthy service delivery in spite of changes in its environment [CdL12]. In architecture-based domains, Pelliccione *et al.* applied model checking at the software architecture level to verify properties of the system, its components, and the interactions among components [PIM09, PTBP08]. Filieri *et al.* have developed a runtime probabilistic model checking technique to detect harmful reconfigurations. To deal with unplanned adaptations, Inverardi *et al.* proposed a theoretical assume-guarantee framework to define under which conditions to perform adaptation by still preserving the desired invariants [IPT09]. Zhang and Cheng developed AMOEBA [ZGC09], a modular model checker to separately verify SAS functional properties in terms of LTL and the adaptive logic in terms of A-LTL (adapt-LTL). AMOEBA-RT [GCZ08] verifies runtime properties of SAS properties. Model checking has also been applied in the domain of agent-based systems, for instance to assure adaptability to unforeseen conditions, behavioral properties, and performance [Gor01]. Finally, Murata used Petri Nets to enable the analysis of properties, such as the reachability of a certain state or deadlock-freeness [Mur89]. Some of these analysis methods have been extended to enhanced versions of Petri Nets, such as Colored Petri Nets [Jen03] and applied to check properties such as performance [Wel02] or safety [CHC96].

Rule-Based Analysis and Verification.   Several approaches based on formal methods, especially graph-based formalisms, have been proposed to leverage rule-based analysis and verification of software properties. In particular, Becker and Giese proposed a graph-transformation based approach to model SASs at a high-level of abstraction. Their approach considers different level of abstractions according to the three-layer SAS reference architecture proposed by Kramer and Magee [KM07]. In their approach, Becker and Giese check the correctness of the modeled SAS using simulation and invariant-checking techniques. Invariant checking is mainly used to verify that a given set of graph transformations will never reach a forbidden state. This verification process exposes a linear complexity on the number of rules and properties to be checked [BBG^{+}06]. In another approach, Giese *et al.* used triple graph grammars as a formal semantics for specifying models, their relation, and transformations. These models can be used as a basis for analyzing the fulfillment of desired properties [GHL10]. In the self-healing domain, Bucchiarone *et al.* proposed an approach to model and verify self-repairing system architectures [BPVR09]. In their approach, dynamic software architectures are formalized as typed hyper-graph grammars. This formalization enables verification of correctness and completeness of self-repairing systems. This approach was extended later by Ehrig *et al.* [EER^{+}10] to model self-healing systems using algebraic graph transformations and graph grammars enriched with graph constraints. This extension enables formal modeling of consistency and operational properties. In the quality-driven component-based software engineering domain, Tamura *et al.* [TCCD12, Tam12] formalized models for component-based structures and reconfiguration rules using typed and attributed graph transformation systems to preserve QoS contracts. Based on this formalization, they provide a means for formal analysis and verification of self-adaptation properties, both at design time and runtime by integrating the Attributed Graph Grammar (AGG) system in their framework.

Synthesis. Another interesting avenue of research is to use synthesis techniques for assuring SASs. The goal of these techniques is to generate the "correct" assembly code for the (pre-selected and pre-acquired) components that constitute the specified system, in such a way that it is possible to guarantee that the system exhibits the specified interactions only. Inverardi *et al.* [IST11] proposed a synthesis-based approach for networking. This approach considers application-layer connectors by referring to two conceptually distinct notions of connector: *coordinator* and *mediator*. The former is used when the networked systems to be connected are already able to communicate but they need to be specifically coordinated to reach their goal(s). The latter goes a step further by representing a solution for both achieving correct coordination and enabling communication between highly heterogeneous networked systems. This work has been extended to also handle non-functional properties [DMIS13]. La Manna *et al.* [PGGB13] proposed an approach for reasoning about safeness of dynamic updates based on specification changes.

Semantic Web. A key challenge for establishing runtime assurance of SASs is the preservation of the relevance of runtime monitoring infrastructures with respect to assurance criteria and the system's execution environment. Specifically, monitoring strategies and infrastructures must adapt themselves dynamically. Models at runtime are also required to support self-adaptation of context management infrastructures (i.e., the third level of dynamics in SASs that was presented in Sect. 3.1). To manage context dynamically, the explicit mapping between assurance concerns and relevant context must be complemented with an explicit mapping between relevant context and infrastructure elements of the monitoring infrastructure. In this way, whenever changes in assurance criteria or relevant context occur, the dynamic adaptation of a representation of the monitoring strategy will trigger the adaptation of context sensors, context providers, and context monitors accordingly. Ramirez and Cheng [RCM10] used a goal-based approach to adapt the monitoring infrastructure to support the changing execution context for an SAS. Resource description framework (RDF) graphs, from semantic web, are good candidates to be used as effective M@RT in the assessment of SASs. Models at runtime in the form of RDF graphs can be exploited to represent relevant context, monitoring strategies, system requirements including assurance criteria, as well as to support changes in context management strategies at runtime. Ontologies and semantic-web based rules, defined according to the application domain, provide the means required to infer changes in the monitoring infrastructure according to changes in requirements, assurance criteria or context [VMT11a, Vil13].

5.2 Classifying Assurance Methods According to Non-Functional Criteria

In this subsection, we classify surveyed runtime assurance approaches according to the non-functional requirements they address as assurance criteria.

Safety.   For systems that are self-adaptive or even self-organizing, the application of traditional safety assurance approaches is currently infeasible. This obstacle is mostly due to the fact that these approaches rely heavily on a complete understanding of the system and its environment, which is difficult to attain for adaptive systems and as of yet impossible for open systems. Open systems, in contrast to self-adaptive systems that are generally closed systems, do not use measured outputs to determine control inputs required to adjust their behavior [HDPT04]. Therefore, open systems necessarily require a complete and accurate model of the system and its environment from which the control input must be derived. These models are generally impractical given that they must be robust to changes in the system and its environment and use no feedback mechanism to adjust themselves. A general solution is to shift parts of the safety assurance measures into runtime when all required information about the current state of the application can be obtained. Rushby [Rus07] developed a strategy where development-time analysis techniques for certification are used at runtime, but the actual certification is performed as needed just-in-time. Based on this work, he later coined the notion of runtime certification [Rus08], using runtime verification techniques to partially perform certification at runtime. Following the same core idea of shifting portions of the assurance measures into runtime, Schneider *et al.* [ST13] introduced the concept of conditional safety certificates (ConSerts). ConSerts are predefined modular safety certificates that have a runtime representation to enable dynamic evaluations in the context of open adaptive systems. Some initial ideas concerning the extension of ConSerts regarding other certifiable non-functional properties such as security have also been published [SBT11]. Priesterjahn and Tichy [PT09] proposed a different approach based on the application of hazard analysis techniques during runtime. This approach is closely related to their previous work where they introduced a development-time hazard analysis approach for analyzing all configurations that a self-adaptive system can reach during runtime [GT06]. A corresponding extension also considers the time between the detection of a failure and its reconfiguration [PSWTH11].

Performance.   Regression models and queuing network models (QNM) are M@RT commonly used to reason about performance-based assurance properties relating to response time, throughput, or utilization. For example, Hellerstein *et al.* [HDPT04] and Lu *et al.* [LAL⁺03] described dynamic regression models in the context of autonomic computing and self-optimization. Menascé and Bennani [MB03] used QNM as predictive models for avoiding bottleneck saturation and for online capacity sizing. Ghanbari *et al.* [GSLI11] used dynamically tuned layered queuing models, which are software specific versions of QNMs, for online performance problem determination and mitigation in cloud computing. More recently, Barna *et al.* [BLG11] reported performance load and stress testing methods on online tuned runtime performance models.

Reliability and Availability.   Run-time assurance methods for reliability and availability properties use discrete time Markov chains that are synchronized with the system and its usage profile. For example, service-based systems built using the QoSMOS (QoS Management and Optimization of Service-based systems) framework [CGK⁺11] translate high-level QoS requirements specified by their administrators into probabilistic temporal logic formulae that are then formally and automatically analyzed to identify and enforce optimal system configurations. The QoSMOS self-adaptation mechanism can handle reliability and performance-related QoS requirements. QoSMOS [FGT11, MG10] uses the KAMI approach [EGMT09] to keep the model, including its parameters, and the system consistent; it uses probabilistic model checking at runtime to evaluate whether the system satisfies the current reliability requirements.

Security. Security considerations revolve around self-protection goals of an SAS, including confidentiality, integrity, authenticity, and authorization [BCdL11, KHW+01]. Run-time assurance of these goals is important in SASs since adaptation may produce emergent behavior that violates one or more other critical system properties. In particular, security assurance must be achieved without compromising system goals unrelated to security [RZN05, HMPB00]. For example, security considerations, such as confidentiality may conflict with availability goals. While the former, confidentiality, aims to protect the information in the system from unauthorized access, the latter, availability, is intended to ensure access to the system and the information a user is authorized to access. One way of counteracting an intrusion is by limiting access to the parts of the system that are affected by an attack. This approach clearly can have negative impact on availability. It is therefore important that, within an SAS, any remedial interventions invoked to preserve security goals also preserve the system properties not related to security. Achieving this balance requires decisions to be made at runtime based on evidence regarding the satisfaction of security goals obtained from analyzing the system and its environment, including user behavior.

Run-time security of an SAS involves not only protecting the target system, but it also means that the adaptation process and the policies governing the adaptation are protected from malicious attacks (e.g., preventing attackers from hijacking its adaptation mechanisms and policies) [Ais03, BJY11, OMH+11]. Adaptation methods, data, policies and certificates must be properly protected to ensure confidentiality, authenticity, and trusted communication of the entire adaptation process and its drivers. The components of every MAPE-MART loop depicted in Figure 2 must also be protected accordingly.

While an SAS is expected to make its adaptation decisions autonomously, a key question is how and how much to empower users with privacy and data security control (e.g., when user context is involved in adaptation decisions). The Surprise [MTVM12] approach (i) allows users to configure access permissions to their sensitive personal information to third parties, selectively and with different levels of granularity; (ii) supports changes in these configurations at runtime to add or remove third parties or permissions, and (iii) realizes partial encryption to share non-sensitive data with third parties who have not been explicitly authorized access, while protecting user identity. The Surprise approach is an exemplar of the application of M@RT to the preservation of privacy and security policies in user-driven SASs.

Security assurance, like other assurance goals at runtime, relies on the definition of high-level policies that must be preserved during adaptation. To achieve this security assurance, the Self-Adaptive Authorization Framework (SAAF) uses a feedback loop that continuously monitors the decisions made by the system's authorization process [BCdL11] . The knowledge gained is used to adjust the authorization policy at runtime, making it more restrictive to constrain user behavior or loosening it to endorse users. Dynamic conflict resolution is particularly important in the context of security assurance but many existing approaches, e.g. [HMPB00], resolve conflicts using priority levels assigned at design time. Instead, the ATNAC (Adaptive Trust Negotiation and Access Control) framework [RZN05] allows access control policies to be dynamically adjusted depending on a set of trust-associated attributes observed at runtime. Formal methods have also been used successfully in this context. For example, the Willow Architecture [KHW+01], a dynamic reconfiguration framework for critical distributed systems, enables systems to continue working with reduced functionality while under a security attack. The use of formal methods enables autonomous handling of conflicts at runtime during reconfiguration.

Usability.   In applications with adaptive user interfaces, it is often impossible to test each adaptation state with real users. Therefore, automated usability evaluation of such user interfaces often relies on models of the user or user interactions to evaluate states of user interfaces automatically [IH01]. Quade *et al.* [QBL+11] introduced an approach that evaluates the usability of the current state of a user interface using M@RT. The evaluation is based on a simulation of user interactions based on the model of the user interface and a model of the user. Having these techniques available at runtime enables a more detailed modeling of the user as the model can be checked against data from the actual user interaction.

6   Compelling Applications for Models at Runtime

This section introduces application exemplars for which M@RT play a major role in the assurance of functional and non-functional assurance criteria. The goal of this section is to provide a catalogue of "killer applications" useful to motivate case studies on the assurance of SASs where M@RTare used as a foundation.

Kaleidoscope.   Kaleidoscope [9]is a multi-channel multimedia video streaming and video on demand system. Imagine an Olympics game or a football match where millions of users are simultaneously streaming, watching and querying videos about the event. The Kaleidoscope application aims to provide/share best quality video for its users. As such, Kaleidoscope must act as a proxy server that is used to store and forward multimedia content to user devices. A device can be a notebook, a smartphone, or a personal digital assistant (PDA). Kaleidoscope must detect both the video source and the user target device. Kaleidoscope must adapt at runtime from one configuration variant to another in order to provide the best quality video to users concurrently and reliably. The broadcast is fetched from a video source via TV cable (e.g., TV broadcast) or either wired or wireless (e.g., Webcast) Internet connection.

Latency and capacity (i.e., bandwidth) are important assurance criteria in Kaleidoscope since high-quality video streaming is a major functional requirement. To guarantee functional requirements under the desired quality conditions, Kaleidoscope must

---

[9] http://www.savinetwork.ca

adapt itself by reconfiguring its network and software architecture to minimize latency and maximize capacity. In this scenario, M@RT are useful for a variety of purposes. For example, predictive models can be used to anticipate latency and required capacity in the near future to perform preventive adaptations and thus avoid the violation of the desired qualities. Another example is the use of runtime formal models such as those exploited in rule-based analysis and verification to guarantee the reliable re-configuration of the system.

Autonomous Vehicle Service. Google driverless cars are now licensed in California, Florida and Nevada.[10] Google engineers and scientists achieved this amazing feat in a short five years after DARPA formulated the Great and Urban Challenges on autonomic cars.[11]

It is speculated that driverless cars could come from and go to parking lots, or deliver packages. In a carpooling scenario, autonomous vehicles booked by users could serve the user at a specific time and destination. Best routes will be planned intelligently based on current context information such as traffic conditions and weather. Ordering, booking, and payment will be performed via smartphone applications. Elderly people will become mobile again, as they will be have greater access to services using an autonomic vehicle.

Increasingly, cars are being equipped with intelligent driver assistance for anticipating potential hazards early and avoiding collisions. Intelligent, yet safe autonomous driving software systems require effective methods to ensure their required qualities. Even though the functions of these vehicles are perceived as "intelligent", they typically rely on standard algorithms from sensor fusion, context management, and control theory. In particular, these systems require special attention to context management infrastructures to guarantee the reliability of sensors and monitors. Autonomous vehicle software use models at several levels, especially for understanding relevant context situations: models are required to represent entities that affect the behavior of the car, to specify quality of sensors, and to model context uncertainty. Given the dynamic nature of context information, these models must be available and manageable at runtime. Another category of important models are those that specify typical vehicle behavior used to understand unusual behavioral patterns.

Models for autonomous vehicle software are typically developed implicitly and coded manually into the running system. In order to rigorously address the assured behavior of these systems, these models need to be managed explicitly and rigorously throughout the software life cycle, including at runtime.

Autonomous Agricultural Operations. *Precision agriculture*[12] is an approach to realize a comprehensive farming management concept. One of the main issues addressed

---

[10] http://www.forbes.com/sites/ptc/2013/11/06/
why-google-and-others-see-a-future-with-driverless-cars/
print/
[11] http://www.tartanracing.org/challenge.html
[12] https://www.ispag.org

by precision agriculture is the optimization of the productivity and efficiency when operating on the field, by tailoring soil and crop management to match the conditions at each location. This level of customization can be achieved through the use of different information sources such as GPS, satellite imagery, and IT systems. More recently, efforts have been underway to further improve productivity and efficiency by increasing the amount of automation on the field to the point of autonomous operation. Examples are harvesting fleets comprising several harvesters but only one is operated by a human, autonomous tractors that pick up the crop from the harvesters, and tractor implement automation (TIA) where tractors are controlled by implements to execute implement-specific tasks. These application scenarios have in common that different vehicles or machines are combined on the field in order to fulfill (partially) autonomous tasks. The assurance and certification of important properties, such as safety and security are clearly critical in this context. Furthermore, traditional assurance techniques are not applicable without significant modifications. A first step to this problem is to shift parts of the assurance measures into runtime. This strategy can be achieved by means of suitable M@RT and corresponding management facilities integrated into these systems.

Ambient Assisted Living.   The number and capabilities of devices available at home are growing steadily. *Ambient Assisted Living (AAL)* is intended to use these technologies to assist users with disabilities in their daily tasks, such as monitoring health conditions and detecting emergency situations.[13] Software applications in this domain are not only critical, but also highly dynamic. On the one hand, human lives can be compromised. On the other hand, every home is different and can contain different devices that could be leveraged by AAL services. New generations of devices are produced on a regular basis requiring AAL services to evolve continuously to keep up to date with new technical developments. Moreover, similar devices produced by different vendors may differ considerably in their capabilities and interfaces. Nevertheless AAL systems must be able to use these devices as soon as they become available at the user's home in an effective and safe manner.

In addition to variations in devices, users of AAL systems are subject to considerable variation. An AAL service must deal with an arbitrary number of people living at the same home, their disabilities and capabilities, and their current environmental conditions. Therefore, the system is required to adapt itself according to current users and their environment. Moreover, these systems must be sufficiently flexible to support future extensions, such as the integration of new sensors or actuators for new applications. Most importantly, these adaptations must be performed seamlessly and reliably to guarantee user safety.

To deal with these complex dynamics, AAL software requires M@RT to reason about users and their context in order to correctly and safely deliver services. Moreover, it is important to maintain a causal connection between these models and both the target systems and adaptation mechanisms. Given the potential risks to human lives, assurance is a major concern that must be guaranteed to prevent hazardous operation before, during, and after adaptation [ZC06a, VMT+11b]. M@RT can be essential in the management

---

[13] http://www.aal-europe.eu

of AAL software for capturing the environment, monitoring the user interaction, and reasoning about possible adaptive behavior and their impact.

The Guardian Angels Project.   In the context of AAL, the "Guardian Angels for a Smarter Planet" project[14] is a good example to illustrate the potential benefits from using M@RT to address SAS assurance. The following details are based on information from the Publications Office of the European Union[15]:

The overarching objective of the Guardian Angels Flagship Initiative is to provide information and communication technologies to assist people in all stages of life. Guardian Angels are envisioned as personal assistants. They are intelligent (thinking), autonomous systems (or even systems-of-systems) featuring sensing, computation, and communication, and delivering features and characteristics that go well beyond human capabilities. It is intended that these systems will provide assistance from infancy through old age. A key feature of these Guardian Angels will be their zero power requirements as they will scavenge for energy. Example services include individual health support tools, local monitoring of ambient conditions for dangers, and emotional applications. Scientific challenges for supporting their research challenges include energy-efficient computing and communication; low-power sensing, bio-inspired energy scavenging, and zero-power human-machine interfaces.

These devices, by their very nature, will need to be adaptive in terms of functional and non-functional properties. In addition, they will be used in critical situations that require high levels of dependability and hence the highest levels of safety assurance.[16] The development of M@RT can support runtime decision making and certification for this important and innovative application area.

7 Conclusions

This chapter presented a research agenda for assurance at runtime with M@RT as a foundation. It grew out of stimulating discussions among the participants of the 2011 Schloss Dagstuhl Seminar on Models@run.time. In particular, we report on the findings of the breakout group Assurance@run.time as well as online discussions among the authors over the past two years while writing this chapter.

In an instrumented, interconnected and intelligent world, self-adaptive software systems proliferate. A key goal is to provide assurance at runtime when such systems adapt at runtime due to changes in their execution environment or their requirements. Traditionally software engineering, as opposed to control engineering, has concentrated on design-time assurance. Thus, a key challenge for the software engineering community is to develop runtime assurance techniques for self-adaptive systems that provide high performance, high confidence, and reconfigurable operation in the presence of uncertainties. One of the most promising avenues of research in this area is to use M@RT

---

[14] http://www.ga-project.eu

[15] Publications Office of the European Union: FET Flagship Pilots, Community Research and Development Information Service (CORDIS), http://cordis.europa.eu/fp7/ict/programme/fet/flagship/6pilots_en.html, 2012.

[16] http://www.ga-project.eu/science/software

as a foundation for developing runtime assurance techniques. Of all the subfields of assurance, V&V has probably made the most progress in transitioning design time models and techniques to runtime. While not all design-time assurance tasks can be transitioned to runtime, a significant opportunity exists to conduct assurance tasks at runtime, thereby making the overall SAS more resilient, reliable, responsive, secure, and cost-effective. One of the most formidable challenges for researchers in the field of runtime software assurance is to investigate techniques that guarantee certifiable trust for highly-adaptive systems.

This research agenda on runtime assurance techniques provides excellent starting points for research communities dealing with SASs, including Models@runtime, Run-time V&V, Requirements engineering@runtime, SEAMS, SASO (International Conference on Self-Adaptive and Self-Organizing Systems), and ICAC (International Conference on Autonomic Computing). Given the increasing use of SAS for high-assurance application domains, such as intelligent vehicles, power grid management, telecommunication infrastructure, financial systems, healthcare management systems, etc., it is paramount that these communities and related communities work together to address the assurance of SASs. M@RT is a key enabling technology to accelerate progress in this area.

References

[ABH⁺10] Abrial, J.-R., Butler, M., Hallerstede, S., Hoang, T.S., Mehta, F., Voisin, L.: Rodin: An open toolset for modelling and reasoning in Event-B. Software Tools for Technology Transfer (STTT) 12(6), 447–466 (2010)

[Abr88] Abrial, J.R.: The B Tool. In: Bloomfield, R.E., Marshall, L.S., Jones, R.B. (eds.) VDM 1988 VDM — The Way Ahead. LNCS, vol. 328, pp. 86–87. Springer, Heidelberg (1988)

[Acc04] Accelera. Property Specification Language Reference Manual, Version 1.1 (2004)

[ACR⁺11] Autili, M., Cortellessa, V., Di Ruscio, D., Inverardi, P., Pelliccione, P., Tivoli, M.: Eagle: Engineering software in the ubiquitous globe by leveraging uncertainty. In: Proceedings of the 19th ACM SIGSOFT Symposium and 13th European Conference on Foundations of Software Engineering (ESEC/FSE 2011), pp. 488–491 (2011)

[AIP07] Autili, M., Inverardi, P., Pelliccione, P.: Graphical scenarios for specifying temporal properties: An automated approach. Automated Software Engineering (ASE 2007) 14, 293–340 (2007)

[Ais03] Aissi, S.: Runtime environment security models. Intel Technology Journal 7(1), 60–67 (2003)

[ALRL04] Avizienis, A., Laprie, J.-C., Randell, B., Landwehr, C.: Basic concepts and taxonomy of dependable and secure computing. IEEE Transactions on Dependable and Secure Computing (TDSC) 1(1), 11–33 (2004)

[ASaP13] Angelopoulos, K., Silva Souza, V.E., Pimentel, J.A.: Requirements and architectural approaches to adaptive software systems: A comparative study. In: Proceedings of the 8th ACM/IEEE International Symposium on Software Engineering for Adaptive and Self-Managing Systems (SEAMS 2013), pp. 23–32 (2013)

[ASM80] Abrial, J.-R., Schuman, S.A., Meyer, B.: A specification language. In: McNaughten, R., McKeag, R.C. (eds.) On the Construction of Programs, pp. 343–406. Cambridge University Press (1980)

[AW94]   Aström, K.J., Wittenmark, B.: Adaptive Control, 2nd edn. Addison-Wesley (1994)

[AZ12]   Abeywickrama, D.B., Zambonelli, F.: Model checking goal-oriented requirements
            for self-adaptive systems. In: Proceedings of the Engineering of Computer Based
            Systems (ECBS 2012), pp. 33–42 (2012)

[BAMP81]   Ben-Ari, M., Manna, Z., Pnueli, A.: The temporal logic of branching time. In: Pro-
            ceedings of the 8th ACM SIGPLAN-SIGACT Symposium on Principles of Pro-
            gramming Languages (POPL 1981), pp. 164–176 (1981)

[BBF09]   Blair, G., Bencomo, N., France, R.B.: Models@run.time. IEEE Computer 42,
            22–27 (2009)

[BBG+06]   Becker, B., Beyer, D., Giese, H., Klein, F., Schilling, D.: Symbolic invariant ver-
            ification for systems with dynamic structural adaptation. In: Proceedings of the
            28th ACM/IEEE International Conference on Software Engineering (ICSE 2006),
            pp. 72–81 (2006)

[BCD97]   Blair, G., Coulson, G., Davies, N.: Adaptive middleware for mobile multime-
            dia applications. In: Proceedings of the 8th International Workshop on Network
            and Operating System Support for Digital Audio and Video (NOSSDAV 1997),
            pp. 259–273 (1997)

[BCdL11]   Bailey, C., Chadwick, D.W., de Lemos, R.: Self-adaptive authorization framework
            for policy based RBAC/ABAC models. In: Proceedings of the 9th IEEE Inter-
            national Conference on Dependable, Autonomic and Secure Computing (DASC
            2011), pp. 37–44 (2011)

[BDM+11]   Balasubramanian, S., Desmarais, R., Müller, H.A., Stege, U., Venkatesh, S.: Char-
            acterizing problems for realizing policies in self-adaptive and self-managing sys-
            tems. In: Proceedings of the 6th ACM/IEEE International Symposium on Software
            Engineering for Adaptive and Self-Managing Systems (SEAMS 2011), pp. 70–79
            (2011)

[Ber08]   Berry, D.M.: Ambiguity in natural language requirements documents. In: Martell,
            C. (ed.) Monterey Workshop 2007. LNCS, vol. 5320, pp. 1–7. Springer, Heidelberg
            (2008)

[BG10]   Baresi, L., Ghezzi, C.: The disappearing boundary between development-time and
            run-time. In: Proceedings of the Workshop on Future of Software Engineering Re-
            search (FoSER 2010), pp. 17–22. ACM (2010)

[BHTV06]   Baresi, L., Heckel, R., Thöne, S., Varró, D.: Style-based modeling and refinement
            of service-oriented architectures. Software and System Modeling 5(2), 187–207
            (2006)

[BJ78]   Bjorner, D., Jones, C.B. (eds.): The Vienna Development Method: The Meta-
            Language. LNCS, vol. 61. Springer, Heidelberg (1978)

[BJY11]   Bauer, A., Jürjens, J., Yu, Y.: Run-time security traceability for evolving systems. Computer Journal 54(1), 58–87 (2011)

[BKLW95]   Barbacci, M., Klein, M.H., Longstaff, T.A., Weinstock, C.B.: Quality attributes. Technical Report CMU/SEI-95-TR-021, CMU/SEI (1995)

[BLG11]   Barna, C., Litoiu, M., Ghanbari, H.: Autonomic load-testing framework. In: Proceedings of the 8th ACM/IEEE International Conference on Autonomic Computing (ICAC 2011), pp. 91–100 (2011)

[BLPV95]   Bormann, J., Lohse, J., Payer, M., Venzl, G.: Model checking in industrial hardware design. In: Proceedings of the 32nd ACM/IEEE Conference on Design automation (DAC 1995), pp. 298–303 (1995)

[BPS10]   Baresi, L., Pasquale, L., Spoletini, P.: Fuzzy goals for requirements-driven adaptation. In: Proceedings of the 18th IEEE International Requirements Engineering Conference (RE 2010), pp. 125–134 (2010)

[BPVR09]   Bucchiarone, A., Pelliccione, P., Vattani, C., Runge, O.: Self-repairing systems modeling and verification using AGG. In: Proceedings of the Joint Working IEEE/IFIP Conference on Software Architecture 2009 & European Conference on Software Architecture (WICSA/ECSA 2009), pp. 181–190 (2009)

[BSG+09]   Brun, Y., et al.: Engineering self-adaptive systems through feedback loops. In: Cheng, B.H.C., de Lemos, R., Giese, H., Inverardi, P., Magee, J. (eds.) Software Engineering for Self-Adaptive Systems. LNCS, vol. 5525, pp. 48–70. Springer, Heidelberg (2009)

[BWS+10]   Bencomo, N., Whittle, J., Sawyer, P., Finkelstein, A., Letier, E.: Requirements reflection: Requirements as runtime entities. In: Proceedings of the ACM/IEEE 32nd International Conference on Software Engineering (ICSE 2010), pp. 199–202 (2010)

[CdL12]   Cámara, J., de Lemos, R.: Evaluation of resilience in self-adaptive systems using probabilistic model-checking. In: Proceedings of the 7th ACM/IEEE International Symposium on Software Engineering for Adaptive and Self-Managing Systems (SEAMS 2012), pp. 53–62 (2012)

[CE82]   Gupta, M., Rao, R.S., Pande, A., Tripathi, A.K.: Design and synthesis of synchronization skeletons using branching time temporal logic. In: Meghanathan, N., Kaushik, B.K., Nagamalai, D. (eds.) CCSIT 2011, Part I. CCIS, vol. 131, pp. 318–328. Springer, Heidelberg (2011)

[CGK+11]   Calinescu, R., Grunske, L., Kwiatkowska, M.Z., Mirandola, R., Tamburrelli, G.: Dynamic QoS management and optimization in service-based systems. IEEE Transactions on Software Engineering (TSE) 37(3), 387–409 (2011)

[CGP01]   Clarke, E.M., Grumberg, O., Peled, D.A.: Model checking. MIT Press (2001)

[CGP02]   Chandra, S., Godefroid, P., Palm, C.: Software model checking in practice: An industrial case study. In: Proceedings of the 24th ACM/IEEE International Conference on Software Engineering (ICSE 2002), pp. 431–441 (2002)

[CHC96]   Cho, S.M., Hong, H.S., Cha, S.D.: Safety analysis using coloured Petri nets. In: Proceedings of the Asia Pacific Software Engineering Conference (APSEC 1996), pp. 176–193 (1996)

[Cle96]   Clements, P.C.: A survey of architecture description languages. In: Proceedings of the 8th IEEE International Workshop on Software Specification and Design (IWSSD 1996), pp. 16–26 (1996)

[CNdRW06] Chantree, F., Nuseibeh, B., de Roeck, A., Willis, A.: Identifying nocuous ambiguities in natural language requirements. In: Proceedings of 14th IEEE International Requirements Engineering Conference (RE 2006), pp. 59–68 (2006)

[CPL09] Chung, L., do Prado Leite, J.C.S.: On non-functional requirements in software engineering. In: Borgida, A.T., Chaudhri, V.K., Giorgini, P., Yu, E.S. (eds.) Conceptual Modeling: Foundations and Applications. LNCS, vol. Conceptual Modeling: Foundations and Applications, pp. 363–379. Springer, Heidelberg (2009)

[CSBW09] Cheng, B.H.C., Sawyer, P., Bencomo, N., Whittle, J.: A goal-based modeling approach to develop requirements of an adaptive system with environmental uncertainty. In: Schürr, A., Selic, B. (eds.) MODELS 2009. LNCS, vol. 5795, pp. 468–483. Springer, Heidelberg (2009)

[CVM14] Castañeda, L., Villegas, N.M., Müller, H.A.: Self-adaptive applications: On the development of personalized web-tasking systems. In: Proceedings of the 9th ACM/IEEE International Symposium on Software Engineering for Adaptive and Self-Managing Systems, SEAMS 2014 (in press, 2014)

[Dah10] Dahm, W.J.A.: Technology Horizons a Vision for Air Force Science & Technology During 2010-2030. Technical report, U.S. Air Force (2010)

[DDKM08] Dawson, D., Desmarais, R., Kienle, H.M., Muller, H.A.: Monitoring in adaptive systems using reflection. In: Proceedings of the 3rd ACM/IEEE International Workshop on Software Engineering for Adaptive and Self-Managing Systems (SEAMS 2008), pp. 81–88 (2008)

[DMIS13] Di Marco, A., Inverardi, P., Spalazzese, R.: Synthesizing self-adaptive connectors meeting functional and performance concerns. In: Proceedings of the 8th ACM/IEEE International Symposium on Software Engineering for Adaptive and Self-Managing Systems (SEAMS 2013), pp. 133–142 (2013)

[EER+10] Ehrig, H., Ermel, C., Runge, O., Bucchiarone, A., Pelliccione, P.: Formal analysis and verification of self-healing systems. In: Rosenblum, D.S., Taentzer, G. (eds.) FASE 2010. LNCS, vol. 6013, pp. 139–153. Springer, Heidelberg (2010)

[EGMT09] Epifani, I., Ghezzi, C., Mirandola, R., Tamburrelli, G.: Model evolution by runtime parameter adaptation. In: Proceedings of the 31st ACM/IEEE International Conference on Software Engineering (ICSE 2009), pp. 111–121 (2009)

[EKM11] Esfahani, N., Kouroshfar, E., Malek, S.: Taming uncertainty in self-adaptive software. In: Proceedings of the 19th ACM SIGSOFT Symposium and the 13th European Conference on Foundations of Software Engineering (ESEC/FSE 2011), pp. 234–244 (2011)

[EM13] Esfahani, N., Malek, S.: Uncertainty in self-adaptive software systems. In: de Lemos, R., Giese, H., Müller, H.A., Shaw, M. (eds.) Self-Adaptive Systems. LNCS, vol. 7475, pp. 214–238. Springer, Heidelberg (2013)

[FA11] Fraser, G., Arcuri, A.: Evosuite: Automatic test suite generation for object-oriented software. In: Proceedings of the 19th ACM SIGSOFT Symposium and the 13th European Conference on Foundations of Software Engineering (ESEC/FSE 2011), pp. 416–419 (2011)

[FDB+08] Fleury, F., Dehlen, V., Bencomo, N., Morin, B., Jezequel, J.M.: Modeling and validating dynamic adaptation. In: Proceedings of the International Workshop on Models@RunTime (M@RT 2008), pp. 97–108 (2008)

[FDC14a] Fredericks, E.M., Devries, B., Cheng, B.H.C.: AutoRELAX: Automatically RELAXing a goal model to address uncertainty. Empirical Software Engineering (in press, 2014)

[FDC14b]   Fredericks, E.M., Devries, B., Cheng, B.H.C.: Towards run-time adaptation of test cases for self-adaptive systems in the face of uncertainty. In: Proceedings of the 9th ACM/IEEE International Symposium on Software Engineering for Adaptive and Self-Managing Systems, SEAMS 2014 (in press, 2014)

[FF95]   Fickas, S., Feather, M.S.: Requirements monitoring in dynamic environments. In: Proceedings of the Second IEEE International Symposium on Requirements Engineering (RE 1995), pp. 140–147 (1995)

[FFvLP98]   Feather, M.S., Fickas, S., van Lamsweerde, A., Ponsard, C.: Reconciling system requirements and runtime behavior. In: Proceedings of the 9th International Workshop on Software Specification and Design (IWSSD 1998), pp. 50–59. IEEE (1998)

[FGT11]   Filieri, A., Ghezzi, C., Tamburrelli, G.: Run-time efficient probabilistic model checking. In: Proceedings of the 33rd ACM/IEEE International Conference on Software Engineering (ICSE 2011), pp. 341–350 (2011)

[FRC13a]   Fredericks, E.M., Ramirez, A.J., Cheng, B.H.C.: Towards run-time testing of dynamic adaptive systems. In: Proceedings of the 8th ACM/IEEE International Symposium on Software Engineering for Self-Adaptive Systems (SEAMS 2013), pp. 169–174 (2013)

[FRC13b]   Fredericks, E.M., Ramirez, A.J., Cheng, B.H.C.: Validating code-level behavior of dynamic adaptive systems in the face of uncertainty. In: Ruhe, G., Zhang, Y. (eds.) SSBSE 2013. LNCS, vol. 8084, pp. 81–95. Springer, Heidelberg (2013)

[GCH⁺04]   Garlan, D., Cheng, S.-W., Huang, A.-C., Schmerl, B., Steenkiste, P.: Rainbow: Architecture-based self-adaptation with reusable infrastructure. IEEE Computer 37(10), 46–54 (2004)

[GCZ08]   Goldsby, H.J., Cheng, B.H.C., Zhang, J.: AMOEBA-RT: Run-time verification of adaptive software. In: Giese, H. (ed.) MODELS 2008. LNCS, vol. 5002, pp. 212–224. Springer, Heidelberg (2008)

[GH04]   Gomaa, H., Hussein, M.: Software reconfiguration patterns for dynamic evolution of software architectures. In: Proceedings of the Fourth IEEE/IFIP Working Conference on Software Architecture (WICSA 2004), pp. 79–88 (2004)

[GHL10]   Giese, H., Hildebrandt, S., Lambers, L.: Toward bridging the gap between formal semantics and implementation of triple graph grammars. In: Proceedings of the Workshop on Model-Driven Engineering, Verification, and Validation (MOD-EVVA 2010), pp. 19–24. IEEE (2010)

[Gor01]   Gordon, D.F.: APT agents: Agents that are adaptive, predictable, and timely. In: Rash, J.L., Rouff, C.A., Truszkowski, W., Gordon, D.F., Hinchey, M.G. (eds.) FAABS 2000. LNCS (LNAI), vol. 1871, pp. 278–293. Springer, Heidelberg (2001)

[Gru11]   Grunske, L.: An effective sequential statistical test for probabilistic monitoring. Information & Software Technology (IST) 53(3), 190–199 (2011)

[GSLI11]   Ghanbari, H., Simmons, B., Litoiu, M., Iszlai, G.: Exploring alternative approaches to implement an elasticity policy. In: Proceedings of the IEEE International Conference on Cloud Computing (CLOUD 2011), pp. 716–723 (2011)

[GT06]   Giese, H., Tichy, M.: Component-based hazard analysis: Optimal designs, product lines, and online-reconfiguration. In: Górski, J. (ed.) SAFECOMP 2006. LNCS, vol. 4166, pp. 156–169. Springer, Heidelberg (2006)

[GZ09]   Grunske, L., Zhang, P.: Monitoring probabilistic properties. In: Proceedings of the 7th Joint Meeting of the European Software Engineering Conference and the ACM SIGSOFT International Symposium on Foundations of Software Engineering (ESEC/FSE 2009), pp. 183–192 (2009)

[Har87]   Harel, D.: Statecharts: A visual formalism for complex systems. Science of Computer Programming 8(3), 231–274 (1987)

[HDPT04]   Hellerstein, J.L., Diao, Y., Parekh, S., Tilbury, D.M.: Feedback Control of Computing Systems. John Wiley & Sons (2004)

[HMPB00]   Hashii, B., Malabarba, S., Pandey, R., Bishop, M.: Supporting reconfigurable security policies for mobile programs. Computer Networks 33(1-6), 77–93 (2000)

[HT04]   Harel, D., Thiagarajan, P.S.: Message sequence charts. UML for Real, 77–105 (2004)

[IBM06]   IBM Corporation. An architectural blueprint for autonomic computing. Technical report, IBM Corporation (2006)

[IEE90]   IEEE. IEEE standard glossary of software engineering terminology. IEEE Std 610.12-1990 (1990)

[IH01]   Ivory, M.Y., Hearst, M.A.: The state of the art in automating usability evaluation of user interfaces. ACM Computer Survey 33(4), 470–516 (2001)

[Inv07]   Inverardi, P.: Software of the future is the future of software? In: Montanari, U., Sannella, D., Bruni, R. (eds.) TGC 2006. LNCS, vol. 4661, pp. 69–85. Springer, Heidelberg (2007)

[IPT09]   Inverardi, P., Pelliccione, P., Tivoli, M.: Towards an assume-guarantee theory for adaptable systems. In: Proceedings of the 4th ACM/IEEE Workshop on Software Engineering for Adaptive and Self-Managing Systems (SEAMS 2009), pp. 106–115 (2009)

[IST11]   Inverardi, P., Spalazzese, R., Tivoli, M.: Application-layer connector synthesis. In: Bernardo, M., Issarny, V. (eds.) SFM 2011. LNCS, vol. 6659, pp. 148–190. Springer, Heidelberg (2011)

[Jen03]   Jensen, K.: Coloured Petri Nets: Basic Concepts, Analysis Methods and Practical Use. EATCS Series, vol. 1. Springer (2003)

[JT96]   Jonsson, B., Tsay, Y.-K.: Assumption/guarantee specifications in linear-time temporal logic. Theoretical Computer Science 167(1-2), 47–72 (1996)

[KC03]   Kephart, J.O., Chess, D.M.: The vision of autonomic computing. IEEE Computer 36(1), 41–50 (2003)

[KHW⁺01]   Knight, J.C., Heimbigner, D., Wolf, A.L., Carzaniga, A., Hill, J., Devanbu, P., Gertz, M.: The Willow architecture: Comprehensive survivability for large-scale distributed applications. Technical Report CU-CS-926-01, Department of Computer Science, University of Colorado (2001)

[KM90]   Kramer, J., Magee, J.: The evolving philosophers problem: Dynamic change management. IEEE Transactions on Software Engineering (TSE) 16(11), 1293–1306 (1990)

[KM07]   Kramer, J., Magee, J.: Self-managed systems: An architectural challenge. In: Future of Software Engineering (FOSE 2007), pp. 259–268. IEEE (2007)

[LAL⁺03]   Lu, Y., Abdelzaher, T., Lu, C., Sha, L., Liu, X.: Feedback control with queueing-theoretic prediction for relative delay guarantees in web servers. In: Proceedings of the 9th IEEE Real-Time and Embedded Technology and Applications Symposium (RTAS 2003), p. 208 (2003)

[MAB⁺02]   Murray, R.M., Aström, K.J., Boyd, S.P., Brockett, R.W., Burns, J.A., Dahleh, M.A.: Control in an information rich world (2002)

[Mae87]   Maes, P.: Concepts and experiments in computational reflection. ACM SIGPLAN Notices 22(12), 147–155 (1987)

[MB03]   Menascé, D.A., Bennani, M.N.: On the use of performance models to design self-managing computer systems. In: Proceedings of the 29th International Computer Measurement Group Conference (CMG 2003), pp. 7–12 (2003)

[MG10]   Meedeniya, I., Grunske, L.: An efficient method for architecture-based reliability evaluation for evolving systems with changing parameters. In: Proceedings of the 21st IEEE International Symposium on Software Reliability Engineering (ISSRE 2010), pp. 229–238 (2010)

[MKS09]   Müller, H.A., Kienle, H.M., Stege, U.: Autonomic computing: Now you see it, now you don't—design and evolution of autonomic software systems. In: De Lucia, A., Ferrucci, F. (eds.) ISSSE 2006-2008. LNCS, vol. 5413, pp. 32–54. Springer, Heidelberg (2009)

[MPP09]   Morandini, M., Penserini, L., Perini, A.: Operational semantics of goal models in adaptive agents. In: Proceedings of the 8th International Conference on Autonomous Agents and Multiagent Systems—Volume 1 (AAMAS 2009), pp. 129–136. IFAA-MAS (2009)

[MPS08]   Müller, H.A., Pezzè, M., Shaw, M.: Visibility of control in adaptive systems. In: Proceedings of the 2nd International Workshop on Ultra-Large-Scale Software-Intensive Systems (ULSSIS 2008). ACM (2008)

[MTVM12]   Muñoz, J.C., Tamura, G., Villegas, N.M., Müller, H.A.: Surprise: User-controlled granular privacy and security for personal data in smartercontext. In: Proceedings of the 22nd Conference of the Center for Advanced Studies on Collaborative Research (CASCON 2012), pp. 128–142. ACM (2012)

[Mur89]   Murata, T.: Petri nets: Properties, analysis and applications. Proceedings to the IEEE 77(4), 541–580 (1989)

[MV14]   Müller, H., Villegas, N.: Runtime evolution of highly dynamic software. In: Mens, T., Serebrenik, A., Cleve, A. (eds.) Evolving Software Systems, pp. 229–264. Springer (2014)

[NPB+09]   Nguyen, C., Perini, A., Bernon, C., Pavón, J., Thangarajah, J.: Testing in multi-agent systems. In: Proceedings of the 10th International Workshop on Agent Oriented Software Engineering (AOSE 2009), pp. 180–190 (2009)

[NPT+09]   Nguyen, C., Perini, A., Tonella, P., Miles, S., Harman, M., Luck, M.: Evolutionary testing of autonomous software agents. In: Proceedings of the 8th International Conference on Autonomous Agents and Multiagent Systems—Volume 1 (AAMAS 2009), pp. 521–528. IFAAMAS (2009)

[OGT+]   Oreizy, P., Gorlick, M.M., Taylor, R.N., Heimbigner, D., Johnson, G., Medvidovic, N., Quilici, A., Rosenblum, D.S., Wolf, A.L.: An architecture-based approach to self-adaptive software. IEEE Intelligent Systems, 14

[OMH+11]   Ouedraogo, M., Mouratidis, H., Hecker, A., Bonhomme, C., Khadraoui, D., Dubois, E., Preston, D.: A new approach to evaluating security assurance. In: Proceedings of the 7th IEEE International Conference on Information Assurance and Security (IAS 2011), pp. 215–221 (2011)

[PGGB13]   La Manna, V.P., Greenyer, J., Ghezzi, C., Brenner, C.: Formalizing correctness criteria of dynamic updates derived from specification changes. In: Proceedings of the 8th ACM/IEEE International Symposium on Software Engineering for Adaptive and Self-Managing Systems (SEAMS 2013), pp. 63–72 (2013)

[PIM09]   Pelliccione, P., Inverardi, P., Muccini, H.: CHARMY: A framework for designing and verifying architectural specifications. IEEE Transactions on Software Engineering (TSE) 35, 325–346 (2009)

[Pnu81]   Pnueli, A.: A temporal logic of concurrent programs. Theoretical Computer Science 13, 45–60 (1981)

[PPS09]   Peled, D., Pelliccione, P., Spoletini, P.: Model Checking. In: Wiley Encyclopedia of Computer Science and Engineering, 6th edn., 5-Volume Set, vol. 3, pp. 1904–1920. John Wiley (2009)

[PS11]   Pasquale, L., Spoletini, P.: Monitoring fuzzy temporal requirements for service compositions: Motivations, challenges, and experimental results. In: Proceedings of the International Workshop on Requirements Engineering for Systems, Services and Systems of Systems (RESS 2011), pp. 63–69. IEEE (2011)

[PSWTH11] Priesterjahn, C., Sondermann-Wölke, C., Tichy, M., Hölscher, C.: Component-based hazard analysis for mechatronic systems. In: Proceedings of the IEEE International Symposium on Object/Component/Service-oriented Real-time Distributed Computing (ISORC 2011), pp. 80–87 (2011)

[PT09]   Priesterjahn, C., Tichy, M.: Modeling safe reconfiguration with the fujaba real-time tool suite. In: Proceedings of the 7th International Fujaba Days, pp. 20–14 (2009)

[PTBP08]   Pelliccione, P., Tivoli, M., Bucchiarone, A., Polini, A.: An architectural approach to the correct and automatic assembly of evolving component-based systems. Journal of Systems Software 81, 2237–2251 (2008)

[QBL$^+$11] Quade, M., Blumendorf, M., Lehmann, G., Roscher, D., Albayrak, S.: Evaluating user interface adaptations at runtime by simulating user interaction. In: Proceedings of the 25th BCS Conference on Human Computer Interaction (HCI 2011), pp. 497–502 (2011)

[QJP11]   Qureshi, N.A., Jureta, I.J., Perini, A.: Requirements engineering for self-adaptive systems: Core ontology and problem statement. In: Mouratidis, H., Rolland, C. (eds.) CAiSE 2011. LNCS, vol. 6741, pp. 33–47. Springer, Heidelberg (2011)

[QLP11]   Qureshi, N.A., Liaskos, S., Perini, A.: Reasoning about adaptive requirements for self-adaptive systems at runtime. In: Proceedings of the 2nd International Workshop on Requirements@run.time (RE@run.time 2011), pp. 16–22 (2011)

[QP10]   Qureshi, N.A., Perini, A.: Requirements engineering for adaptive service based applications. In: Proceedings of the 18th IEEE International Requirements Engineering Conference (RE 2010), pp. 108–111 (2010)

[QS82]   Queille, J.-P., Sifakis, J.: Specification and verification of concurrent systems in CESAR. In: Dezani-Ciancaglini, M., Montanari, U. (eds.) International Symposium on Programming 1982. LNCS, vol. 137, pp. 337–351. Springer, Heidelberg (1982)

[RC10a]   Ramirez, A.J., Cheng, B.H.C.: Adaptive monitoring of software requirements. In: Proceedings of the Workshop on Requirements at Run Time (RE@RunTime 2010), pp. 41–50. IEEE (2010)

[RC10b]   Ramirez, A.J., Cheng, B.H.C.: Design patterns for developing dynamically adaptive systems. In: Proceedings of the 5th ACM/IEEE Workshop on Software Engineering for Adaptive and Self-Managed Systems (SEAMS 2010), pp. 49–58 (2010)

[RC11]   Ramirez, A.J., Cheng, B.H.C.: Automatic derivation of utility functions for monitoring software requirements. In: Whittle, J., Clark, T., Kühne, T. (eds.) MODELS 2011. LNCS, vol. 6981, pp. 501–516. Springer, Heidelberg (2011)

[RCBS12]   Ramirez, A.J., Cheng, B.H.C., Bencomo, N., Sawyer, P.: Relaxing claims: Coping with uncertainty while evaluating assumptions at run time. In: France, R.B., Kazmeier, J., Breu, R., Atkinson, C. (eds.) MODELS 2012. LNCS, vol. 7590, pp. 53–69. Springer, Heidelberg (2012)

[RCM10]   Ramirez, A.J., Cheng, B.H.C., McKinley, P.K.: Adaptive monitoring of software requirements. In: Proceedings of the First International Workshop on Requirements@run.time (RE@run.time 2010), pp. 41–50 (2010)

[RFJB12]   Ramirez, A.J., Fredericks, E.M., Jensen, A.C., Cheng, B.H.C.: Automatically RELAXing a goal model to cope with uncertainty. In: Fraser, G., Teixeira de Souza, J. (eds.) SSBSE 2012. LNCS, vol. 7515, pp. 198–212. Springer, Heidelberg (2012)

[RJC12]   Ramirez, A.J., Jensen, A.C., Cheng, B.H.C.: A taxonomy of uncertainty for dy-
            namically adaptive systems. In: Proceedings of the 7th ACM/IEEEE International
            Symposium on Software Engineering for Adaptive and Self-Managing Systems
            (SEAMS 2012), pp. 99–108 (2012)
[Rus07]   Rushby, J.: Just-in-time certification. In: Proceedings of the 12th IEEE Interna-
            tional Conference on Engineering of Complex Computer Systems (ICECCS 2007),
            pp. 15–24 (2007)
[Rus08]   Rushby, J.: Runtime certification. In: Leucker, M. (ed.) RV 2008. LNCS, vol. 5289,
            pp. 21–35. Springer, Heidelberg (2008)
[RZN05]   Ryutov, T., Zhou, L., Neuman, C.: Adaptive trust negotiation and access control.
            In: Proceedings of the 10th ACM Symposium on Access Control Models and Tech-
            nologies (SACMAT 2005), pp. 139–146 (2005)
[SAS14]   Proceedings of the ACM/IEEE International Conference on Self-Adaptive and
            Self-Organizing Systems (2007-2014)
[SBT11]   Schneider, D., Becker, M., Trapp, M.: Approaching runtime trust assurance in open
            adaptive systems. In: Proceedings of the 6th ACM/IEEE International Sympo-
            sium on Software Engineering for Adaptive and Self-Managing Systems (SEAMS
            2011), pp. 196–201 (2011)
[SCF⁺06]   Sottet, J.-S., Calvary, G., Favré, J.-M., Coutaz, J., Demeure, A., Balme, L.: Towards
            model driven engineering of plastic user interfaces. In: Bruel, J.-M. (ed.) MoDELS
            2005. LNCS, vol. 3844, pp. 191–200. Springer, Heidelberg (2006)
[SMB⁺09]   Simanta, S., Morris, E., Balasubramaniam, S., Davenport, J., Smith, D.B.: Informa-
            tion assurance challenges and strategies for securing SOA environments and web
            services. In: Proceedings of the 3rd IEEE Annual Systems Conference (SysCon
            2009), pp. 173–178 (2009)
[SSLRM11]   Souza, V.E.S., Lapouchnian, A., Robinson, W.N., Mylopoulos, J.: Awareness re-
            quirements for adaptive systems. In: Proceedings of the 6th International Sympo-
            sium on Software Engineering for Adaptive and Self-Managing Systems (SEAMS
            2011), pp. 60–69 (2011)
[ST13]   Schneider, D., Trapp, M.: Conditional safety certification of open adaptive systems.
            ACM Transactions on Autonomous and Adaptive Systems 8(2), 1–20 (2013)
[Tam12]   Tamura, G.: QoS-CARE: A Reliable System for Preserving QoS Contracts through
            Dynamic Reconfiguration. PhD thesis, University of Lille 1 - Science and Tech-
            nology and Universidad de Los Andes (2012)
[TCCD12]   Tamura, G., Casallas, R., Cleve, A., Duchien, L.: QoS contract-aware reconfigu-
            ration of component architectures using e-graphs. In: Barbosa, L.S., Lumpe, M.
            (eds.) FACS 2010. LNCS, vol. 6921, pp. 34–52. Springer, Heidelberg (2012)
[TVM⁺12]   Tamura, G., et al.: Towards Practical Runtime Verification and Validation of Self-
            Adaptive Software Systems. In: de Lemos, R., Giese, H., Müller, H.A., Shaw,
            M. (eds.) Software Engineering for Self-Adaptive Systems. LNCS, vol. 7475,
            pp. 108–132. Springer, Heidelberg (2013)
[TVM⁺13]   Tamura, G., Villegas, N.M., Müller, H.A., Duchien, L., Seinturier, L.: Improving
            context-awareness in self-adaptation using the dynamico reference model. In: Pro-
            ceedings of the 8th International Symposium on Software Engineering for Adaptive
            and Self-Managing Systems (SEAMS 2013), pp. 153–162 (2013)
[Uni99]   International Telecomunication Union. ITU-T Recommendation Z.100: Specifica-
            tion and Description Language, SDL (1999)
[Vil13]   Villegas, N.M.: Context Management and Self-Adaptivity for Situation-Aware
            Smart Software Systems. PhD thesis, Department of Computer Science, University
            of Victoria, Canada (February 2013)

[vLDL98]   van Lamsweerde, A., Darimont, R., Letier, E.: Managing conflicts in goal-driven requirements engineering. IEEE Transactions on Software Engineering (TSE) 24(11), 908–926 (1998)

[VMM+11]   Villegas, N.M., Müller, H.A., Muñoz, J.C., Lau, A., Ng, J., Brealey, C.: A dynamic context management infrastructure for supporting user-driven web integration in the personal web. In: Proceedings of the Conference of the Center for Advanced Studies on Collaborative Research (CASCON 2011), pp. 200–214. ACM (2011)

[VMT11a]   Villegas, N.M., Müller, H.A., Tamura, G.: Optimizing run-time SOA governance through context-driven SLAs and dynamic monitoring. In: Proceedings of the IEEE International Workshop on the Maintenance and Evolution of Service-Oriented and Cloud-Based Systems (MESOCA 2011), pp. 1–10 (2011)

[VMT+11b]   Villegas, N.M., Müller, H.A., Tamura, G., Duchien, L., Casallas, R.: A framework for evaluating quality-driven self-adaptive software systems. In: Proceedings of the 6th ACM/IEEE International Symposium on Software Engineering for Adaptive and Self-Managing Systems (SEAMS 2011), pp. 80–89 (2011)

[VTM+12]   Villegas, N.M., Tamura, G., Müller, H.A., Duchien, L., Casallas, R.: DYNAMICO: A reference model for governing control objectives and context relevance in self-adaptive software systems. In: de Lemos, R., Giese, H., Müller, H.A., Shaw, M. (eds.) Software Engineering for Self-Adaptive Systems. LNCS, vol. 7475, pp. 265–293. Springer, Heidelberg (2013)

[Wel02]   Wells, L.: Performance analysis using coloured Petri nets. In: Proceedings of the 10th IEEE International Symposium on Modeling, Analysis, and Simulation of Computer and Telecommunications Systems (MASCOTS 2002), pp. 217–224 (2002)

[WIdlIA12]   Weyns, D., Usman Iftikhar, M, de la Iglesia, D.G., Ahmad, T.: A survey of formal methods in self-adaptive systems. In: Proceedings of the Fifth International C* Conference on Computer Science and Software Engineering (C3S2E 2012), pp. 67–79. ACM (2012)

[WMA10]   Weyns, D., Malek, S., Andersson, J.: Forms: A formal reference model for self-adaptation. In: Proceedings of the 7th IEEE International Conference on Autonomic Computing (ICAC 2010), pp. 205–214 (2010)

[WSB+09]   Whittle, J., Sawyer, P., Bencomo, N., Cheng, B.H.C., Bruel, J.-M.: RELAX: Incorporating uncertainty into the specification of self-adaptive systems. In: Proceedings of the 17th IEEE International Requirements Engineering Conference (RE 2009), pp. 79–88 (2009)

[WSB11]   Welsh, K., Sawyer, P., Bencomo, N.: Towards requirements aware systems: Run-time resolution of design-time assumptions. In: Proceedings of the 26th ACM/IEEE International Conference on Automated Software Engineering (ICSE 20011), pp. 560–563 (2011)

[ZC05]   Zhang, J., Cheng, B.H.C.: Specifying adaptation semantics. In: Proceedings of the 2005 Workshop on Architecting Dependable Systems (WADS 2005), pp. 1–7. ACM (2005)

[ZC06a]   Zhang, J., Cheng, B.H.C.: Model-based development of dynamically adaptive software. In: Proceedings of the 28th ACM/IEEE International Conference on Software Engineering (ICSE 2006), pp. 371–380 (2006)

[ZC06b]   Zhang, J., Cheng, B.H.C.: Using temporal logic to specify adaptive program semantics. Journal of Systems and Software (JSS) 79(10), 1361–1369 (2006); Architecting Dependable Systems

[ZCYM05]   Zhang, J., Cheng, B.H.C., Yang, Z., McKinley, P.K.: Enabling safe dynamic component-based software adaptation. In: de Lemos, R., Gacek, C., Romanovsky, A. (eds.) Architecting Dependable Systems III. LNCS, vol. 3549, pp. 194–211. Springer, Heidelberg (2005)

[ZGC09]   Zhang, J., Goldsby, H.J., Cheng, B.H.C.: Modular verification of dynamically adaptive systems. In: Proceedings of the 8th ACM International Conference on Aspect-Oriented Software Development (AOSD 2009), pp. 161–172 (2009)

[ZJ97]   Zave, P., Jackson, M.: Four dark corners of requirements engineering. ACM Transactions on Software Engineering Methodology (TOSEM) 6(1), 1–30 (1997)

Model-driven, Moving-Target Defense
for Enterprise Network Security

Scott A. DeLoach, Xinming Ou, Rui Zhuang, and Su Zhang

Department of Computing and Information Sciences
Kansas State University
234 Nichols Hall, Manhattan, KS USA 66506
{sdeloach,xou,rui,szhang}@ksu.edu
http://cis.ksu.edu/

Abstract. This chapter presents the design and initial simulation results for a prototype moving-target defense (MTD) system, whose goal
is to significantly increase the difficulty of attacks on enterprise networks. Most networks are static, which gives attacker's a great advantage. Services are run on well-known ports at fixed, easily identifiable
IP addresses. The goal of an MTD system is to eliminate the static nature of networks by continuously adapting their configuration over time
in ways that seems random or chaotic to attackers, thus negating their
advantage. The novelty of our approach lies in the use of runtime models
that explicitly capture a network's operational and security goals, the
functionality required to achieve those goals, and the configuration of
the system. The MTD system reasons over these models to determine
how to make changes to the system that are invisible to users but appear
chaotic to an attacker. Our system uses these runtime models to analyze both known and unknown vulnerabilities to ensure that adaptations
occur often enough and in the right ways to protect the system against
external attacks.

Keywords: Runtime models, moving target defense, adaptive systems,
network security.

1 Introduction

In cyber space, attackers have time to study our networks to determine potential
vulnerabilities and choose the time of attack to gain the maximum benefit. Additionally, once an attacker acquires a privilege, that privilege can be maintained
for a long time without being detected [4]. The static nature of current networks
makes it easy to attack and breach a system and to maintain illegal access privileges for extended periods of time. To combat this advantage, a promising new
approach to network security has been suggested called the moving target defense (MTD) [20]. While there are many facets of MTD, for computer networks,
one can broadly interpret MTD as the fact that the network constantly changes
its configuration to reduce/shift the attack surface area available for exploitation by attackers. An MTD system will make attacking a system more difficult

N. Bencomo et al. (Eds.): Models@run.time, LNCS 8378, pp. 137–161, 2014.
© Springer International Publishing Switzerland 2014

because the attacker will spend more time scanning the network for potential vulnerabilities and will not be able to maintain illegally acquired privileges for long. While promising, little research has been done to show that MTDs can work effectively in realistic networked systems.

Current approaches to network defense rely on reacting to attacker's efforts to penetrate the system. Similarly, current adaptive systems react to a variety of stimuli (e.g., system failure or new tasks) to trigger their adaptations. Thus, to be effective, MTD research must push beyond the existing state-of-the-art in both network security and adaptive systems in order to allow the system to adapt proactively without negatively affecting system functionality. Our vision is that an MTD system should be able to reason about its current configuration and make changes that are invisible to a valid user but appear chaotic to an attacker. In order to reason about its current configuration, runtime models that reflect the current configuration are needed that capture the modifiable aspects of the system and their relationship to the overall goals of the system. The *modifiable aspects* of the system are parts of the configuration that may be changed such as IP addresses, ports, firewall settings, host assignments, protocols, routing, virtual machines used, and software application type, versions, etc.

The research challenges in MTD systems are significant. First, we must find a way to model both the requirements, design, and current configuration (implementation) of the system in such a way as to allow automated reasoning. Second, we must provide a mechanism that supports automated reconfiguration of the system to include reassigning host addresses and returning the services to known good configurations. Third, we provide a mechanism that allows services to find the services they depend on in the midst of wide-spread system reconfiguration. Fourth, we must provide an adaptation mechanism (algorithm) that can adapt multiple aspects of the network's configuration in a way the mitigates the effect of attacks against critical network resources. And finally, we must integrate intrusion detection and risk assessment methodologies so that the system adaptation can respond to attack and risk indicators in a way that continues to appear random and chaotic to the attacker. This paper seeks to describe our initial approach at modeling the network requirements and design and demonstrate that an MTD based approach has potential for significantly increasing the difficulty of attacks on enterprise networks.

2   Moving Target Defense System

The high-level architecture of a simple MTD system that adapts randomly is shown in Figure 1 within the dashed box. Here, an *Adaptation Engine* orders (what appears to be) random adaptations to the network configuration at random intervals. These adaptations are carried out by a *Configuration Manager* that controls the configuration of the *Physical Network*. The key to these apparently random adaptations is that they are based on a *Logical Mission Model*, which is a runtime model that captures the Physical Network's current configuration as well as the functional requirements of the network. Since purely random

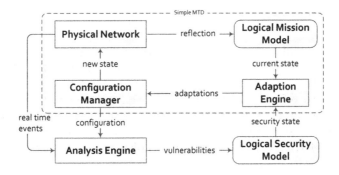

Fig. 1. Moving Target Defense System

adaptations would quickly yield the system inoperable, the adaptations must be made with an understanding of the requirements of the system in light of the current configuration. Specifically, the Logical Mission Model includes two runtime models: an organization model and a goal model. The *organizational model* captures the current configuration including the required functionalities in the system and the physical hardware capabilities. The *goal model* captures the system level requirements and the importance of the various requirements. We use the Organizational Model for Adaptive Complex Systems (OMACS) developed previously [10] for the organizational model and a new goal model, the Value-based Goal Model (VGM) [11], which is designed to capture requirements of long-lived, service-based systems.

While a simple MTD system holds promise, our ultimate vision for MTD systems uses apparently random changes in conjunction with intelligent control, where adaptations can occur randomly or based on risk indicators such as vulnerability scanning results and alerts from intrusion detection systems. The intelligent MTD system architecture extends the simple MTD architecture in Figure 1 by adding an *Analysis Engine* that takes real-time events from the Physical Network and the current configuration from the Configuration Manager to determine possible vulnerabilities and on-going attacks. The Adaptation Engine is extended to look at the network's current state along with its security state, as captured in the Logical Security Model. The *Logical Security Model* also consists of two runtime models: a goal model and a model of system vulnerabilities. The goal model uses the VGM like the Logical Mission Model; however, instead of capturing required functionalities, the Logical Security Model's VGM is used to capture the security goals of the system. The system vulnerability model is captured in the form of a novel *Conservative Attack Graph* (CAG), which captures both known and unknown system vulnerabilities and how an attacker might move through the system to gain specific privileges. If there are security issues that need to be addressed, the Adaption Engine uses these two models to determine an appropriate set of adaptations and sends them to the Configuration Manager (along with "random" adaptations) to implement.

2.1   Nomenclature

The terminology differences between enterprise networks, network security, and the abstract models we use in our research can be confusing. Therefore, for the remainder of the paper, we try to consistently use the following terms. We use the term *role* to refer to network services (e.g., web server, e-mail server, db servers) and the term *resource* to refer to the physical components of the system (e.g., computer hosts, firewalls, servers). The term resources is also equated to agents when referring to the OMACS model discussed in Section 4.2.

2.2   Resource Mapping System

One problem with a "moving" system is ensuring that system resources can locate each other after adaptations occur. Thus, to make these changes invisible to the system itself, a *Resource Mapping System* (RMS) is required, which also serves as a hardened system core that the attacker must penetrate to exploit the system. Current networks are so complex that even their system administrators have no clear understanding of the service dependencies [6,3,15]. In such complex systems, attacks can follow many patterns making their identification and prevention difficult. This is evidenced by research that shows an exponential increase in the number of attack paths in even moderate-sized networks [21,17]. The RMS interacts with the Configuration Manager, which pushes the current configuration to the RMS components. All communication between system roles must go through the RMS so that communications can be maintained even as the location of the roles change.

As shown in Figure 2, each role is assigned to a single virtual machine (VM), which has a dedicated RMS component that handles all communication with other roles. Each dedicated RMS component only knows the locations of the roles it needs to communicate with as defined by the role's communication requirements in the Role model (See Section 5). All communications between mission critical roles are controlled by RMS even as their locations change dynamically. In some sense the RMS functions like an end-host firewall with highly restrictive policies for critical roles; critical roles can be isolated on VMs with only the minimal ports open. Compared with traditional firewalls, the RMS provides flexibility for non-critical roles, while increasing protection for critical roles.

In modern virtual environments, isolating individual services on separate VMs provides the ability to tailor the VM's operating system to specific services and thus limit potential vulnerabilities. We believe that tailoring a VM's security environment while controlling communications via the RMS will provide a highly tailored security environment that will make successful attacks more difficult. However, due to its knowledge of the entire system configuration, the Configuration Manager is the key vulnerability of our design. We currently assume the Configuration Manager runs on a trusted host and significant resources are used to ensure its safety.

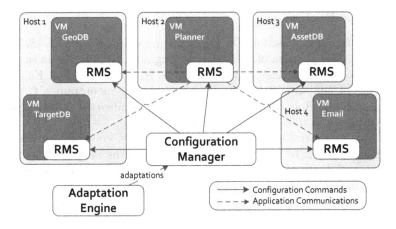

Fig. 2. RMS System

2.3   Adaptation Engine

The assignment of roles to resources allows the system to adapt autonomously while ensuring all mission goals are still supported. In traditional adaptive system, the adaptation algorithm would attempt to provide optimal or near optimal configurations [4]. However, since the goal of MTDs is to produce non-predictable configurations, we must consider alternative approaches. Instead of seeking optimal configurations (in terms of system performance), which tends to produce the same configuration over and over, we must develop algorithms that find near optimal configurations that are significantly different in some aspect.

Since the Adaptation Engine is the main decision making apparatus for the MTD, it must be able to control the various modifiable aspects of the system such as the assignment of roles to resources, IP addresses and ports, firewall settings, applications (types, versions, etc.), VM types, and protocols between roles. The assignment of roles to resources is similar to our existing reassignment algorithms [10] and is based on ensuring the resources have the appropriate capabilities to play the role. Since we use unique VMs for each role, we can assign any available IP address on the network to a new VM. If the role's communication is supported by the RMS, the port number can also be randomly selected. Firewall settings can be updated based on the knowledge of which VMs actually need to communicate. Specific application types (e.g., Apache, Oracle, Hiawatha, etc.), versions, or VM types can also be specified by the Adaptation Engine. Finally, we can consider adapting the protocols for various critical roles that communicate via the VM. Such protocol changes could be minor while still allowing the RMS to easily detect compromised VMs or physical resources. A further discussion of how the models are used in the adaptation process is given in 4.5 after the models are presented.

2.4   Analysis Engine

The Analysis Engine is based on Dr. Ou's existing work on MulVAL [22,21] and SnIPS [23,28]. The purpose of the Analysis Engine is to infer the most critical vulnerabilities and most likely attack activities so the Adaptation Engine can make intelligent adaptation choices. The Analysis Engine outputs a CAG that is derived from the Role model (see Section 5) dependencies and incorporates real-time evidence to infer the network's security state.

Traditional enterprise security risk assessment uses vulnerability scans and firewall configurations to identify potential attack paths into the system. This has a number of disadvantages, such as the inability to mitigate risk due to unknown threats (e.g., zero-day vulnerabilities). Intrusion detection system (IDS) and Security Information and Event Management System (SIEM) are typically deployed for the purpose of situational awareness and forensics. The analysis engine in our envisioned system will take input from these traditional sources but map them to the unique conservative attack graph (CAG) model due to the dynamic nature of the adaptation. The unique advantage moving-target brings to security analysis is that the usable attack surface is greatly reduced due to shifting, and the false-positive challenge in intrusion detection can be mitigated by proactively adapting the system even with less than certain attack indicators.

The CAG model is also used in our simulation study of the effectiveness of the system against both known and unknown attacks. In our model we assume each host could contain exploitable vulnerabilities and for this reason there is no distinction between known and unknown vulnerabilities in our simulation. When a CAG is used in deployed systems, however, such distinctions will matter and we intend to build models to capture the impact of both known and unknown vulnerabilities in the moving-target system as part of our future work.

3   Example System

To demonstrate that MTD systems can be effective for network security defense, we simulated an MTD system using a simple military mission planning system that allows authorized users to access a mission planner. We provide an overview of that system here and use it to illustrate our proposed runtime models in Section 4. The mission planning system, shown in Figure 3, supports users located both inside and outside the local network. The system allows users to access three different databases in order to construct a specific mission. The databases that the planner accesses are an *asset database* that includes the types and numbers of assets available to carry out planning, a *target database* that includes the intelligence on targets of interest, and a *geographical database* that includes maps and geographical information about the areas required for planning appropriate ingress, target attack, and egress routes.

In this system, the likely targets of interest are not the Authorizer or Planner systems, but the data behind them. Specifically, the TargetDB and AssetDB have the most potentially important data, thus, they would likely be the targets of an attack. In our simulation, we assume the TargetDB is the main focus.

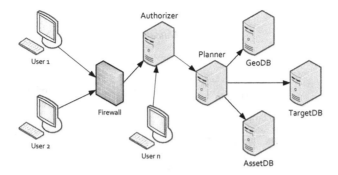

Fig. 3. Mission Planning System

4   Runtime Models

The key to our MTD approach lies in novel runtime models based on human organizations that explicitly capture a system's goals, the functionality required to achieve those goals, and the logical and physical configuration of the system. These runtime models allow the system to reason about its current state and make changes that are invisible to the user but appear chaotic and significantly increase the difficulty for an attacker. Key runtime models include:

- a Value-based Goal model (VGM) that captures the system's mission and security requirements
- an OMACS model that captures the physical resources in the system, their capabilities, the software functions available carry out system goals, and the current assignment of functions to physical resources
- a Conservative Attack Graph (CAG) that captures both known and unknown vulnerabilities based on the current system configuration

4.1   Value Based Goal Model (VGM)

It has recently been recognized by the adaptive systems community that the key to highly efficient and effective adaptive systems is explicitly modeling the requirements or objectives of the system [5,25], a position we have espoused for several years [9,10,12]. Specifically, we capture the system objectives as goals, which allows the system to adapt while still ensuring it can support its overall goals. As there are trade offs during adaptation, understanding which goals are the most important is critical to ensuring the system adapts appropriately. Thus we capture the system's mission and security goals in a novel Value-based Goal model (VGM), which allows us to determine the effect of attacks and adaptations on system functionality and security [18].

Formally, a VGM is a tree whose nodes are value-based goals rooted at goal g_0, as shown in Figure 4 where g_0 is the *Mission Goal*. Typically, g_0 represents the overall operational goal of the network or the overall goal of system security.

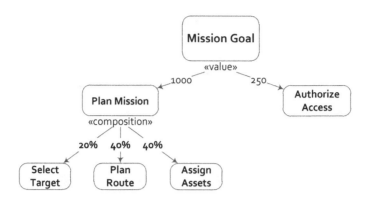

Fig. 4. Value-Based Goal Model

Goals are typically defined as some desired state of the world, and this is true of value-based goals as well. However, value-based goals are not achievement goals whose state must be attained by the system, but instead are maintenance goals whose state must be preserved by the system [8]. Thus instead of achieving goals, the objective of a value-based system is to maintain the maximal value of a set of goals expressed in a unique decomposition and value aggregation approach.

The key to determining the overall value of a VGM tree is to know which goals are currently maintained. Thus, we define a set called the *maintained set* that captures the current set of goals maintained by the system. The maintained set is computed by first determining the leaf goals in the maintained set and then computing the parent goals that are in the maintained set. The value of a VGM is based on the current set of goals in the maintained set. Thus, the current value of the VGM as well as future values of the VGM with different maintained sets can be computed. The current value of any goal that is not maintained is zero.

The root goal, g_0, of a value-based goal model represents the overall value of the system. Goal g_0 is always a *value goal*, which is decomposed into a set of sub-goals, each of which are assigned a maximum value. The current value of the g_0 is simply the sum of the values of its children, which can range from 0 to their maximum values. The root value goal is decomposed into one or more of the following types of goals: Composition, AND, OR, or Leaf.

If a goal is a *Composition goal*, all of its sub-goals contribute a percentage to its value. Thus, each sub-goal of a Composition goal has an associated contribution value and the contributions of all sub-goals of a Composition goal must equal 1.0. The current value of a Composition goal is the sum of the sub-goal contributions that are currently maintained.

An *AND goal* denotes the case when all sub-goals must be maintained in order for the parent goal to be maintained and contribute its maximum value. In some cases, the current values of an AND goal's sub-goals may be maintained, but not at the maximum value. Thus, we define the current value of an AND goal to be the minimum value of all its sub-goals (if one is not maintained its value is 0).

The maximum values of each sub-goal of an AND goal is the maximum value of the AND goal since the failure to maintain any one of the sub-goals reduces the value of the parent to zero.

An *OR goal* is similar to an AND goal as its value is based on a Boolean operator, in this case logical OR. Thus, if any sub-goal of an OR goal is maintained, then the OR goal itself is maintained. However, unlike the AND goal, each sub-goal has an individual contribution value associated with it, stated in terms of a percentage (0 to 100) of the OR goal's maximum value. The notion of an OR goal is that there may be multiple ways to maintain a specific goal, although some may be better than others.

Leaf goals have no sub-goals and contribute to the overall value of the goal tree based on their parent's type. Actually, only Leaf goals are actively maintained by the system. As the system maintains (or fails to maintain) Leaf goals, the overall value is aggregated based on parent goal types until a final value for the system is computed. Using the description above, it should be noted that the value of a system is not simply the value of all its Leaf goals and thus care should be taken when using the values of Leaf goals independently of their parent goals. In many cases, the value of a Leaf goal (that are sub-goals of AND/OR goals directly or indirectly) can only be computed in light of a specific configuration.

In an MTD, a VGM captures the relative importance of the system goals in case trade-offs must be made. As shown in Figure 4, our example system's objectives are decomposed into two main goals: allowing external users access to the system (Authorizer) and allowing users to plan missions (Plan Mission). The Plan Mission goal is decomposed into a set of subgoals, where each subgoal is weighted to express its contribution to its parent goal. Thus, based on the system's VGM, if there are not enough resources to achieve all goals, the *Plan Mission* goal is more important than the *Authorize Access* goal and thus the system should try to support the *Plan Mission* goal.

4.2   Organization Model for Adaptive Complex Systems (OMACS)

The Organization Model for Adaptive Computational Systems (OMACS) [10] is a model that defines the knowledge required to allow a team of agents to reorganize in response to agent failure or changing team goals. While adapting to failure and changing goals can be a benefit in a network-based system, our objective in using OMACS as the basis for our MTD system is to use this knowledge to ensure the adaptations carried out in a defensive effort do not inhibit the system's ability to achieve its goals. As shown in Figure 5, the key entities in OMACS include a set of goals, roles, agents, and capabilities. For our MTD system, the *goals* represent the functional requirements of the system, *roles* represent services (such as the applications, web servers and database servers), *agents* represent physical resources such as computer hosts, and *capabilities* represent agent attributes such as memory, bandwidth, and installed software. This information is used to compute the assignments (configurations) that tell agents the roles they are assigned to play in order to achieve system goals.

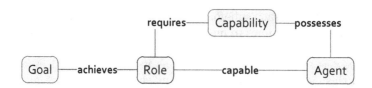

Fig. 5. Key OMACS Entities

Organizations are generally formed with some specific objective or goal in mind. In OMACS, the overall goal of an organization is represented by a set of goals that the organization is trying to achieve. The relationship between the various goals is not handled directly by OMACS but is entrusted to the VGM. More specifically, OMACS goals are the leaf goals in a VGM model. Goals are achieved by agents playing specific roles within the organization.

Every OMACS organization has a set of agents, which in a computer network are the physical computer hosts available for use. Agents possess capabilities that are required to play roles for the network.

In general, OMACS roles denote a set of responsibilities or the expected behaviors. In our approach, we use roles to describe services such as the applications, web servers and database servers required to support (and thus maintain) various system goals as shown in Figure 6. Each role has two types of characteristics that are critical to effective system adaptation: requirements and attributes. The specific requirements and attributes of each role are used by the Adaptation Engine to select the appropriate agent to carry out those roles. Each role has a set of required capabilities such as processing power, memory amount, bandwidth, and installed software. In a minor extension to OMACS, MTD roles also contain a set of attributes that give the RMS and the assigned physical resource (and its VM) precise directions on how to setup and run that role. To support the assignment process, OMACS defines the *achieves* function, which takes as input a goal and a role, and returns a value that reflects how well the given role achieves the given goal type.

Roles are defined in a Role model as shown in Figure 6. The Role model not only captures the requirements and attributes of each role, but also defines the communications that must be allowed between roles, which is critical to the definition of the CAG and the operation of the RMS system. In our example system, each mission leaf goal from Figure 4 is supported by a role, namely the Planner, AssetDB, TargetDB, GeoDB, and Authorizer roles. The relationship between goals and roles is formally captured in the *achieves* relation. When the system is running, these roles are assigned to physical resources such hosts or VMs while their communications are supported by the RMS.

Before a role is assigned to an agent (i.e., before a service is deployed on a host), the agent must meet the requirements for that role. Capabilities are essential in determining the roles that each agent is capable of playing. Capabilities are used to represent a wide variety of abilities. In a computer network, capabilities are used to model the hardware and software capabilities of a network

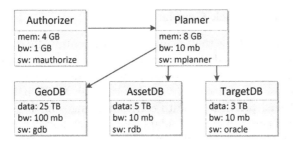

Fig. 6. Role Model

resource such as processing power, memory amount, bandwidth, and installed software. If an agent has all the required capabilities to play a role, the role capability function (rcf) is used to compute how well the agent can play that role, thus allowing designers to indicate the importance of specific capabilities to each role.

To determine the best overall set of assignments (configurations) for a specific set of goals, OMACS defines an organization assignment function (oaf). The oaf determines the effectiveness of a given set of assignments and assigns it a value. In normal systems, the optimal oaf value is selected when a reorganization (in our case an adaptation) is required. However, in an MTD system, we must use non-optimal configurations since our goal is to produce a constantly changing attack surface. A complete definition of OMACS can be found in [10].

4.3   Physical Resource Model

The capabilities of OMACS agents are taken from the Physical Resource model, which captures the configuration of available resources (e.g., computers, firewalls, servers, etc.) that support the operational system. Each resource in the physical resource model has a particular set of capabilities that can be used to play roles in the operational system. A role's physical capability requirements and the assigned role attributes are compared with resource capabilities to determine if the role can be assigned to that resource. In addition, role communication requirements are used to modify firewall (RMS) configuration as needed. With the advent of virtual machines (VMs), virtual resources can be created when and where (logically) required. The use of VMs supports the movement of roles between physical resources. In addition, the use of VMs allows a single role to be executed on a single VM and thus makes the security configuration of the VMs simpler and more secure.

As a side benefit, the ability to adapt by changing the mapping of goals to roles to physical resources also allows the MTD to respond effectively to changes and failures in the physical configuration of the network. If a role is running on a resource that fails, the MTD must identify that a goal is no longer being supported and assign that role to a new resource.

4.4 Conservative Attack Graphs

An integral effect of MTDs is that an attacker must continually regain the knowledge and privileges obtained through prior attacks. This effect invalidates the typical monotonicity assumption found in most attack-graph work where an attacker cannot lose a privilege after gaining it. In an MTD, it becomes important to model losing privileges due to constant changes in the system configuration. The frequency and type of adaptations affect how far an attacker can move forward in a system. Modeling such dynamism requires a state-machine model, rather than the commonly used dependency attack graph. Previous state-enumeration attack graphs were not scalable to large attack graphs. However, we do not need to apply a fine-grained attack-graph models to analyze the effect of MTDs since MTDs do not attempt to counter known vulnerabilities, but use dynamism to counter *assumed* vulnerabilities at every node. Thus, we use a conservative attack graph (CAG), which assumes the existence of unknown vulnerabilities without enumerating all possible vulnerabilities. This assumption actually makes the model smaller and lends itself to stochastic analysis through a state-machine model.

Figure 7 shows the CAG for our example. The topology of the CAG is partially derived from the dependencies specified in the Role model. As shown in Figure 6, the Authorizer role initiates interactions (depicted by the arrows between roles) with the Planner role, which initiates interactions with the TargetDB, GeoDB, and AssetDB roles. Because the RMS system limits communication between system roles, we can assume that the only paths between roles are those allowed by the RMS. Thus, the only legitimate access paths in the system are (1) from the Internet to the Authorizer, (2) from the Authorizer to the Planner, and (3) from the Planner to the three database servers (TargetDB, GeoDB, and AssetDB). Thus, our CAG captures these logical access paths.

The RMS components on the VMs implement the network communication policy derived from the Role model to adhere to the logical paths. If an RMS component is compromised, the attacker would potentially be able to bypass this control and try to access roles not exposed to the VM. However, in such situations the compromised RMS would not know the location of those roles and thus the attacker would have to correctly guess the IP and address (among other aspects), which is a low-probability event. Thus, if an RMS is compromised, the only realistic attack path is along the paths of the CAG.

4.5 Model-Driven Adaptation

This section shows how the Adaptation Engine uses the models to make adaptations to the system configuration. All adaptations are initiated by a triggering mechanism. In an MTD system, the trigger could be a timer (for random adaptations), a goal modification (addition, deletion, or changing of various goal values), or a change in the current state of the system (either software/hardware failure or identification of a potential intrusion). The end goal of an adaptation is to produce a configuration that ensures that system goals are achieved at the

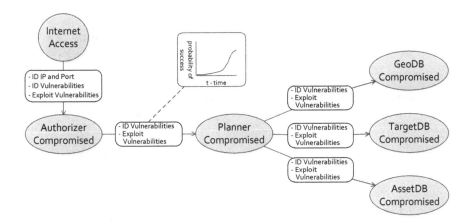

Fig. 7. Conservative Attack Graph

highest possible value. Here we assume all goals are achievable by the available roles and agents; however, if they are not, the least valuable goals can be dropped until a valid configuration is obtained.

For the initial configuration, a role (a service) is selected that achieves each goal and is assigned to an agent (a host) that provides the capabilities required to carry out that role. This configuration is given to the Configuration Manager, who makes the physical assignments and provides the appropriate knowledge to the RMS components.

If a failure occurs, goals that are no longer being achieved due to the failure are reassigned to new role-agent pairs. If a potential intrusion is detected, the goals and roles of the agents that are involved in the potential intrusion (source or destination) are reassigned to new role-agent pairs. When goals are added, new assignments must be made while when goals are deleted, old assignments may be removed. When a random adaptation is triggered, the Adaptation Engine selects a specific goal-role-agent assignment in the system to modify along with a specific modifiable aspect and a new assignment for the goal is generated. In all cases, the changes determined by the Adaptation Engine are passed on to the Configuration Manager who makes the appropriate changes in the physical system.

The key to random adaptation is ensuring that adaptations are as unpredictable as possible within a reasonable cost. Ideally, the probability of adapting a particular aspect and agent would be represented as a uniform probability distribution across the entire domain of the configuration space, thus maximizing the entropy of the system [27]. However, a system with maximum entropy would likely degrade system performance to the point where the system performance would be unusable. Therefore, we plan to investigate approaches that allow for a trade off between system entropy and performance/cost.

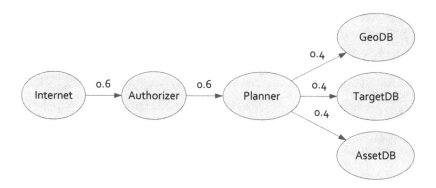

Fig. 8. Simplified Conservative Attack Graph for Simulation

5   Simulation Results

To determine if our approach has merit, we developed three high-level simulations to reflect the MTD approach discussed above. The first simulation, which we call the RMS-only Simulation, was developed to evaluate the effectiveness of our MTD approach using an existing network simulator called NeSSi2 [26]. NeSSi2 is an open-source, discrete-event based network security simulator with extensive support for constructing complex application-level scenarios based on a simulated TCP/IP protocol stack [26]. In this simulation, we assumed the user had full knowledge of the logical system configuration and only attacked through the RMS system. In the second and third simulations (which we term *broad attack simulations*), while the attacker still has full knowledge of the logical system configuration, the attacker also attempts attacks between nodes not directly connected via the RMS system. For these broad attack simulations, we developed a unique event-driven simulator. In the first two simulations, we assumed only a basic MTD system that adapted randomly at a specified time interval. However, in the last simulation, we upgraded the MTD to an intelligent MTD system that could detect when attacks were attempted outside the RMS system.

The overview of the simulated network is shown in Figure 8. The edges in the graph (with the exception of the Internet to Authorizer edge) show the valid paths supported by the RMS. We assume the attacker is located at the Internet node and wishes to attack the TargetDB. In the first simulation, we assume the attacker can only attack along the valid RMS paths. However, in the second and third simulations, we assume that attacker attempts to attack through valid RMS paths as well as directly between hosts (e.g., Authorizer to TargetDB).

To simplify our simulations, we made several assumptions.

1. Adaptations are applied at a specified time interval and are random in nature (which is extended in the third simulation to include intelligent adaptation).
2. Adaptations are limited to VM refreshing, which also includes changing the VM's IP address.

3. All VMs assigned to play a given role have the same configuration except for its ID and IP address.
4. Once a node is compromised, the attacker can immediately use the RMS to attack the next node in the attack path.
5. The attacker knows the basic system architecture as defined by the Logical Mission Model and thus the attack is restricted to the VMs playing those five roles.
6. The attacker knows immediately when a resource it has compromised has been refreshed.

While these assumptions make the simulation easier, they are also tilted toward the attacker since we do not use advanced variability techniques (software versions, operating systems, etc.), which would make compromises more difficult, and we assume the attacker knows the system design and can immediately compromise the RMS.

5.1   RMS-only Attack Simulation

The three main components of the RMS-only testbed include the Defense component, the Attack component and the Ground Truth component as shown in Figure 9. The *Defense component* contains the Configuration Manager, three physical resources (hosts) and five active VMs, which can be assigned to play host to any of the five roles: Authorizer Planner, TargetDB, AssetDB, or GeoDB. At a preset time interval, Δt, the Configuration Manager selects an adaption by randomly picking an existing role and refreshing its VM which includes modifying its address. Then, the Configuration Manager notifies the affected hosts of the changes and updates the Ground Truth component with new current configuration.

The *Attack component* simulates the attacker and uses the CAG shown in Figure 8 to allow it to know exactly where to attack to achieve its goal, the TargetDB. Since the only available attack path is to penetrate from the Internet to the Authorizer, from the Authorizer to the Planner, and then from Planner to the TargetDB. The edge values in the CAG denote the attacker's probability of attack success between nodes assuming both nodes remain static. As shown, the attacker has a 40% chance of compromising the TargetDB if (1) it has already compromised the Planner and (2) the Configuration Manager does not adapt either the Planner or the TargetDB during the time step. In a real system, these probabilities would be based on the current probability of unknown and known vulnerabilities of the roles and would likely increase over time. The success of attacks is determined randomly based on the probabilities in the CAG as well as whether or not the nodes in the attack have been refreshed during the attack.

The *Ground Truth component* maintains the current CAG. The Ground Truth component receives adaptation information from Configuration Manager and updates the CAG as required. It also supplies the current CAG to the Attack component when requested. The Attack component, Defense component, and Ground Truth component are implemented as NeSSi2 components along with

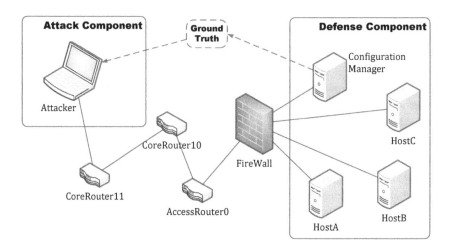

Fig. 9. Network Topology

the three host resources: hostA, hostB, and hostC. These six components are loaded onto the corresponding nodes as shown in Figure 9. The hosts do not actually perform their assigned role responsibilities, but merely exist to give the attacker something to attack. The results of our initial experiments are presented in the next section.

RMS-only Attack Simulation Results. We conducted two different experiments (denoted 1a and 1b) to see how the frequency of system adaptation would impact attack success. Within each experiment, we included a control scenario where no adaptation occurred. Attacks were launched from the Internet towards the TargetDB. Each attack consisted of *single step attacks* from the Internet to the Authorizer, the Authorizer to the Planner, and from the Planner to the TargetDB. Once the TargetDB was compromised, the attack was counted as a successful. If a single step attack failed, the attacker remained at the current VM and retried the attack until successful or until the MTD system refreshed the VM. In each experiment, we performed 1000 single step attacks with a fixed Δt between each single step attack of 100 time intervals. We ran the 1000 single step attacks against an MTD system using 5 different time intervals (20, 50, 100, 200 and ∞) between each adaptation. Note that an ∞ adaptation interval corresponds to a completely static system.

In the experiment 1a, we assumed that in order to stop a single step attack from succeeding, the MTD must refresh either the node under attack or the node from which the attack was launched during the attack (100 time intervals). Therefore, if there was an single step attack occurring from the Planner to the TargetDB, it could be stopped if either the Planner, or TargetDB roles were refreshed by the MTD system during the attack. However, the attacker would remain on the network unless the actual VM it was residing on was refreshed. Figure 10 shows the ability of the MTD to deter a successful attack from the

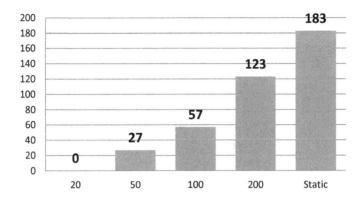

Fig. 10. Attack Success Against TargetDB (assuming only refresh of current node or attacked node inhibits attack)

Internet through the Authorizer and the Planner to the TargetDB. When the configuration is static, the number of successful attacks (of each round of 1000 single step attacks) is 183. Essentially, since no refreshing was going on, this is maximum number of successful attacks given the probabilities of single step attack success. Once the MTD system is activated, the number of successful attacks decrease. With an adaptation interval of 200, the number of successful attacks is reduced to 123, while an interval of 100 reduces it to 57, and an interval of 20 eliminates all successful attacks against the TargetDB. Figure 10 clearly shows that as the adaptation interval is reduced, the effect of the MTD defense is clearly visible.

In the experiment 1b, we assumed that in order to stop an attack from succeeding, the MTD could refresh any node on the path to the node being attacked during the attack (100 time intervals). Thus in this version, if there was an single step attack occurring from the Planner to the TargetDB, it could be stopped if either the Authorizer, Planner, or TargetDB roles were refreshed during the attack. Figure 11 shows the ability of the MTD to deter a completed attack from the Internet through the Authorizer and the Planner to the TargetDB. When the configuration is static, the number of completed attacks (out of 1000) is 168, while an adaptation interval of 200 reduces that number to 107, 100 reduces it to 41, and an adaptation interval of 20 again eliminates all successful attacks against the TargetDB. Again, Figure 11 clearly shows that as the adaptation interval is reduced, the effect of the MTD defense is obvious.

5.2   Broad Attack Simulation System

In the broad attack simulation, the attacker is again attempting to compromise the TargetDB. Since the attacker knows the details of the system configuration, it can use the RMS to its advantage; however, the attacker also attacks outside the RMS to stress the MTD defenses. For these simulations, we assume a sophisticated attacker who automatically attacks each available node in the network

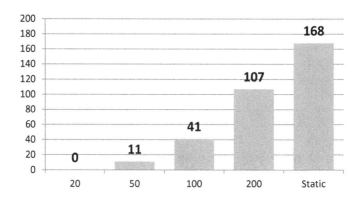

Fig. 11. Attack Success Against Target DB (assuming refresh of any node in path inhibits attack)

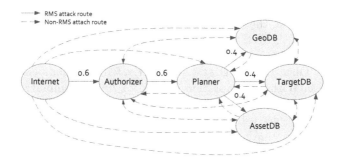

Fig. 12. Attack Success Probabilities in Broad Attack Simulation (dashed lines have a probability of p/65,536 where p is the probability of successfully attacking the role through the RMS)

from its current location using the RMS or by attempting to guess the address and port of an available node. Therefore, the attacker is not limited to the RMS routes and thus the attack routes form a completely bidirectionally connected graph (except for the Internet node, which only has arrows to nodes into the network) as shown in Figure 12. However, since the RMS will *not* respond to standard network requests for mapping information, this eliminates the ability for the attacker to automatically map the address space.

The probabilities associated with each attack depend on the node from which the attack originates and the node being attacked. All attacks along the RMS maintain their probabilities as shown in Figure 12. However, the dashed lines, which denote attacks outside the RMS, have a much lower probability due to the fact that the attacker must guess the appropriate port for the attack to even have a chance to succeed. Therefore, each dashed line has an attack success probability of $p/65,536$ where p is the probability of successfully attacking that node through the RMS. Thus, all attacks against the TargetDB from any node but the Planner would have a $0.4/65,536$ probability of success. While this might seem like a very low probability, we believe that it is actually the upper bound for such an attack. Since the VMs addresses are being modified over time, the attacker will also have to guess the VM address. However, since it is hard to determine the specific range over which the addresses be assigned, we assume the attacker can guess that in some way (once again giving the benefit to the attacker as opposed to the MTD system).

The simulation starts with the attacker at the Internet node. From the Internet node, the attacker attempts to attack each node in the network. The success of each attack is determined based on the probability of success of the attack and whether either the node being attacked and the node from which the attack originated was refreshed during the attack. If any of the attacks were successful, the newly compromised nodes are used to mount new attacks. Again, we assume we try to attack all uncompromised nodes from each newly compromised node. This process continues until the TargetDB becomes compromised, or the attacker has no compromised nodes in the network (other than the Internet).

Broad Attack Simulation Results. We conducted 1000 runs (as opposed to single step attacks used in the RMS only experiments) of the broad attack simulation against various frequencies of MTD adaptation to determine its impact against attack success. Since the broad attack simulation allowed the attacker to keep attempting to attack network nodes as long as the attacker had access to a compromised network node, each run consisted of a sequence of attacks starting with the initial attack from the Internet to the Authorizer node and continuing until either (1) the attacker did not have access to a compromised node in the network or (2) the attacker successfully compromised the TargetDB. As with the previous experiments, we included a *static* control scenario where no adaptation occurred. In each experiment, we again assumed a fixed Δt between each attack of 100 time intervals. For each experiment, we ran the 1000 runs using 5 different adaptation intervals (20, 50, 100, 200 and ∞).

Figure 13 shows the ability of the MTD to deter an attack from the Internet through the network to the TargetDB. When the configuration is static, the number of completed attacks (out of 1000) is 588, which is close the expected 60% rate given that the probability of compromising the Authorizer node from the Internet is 0.6. This is due to the fact that if the attacker compromised the Authorizer node on the first attack, with a static network, the attacker will remain on the Authorizer node attacking various network nodes until the TargetDB is eventually compromised. We also noted that no attacks outside the RMS actually succeeded, which was expected given the extremely low probability of success. When we introduced our random adaptations, we found that an adaptation interval of 200 reduced the number of successful attacks against the TargetDB to 421, an adaptation interval of 100 reduced that number to 57, an adaptation interval of 50 allowed only 24 successful attacks, and an adaptation

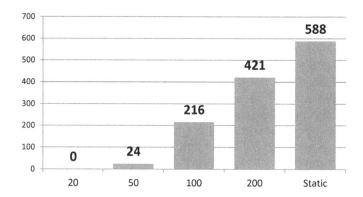

Fig. 13. Attack Success Against TargetDB for Broad Attack Simulation Against Simple MTD

interval of 20 totally eliminated the ability of the attacker to compromise the TargetDB. Once again, Figure 13 clearly shows that as the adaptation interval is reduced, the effect of the MTD defense is clearly visible.

5.3 Intelligent MTD Simulation System

To help determine the effect of an intelligent MTD system, we again used our broad attack simulation where the attacker attempts to compromise the TargetDB. In fact, the experimental setup was the same as for the broad attack simulation presented above with one exception. To simulate an intelligent MTD system, we assumed that whenever the attacker attempted an attack outside the RMS, that such an attack could trigger an alert based on some probability of detection, p_d. Since the RMS is set up to allow only communication from known nodes on exactly one port, we believe the implementation of such detectors would be both practical and efficient. When detected, alerts would be sent directly to the Adaptation Engine, which would request that Configuration Manager immediately refresh the VM from which the detected attack originated. In addition, random adaptations continued to occur at the same predetermined intervals Δt as used in the previous experiments.

Intelligent MTD Simulation Results. The result of the intelligent MTD simulation is shown in Figure 14; note that the graph is logarithmic to show proper detail. Since the attacker indiscriminately attacks all nodes in the network without necessarily attempting to go through the RMS system, thus raising many alerts, the success rate of the attacker is reduced significantly. At a 100% probability of detection, the attacker is always immediately detected and removed from the system, thus the attack success rate is 0%. However, even with lower p_d values, the reduction in attack success is significant. Even in the static case, with a p_d of 50%, the number of successful attacks is reduced from 616 (61.2%) to 32 (3.2%). We believe this shows the power of using an RMS with an

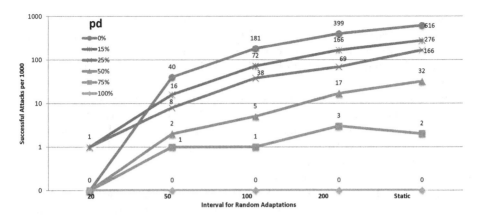

Fig. 14. Attack Success Against TargetDB for Broad Attack Simulation Against Intelligent MTD

intelligent MTD system. The RMS minimizes the attack surface to such a degree that attacks outside the RMS are easily detected and significantly decrease the attackers likelihood of success.

When compared with the attack success rate of the simple MTD system (which is represented by the line in Figure 14 with $p_d = 0\%$), we see that the intelligent MTD system performs significantly better since the simple MTD system. We do see a slight anomaly in the data since at an adaptation interval of 20, when the p_d is both 15% and 25%, we see 1 successful attack while there are 0 successful attacks with a p_d of 0%. Although the probability of success is extremely low, the attacker can succeed. We believe that with more runs (than 1000) the data would have normalized. Overall, while not conclusive, this experiment clearly shows the need for further investigation into the costs and benefits of intelligent MTD systems.

5.4   Discussion

The design of our MTD is based on knowing the current situation, which is captured in a set of runtime models. These runtime models allow the system to reason over the current state of the system and produce adaptations to confuse and rebuff potential attackers. The system design shows how a set of runtime models can be combined to model and reason over multiple aspects of a complex problem. Specifically, this system includes models for the system configuration, the system objectives (operational and security), and entities external to the system (the attackers).

The simulation presented here is our first, and one of the first anywhere, simulation of an MTD architecture for enterprise network security. As such, the simulation implemented only a simple MTD system and did not use the full power of its runtime models. However, the results demonstrate the potential effectiveness of MTDs for enterprise computer networks. Therefore, we plan to continue to simulate more complex systems (in terms of nodes and interconnections), increase the sophisticated of the attackers, and integrate in the full power of an intelligent MTD system based on runtime models. In addition, we are currently building a real world MTD test bed using existing visualization technologies.

This system also demonstrates the applicability of the OMACS model to new and novel applications. The OMACS model was originally envisioned as a metamodel to capture multiagent systems. However, it quickly became clear that by looking at existing research on human organizations, the model could be made much more general. Since its inception, OMACS has been applied to multiagent systems, cooperative robotics, human-robot teams, sensor networks, and power distribution systems. In fact, the claim could be made that OMACS can be applied to any domain in which distributed agents (natural or artificial) need to coordinate their actions to achieve shared objectives and adapt to the current state of the environment or their problem solution.

6   Related Work

6.1   State of Practice

Network configuration currently tends to be static and routine assumptions are made about the location of services in terms of fixed URL's or IP addresses. Such static configuration is largely due to the use of legacy system components. The benefit of static configurations appear to be ease of management and programming. However, it has been observed that the static network configurations (i.e, service dependencies) have actually made it harder to manage systems, especially when changes must be made [3,15,6]. The state of the practice in computer network defense relies upon firewalls in both network and application layers, intrusion detection and prevention systems, and anti-malware products that provide defense in depth. Unfortunately, once a method is found to circumvent these mechanisms, the attacker can keep attained privileges until discovered. In addition, the attacker can generally use the same methods to circumvent other similar defenses. Here, the lack of dynamism is an important contributor to the ease with which an attacker can launch a successful cyber attack.

6.2   Moving Target Defenses

Most of the prior work on MTDs in a network context has been related to low-level techniques such as IP address shifting and network routing and topology control. In the late 90s, BBN developed approaches to active network defense [16,2] that gave the illusion that the addresses and port numbers used by the network's computers changed dynamically. While these techniques significantly increased the attacker's effort by making it almost impossible to map the network [16], they required all trusted computers be shielded by special processes and displayed had several application interoperability issues [19]. More recently, a network address space randomization scheme to thwart hit list worms [1], which configured DHCP servers to expire the leases of hosts at various intervals to support address randomization. In [7], an approach to dynamically changing network packet routes so that observable traffic patterns change was proposed to make network mapping more difficult and to make packet sniffing less effective. In each of these cases, only the network addresses were changed or made to look like they changed and only served to confuse attackers without the ability to automatically remove them from the system once they compromised a resource.

In a different approach to MTD, Roeder and Schneider [24] propose to use *proactive obfuscation* to create application replicas with identical functionality but dissimilar vulnerabilities that react differently to identical attacks. The authors showed that with sufficient entropy in the executables, the approach effectively thwarted known attacks without greatly increasing costs. We anticipate that proactive obfuscation could be employed in our MTD approach to increase the difficulty of initial compromise as well as the ease with which attackers could reacquire resources after being removed from the system.

7   Conclusions

In this paper we presented a preliminary design of an MTD system that uses runtime models of a network's requirements, design, and implementation to allow it to adapt its configuration to increase the difficulty of attacks on the network. We conducted several simulation-based experiments to study the effects of randomly adapting the system in reducing attacker's success likelihood. Our results showed a reduction in attack success as the rate of adaptation increased. In addition, we conducted simulations that showed the effect of adding intelligence to the decision of when and where to adapt in the form of detectors that could detect when an attack occurred outside the normal RMS system. Our results showed that even with less than perfect detectors, significant improvements in network security can be made. These results clearly demonstrate the potential for both simple and intelligent MTD systems and are preliminary steps toward developing a comprehensive evaluation and analysis framework for MTD systems.

Acknowledgments. This work was supported by the Air Force Office of Scientific Research under award no. FA9550-12-1-0106, and U.S. National Science Foundation under award no. 0954138 and 1018703. Any opinions, findings and conclusions or recommendations expressed in this material are those of the authors and do not necessarily reflect the views of the above agencies.

References

1. Antonatos, S., Akritidis, P., Markatos, E.P., Anagnostakis, K.G.: Defending against hitlist worms using network address space randomization. Computer Networks: The International Journal of Computer and Telecommunications Networking 51, 3471–3490 (2007)

2. Atighetchi, M., Pal, P., Webber, F., Jones, C.: Adaptive Use of Network-Centric Mechanisms in Cyber-Defense. In: Proceedings of the Sixth IEEE International Symposium on Object-Oriented Real-Time Distributed Computing (ISORC 2003), pp. 183–192. IEEE Computer Society, Washington, DC (2003)
3. Bahl, P., Chandra, R., Greenberg, A., Kandula, S., Maltz, D.A., Zhang, M.: Towards highly reliable enterprise network services via inference of multi-level dependencies. In: Proceedings of the 2007 Conference on Applications, Technologies, Architectures, and Protocols for Computer Communications (SIGCOMM 2007), pp. 13–24. ACM, New York (2007)
4. Barrett, D.: Hackers Penetrate Nasdaq Computers. Wall Street Journal, http://online.wsj.com/article/ SB10001424052748704709304576124502351634690.html (February 5, 2011)
5. Bencomo, N., Whittle, J., Sawyer, P., Finkelstein, A., Letier, E.: Requirements reflection: Requirements as runtime entities. In: Proceedings of the 32nd ACM/IEEE International Conference on Software Engineering (ICSE 2010), vol. 2, pp. 199–202. ACM, New York (2010)
6. Chen, X., Zhang, M., Mao, Z.M., Bahl, V.: Automating Network Application Dependency Discovery: Experiences, Limitations, and New Solutions. In: Proceedings of the 8th USENIX Conference on Operating Systems Design and Implementation (OSDI 2008), pp. 117–130. USENIX Association, Berkeley (2008)
7. Compton, M.D., Hopkinson, K.M., Peterson, G.L., Moore, J.T.: Network Obfuscation Through Polymorphic Routing and Topology Control. IEEE Transactions on Dependable and Secure Computing (2012) (in preparation)
8. Dardenne, D., van Lamsweerde, A., Fickas, S.: Goal-directed requirements acquisition. Science of Computer Programming 20, 3–50 (1993)
9. DeLoach, S.A., Miller, M.: A Goal Model for Adaptive Complex Systems. International Journal of Computational Intelligence: Theory and Practice 5, 83–92 (2010)
10. DeLoach, S.A., Oyenan, W., Matson, E.T.: A Capabilities-Based Model for Artificial Organizations. Journal of Autonomous Agents and Multiagent Systems 16, 13–56 (2008)
11. DeLoach, S.A., Ou, X.: A Value Based Goal Model. Multiagent and Cooperative Robotics Laboratory Technical Report No. MACR-TR-2011-01. Kansas State University (2011)
12. DeLoach, S.A., Wood, M.F., Sparkman, C.H.: Multiagent Systems Engineering. The Intl. Journal of Software Engineering and Knowledge Engineering 11, 231–258 (2001)
13. Grimaila, M.R., Fortson, L.W., Sutton, J.L.: Design Considerations for a Cyber Incident Mission Impact Assessment (CIMIA) Process. In: Proceedings of the 2009 International Conference on Security and Management, SAM 2009 (2009)
14. Hellesen, D., Grimaila, M.R.: Information Asset Value Quantification. In: Proceedings of the 2010 International Conference on Information Warfare and Security (ICIW 2010), pp. 138–147 (2010)
15. Joukov, N., Pfitzmann, B., Ramasamy, H.V., Devarakonda, M.V.: Application-storage discovery. In: Proceedings of the 3rd Annual Haifa Experimental Systems Conference (SYSTOR). ACM, New York (2010)
16. Kewley, D.L., Bouchard, J.F.: DARPA Information Assurance Program dynamic defense experiment summary. Systems, Man and Cybernetics, Part A: Systems and Humans 31, 331–336 (2001)
17. Lippmann, K.W., Ingols, C., Piwowarski, S.K., Kratkiewicz, K.J., Artz, M., Cunningham, R.K.: Evaluating and strengthening enterprise network security using attack graphs. Technical Report. MIT Lincoln Laboratory (2005)

18. McQueen, M., McQueen, T., Boyer, W., Chaffin, M.: Empirical estimates and observations of 0day vulnerabilities. In: 42nd Hawaii International Conference on System Sciences, pp. 1–12 (2009)
19. Michalski, J., Price, C., Stanton, E., Chua, E.L., Seah, K., Heng, W.Y., Pheng, T.C.: Final Report for the Network Security Mechanisms Utilizing Network Address Translation LDRD Project. Technical Report SAND2002-3613. Sandia National Laboratories (2002)
20. National Cyber Leap Year Summit 2009, Co-Chairs' Report. (September 16, 2009)
21. Ou, X., Boyer, W.F., McQueen, M.A.: A scalable approach to attack graph generation. In: 13th ACM Conference on Computer and Communications Security, pp. 336–345. ACM, New York (2006)
22. Ou, X., Govindavajhala, S., Appel, A.W.: MulVAL: A logic-based network security analyzer. In: 14th USENIX Security Symposium, Baltimore, Maryland, U.S.A (August 2005)
23. Ou, X., Rajagopalan, S.R., Sakthivelmurugan, S.: An empirical approach to modeling uncertainty in intrusion analysis. In: Annual Computer Security Applications Conference, pp. 494–503 (December 2009)
24. Roeder, T., Schneider, F.B.: Proactive obfuscation. ACM Trans. Comput. Syst. 28, 4:1–4:54 (2010)
25. Sawyer, P., Bencomo, N., Whittle, J., Letier, E., Finkelstein, A.: Requirements-Aware Systems: A Research Agenda for RE for Self-adaptive Systems. In: Proceedings of 18th IEEE International Requirements Engineering Conference, pp. 95–103. IEEE Press, New York (2010)
26. Schmidt, S., Bye, R., Chinnow, J., Bsufka, K., Camtepe, A., Albayrak, S.: Application-level Simulation for Network Security. SIMULATION 86, 311–330 (2010)
27. Shannon, C.E.: A Mathematical Theory of Communication. Bell Syst. Technical Journal 27(3), 379–423 (1948)
28. Sundaramurthy, S.C., Zomlot, L., Ou, X.: Practical IDS alert correlation in the face of dynamic threats. In: International Conference on Security and Management (2011)

ModelLAND: Where Do Models Come from?

Marco Autili, Davide Di Ruscio, Paola Inverardi,
Patrizio Pelliccione, and Massimo Tivoli

Dipartimento di Ingegneria e Scienze dell'Informazione e Matematica
Università dell'Aquila, Italy
{marco.autili,davide.diruscio,paola.inverardi,patrizio.pelliccione,
massimo.tivoli}@univaq.it

Abstract. The way in which software systems are produced is radically changing, by increasingly promoting the (re-)use of existent software artifacts. A flourishing of model-based engineering techniques has been defined for building, managing, verifying, validating and controlling software systems. Most approaches build on the assumption that suitable models of software artifacts exist. However, when moving from theory to practice, a question raises up: *where do models come from?*

The thesis of this paper is that there is the need of explore techniques to automatically extract models from existent software. This paper proposes a general overview of the exploring problem and shows two different techniques, tailored to specific domains, to automatically build models (of different nature) from software artifacts.

1 Introduction

In recent years a growing emphasis on the use of models emerged in the Software Engineering (SE) community. Traditionally, in the software development process, models represent abstractions of the system under implementation and are developed independently from the system, that is, from requirements specification *etc.* This has led to the standard dichotomy between verification and validation of a system, being verification related to the correspondence between models and implemented system, whereas validation between user expectations and the implemented system. In the literature it is often given for granted that such models exist or that they can be easily defined. However, this assumption is far from being realistic, and one key issue is to consider how to obtain such models.

Indeed, the system development paradigm we are facing in the future promotes more and more the (re-)use of existent software artifacts, whose availability is growing at a fast pace. Available software ranges from white-box software for which source code and internal perspective is available, to black-box software for which all we know is, *e.g.*, a description (often informal) of the functionalities or their published known interfaces. In any case, to foster a correct reuse with respect to a given goal, we should know the actual functional and non-functional runtime behavior of the software being reused. This calls for the production,

N. Bencomo et al. (Eds.): Models@run.time, LNCS 8378, pp. 162–187, 2014.

the management and the maintenance of models all along the software life time in order to assist the system realization, its validation and evolution out of abstractions of existent software [21,23,11,6]. Unfortunately, in general, the runtime behavior is only and can only be partially known also in terms of aggregated artifacts, like specifications of both interface and behavior (see [4,21] and references therein). In this setting, techniques must be employed to explore the available software, extract observations, and produce models that, according to a given goal, abstract the actual runtime behavior with the best possible accuracy. Different elicitation techniques can then be applied to achieve a combination of models that abstract the software under exploration from different perspectives and with different costs.

In this paper we are interested in models that are automatically extracted from existent software. They represent by definition different observations of the system that are consistent with the effective behavior of the system itself. This approach is comforted by an increasingly number of research contributions that concern the elicitation of observational models from software artifacts. These approaches range from machine learning ones to static and dynamic analysis to running traces observations.

The common characteristics of the models resulting from the application of diverse techniques is that they always contain the result of the corresponding observations but in general represent an approximation of a portion of the system itself. Such observations are defined according to a goal G. Starting from a set of observations, the problem is to define synthesis algorithms that are able to produce a "correct" approximation of the system that is cost-effective with respect to the goal G.

The paper is organized as follows. Section 2 provides the context of the paper by presenting a software development process of the near future, called EAGLE. Section 3 briefly surveys those explore techniques that are closer to the EAGLE view. Section 4 presents a general overview of the exploring problem. In order to show how this general overview could be applied, Sections 5 and 6 present two instantiations of it. Specifically, Section 5 presents an exploration technique to automatically produce behavior protocols of running Web-Services (WSs), and Section 6 presents an explore technique to automatically produce a model of a running Linux system. The paper concludes with final remarks in Section 7.

2   Software Development Process of the Near Future

As firstly stated in [21] and then mentioned in [23,11,6], the software development process life cycle needs to be rethought by breaking the traditional division among development phases, e.g., [4] and SMSCom[1]. This is achieved by moving some development activities from design-time to deployment- and run-time, hence asking for new and more efficient techniques to support run-time activities.

---

[1] ERC Advanced Investigator Grant N. 227977 [2008-2013],
http://deepse.dei.polimi.it/smscom/index.html

Recent approaches recognize the need to produce, manage and maintain software models all along the software life time in order to assist the realization and validation of system adaptations while the system is in execution [21,11]. EA-GLE [4] builds on the model-based software production paradigm and focuses on the inherent incompleteness of information about requirements, execution context, and existing software. This evidence promotes the use of an experimental approach, as opposed to a creationistic one, to the production of dependable software. In fact, software development has been so far biased towards a creationist view: a producer is the owner of the artifact, and with the right tools she can supply any piece of information (interfaces, behaviors, contracts, *etc.*). The Digital Space promotes a different experimental view: the knowledge of a software artifact is limited to what can be observed of it. In other words software developers will less and less know the precise behaviour of a third party software service, nevertheless they will use it to build their own application. This very same problem recognized in the software engineering domain [16] is faced in many other computer science domain, *e.g.*, exploratory search [41] and search computing [12].

In order to face this problem and provide a producer with a supporting framework to realize software applications, we propose a process that implements a radically new perspective (first results might be found in [5]). Figure 1 shows a graphical overview of this process. It builds around *elicit* and *integrate* phases, and both of these phases embed validation activities devoted to ensure that the produced artefacts satisfy the goal. To support dynamic evolution, these two phases are eternally iterated by maintaining continuously the experimental view mentioned above. In this way the produced software is continuously tuned and adapted towards customer needs by learning from real customer usage data [33].

Elicit: given a software service S, elicitation techniques must be defined to produce models as much complete as possible with respect to an opportunistic goal G. This means that we admit models that may exhibit a high degree of incompleteness, provided that they are accurate enough to satisfy user needs and preferences (as modelled by G). The goal G can be specified in different ways depending, *e.g.*, on the technical requirements on the software-to-be and assumptions on its environment. In any case, for the elicit and integrate phases to be automated, a goal G specification is a machine-readable model achieved by the producer through an operationalization of the needs and preferences of the user [37]. Validation of the elicited models is embedded in the elicitation process. That is, validation of the model against the run-time behaviour of its corresponding explored software is achieved through experimental verification of what the model expresses against what the explored software actually does at run-time. As discussed above, this process is carried on in a goal-oriented way. Thus it is not relevant to come out with a model completely conforming to the software run-time behaviour, rather it is sufficient to have a confidence that the model reflects the only software run-time behaviour needed for achieving the specified goal.

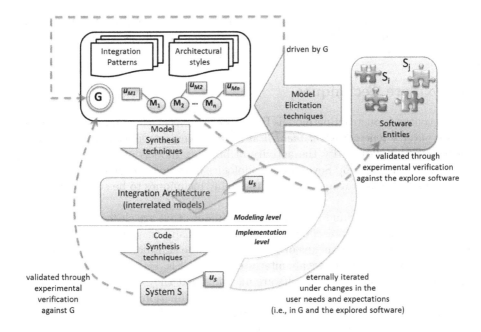

Fig. 1. Elicit and Integration activities of EAGLE

Integrate: it assists the producer in creating the appropriate integration means to compose the observed software together in order to produce an application that satisfies G. Referring to Figure 1, $M_1, M_2, \ldots, M_n$, obtained through the elicit phase, represent models of the services to be integrated; each of these models exhibits its own degree of uncertainty $u_{M_1}, u_{M_2}, , u_{M_n}$, respectively. Multiple models may exist for each service (*e.g.*, behavioural, stochastic or Bayesian), each representing a specific view of the service. Model transformation techniques can ensure coherence and consistency among the different views, hence providing an adequate and systematic support to model interoperability [19]. These models are the input of model synthesis techniques together with the goal G. Suitably instantiating architectural patterns and styles [35] and integration patterns [42], the output is an Integration Architecture (IA) that interrelates the elicited models together with additional integrator models as synthesized by EAGLE. Integrator models, besides guaranteeing correctness of the interaction logic, *e.g.*, deadlock freeness and performance system requirements, can compensate the lack of knowledge of the composed software by also adding extra logic through connectors, mediators and adapters [36,22,29,24], hence enhancing dependability. IA plays a crucial role in influencing the overall uncertainty degree of the final integrated system S, as different IAs may result in different uncertainty degrees for S, namely u_S. Once obtained an integration architecture, code synthesis techniques provided by EAGLE generate integration code that guarantees, during the system lifetime, the specified goal under a controlled uncertainty degree. Analogously to what is done for the explore phase, also here the validation of the integrated system against G is done through experimental verification. That is, the IA the integrated system relies on is automatically synthesized correct-by-construction with respect to the specified goal.

3 Explore Techniques

The activity of constructing models from observations is a long-standing practice in computer science. *System identification* has been introduced as long ago as 1956 by Zadeh to identify the activity of building models of dynamic systems from observed data [26]. Several methodologies have been developed in different areas and, in the literature, there are too many techniques to be surveyed in one paper only.

In order to identify and discuss those techniques that are closer to the EAGLE view, which has been presented in Section 2, we can consider both the kind of models to be elicited by means of exploration of the considered software and the type of explore techniques we are interested on. That is, EAGLE primarily focuses on behavioural models of the software meaning that they describe the run-time behaviour of a software entity in terms of both its functional and non-functional characteristics. For instance, automata-based models describing the interaction protocol that a software component performs with its environment fall in this class of models, as well as probabilistic automata if one is interested on reasoning about, e.g., the reliability of a piece of software. Contrarily, "structural" models such as *UML Class Diagrams* can clearly ease the explore phase but, for the software integration and actual code synthesis to be fully automated, if considered in isolation, they are not of particular interest as output of the explore phase itself. Being more interested on the elicitation of (run-time) behavioural models and aiming at accounting also for the integration of third-party software entities, for which very often the code and their internal characteristics are not accessible from outside, EAGLE mainly focuses on either *black-box* or *grey-box* explore techniques. This means that the considered techniques take as input a description of the software whose level of abstraction is far from the one of the actual implementation code. For instance, interface descriptions such as WSDL for web-services or execution traces obtained via logging activities are suitable examples of input for the explore techniques considered by EAGLE.

Before providing an overview of the considered techniques, we discuss the core concepts underlying the explore phase as follows.

- **Model** - it represents an abstraction of the system which should be inferred by the explore phase. In general, a model can be of different nature, such as the system's (i) Software Architecture model, (ii) control flow, (iii) data flow, or (iv) type structure. In [34] a model is defined as "a set of statements about a system under study". Bézivin and Gerbé in [10] define a model as "a simplification of a system built with an intended goal in mind. The model should be able to answer questions in place of the actual system". According to Mellor et al. [31] a model "is a coherent set of formal elements describing something (e.g., a system, bank, phone, or train) built for some purpose that is amenable to a particular form of analysis" such as communication of ideas between people and machines, test cases generation, transformation into an implementation, etc. The MDA guide [32] defines a model of a system as "a description or specification of that system and its environment for some certain purposes. A model is often presented as a combination of drawings and text. The text may be in a modeling language or in a natural language". These formulations do not conflict but rather complement one another and represent the various aspects of the fundamental philosophical category of software. Despite these general views of the model concept, as explained above, EAGLE focuses on behavioural models (both functional and non-functional) of the observed software.

– **Observation** - it represents the information that is grasped from the system in order to build a model of it. In general, observations can be built by directly observing the system S, such as its source code or its bytecode as usually done by, e.g., *reverse engineering* approaches, or by observing the semantics of S, i.e., its executions, such as log files or performed tests as usually done by, e.g., *machine learning* approaches. Moreover, observations depend on the techniques that are used to grasp information about the observed system, e.g., white-box, grey-box, or black-box techniques. As discussed above, EAGLE focuses on black-box/grey-box explore techniques and, hence, the exploited notion of observation is the one related to observing the semantics of the software.

– **Uncertainty** - a key challenge for explore techniques is the ability to assess their goodness in terms of the *degree of uncertainty* of the elicited models. Informally, the notion of uncertainty is related to a measure of the gap between what is expressed by an elicited model and what the corresponding observed software actually does at run-time. A useful basis for empirically comparing candidate techniques has been provided in a competition to spur the development of inference techniques for FSMs of software systems [38]. The work in [27] presents an empirical comparative study between techniques that infer simple automata and techniques that infer automata extended with information about data-flow. We believe that the problem of providing methods and metrics to express the uncertainty of a model with respect to the system and the goal is of primary importance. The work in [18] can be considered as a first attempt in this direction. This work is applied in a white-box component setting. As inferred system model, a three-valued interface LTS is generated. It explicitly labels states as unknown to reflect the fact that the given sequence of method invocations leads to a component state that the analysis could not mark as safe or unsafe. As far as the use of partial behavioural models is concerned, it should be noted that the degree of uncertainty in behavioral models may heavily affect the capability of non-functional analysis techniques. Indeed non-functional (*e.g.*, performance, reliability) models take most of their structure and parameters from software behavior representation. However, this problem is not new, and it has been mitigated by the wide experience in using (in this domain) stochastic models suited for representing uncertainty.

In the following, we provide an overview of some examples of explore techniques, which are closer to the EAGLE view in the sense discussed above. That is, they are black-box/grey-box techniques able to elicit behavioural models of the software. The reader interested on white-box techniques can refer to [40,39,2] and references therein.

Bertolino et al. [8]: StrawBerry is an approach to produce a behavior protocol of a WS starting from its WSDL. The automaton that is produced by StrawBerry models the interaction protocol that a client has to follow in order to correctly interact with the WS. This automaton explicitly models also the information that has to be passed to the WS operations. StrawBerry makes use of two phases, namely synthesis and testing. The synthesis stage is driven by data type analysis, through which a preliminary dependencies automaton is inferred. Once synthesized, this dependencies automaton is validated through testing against the WS to verify conformance, and finally transformed into an automaton defining the behavior protocol. StrawBerry is a black-box and extra-procedural technique. It is black-box since it takes into account only the WSDL of the WS. It is extra-procedural since it focuses on synthesizing a model of the behavior that is assumed when interacting with the WS from outside, as opposed to intra-procedural methods that synthesize a model of the implementation logic of the single WS operations. The uncertainty of the models elicited by StrawBerry relies on testing and therefore it is subject to possible inaccuracies especially depending on the semantics of data (method invocation parameters). StrawBerry is detailed in Section 5.

Di Ruscio et al. [15]: EVOSS is an approach to automatically produce a model of a running Linux system. The construction of a model is automatically performed by means of proper model injectors which are able to observe the system configuration to be upgraded, and the packages involved in the considered upgrade plan, and to create the corresponding models. Information that are used to build the model are obtained by querying the running Linux system via *bash* command line tools that gather information like the installed packages, running services, *etc.* The elicited model is accurate enough, meaning that the uncertainty is related to the identified level of abstraction only. EVOSS is detailed in Section 6.

Hungar et al. [20]: LearnLib is a framework to automatically construct a finite automaton through automata learning and experimentation. Active automata learning tries to automatically construct a finite automaton that matches the behavior of a given target automaton on the basis of active interrogation of target systems and observation of the produced behavior. Active automata learning originally has been conceived for language acceptors in the form of deterministic finite automata (DFAs) (*cf.* Angluin's L^* algorithm [3]). The uncertainty of the elicited automaton relies on the goodness of the L^* algorithm, which performs active automata learning. Thus, since automata learning converges by exactly inferring the target automaton for the considered system, the degree of uncertainty is due to the possible incompleteness of the set of data instances used to query the running system.

Krogmann et al. [25]: The work presents a comprehensive approach for building parametrized behaviour models of existing black-box components for performance prediction. Those parameters represent three performance-influencing factor, *i.e.*, usage, assembly, and deployment context; this makes the models sensitive to changing load situations, connected components, and the underlying hardware. The approach makes use of static and dynamic analysis and search-based approaches, namely genetic programming. These techniques take as input monitoring data, runtime bytecode counts, and static bytecode analysis. The inferred model is accurate although it represents an approximation of the semantics of the considered system. The uncertainty degree can be measured in terms of a "prediction error". It is given by the deviation between monitored values (e.g., data/bytecode counts) and values predicted by the mathematical expression found by the genetic search, the prediction techniques is based on.

Ghezzi et al. [17]: SPY is an approach to infer a formal specification of stateful black-box components that behave as data abstractions (Java classes that behave as data containers) by observing their run-time behavior. SPY proceeds in two main stages: first, SPY infers a partial model of the considered Java class; second, through graph transformation, this partial model is generalized to deal with data values beyond the ones specified by the given instance pools. The inferred model is partial since it models the intentional behavior of the class with respect to only a set of instance pools provided as input, which are used to get values for method parameters, and an upper bound on the number of states of the model. The accuracy of the generalized model, that is the output of the SPY approach, depends on two assumptions. First assumption: the value of method parameters does not impact the implementation logic of the methods of a class; usually, this is the case for classes implementing abstract data types but it is not the case for other kind of classes. Second assumption: the behavior observed during the partial model inference process enjoys the so called "continuity property" (i.e., a class instance has a kind of "uniform" behavior). This property allows the generalization of the partial model. Thus the elicited model is accurate with respect to a fixed bound on the number of states of the model to be inferred. This means that the uncertainty of the model depends on the inherent incompleteness of it, which is due to this fixed bound. However, for Java classes that enjoy the so-called continuity property, it is possible to find a bound on the number of states that allows the inference technique to produce a complete model.

Lorenzoli et al. [28]: GK-Tail is a technique to automatically generate behavioral models from (object-oriented) system execution traces. GK-Tail assumes that execution traces are obtained by monitoring the system through message logging frameworks. For each system method, an Extended Finite State Machine (EFSM) is generated. It models the interaction between the components forming the system in terms of sequences of method invocations and data constraints on these invocations. The correctness of these data constraints depends on the completeness of the set of monitored traces with respect to all the possible system executions that might be infinite. Furthermore, since the set of monitored traces represents only positive samples of the system execution, this approach cannot guarantee the complete correctness of the inferred data constraints. GK-Tail is an intra-procedural approach since it synthesizes an intra-system interaction model. As far as uncertainty is concerned, the more the set of given execution traces is complete and the more the inferred model is accurate.

Berg et al. [7]: This work presents an approach for inferring state machines with an infinite state space. By observing the output that the system produces when stimulated with selected inputs, they extend existing algorithms for regular inference (which infer finite state machines) to deal with infinite-state systems. More precisely, with the aim of fully supporting the generation of models with data parameters, they consider a general theory for inference of infinite-state machines with input and output symbols from potentially infinite domains. To this purpose, the behavior protocol of the system is first observed by considering a small domain of data for the input parameters. Then, by exploiting classical regular inference algorithms, a finite-state Mealy machine is generated to model the behavior of the system on the small domain. Finally, the generated Mealy machine is folded into a smaller symbolic model. This approach makes the problem of dealing with an infinite state space tractable, but may suffer a higher degree of model approximation. As far as uncertainty is concerned, analogously to the work described in [20], the more the set of data instances used to query the running system is complete and the more the inferred model is accurate.

Meinke [30]: This work describes a learning-based black-box testing approach in which the problem of testing functional correctness is reduced to a constraint solving problem. Functional correctness is modeled by pre- and post-conditions that are first-order predicate formulas. A successful black-box test is an execution of the program on a set of input values satisfying the pre-condition, which terminates by retrieving a set of output values violating the post-condition. Black-box functional testing is the search for successful tests with respect to the program pre- and post-conditions. As *coverage* criterion the authors formulate a convergence criterion on function approximation. The testing process is an iterative process: at a generic testing step, if a successful test has to be still found, the approach described in [30] exploits the input and output assignments obtained by the previous test cases in order to build an approximation of the system under testing and try to infer a valid input assignments that can lead the system to produce an output either violating the post-condition or useful to further refine the system approximated model. The uncertainty of the inferred model depends on the type of the approximation functions chosen in order to deal with the different data types.

Dallmeier et al. [14]: This work presents an approach that, through a combination of systematic test case generation (by means of the TAUTOKO tool) and typestate mining, infers models of program behavior in the form of finite state automata describing transitions between object states. The generation of test cases permits to cover previously unobserved behavior, and systematically extends the execution space, and enriches the inferred behavior model. In this sense, it can be said this approach goes in an opposite direction with respect to the `StrawBerry` approach [8]. In fact, the latter first produces a exhaustive behavior model containing both legal and illegal interactions, and then refines it (through testing) in order to cut the illegal interactions. By explicitly accounting for exceptional behavior, the models generated by the approach in [14] may tend to be more close to completeness. As far as uncertainty is concerned, the inferred models can be almost as good as manually (by the class developer) specified models.

Summary on behavior model elicitation techniques – Table 3 summarizes the key characteristics of the considered techniques in terms of the core concepts discussed above for the explore phase. This summary represents the basis for scratching, in the next section, a preliminary foundational treatment of the exploring problem.

The first column of the table contains a reference to the considered technique. The second column describes the domain in which the technique is used. The column named *Input (Observations)* describes the input elements that are required to use the technique. For instance, in the case of `StrawBerry`, the input is the WSDL description but also a running service that can be freely invoked. The column *Output (Model)* represents a description of the model that is produced by the technique. The column *Observed subject* describes what is observed of the system, i.e., the system itself (S) or its semantics, for instance in terms of its behaviour. The column named *Type* describes whether the technique is black box, grey box, or white box. Finally, the *Techniques used* column describes the techniques that are used to observe the system and to construct the model.

Table 1. Explore techniques overview

	Domain	Input (Observations)	Output (Model)	Obser. subject	Type	Techniques used
Bertolino et al. [8]	SOAP-based WSs	WSDL + running WS	Behaviour protocol automaton enriched with method invocation parameters	Sem. of S	Black box	Syntactic analysis, testing, and synthesis
Di Ruscio et al. [15]	Linux distributions	Packages and running system	Model of the system configuration (mainly structural aspects)	S	Grey box	Text-to-Model transformation

Hungar et al. [20]	"Testable" software systems	Alphabet of actions + running system	Finite state automaton	Sem. of S	Black box	Active automata learning and experimentation
Krog-mann et al. [25] [8]	Monitorable software components	Data from monitoring + component bytecode	Parametrized behaviour models for performance prediction	Sem. of S	Grey box	Static and dynamic analysis + genetic programming
Ghezzi et al. [17]	Java classes implementing abstract data types	Public interface of the considered class + instance pool for the method parameters	A finite state automaton dealing with data beyond the ones contained in the given instance pool	Sem. of S	Black box	Dynamic analysis + graph transformation
Lorenzoli et al. [28]	Monitorable java classes	Execution traces	A set of Extended Finite State Machines, one for each method in the public interface of the class	Sem. of S	Grey Box	Static analysis of execution traces (obtained via run-time behaviour monitoring)
Berg et al. [7]	"Testable" software systems	Alphabet of actions + running system	An infinite state automaton	Sem. of S	Black box	An extension of active automata learning for infinite state automata
Meinke [30]	"Testable" software systems	A functional model of the system in terms of a first-order logic formula of pre- and post-conditions + running system	a set of successful tests	Sem. of S	Black box	Black-box testing + constraints solving + functional approximation

Dallmeier et al. [14]	Java classes	sample executions + regression test suites + executable Java classes	Typestate specifications, i.e., finite state automata describing transitions between object states	Sem. of S	Black box	Test case generation + dynamic specification mining

4 Elicit Phase: Eliciting Models from Software Artifacts

In this section we continue the work done at the beginning of Section 3 with the aim at identifying basic elements and functions that regulate the explore phase of the EAGLE process. As shown in Figure 2, given a system S, elicitation techniques must be defined to produce models according to a goal G and under some cost restrictions. Thus, elicitation composed of two phases, namely observation and construction.

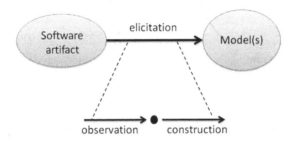

Fig. 2. Elicit phase

Observation, driven by G, produces a set of observations of the system. More specifically, the set of observations is defined with the aim at extracting the aspects of the system that are relevant according to the goal G. G is a formula expressed in some formalism whose validity can be proven on the abstractions of the system. This abstraction can be constructed starting from the set of observations. Different goals require different kind of observations. Observations are included in the system by construction. Observations are an abstraction of S or of the semantics of S in terms both of output data and quantitative aspects, *e.g.*, response time once executed with a provided input in the execution context.

Construction, driven by G, takes as input the set of observations and produces a system model. This model contains the observed behaviors and typically enriches them with an inference step.

In the ideal case, the objective of the explore phase is to produce models that are correct and complete with respect to the goal G, *i.e.*, G holds on the elicited model *iff* it holds on S. This ideal situation is shown in Figure 3.(a), where the complete inclusion of the model(s) ellipse wants to informally represent that the "knowledge" of the system, as abstracted by the elicited model, is correct and complete with respect to validating G. Unfortunately, in the real case, the correctness and completeness of the models cannot be always achieved. For instance, it may be the case that achieving a correct and complete model implies performing (possibly) infinite observations.

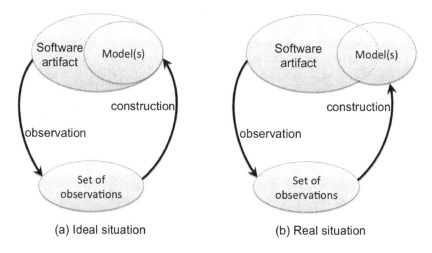

(a) Ideal situation   (b) Real situation

Fig. 3. Software artifact, observations, and model

The real situation is shown in Figure 3.(b) in which models are neither correct nor complete. This is because the set of observations is always finite and typically the construction phase has to infer something in order to produce the model. For instance, let us assume that we aim at constructing a behavior model of the system. Then, let us assume also that the observations are system traces, *e.g.*, observed by monitoring the system. What one aims at is to get complete models up to a certain length of the observation (*i.e.*, number of events observed). However, the behavior model has to be produced to represent the functioning of the system even while running more than the observed length. This requires an inference phase, *e.g.*, performed by means of a synthesis step [36], that may add uncertainty. Obviously, the more you observe the more accurate you can be and the more "costly" will be.

Then, according to the EAGLE process presented in Section 2, elicitation has associated a cost and is subject to uncertainty. Informally, the elicitation technique, *elicitation*$_i$ can be seen as a function that takes as input a system S, a goal G, a cost c that we are willing to pay, and produces a model with associated a degree of uncertainty, $M_{i,u}$:

$$elicitation_i(S, G, c) = M_{i,u}$$

As described before, the $elicitation_i$ function makes use of the $observation_k$ and $construction_j$ functions. The observation technique $observation_k$ takes as input the system S, the goal G, and the cost we are willing to pay for the observation phase, c_1, and produces a set of observations O_k under an uncertainty $u_{k,1}$:

$$observation_k(S, G, c_1) = (O_k, u_{k,1})$$

The construction technique $construction_j$ takes as input the observations produced under an uncertainty degree $(O_k, u_{k,1})$, the goal G, and the cost we are willing to pay for the construction phase, c_2, and produces a model with associated a degree of uncertainty, $M_{i,u}$.

$$construction_j((O_k, u_{k,1}), G, c_2) = M_{i,u}$$

Therefore:

$$elicitation_i(S, G, c) = construction_j(observation_k(S, G, c_1), G, c_2) = M_{i,u}$$

with the cost $c = c_1 + c_2$.

The uncertainty of a system is typically measured with a system metric. The metrics adopted to reason on uncertainty are different depending on the sources of uncertainty they refer to [5]. As discussed in [5], this calls for a tradeoff between different metrics, each associated to a specific functional or non-functional aspect: a designer might decide to decrease the uncertainty in one direction whereas increase the uncertainty in other directions.

Furthermore, an important aspect concerns the relationship between the goal and the cost that we are willing to pay, which to some extent can allow us to "control" the resulting uncertainty of the model. In this sense our notion of explore phase can be seen as a sort of selected exploration that can make feasible the elicitation of models with an acceptable uncertainty degree whenever a "goal-independent" exploration would fail, meaning that the elicitation problem would be intractable. For instance, let us consider the *Amazon E-commerce WS* (AEWS) as software system to be explored and let us exploit StrawBerry (see Section 5) as explore technique without considering a specified goal. All we know is a WSDL descrition of AEWS[2] that we can use to elicit its behaviour protocol automaton via StrawBerry. The AEWS WSDL description is made of 85 XML Schema type definitions and 23 WSDL operation definitions[3].

In a previous case study described in [8], by using StrawBerry, we have been able to elicit the behavior protocol automaton of the AEWS. Figure 4 shows an

---

[2] http://webservices.amazon.com/AWSECommerceService/
AWSECommerceService.wsdl

[3] We are referring to the 2009 AEWS version.

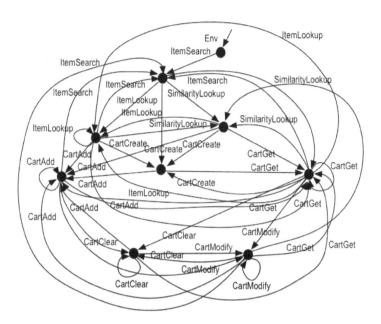

Fig. 4. An excerpt of the AEWS behaviour protocol as elicited by a "goal-independent" explore phase

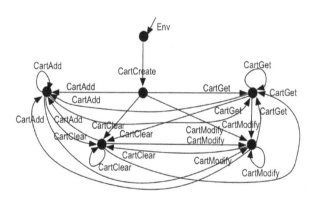

Fig. 5. AEWS behaviour protocol as elicited by a goal-oriented explore phase

excerpt of it concerning all the "item search" and "cart management" operations (for the sake of readability, data parameters in the operation labels are omitted). Indeed, the entire automaton elicited by **StrawBerry** is made of 24 states and 288 transitions. To elicit it, **StrawBerry** produced 10^6 test cases and executed them in 10^{-2} secs. for each, which means few hours of testing. Note that this is perfectly acceptable for off-line analysis but not usable for dynamic analysis and, hence, for the kind of revolutionary process envisioned by EAGLE.

Repeating the experiment by considering a goal specification expressing the fact that the EAGLE user (e.g., the developer of the system to be integrated) wishes to *"develop a client for cart management only"*, StrawBerry elicits the automaton shown in Figure 5. It is made of 6 state and 21 transitions only. The elicitation of it required the generation and execution of 10^5 test cases, which means few seconds of testing.

5 StrawBerry: An Explore Technique to Produce Behaviour Protocols from Webservices

By taking as input a syntactical description of the WS signature, expressed by means of the WSDL notation [1], StrawBerry [8] derives in an automated way a partial ordering relation among the invocations of the different WSDL operations. This partial ordering relation is represented as an automaton that we call *Behavior Protocol automaton*. It models the interaction protocol that a client has to follow in order to correctly interact with the WS. This automaton also explicitly models the information that has to be passed to the WS operations.

StrawBerry is a black-box and extra-procedural method. It is black-box since it takes into account only the WSDL of the WS. It is extra-procedural since it focuses on synthesizing a model of the behavior that is assumed when interacting with the WS from outside, as opposed to intra-procedural methods that synthesize a model of the implementation logic of the single WS operations [28,40]. Figure 6 graphically represents StrawBerry as a process that is split in five main activities that realize its **observation** and **construction** phases.

Observation: the observation phase is in turn organized in two sub-phases.

– The *first sub-phase* exploits the information that is available on the webservice, *i.e.*, its WSDL, and performs a syntactic interface analysis (*i.e.*, data type analysis).
  By referring to Figure 6, the *Dependencies Elicitation* activity elicits data dependencies between the I/O parameters of the operations defined in the WSDL. A dependency is recorded whenever the type of the output of an operation matches with the type of the input of another operation. The match is syntactic. The elicited set of I/O dependencies may be optimized under some heuristics [8].
  The elicited set of I/O dependencies (see the *Input/Output Dependencies* artifact shown in Figure 6) is used for constructing a data-flow model (see the *Saturated Dependencies Automaton Synthesis* activity and the *Saturated Dependencies Automaton* artifact shown in Figure 6) where each node stores data dependencies that concern the output parameters of a specific operation and directed arcs are used to model syntactic matches between output parameters of an operation and input parameters of another operation. This

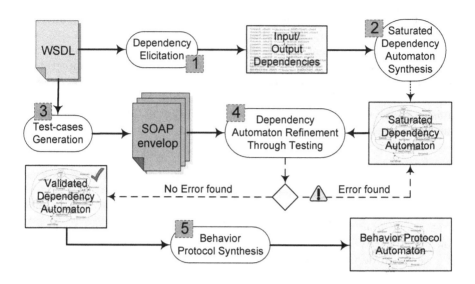

Fig. 6. Overview of the `StrawBerry` method

model is completed by applying a *saturation rule*. This rule adds new dependencies that model the possibility for a client to invoke a WS operation by directly providing its input parameters.

– The *second sub-phase* refines this dependencies automaton by observing the execution of the webservice. More specifically, the dependencies automaton is validated through testing against the WS to verify conformance (see *Dependencies Automaton Refinement Through Testing* activity shown in Figure 6). The testing phase takes as input the SOAP messages produced by the *Test-cases generation* activity. The latter, driven by coverage criteria, automatically derives a suite of test cases (*i.e.*, SOAP envelop messages) for the operations to be tested, according to the WSDL of the WS. In `StrawBerry` tests are generated from the WSDL and aim at validating whether the synthesized automaton is a correct abstraction of the service implementation. Testing is used to refine the syntactic dependencies by discovering those that are semantically wrong. By construction, the inferred set of dependencies is syntactically correct. However, it might not be correct semantically since it may contain false positives (*e.g.*, a string parameter used as a generic attribute is matched with another string parameter that is a unique key). The testing activity is organized into three steps. `StrawBerry` runs positive tests in the first step and negative tests in the second step. Positive test cases reproduce the elicited data dependencies and are used to reject fake dependencies: if a positive test invocation returns an error answer, `StrawBerry` concludes that the tested dependency does not exist. Negative test cases are instead used to confirm uncertain dependencies: `StrawBerry` provides in input to the sink operation a random test case of the expected type. If this test invocation returns an error answer, then `StrawBerry` concludes that the WS was indeed expecting as input the output produced by the source operation, and it confirms the hypothesized dependency as certain. If uncertain dependencies remain after the two steps, `StrawBerry` resolves the uncertainty by assuming that the hypothesized dependencies do not exist. Intuitively, this is the safest choice, given that at the previous step the invoked operation accepted a random input.

Construction: the construction phase consists in a synthesis stage which aims at transforming the validated dependency automaton (a data-flow model) into an automaton defining the behavior protocol (a control-flow model), see the *Behavior Protocol Synthesis* activity in Figure 6. This automaton explicitly models also the data that has to be passed to the WS operations. More precisely, the states of the behavior protocol automaton are WS execution states and the transitions, labeled with operation names plus I/O data, model possible operation invocations from the client of the WS.

Uncertainty in `StrawBerry` meanly consists in the lack of behavioral information in the produced behavior protocol automaton. This lack of information can be attributed to the fact that web service interfaces are not concerned with describing behavioral aspects and thus provide incomplete information to any analysis approach merely focusing on interfaces. Uncertainty in `StrawBerry` can be introduced both in the observation and in the construction phase.

During the observation phase the dependency automaton is constructed by only considering syntactic correspondences and then refined by means of testing. This procedure is not exhaustive and then cannot ensure neither correctness nor completeness. As stated in Section 4, the more you observe (*i.e.*, more invest to the testing phase) the more accurate you can be (*i.e.*, reduce the uncertainty) and the more "costly" will be.

During the construction phase the dependency automaton is transformed into a behavior protocol. The synthesis phase takes as input the observations that have been tested always for a finite length. Whereas, the behavior protocol automaton has to be produced to represent the functioning of the webservice even while running more than the observed length. This calls for an inference step that unavoidably introduces uncertainty. This uncertainty can be reduced by performing tests that validate longer sequences of operation invocations. As usual, this increases the cost of the elicitation phase.

6 EVOSS Injection: An Explore Technique to Produce a Model from a Running Linux System

As another example of elicitation technique, let us consider the case of Free and Open Source Software (FOSS) systems and, in particular, the case of widely used FOSS distributions, like Debian, Ubuntu, Fedora, and Suse. These systems are based on the central notion of software package. Packages are assembled to build a specific software system. The recommended way of evolving such systems is to use package manager tools to perform system modifications by adding, removing, or replacing packages. However, the ability to analyze and predict component behavior during their upgrades, *e.g.*, installation and removal, in FOSS systems is intrinsically difficult and requires techniques, algorithms, and methods which are both expressive and computationally feasible in order to be used in practice. Currently, package managers are only aware of some static aspects of packages that can influence upgrades, and at the same time they completely ignore relevant dynamic aspects, such as potential failures of configuration scripts that are executed during upgrade deployment. Thus, it is not surprising that an apparently innocuous package upgrade can end up with a broken system state [13].

6.1 Overview of Evoss

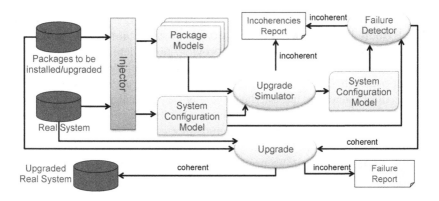

Fig. 7. Overview of the Evoss approach

The Evoss (EVolution of free and Open Source Software) approach[4] [15] enhances the prediction of upgrades in FOSS distributions. In order to make upgrade prediction more accurate, Evoss considers both static and dynamic aspects of upgrades. Static aspects have been modeled by enhancing the expressiveness of the representations with respect to the state of the art of package managers, enabling the detection of a larger number of undesirable configurations, such as the breakage of fine-grained dependencies among packages, currently neglected by package managers. The main dynamic aspects considered are those related to the behavior of package configuration scripts which are executed during upgrade deployment.

---

[4] Evoss, `http://evoss.di.univaq.it`, has been proposed within the FP7/2007–2013 European project Mancoosi, `http://www.mancoosi.org`, grant agreement n. 214898.

An overview of the EVOSS approach is shown in Figure 7. It is a model-driven engineering (MDE) approach [9], which relies on a model-based representation of the current system configuration and of all packages that are meant to be upgraded. This enables EVOSS to *simulate* upgrades as model transformations *before* upgrade deployment. To this end, we encode fine-grained configuration dependencies and abstract over maintainer scripts. This way the models capture all the information needed to anticipate the inconsistent configurations that current tools cannot detect, as they only rely on package metadata.

According to Figure 7, the simulation of a system upgrade is performed by the *Upgrade Simulator* which takes a set of models as input: a *System Configuration Model* and *Package Models* corresponding to the packages which have to be installed/removed/replaced. The *System Configuration Model* describes the state of a given system in terms of installed packages, running services, configuration files, *etc.* In other words, it represents a snapshot of the considered system and maintains in a uniform and explicit way the information that is important for simulation purposes. The *Package Model* provides information about all packages involved in the upgrade, including maintainer script behavior. The output of *Upgrade Simulator* is a new *System Configuration Model* if no errors occur during the simulation, otherwise an *Incoherences Report* is produced. The new *System Configuration Model* is queried and analyzed by the *Failure Detector* component. When *Failure Detector* discovers inconsistencies and they are collected in the *Failure Report*. The real upgrade is performed on the system only if the new system configuration model is coherent.

6.2   The EVOSS Injection

The EVOSS injection aims at building the system configuration and package models. By adhering to the terminology proposed in Section 4 we need proper *observation* and *construction* functions able to create the models required for the simulation. Such functions are presented in the next sections. In EVOSS the elicitation phase is performed by means of proper model injectors which are able to observe the system configuration to be upgraded, and the packages involved in the considered upgrade plan, and to create the corresponding models as described in the following.

Observation: concerning the system configuration, the observation is performed by executing specific shell commands able to query the system and gather the required information. For instance, to retrieve all the packages that are installed in a Debian-based system, the following shell command can be executed:

```
dpkg --get-selections
```

and an output like the following is obtained:

```
acl                 install
acpi                install
acpi-support        install
acpid               install
                ...
zip                 install
zlib1g              install
```

Other specific shell commands and ad-hoc scripts can be executed in order to retrieve data which are not directly available in the system, like implicit dependencies among packages that occur, for instance, because of their configuration files, which are not considered in the package metadata.

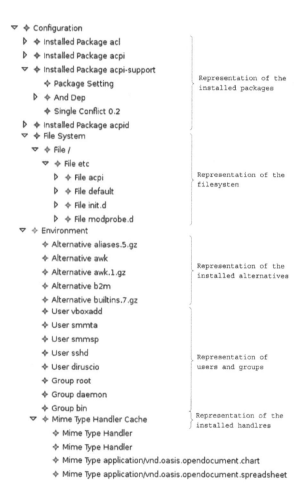

Fig. 8. Sample configuration model

Concerning, the packages involved in a given upgrade plan, their models are obtained by means of another observation function that still is based on specific shell commands. For instance, the following command:

```
dpkg -s swi-prolog
```

retrieves all the metadata of the `swi-prolog` package. Additional tools are required to retrieve also the configuration scripts of the package that are required for simulation purposes.

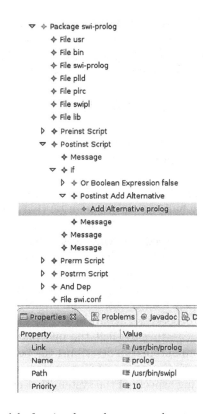

Fig. 9. Model of a simple package named `swiprolog-5.7.59`

Construction: once the system and the packages involved in the upgrade plan have been observed, the corresponding models can be created. In EVOSS the creation of models has been implemented by using the Eclipse Modeling Framework (EMF)[5]. An example of a system configuration model, automatically obtained from a running system, is shown in Figure 8. The model has been created by considering the observations which have been obtained as previously discussed.

---

[5] Eclipse Modeling Framework: `http://www.eclipse.org/emf`

Figure 9 shows a fragment of a simple package named `swiprolog-5.7.59`. The model represents the files contained in the package, the dependencies with other packages and the maintainer scripts which are executed during the upgrade. In EVOSS, maintainer scripts are expressed by means of a DSL [15] that mainly provides macros representing recurring script fragments. According to model in Figure 9, the post-installation script of the package `swiprolog-5.7.59` consists of four DSL statements. The statement that can affect the system configuration during the package installation is the `if` statement. Its `then` block contains the `addAlternative` statement that, once executed, creates a new alternative called `prolog`, which points to the executable `/usr/bin/swipl`.

Uncertainty in EVOSS is represented by the lack of information related to both system configurations and packages. In particular, models represent abstractions of the system to be upgraded and of the packages involved in the given upgrade plan. The cost to be paid for obtaining such models is proportional to the amount of information to be represented, thus to the time required to gather such information. Further details about the performance of the EVOSS approach might be found on [15].

7   Concluding Remarks

Techniques for building, managing, verifying, validating and controlling modern software systems typically build on the assumption that suitable models of software artifacts exist. Unfortunately, in the practice this assumption turns out to be unfounded. It emerges the need of having explore techniques to automatically extract models from existent software. This paper proposes a general overview of the exploring problem. This overview has been conceived by studying existing techniques that concern the elicitation of observational models from software artifacts. Moreover, the paper describes two different techniques to automatically construct models by observing software artifacts. The first technique, called `StrawBerry`, makes use of testing to elicit the information that are needed to automatically synthesize an automaton describing the behavior of a web-service. The second technique queries a running Linux system and automatically constructs a model representing aspects of the system that enable the simulation of system upgrades.

On the future work side, we aim at defining a general theory that regulates the exploring problem and explains relations among software artifacts, observations, goal, and produced models.

Acknowledgment. This work is supported by the European Community's Seventh Framework Programme FP7/2007-2013 under grant agreements: number 257178 (project CHOReOS - Large Scale Choreographies for the Future

Internet - www.choreos.eu), and number 231167 (project CONNECT - Emergent Connectors for Eternal Software Intensive Networked Systems - http://connect-forever.eu/).

References

1. WSDL: Web Services Description Languages v1.1 spec., http://www.w3.org/TR/2001/NOTE-wsdl-20010315
2. Alur, R., Cerný, P., Madhusudan, P., Nam, W.: Synthesis of interface specifications for Java classes. In: POPL, pp. 98–109 (2005)
3. Angluin, D.: Learning regular sets from queries and counterexamples. Inf. Comput. 75, 87–106 (1987)
4. Autili, M., Cortellessa, V., Di Ruscio, D., Inverardi, P., Pelliccione, P., Tivoli, M.: Eagle: Engineering software in the ubiquitous globe by leveraging uncertainty. In: Proceedings of the 19th ACM SIGSOFT Symposium and the 13th European Conference on Foundations of Software Engineering, ESEC/FSE 2011, pp. 488–491. ACM, New York (2011)
5. Autili, M., Cortellessa, V., Di Ruscio, D., Inverardi, P., Pelliccione, P., Tivoli, M.: Integration architecture synthesis for taming uncertainty in the Digital Space. In: Calinescu, R., Garlan, D. (eds.) Monterey Workshop 2012. LNCS, vol. 7539, pp. 118–131. Springer, Heidelberg (2012)
6. Baresi, L., Ghezzi, C.: The disappearing boundary between development-time and run-time. In: Proceedings of FoSER 2010, pp. 17–22. ACM (2010)
7. Berg, T., Jonsson, B., Raffelt, H.: Regular Inference for State Machines Using Domains with Equality Tests. In: Fiadeiro, J.L., Inverardi, P. (eds.) FASE 2008. LNCS, vol. 4961, pp. 317–331. Springer, Heidelberg (2008)
8. Bertolino, A., Inverardi, P., Pelliccione, P., Tivoli, M.: Automatic synthesis of behavior protocols for composable web-services. In: Proceedings of The 7th Joint Meeting of the European Software Engineering Conference (ESEC) and the ACM SIGSOFT Symposium on the Foundations of Software Engineering (FSE), pp. 141–150 (August 2009)
9. Bézivin, J.: On the Unification Power of Models. SOSYM 4(2), 171–188 (2005)
10. Bézivin, J., Gerbé, O.: Towards a Precise Definition of the OMG/MDA Framework. In: Automated Software Engineering (ASE 2001), Los Alamitos, CA, pp. 273–282. IEEE Computer Society Press (2001)
11. Blair, G., Bencomo, N., France, R.B.: Models@run.time. Computer 42, 22–27 (2009)
12. Ceri, S., Braga, D., Corcoglioniti, F., Grossniklaus, M., Vadacca, S.: Search computing challenges and directions. In: Dearle, A., Zicari, R.V. (eds.) ICOODB 2010. LNCS, vol. 6348, pp. 1–5. Springer, Heidelberg (2010)
13. Crameri, O., Knezevic, N., Kostic, D., Bianchini, R., Zwaenepoel, W.: Staged deployment in mirage, an integrated software upgrade testing and distribution system. SIGOPS Oper. Syst. Rev. 41(6), 221–236 (2007)
14. Dallmeier, V., Knopp, N., Mallon, C., Fraser, G., Hack, S., Zeller, A.: Automatically generating test cases for specification mining. IEEE Transactions on Software Engineering 38(2), 243–257 (2012)
15. Di Cosmo, R., Di Ruscio, D., Pelliccione, P., Pierantonio, A., Zacchiroli, S.: Supporting software evolution in component-based FOSS systems. Sci. Comput. Program. 76(12), 1144–1160 (2011)

16. Garlan, D.: Software engineering in an uncertain world. In: Proc. of FSE/SDP 2010, pp. 125–128 (2010)
17. Ghezzi, C., Mocci, A., Monga, M.: Synthesizing Intentional Behavior Models by Graph Transformation. In: ICSE 2009, Vancouver, Canada (2009)
18. Giannakopoulou, D., Rakamarić, Z., Raman, V.: Symbolic learning of component interfaces. In: Miné, A., Schmidt, D. (eds.) SAS 2012. LNCS, vol. 7460, pp. 248–264. Springer, Heidelberg (2012)
19. Hilliard, R., Malavolta, I., Muccini, H., Pelliccione, P.: On the composition and reuse of viewpoints across architecture frameworks. In: 10th Working IEEE/IFIP Conference on Software Architecture (WICSA) & 6th European Conference on Software Architecture (ECSA) - WICSA/ECSA 2012, (August 2012)
20. Hungar, H., Margaria, T., Steffen, B.: Test-based model generation for legacy systems. In: Proceedings of International Test Conference ITC 2003, September 30-October 2, vol. 1, pp. 971–980 (2003)
21. Inverardi, P.: Software of the future is the future of software? In: Montanari, U., Sannella, D., Bruni, R. (eds.) TGC 2006. LNCS, vol. 4661, pp. 69–85. Springer, Heidelberg (2007)
22. Inverardi, P., Spalazzese, R., Tivoli, M.: Application-layer connector synthesis. In: Bernardo, M., Issarny, V. (eds.) SFM 2011. LNCS, vol. 6659, pp. 148–190. Springer, Heidelberg (2011)
23. Inverardi, P., Tivoli, M.: The Future of Software: Adaptation and Dependability. In: De Lucia, A., Ferrucci, F. (eds.) ISSSE 2006-2008. LNCS, vol. 5413, pp. 1–31. Springer, Heidelberg (2009)
24. Inverardi, P., Tivoli, M.: Automatic synthesis of modular connectors via composition of protocol mediation patterns. In: 35th International Conference on Software Engineering, ICSE 2013 (2013)
25. Krogmann, K., Kuperberg, M., Reussner, R.: Using genetic search for reverse engineering of parametric behavior models for performance prediction. IEEE Trans. Softw. Eng. 36(6), 865–877 (2010)
26. Ljung, L.: Perspectives on system identification. Annual Reviews in Control 34(1), 1–12 (2010)
27. Lo, D., Mariani, L., Santoro, M.: Learning extended fsa from software: An empirical assessment. Journal of Systems and Software 85(9), 2063–2076 (2012); Selected papers from the 2011 Joint Working IEEE/IFIP Conference on Software Architecture (WICSA 2011)
28. Lorenzoli, D., Mariani, L., Pezzè, M.: Automatic Generation of Software Behavioral Models. In: ICSE 2008, pp. 501–510. ACM, NY (2008)
29. Mateescu, R., Poizat, P., Salaun, G.: Adaptation of service protocols using process algebra and on-the-fly reduction techniques. IEEE Transactions on Software Engineering 38(4), 755–777 (2012)
30. Meinke, K.: Automated Black-box Testing of Functional Correctness using Function Approximation. SIGSOFT Softw. Eng. Notes 29(4), 143–153 (2004)
31. Mellor, S.J., Clark, A.N., Futagami, T.: Guest Editors' Introduction: Model-Driven Development. IEEE Software 20(5), 14–18 (2003)
32. Object Management Group (OMG). MDA Guide version 1.0.1, OMG Document: omg/2003-06-01 (2003)
33. Olsson, H.H., Alahyari, H., Bosch, J.: Climbing the "stairway to heaven" – a mulitiple-case study exploring barriers in the transition from agile development towards continuous deployment of software. In: 2010 36th EUROMICRO Conference on Software Engineering and Advanced Applications, pp. 392–399 (2012)

34. Seidewitz, E.: What Models Mean. IEEE Software 20(5), 26–32 (2003)
35. Taylor, R.N., Medvidovic, N., Dashofy, E.M.: Software Architecture: Foundations, Theory, and Practice. Wiley (2009)
36. Tivoli, M., Inverardi, P.: Failure-free coordinators synthesis for component-based architectures. Sci. Comput. Program. 71(3), 181–212 (2008)
37. van Lamsweerde, A.: Requirements Engineering: From System Goals to UML Models to Software Specifications. Wiley (March 2009)
38. Walkinshaw, N., Lambeau, B., Damas, C., Bogdanov, K., Dupont, P.: Stamina: A competition to encourage the development and assessment of software model inference techniques. Empirical Software Engineering, 1–34 (2012)
39. Wasylkowski, A., Zeller, A.: Mining temporal specifications from object usage. Automated Software Engg. 18(3-4), 263–292 (2011)
40. Wasylkowski, A., Zeller, A., Lindig, C.: Detecting Object Usage Anomalies. In: ESEC-FSE 2007, pp. 35–44. ACM (2007)
41. White, R.W., Roth, R.A.: Exploratory Search: Beyond the Query-Response Paradigm. Synthesis Lect. on ICRS. Morgan & Claypool Publishers (2009)
42. BobbyWoolf, G.H.: Enterprise Integration Patterns: Designing, Building, and Deploying Messaging Solutions. Addison-Wesley Professional (October 2003)

From Model-Driven Software Development Processes to Problem Diagnoses at Runtime

Yijun Yu[1], Thein Than Tun[1], Arosha K. Bandara[1], Tian Zhang[3],
and Bashar Nuseibeh[1,2]

[1] Department of Computing and Communications, The Open University, UK
[2] Lero, University of Limerick, Ireland
[3] State Key Laboratory for Novel Software Technology, Nanjing University, China

Abstract. Following the "convention over configuration" paradigm, model-driven software development (MDSD) generates code to implement the "default" behaviour that has been specified by a template separate from the input model. On the one hand, developers can produce end-products without a full understanding of the templates; on the other hand, the tacit knowledge in the templates is subtle to diagnose when a runtime software failure occurs. Therefore, there is a gap between templates and runtime adapted models. Generalising from the concrete problematic examples in MDSD processes to a model-based problem diagnosis, the chapter presents a procedure to separate the automated fixes from those runtime gaps that require human judgments.

Keywords: Model-Driven Software Development, Problem Frames.

1 Introduction

Decades after Alan Turing introduced the computing machine that uses a tape of infinitely long '0' and '1' binary numbers to store data and programs [22], abstraction levels of programs have become closer to human understanding of the physical world [13]. High-level programming languages can be automatically translated and optimised into Turing machines by compilers, freeing programmers from having to think in terms of machine instructions [2]. Naturally, one would like to model the physical world, and generate the code for implementing the machine from the model, in the same automated way as compiling source program into binary code. This vision motivates model-driven software development methods (MDSD) [10], using an input model much more abstract than the binary code of Turing machines.

For example, our graphical modeling tool to support the Problem Frames approach (PF) [12] was created using MDSD method, starting from a concise domain-specific language for representing or modeling problem diagrams. Given that diagrammatic notations of the PF have been unambiguously defined by researchers, and graphical editing is one of the exemplars of mature MDSD tools, one would assume that developing the PF modeling tool is a straightforward application of MDSD methods.

N. Bencomo et al. (Eds.): Models@run.time, LNCS 8378, pp. 188–207, 2014.

However, this assumption needs to be checked, both from a requirements engineering (RE) perspective and from a practical, problem solving perspective. From a RE perspective, we need to analyse the requirements of "developing a graphical modeling tool support for Problem Frames approach", as an exercise of both MDSD and Problem Frames. This exercise serves two purposes. First, it tells us whether MDSD directly meets the requirement of "supporting a graphical modeling language"; second, it tells us how such MDSD requirements can be analysed by the PF approach. In doing so, we hope to discover a useful pattern in the problem solving practice that relates the MDSD solutions to the requirements. We also hope to improve our understanding about any generic concerns in the MDSD methodology. From a practical perspective, we would like to explore problems that cannot be solved by the current practices of MDSD.

If such problems exist, the practitioners need a new methodology for diagnosing them. In this chapter, we will show that runtime diagnosis of the gap between models in two minds (of a developer and of a user) must be reconciled. We will also demonstrate the feasibility through a new runtime model diagnosis framework summarised at the end of the chapter.

Background and Terminology of MDSD

To demonstrate the problems, a chain of automated tool support from the Eclipse Modeling project[1] and the terminology used in this chapter will be discussed. Many techniques have been proposed for MDSD. The general idea is to have one metametamodel (e.g., OMG MOF) whose instance is a metamodel or a modeling language. An instance of the metamodel is a program in a domain specific or generic language. For an Eclipse modeling project, the metametamodel is called *ecore*, a sublanguage to define metamodels in the XML interchange (XMI) format. Ecore itself is an instance of the ecore metamodel, which we call *self-defining*. In general, an instance of ecore is called *EMF* model, named after the de facto standard in the Eclipse modeling community. All these languages are supported by a chain of EMF tools[2].

Using an analogy to language engineering, EMF corresponds to the abstract syntax of the language without specifying its concrete syntax. The XMI is only one concrete syntax to represent EMF, and one may choose another concrete syntax such as a textual DSL language or a graphical language. Transformations can be written to convert text to model (T2M), model to model (M2M), and model to text (M2T), following a suite of OMG modeling standards. Since the Ecore modeling language is a generic implementation of the OMG MOF, diagrammatic languages such as UML can also be fully supported.

As an example, the xtext framework[3] is provided to perform the T2M parsing, converting the abstract syntax of a DSL program into its corresponding EMF model. As the by-product of such a transformation, a syntax-highlighting

---

[1] www.eclipse.org/modeling

[2] www.eclipse.org/modeling/emf

[3] http://www.eclipse.org/Xtext/

text editor can be generated for editing the DSL program instances. Similarly, GMF editors can also be generated for editing the EMF models graphically[4]. These feature-rich graphical editors can be generated from the EMF metamodel, the graph definition models that define the graphical notations, and the mappings between the elements on the Ecore to the presentations.

In a nutshell, generating a graphical editor in MDSD is now feasible by providing the language design in an abstract way using the extended BNF rules, plus the mapping decisions to show the modeling elements in appropriate graphical notations.

Example: Describing PF Modeling as a PF Model

Before analysing the general problem, we first describe the requirements and the stakeholders involved in a specific example. In this example, our primary requirement is that "a PF graphical modeling tool must allow users to create and edit problem diagrams as defined by the PF researchers". For the PF modeling tool to be developed, this requirement also involves stakeholders such as users who use the PF modeling tool and researchers who define the PF language.

To solve this problem without using the MDSD approach, a Model-View-Controller (MVC) design pattern or a Workpiece frame [12] can be used.

A Workpiece frame is a general class of problems identified by a requirement of users to edit a piece of work through a tool. Any editing problem fits this frame: the PF Graphical Modeling Tool (see Figure 1) is no exception.

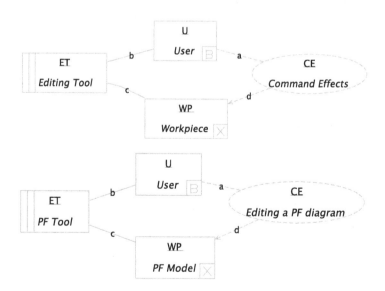

Fig. 1. A Work Piece frame and its instantiation for the PF editing problem

---

[4] www.eclipse.org/modeling/gmf

Basic PF notations A requirement is represented by a dashed ellipse shape, labelled by the name of the requirement and its abbreviation; and a solution to
the problem is represented by a rectangle, marked with double strips on the left.
When marked with a single strip on the left, the domain is "designed" by other
problem solving steps. A physical domain can also be represented by a rectangle
with names and abbreviation labels without the strips. The behaviour type of a
domain node can be classified by a letter mark at the lower-right corner of the
rectangle. For example, a lexical domain marked with "X" indicates a passive
behaviour that does not cause change itself, a biddable domain marked with "B"
indicates an active behaviour that can change by itself non-deterministically, a
causal domain marked with "C" indicates an active behaviour that is determin-
stic. Domains can share an interface between each other. The shared interface is
represented by an undirected solid link, marked with a letter abbreviating a set
of shared phenomena such as events and states. A requirement can constrain a
domain's behaviour, indicated by a dashed arrow to the constrained domains; a
requirement can also refer to a domain, shown as a dashed link between them.

In fact, a textual or graphical editing tool may already meet this requirement.
Most PF diagrams documented in the literature so far were drawn using either a
text editing tool such as LaTeX, or a diagramming tool such as Dia[5]. This raises
many interesting questions: "What can MDSD add to the available solutions for
the PF modeling tool requirement" and "Who can benefit from MDSD"?

Naturally such an investigation brings us to a new type of role – "Developer".
In fact, a developer opts for the MDSD method mainly because it promises two
more quality requirements: "productivity" and "maintainability". It must take
little effort for a developer to create a PF modeling tool from scratch, and it
must take little effort for a developer to adjust the tool when the researcher
makes some refinement to the PF language.

Even with these productivity and maintainability requirements in mind, there
is still one alternative solution to these requirements without resorting to the
MDSD technology: to customise existing functionalities in graphical editing tool
such as Visio, e.g., by creating a new stencil or template for PF notations. In
fact, this is what the graphical drawing tool Dia already offered. So, why do we
still bother with MDSD?

Let us revisit the initial requirement of the "Users" and the "Researchers".
There is one additional requirement "modeling conformance" that a customised
general diagramming tool cannot easily meet. "How can one be sure that the
modeling elements are uniquely named? How can one check whether there is
a single machine node and a single requirement node in a problem diagram?
How can one make sure all the nodes are linked and all the links are connected to certain nodes? How can one make sure the dashed arrows are always
from requirement nodes to the domain nodes?" In short, the key advantage
of providing PF Modeling Tool through MDSD is the additional capability to
satisfy these "domain-specific" modeling requirements. Syntax checking aside,
syntax highlighting, syntax-driven editing, auto completion, pattern matching,

---

[5] http://projects.gnome.org/dia/

transformations, and various form of inconsistency checks such as type checks and uniqueness checks, are amongst the various benefits a MDSD derived PF Modeling tool brings about, in addition to the graphical editing features such as drag-and-drop, zooming, panning, layouting, and printing. Instead of asking "why bother with MDSD", one would ask "why bother with implementing all these nice features yourself" instead.

Note that we had a similar experience in creating other requirements modeling tool using the MDSD approach (e.g., OpenOME for i*). In the following section, we discuss several examples of problems found during the development time of our research prototype.

2   Problems and Concerns in the MDSD Process

Given the analysis so far, we established how a MDSD process benefits the developers in creating and maintaining a PF modeling tool for the PF researchers and users alike.

Now we now look at the darker corners of the MDSD approach, explaining some issues experienced when applying it. A possibly shocking concern we documented here resembles the experience in several non-trivial instances. It is our belief that this may be a general concern for MDSD development.

The poor experience came from the attempt to stretch the tool to support analysing the requirements problems in two complementary modeling languages, namely PF and i* [24]. While the PF approach focuses on understanding the entailment relationship $W, S \vdash R$ between the requirements R, solutions S and the world context domains W, the goal-oriented modeling approach focuses on understanding the relationships between the stakeholders (i.e., the "Who") and their intentional requirements (i.e., the "why"). Since their diagramming tools have been both developed using MDSD, we would consider a generalisation of the graphical modeling tool support.

The first attempt was to use the grammar "mixin" feature in xtext. By inheriting concrete syntax from both grammars of PF and i*, we obtained such a modeling language that can navigate between them: (1) a requirement node in PF could be expanded into a detailed i* diagram where the requirement is one of the goals; (2) an intention node in i* diagrams (goal, task, resource, softgoal) could be expanded into a PF diagram where the requirement corresponding to the expanded goal. After applying the xtext MDSD generation, we then obtained a text-based parser that can transform the concrete syntax into an abstract syntax expressed by the combined EMF model. As a result, the new EMF model was compliant to both the metamodel in PF and the metamodel in i*, making it much easier to perform new kinds of analysis such as programmatic scoping of the contexts for alternatively refined subgoals [5].

However, several subtle problems arose when the two Java code bases generated from the EMF models were used together, complicating the MDSD experience.

Figure 2 summarises the alphabet concern in the "convention over configuration" MDSD paradigm. By "convention", the template code is generated by

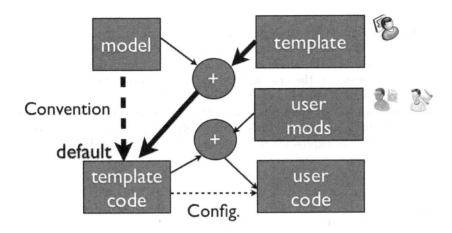

Fig. 2. The additional alphabet (or tacit knowledge) concern in the "convention over configuration" MDSD paradigm. Developers of the templates may not know the requirements of individual programmers, and the individual programmers may not fully understand the rationale behind the default behaviours in the generated template code.

instantiating the templates behind the scenes with the input model; by "configuration" users can further modify the generated code according to their individual requirements. The additional alphabet concern applies because neither does the designer of the templates understand the individual users' requirements, nor do the users fully understand the rationale behind the "default" behaviours.

When the two misunderstand each other, a glitch is inevitable. In the following subsections, we document four example problems that are caused by this kind of misunderstanding as the "additional alphabet" or "tacit knowledge" concern of MDSD.

The "Detached" Requirement Phenomena. The first problem was related to an unwanted behaviour in the graphical editing. As described earlier, a requirement node in PF is an ellipse shape, which should connect to other domain nodes through links by the design of language. However, while moving such a node to an angle not aligned horizontally or vertically with the node on the other side of the link, the end of the link would not be connected to the requirement node, appearing as if they were detached. A search on the developers forum revealed that this problem was to do with the `org.eclipse.draw2d.ChopboxAnchor` class used by default in the generated code, rather than the proper `org.eclipse.draw2d.EllipseAnchor`. The ChopboxAnchor in effect calculates the connection anchors based on a rectangle shaped outline, whilst the EllipseAnchor class uses the ellipse shape instead. After replacing ChopboxAnchor with EllipseAnchor in the generated code, however, we found that the problem were not solved. By tracing the execution in a debugger, we found that the real problem was rooted deeply in the path resolution mechanism at the time of

dynamic class loading. In fact, our customised `uk.ac.open.problem.diagram.`
`edit.parts.` `NodeEditPart` class generated from the MDSD tool was never invoked. Instead, the GMF runtime system loaded a `org.eclipse.gef.`
`NodeEditPart` class in the runtime class library of GEF framework. When such
an "import" statement in the customised class was removed, the GMF editor
loaded our class instead, which solved the problem. However, when we did the
same for the LinkEditPart class, the IDE automatically inserted the unwanted
"import" statement back into the code. Ultimately, we had to explicitly coerce
the class by casting the expression to the NodeEditPart class, prefixed with our
exact package name.

Figure 3 illustrates the "detached" requirement problem in details. First of all,
(a) is observed to behave like a Chopbox with respect to the connections to the
requirement node, this is highlighted as a "runtime abnormal behaviour". The
method implementing this behaviour is all in the generated code. The arrows
point backward along the chain of causality. First, the ChopboxAnchor was
used in the generated method body, which implements a default behaviour.
Furthermore, the parent class of the generated code is one of the predefined
classes in the GMF runtime class library. Without changing that inheritance,
the default behaviour cannot be overridden. Second, (b) is observed to behave
normally, such that the connection to the requirement nodes are not clipped
by the rectangle. The fixing changes required are (1) a customization of the
method default implementation to switch the anchor class to ellipse shape if the
node type is a requirement; (2) the generated import statements are removed
manually, such that the ShapeEditPart class in the domain-specific package is to
be used, overriding the default behaviour of the predefined GMF runtime class
library.

We were wondering why a generated class name such as NodeEditPart clashes
with the runtime library, only to realise that the MDSD tool itself had been
developed using the MDSD approach. Their choice of using "Node" to name a
class of nodes and using "Link" to name a class of links happened to be the same
as ours. In other words, the clash was due to our shared "common sense".

On second thought, this incident could have revealed an interesting type of
pitfall in MDSD, which we called "model feature interaction" [21]. The design
details abstracted away in the language specification could indeed be interacting
with the generated code because they refer to the same name in different names-
paces. The runtime class loader is not smart enough to distinguish them, and
a sophisticated mechanism is needed to prevent this from happening again. For
example, a developer may want to avoid using the names "Node/Link" when
modeling the graphical language. If this is the case, the alphabet of the namespace must be restricted, leading to the following discussions.

In general, when abstracting away design details, the advantages gained must
be revisited. First one needs to maintain the traceability between the abstract description and the concrete implementations, and second, one must be aware that
the designer of the MDSD tools could have introduced some alphabets that may
lead to unwanted behaviours when they are composed with the generated code.

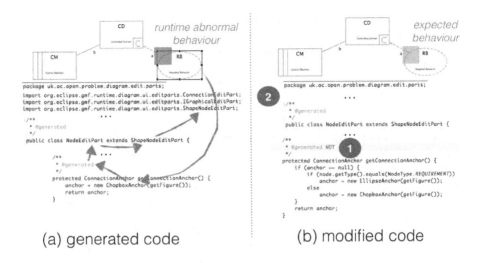

(a) generated code   (b) modified code

Fig. 3. Contrasting the observable problems and the code implementations respectively for the abnormal and correct behaviours

The developer's interpretations of the additional alphabet may not be the same as the original designer's. This might have a serious implication to security problems, adding further difficulty in maintaining and checking the traceability [27].

The Manual Refactoring Phenomena. The second major problem we encountered could be a headache to other developers too. As we discussed earlier, it was fine when MDSD tool were applied separately to PF and i* languages. Each application generates a separate EMF metamodel in Ecore (Ecore is a self-defining metamodel). The PF ecore model was newly "generated" from the concrete syntax in **xtext**, while the i* ecore model was imported from the existing release of OpenOME maintained at the University of Toronto. The generated classes for i* plugins were thereby prefixed by "edu.toronto.cs". The **xtext** tool could not know this, as a result of its code generation, no package prefix was added to the generated classes.

However, the combined metamodel needs to reference the i* classes in hundreds of places. For example, every time a problem node is accessed, it could refer to an i* model element specified in the none-prefixed classes. A subtle but annoying behaviour was caused by this because the generated classes without prefixes were the skeleton code that should work if no customisation had been applied. However, developers at the University of Toronto have made substantial improvements to almost every aspect in the graph editing tool. It is thereby necessary to switch to use the Toronto classes and keep their prefix. Instead of manually renaming all these places where the class names were referenced, we used automated refactoring for the name of generated plugin projects to reintroduce the missing prefix. After such refactorings, we still had to remove the refactored plugin projects such that at runtime the class loader would not get confused by the class paths to throw the ClassNotFound exceptions.

Automated refactoring on Eclipse project names using LTK could have been applied here [28], however, to accommodate every change in the PF language, one must specify which classes need to be renamed to which, and remember to manually change the references to the class names in the plugin specification too. Not a trivial task, without further customising the automated refactoring tool.

The Dependency Injection Phenomena. Instead of Aspect-Oriented Programming (AOP) [14], the designer of MDSD tool xtext uses the Dependency Injection pattern implemented by the Google Guice framework to inject functionalities at runtime. Similar to aspectJ, the new functionalities could be injected into the base system by specifying an adaptor class that uses the reflection mechanism of Java. Unlike aspectJ, the behaviour of the weaved system is somewhat controlled by the base system, in order to make the potential joinpoints explicit.

Ideally such technical details should be hidden from the developers who use MDSD because in principle one would not bother to know how it works if it works. However, one must be aware that the Guice framework assumes that the classes are singletons. If they share the same namespace, e.g., prefixed by the same package names while being located in different plugin projects scope, the dependency injection may still result in runtime conflicts.

As watchful observers for research problems, we were "lucky" enough to experience such a problem when developing the PF/i* integration tool. When we prefix our DSL language "Problem" and our adapted DSL language "Istar" with the same prefix "uk.ac.open", the generated code complained that the IDLink resolution class was not found even though it was present in the packages of the plugin component. After changing the prefix of one of these language into e.g., "uk.ac.open.problem", this conflict was resolved. A side effect was that we obtained a package named "uk.ac.open.problem.problem", in accordance with the particular naming convention adopted by the developer of the MDSD tool (i.e., xtext).

The Template-User Synchronisation Phenomena. When model and code co-evolve, they change concurrently. Since in MDSD, model and generated code are related by transformations, it is required to propagate changes from one end to the other.

To illustrate the problem, we use a constructed example here. Suppose an EMF user initially specifies a simple model that consists of one Entity class with a single name attribute. Using the code generation feature of EMF, she will obtain a *default* implementation which consists of 8 compilation units in Java (Fig. 4).

Fig. 5 lists parts of the generated code. The Entity Java interface has getter and setter methods for the name attribute. They are commented with @generated annotations which indicate that the methods are part of the default implementation. Similarly, such @generated annotations are added to every generated element in the code, e.g., shown in the skeleton of EntityImpl Java class.

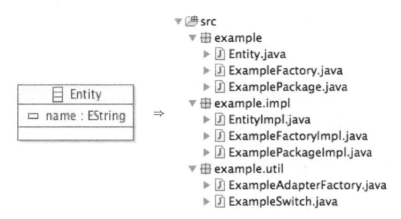

Fig. 4. Default code generated from the EMF meta-model

The annotation @generated defines a *single-trip traceability contract* from the model to the annotated code element. A change in the model or a change in the modelling framework can be propagated to the generated code; however, a change in the generated code will not cause a change to the reflected model and will thus be discarded upon next code generation.

As the default implementation is not always desired, the code generation shall keep user specified changes as long as they are not inside the range of generated traceability, the set of methods marked by @generated that keeps the changes of generated templates. This can be achieved by adapting the @generated annotation into @generated NOT, a non-binding traceability that reflects programmers' intention that it will not be changed when the implementation code is regenerated. Note that such non-binding traceability indicated by @generated NOT is still different from those without any annotation at all: Without such an annotation, EMF will generate new implementation of a method body following the templates.

This workaround does not work when a user parametrises the toString() method to append an additional **type** to the returned result. To guard the method from being overwritten by future code generations, the annotation @generated NOT is used. She also applies a *Rename Method* refactoring, changing the getName method into getID. The modified parts are shown in Fig. 6. Propagating these changes back to the model, the **name** attribute will be renamed into **iD** automatically, following the naming convention that attribute identifiers start with a lower case character.

Code regeneration results in the changes in Fig. 7: the setter methods and the implementations of both getter/setter methods are modified according to the default implementation of the new model. These are expected. However, two unexpected changes are not desirable. First, a compilation error results from the change in the default implementation, where the attribute **name** used in the user controlled code no longer exists. Second, the default implementation of the toString() method is generated with the original signature, which will of course

```
1  package example;
2  import org.eclipse.emf.ecore.EObject;
3  /** @model */
4  public interface Entity extends EObject {
5    /** @model */ public String getName();
6    /** @generated */ void setName(String value);
7  }
```

```
1  package example.impl;
2  import example.Entity;
3  ...
4  /** @generated */
5  public class EntityImpl extends EObjectImpl implements Entity {
6      ...
7      /** @generated */
8      protected String name = NAME_EDEFAULT;
9      ...
10     /** @generated */
11     public String getName() { return name; }
12     /** @generated */
13     public void setName(String newName) { ...    }
14     ...
15     /** @generated */
16     @Override
17     public String toString() {
18         if (eIsProxy()) return super.toString();
19         StringBuffer result = new StringBuffer(super.toString());
20         result.append(" (name: ");
21         result.append(name);
22         result.append(')');
23         return result.toString();
24     }
25 } // EntityImpl
```

Fig. 5. Parts of the generated code in Fig. 4

become dead code since the user has already modified all call sites of `toString()` to reflect the insertion of the new type. Similarly, the user specified `toString()` method can also become dead code, if it is no longer invoked by the new default implementation.

Compilation errors are relatively easy to spot by the programmer with the aid of the Eclipse IDE, but the dead code problems are more subtle because the IDE will not complain. Therefore, it will be more difficult for developers to notice the consequences.

In [25], we have developed a two-layered synchronisation framework, blinkit, to address this problem.

Figure 8 presents an overview of the framework when it is applied to the case study of EMF/GMF, where EMF is the synchronisation framework for vertical traceability and blinkit framework is the horizontal synchronisation counterpart. Examples in [25] indicate that when the complementary changes to templates and user-modified code are conflicting or redundant, our tool can avoid some dead code redundancies and raise some warnings as compilation errors.

So far we have enumerated, using the concrete example, several common MDSD phenomena at the development time. They are all related to the "alphabet mismatch" problem that reveals a gap between the understanding of a model developer and a model user. Since the model developer and user are guessing

```
1  /** @model */
2  public interface Entity extends EObject {
3    /** @model */ public String getNameID();
4    /** @generated */ public void setName();
5  }
6  ...
7  /** @generated */
8  public class EntityImpl extends EObjectImpl implements Entity {
9      /** @generated */
10     public String getNameID() { return name; }
11     ...
12     /** @generated NOT */
13     @Override
14     public String toString(String type) {
15         if (eIsProxy()) return super.toString();
16         StringBuffer result = new StringBuffer(super.toString());
17         result.append(" (name: ");
18         result.append(name);
19         result.append(')');
20         result.append(type);
21         return result.toString();
22     }
23  } //EntityImpl
```

⇓

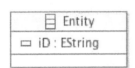

Fig. 6. User modifications to the generated code: insertions are underlined and the deletions are stroked out; the changes are reflected

each other's model in mind, ultimately only runtime reconcilation could resolve their differences.

3   Generalised Problem and Related Work

With the advent of self-adaptive systems, according to Baresi and Ghezzi [6], the boundary between development time and runtime is disappearing. What is typically regarded as development time activities in a MDSD process may now be regarded as runtime activities.

Using the examples presented so far, we identify three gaps in the current research on the runtime problem diagnosis.

Monitoring mismatching requirements. If one would be able to know requirements that are implemented by the default template code, as well as specific requirements customised by individual users, then it can be promising to add runtime monitors to places where the mismatches between the two sets of requirements happen at runtime. More generally, developers and users are often inconsistent in terms of their understanding of requirements. Related to this, Requirements Awareness [18] is a key issue. Without runtime awareness of the

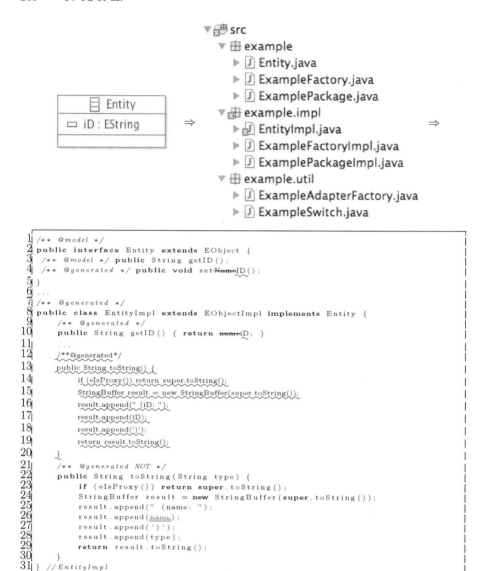

Fig. 7. Regenerated code from the model: insertions are ~~underlined~~ and the deletions are ~~stroked out~~, the compilation error is <u>doubly underlined</u>

requirements of individuals, it is harder for developers and users to agree on the current status of the system with respect to the requirements satisfaction.

In general, the MDSD process would require an additional step to regenerate the solution from the modified model. However, without explicit modeling of the generated code and the template code, it is not possible to automate every change through code generation. Due to the lazy binding of problems and solutions, at runtime such mismatches become even more severe. Current requirements

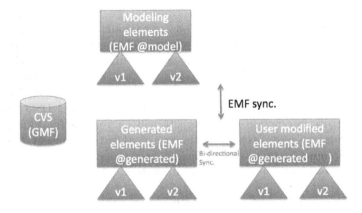

Fig. 8. An overview of the horizontal and vertical traceability links in the bidirectional invariant traceability framework: `blinkit`. V1 and V2 are two revisions of model, template or user codes extracted from the CVS repository of a software development project using EMF code generation.

conflict detection techniques require both models to have similar structures (e.g., mergeable) [15]. If the two models do not have similar structures, the question is how to model them so that they are still verifiable. Another research question is of course to have an explicit encoding of requirements in the templates to prepare for such verifications.

Recently, Akiki et al. [3] proposed the use of interpreted runtime models instead of static models or generative runtime models. Although it is limited in the GUI domain, the proposed solution seems to be promising to bring adaptivity to the runtime systems. A prototype and architecture to support adaptive UI has been developed and demonstrated [4] for adaptive UI of enterprise software applications through service-oriented adaptations.

Runtime traceability. Unlike the use of traceability at development time, runtime traceability of MDSD systems has to listen to the chain of events at the runtime. One example of such mechanisms is the event handler in Java runtime virtual machines. By cascading the listeners to the events, the call traces at the point of failure can give the user a clue about the fault location. However, such a mechanism require developers to be cooperative: explicit exceptions must be thrown or caught in the try-catch blocks. Otherwise, it could be too late to tell where the exception were generated in the first place.

Several machine learning approaches have been proposed to address this issue, for example, by studying the historical events in stack traces [11]. However, runtime traceability requires responsive reactions on the mismatching template and user code which is still not well understood. Earlier work on monitoring and diagnosing software requirements may be helpful to make use of the goal models as a priori knowledge to diagnose problems in the event traces [23]. The challenges we are facing here is that the MDSD processes use more complicated models than goal refinements.

Model interactions problems. As we described earlier, MDSD is a complicated process which may involve more than one metamodel. The "Tao" is to have a megamodel to unify the different metamodel code generation processes [9]. However, different metamodels may be created by different people and thereby inherently embed interaction *bombs* between the tacit knowledge. They are not necessarily compatible to each other, yet may not be notified by the developers and users at the runtime. A mechanism to protect the different MDSD generated code from feature interaction problems [20] will be very useful. One possible direction of research is to investigate the use of AOP technique to detect and resolve undesired interactions between models at runtime. For instance, dynamic aspect weaving techniques provide a mechanism to inject code to resolve runtime conflicts between models.

Recently, Bencome et al. [7] proposed a framework to support on-the-fly inter-operability at runtime by generating emergent middleware that can synthesise multiple runtime behaviour models in labelled transition systems. In order to avoid feature interactions at runtime, uncertainty handling is still regarded as one of the future work. Tun et al [19] addressed the runtime feature interaction problem by encoding the composition frames using the Event Calculus and re-solving the conflicts through a composition controller. However, identifying the composition requirement remains a challenge.

4   Problems Diagnosis at Runtime

This section generalises these runtime concerns into a runtime diagnosis proce-dure which may become a key component of a self-adaptive problem analysis framework.

On basis of our earlier work on runtime adaptive model interpretation middle-ware [3, 4], runtime requirements failure diagnoses [19, 23], and invariant trace-ability [25], we propose a new framework in Figure 9 to consider tacit knowledge for runtime problem diagnosis (PD@runtime). Various sources of information are brought to the attention at the runtime, these include the template development hidden from the users, and the assumptions about the environment hidden from the developers.

The information monitored at runtime includes a context model about the environment [5] and a self-awareness model about the working of the system. A mismatch between the system implementation and the environment expectation is regarded as a system failure or error. To determine what to be included in the system model, at least two kinds of models owned by different stakeholders need to be considered. Generalising from the MDSD process, the template system model captures the knowledge of a developer, whilst the user system model captures the knowledge or at least the perception of a user. Both template and user system models need to be monitored to tell whether any change could lead to a mismatch between the requirements in the way they are understood by the stakeholder. Given that both models are complex, it is usually hard to let either the developer or the user to construct them alone. Instead, the

PD@runtime framework uses a procedure to filter out the changes that can be handled by the underlying automated fixing mechanisms (such as compilers and bidirectional model-transformations [25], such that only information relevant to the requirements mismatch will be passed on to the human stakeholders. Overall, the requirements awareness problem can be defined as the combination of the awareness of system failure and the awareness of the requirements mismatch among stakeholders.

4.1 Meaningful Changes Detection and Propagation

While the template and user models co-evolve, a systematic approach is required to propagate the changes from one end to the other. Earlier we have developed the meaningful change detection tools for identifying changes that are meaningful to different stakeholders [29], as well as the bidirectional transformation framework to propagate the meaningful changes between the template code and the user modifications [25]. The meaningful change detection tool can detect any mismatch between two normalised structures, which covers typically all models that can be described by a computer language. Although the tool is powerful, it requires guidance [26] to learn what kind of information is regarded as meaningful from large datasets. Presumably what is meaningful for one stakeholder may not be meaningful to another. Therefore, we have started a new research agenda to refine the viewpoints of different stakeholders into concrete rules in order to judge the relevance to the other stakeholders.

Once the relevant and meaningful information is defined, the tool generates predefined runtime monitors which can already collect information in such a way that when the abnormal execution traces are obtained, one can trace backwards to track the location of faults. If the faults involve any wrong trust assumption about the environmental contexts, an appropriate adaptation alternative will be switched to at runtime [16,17].

4.2 Feedback Loops

Debugging programs written in a high-level programming language typically requires traceability between the location where error is spotted and the corresponding location in the source code. Because compiler translations add a layer of indirection, if the optimisation option such as -O has been turned on, diagnosing runtime errors become much harder. Programmers would typically *trust* that the optimising transformations do not change the execution behaviour, while debugging the machine code with as few optimizations as possible, e.g., facilitated by the option -g. Since MDSD is motivated by the success of compilers, and the models are at a higher level of abstraction than the high-level programming languages, trust needs to be established by a solid understanding of what to diagnose and where to fix problems. However, the template code that addresses most users' requirements may not be exactly what the individual user wanted. Therefore, whenever such diagnoses trace back into the template code, the problem gets even more difficult.

Since boundary between development-time and runtime is disappearing, the distinction between adaptation and evolution in such systems is also getting blurred. Depending on whether requirements change at runtime, one may separate evolution from adaptation. Yet, the blurring boundary in practice makes it necessary to address MDSD concerns at runtime too. Runtime self-adaptive systems require some form of feedback loops, e.g., using the PID controller [8], to be able to react to quality requirements changes accordingly. It is our hope that the tacit knowledge concern of MDSD can be addressed such that one can also apply the feedback loop mechanisms to the runtime MDSD problems.

Data: E: environment context model, S_D, S_U: developer's and user's system models, $\mu(\Delta)$: meaningful change, $\not\cong$: mismatching judgment, T: system execution traces, C: program code

Result: Traces

while *true* **do**

$\quad (\Delta E, \Delta S, \Delta T, \Delta C) = (E' - E, S' - S, T' - T, C' - C);$

$\quad \mu(\Delta E, \Delta S, \Delta T, \Delta C) = (\mu \Delta E, \mu \Delta S, \mu \Delta T, \mu \Delta C);$

$\quad$ **if** $\mu \Delta T \not\cong \mu \Delta C$ **then**

$\quad\quad$ program_fixed = Abnormal trace fault location and fixing;

$\quad\quad$ **if** *! program_fixed* $\wedge \mu \Delta S \not\cong \Delta E$ **then**

$\quad\quad\quad$ failure_fixed = System failure detected and fixing;

$\quad\quad\quad$ **if** *! failure_fixed* $\wedge \mu \Delta S_D \not\cong \Delta S_U$ **then**

$\quad\quad\quad\quad$ bidirection_transformation = Reconcile requirements mismatch;

$\quad\quad\quad\quad$ **if** *! bidirection_transformation* **then**

$\quad\quad\quad\quad\quad$ inform developer and user about the problem;

$\quad\quad\quad\quad\quad$ $(S'_D, S'_U) = update(S'_D, S'_D);$

$\quad\quad\quad\quad$ **end**

$\quad\quad\quad$ **else if** *bidirectional_transformed* **then**

$\quad\quad\quad\quad$ $(S'_D, S'_U) = bidirectional\_transformed(S'_D, S'_D);$

$\quad\quad\quad$ **end**

$\quad\quad$ **end**

$\quad\quad$ **else if** *failure_fixed* **then**

$\quad\quad\quad$ $(E', S') = failure_fixed(E', S');$

$\quad\quad$ **end**

$\quad$ **end**

$\quad$ **else if** *program_fixed* **then**

$\quad\quad$ $(T', C') = program_fixed(T', C');$

$\quad$ **end**

end

$\quad (E, S, T, C) = (E', S', T', C');$

end

Algorithm 1. An illustration of the PD@runtime procedure

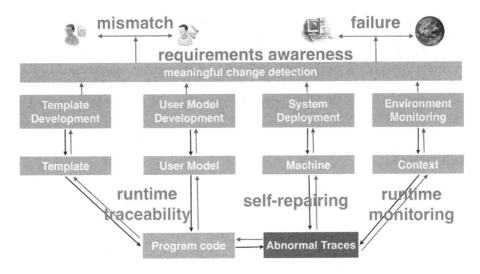

Fig. 9. PD@runtime: tracing the causal chain of events backwards for runtime problem diagnosis for MDSD processes

The following pseudo code describes and summarises the framework into a problem diagnosis at runtime procedure. As one can see, a large part of the procedure can be automated (self-repairing), while some steps still require human on top of the feedback loop to control the overall diagnosis direction.

5   Conclusion

Following the MDSD process blindly at runtime will create more problems in the development than it solves. In summary to the three reported problems, we propose an *additional alphabet* or *tacit knowledge* concern to the MDSD process. The concern can be expressed as follows: "When the MDSD process generates code with additional alphabet introduced (in the form of plugin names, package names, class names, or method names), one must ensure these names are not conflicting with the names (unwittingly) introduced by the developer of the modeling language". To avoid such problems at runtime, it is required to have additional tools to check any violation of the concern.

A more general problem of requirements awareness is derived from the problems we identified from the MDSD process. To tackle it, we show a systematic procedure that uses meaningful changes detection to differentiate the changes in environment contexts (execution traces) and in program implementations (of developer and of user), or in more abstract terms, the mismatches between models of different stakeholders. The procedures is controlled by a feedback loop where automatic fixes are employed with compiler and bidirectional transformations. However, when the automatic fixes are not available, human must be informed to handle the more difficult cases.

Acknowledgement. This work is supported by the ERC Advanced Grant no. 291652 "ASAP: Adaptive Security and Privacy" (2012-2017) - http://www.asap-project.eu. We thank our colleague Michael Jackson for useful discussions on earlier drafts. Most of the work could not have be done without easy-to-use MDSD tools. We have also benefited from fruitful discussions with Jan Koehnlein and anonymous developers through open-source fora (e.g., https://bugs.eclipse.org/bugs/show_bug.cgi? id=326220).

References

1. 15th IEEE International Requirements Engineering Conference, RE 2007, New Delhi, India, October 15-19. IEEE (2007)
2. Aho, A.V., Lam, M.S., Sethi, R., Ullman, J.D.: Compilers: Principles, Techniques, and Tools. Prentice Hall, 2 edn. (August 2006)
3. Akiki, P.A., Bandara, A.K., Yu, Y.: Using interpreted runtime models for devising adaptive user interfaces of enterprise applications. In: Maciaszek, L.A., Cuzzocrea, A., Cordeiro, J. (eds.) ICEIS (3), pp. 72–77. SciTePress (2012)
4. Akiki, P.A., Bandara, A.K., Yu, Y.: RBUIS: Simplifying enterprise application user interfaces through engineering role-based adaptive behaviour. In: The 5th ACM SIGCHI Symposium on Engineering Interactive Computing Systems, EICS 2013, pp. 3–17 (2013)
5. Ali, R., Dalpiaz, F., Giorgini, P.: A goal-based framework for contextual requirements modeling and analysis. Requir. Eng. 15(4), 439–458 (2010)
6. Baresi, L., Ghezzi, C.: The disappearing boundary between development-time and run-time. In: Proceedings of the FSE/SDP Workshop on Future of Software Engineering Research FoSER 2010, pp. 17–22. ACM, New York (2010), http://doi.acm.org/10.1145/1882362.1882367
7. Bencomo, N., Bennaceur, A., Grace, P., Blair, G.S., Issarny, V.: The role of models@run.time in supporting on-the-fly interoperability. Computing 95(3), 167–190 (2013)
8. Chen, B., Peng, X., Yu, Y., Zhao, W.: Are your sites down? requirements-driven self-tuning for the survivability of web systems. In: RE, pp. 219–228. IEEE (2011)
9. Djuric, D., Gasevic, D., Devedzic, V.: The tao of modeling spaces. Journal of Object Technology 5(8), 125–147 (2006)
10. Hailpern, B., Tarr, P.: Model-driven development: The good, the bad, and the ugly. IBM Systems Journal 45(3), 451–461 (2006)
11. Han, S., Dang, Y., Ge, S., Zhang, D., Xie, T.: Performance debugging in the large via mining millions of stack traces. In: Proc. 34th International Conference on Software Engineering (ICSE 2012), http://www.csc.ncsu.edu/faculty/xie/publications/icse12-stackmine.pdf (June 2012)
12. Jackson, M.: Problem Frames: Analyzing and structuring software development problems. Addison Wesley (2001)
13. Jackson, M.: Some notes on models and modelling. In: Borgida, A.T., Chaudhri, V.K., Giorgini, P., Yu, E.S. (eds.) Mylopoulos Festschrift. LNCS, vol. 5600, pp. 68–81. Springer, Heidelberg (2009)
14. Kiczales, G.: Aspect-oriented programming. ACM Comput. Surv. 28(4es), 154 (1996)

15. Sabetzadeh, M., Nejati, S., Liaskos, S., Easterbrook, S.M., Chechik, M.: Consistency checking of conceptual models via model merging. In: RE [1], pp. 221–230
16. Salifu, M., Yu, Y., Bandara, A.K., Nuseibeh, B.: Analysing monitoring and switching problems for adaptive systems. Journal of Systems and Software 85(12), 2829–2839 (2012)
17. Salifu, M., Yu, Y., Nuseibeh, B.: Specifying monitoring and switching problems in context. In: RE [1], pp. 211–220
18. Souza, V.E.S., Lapouchnian, A., Robinson, W.N., Mylopoulos, J.: Awareness requirements for adaptive systems. In: Giese, H., Cheng, B.H.C. (eds.) SEAMS, pp. 60–69. ACM (2011)
19. Tun, T., Laney, R., Yu, Y., Nuseibeh, B.: Specifying software features for composition: A tool-supported approach. Computer Networks 57(12), 2454–2464 (2013), http://oro.open.ac.uk/37468/
20. Tun, T.T., Trew, T., Jackson, M., Laney, R.C., Nuseibeh, B.: Specifying features of an evolving software system. Softw. Pract. Exper. 39(11), 973–1002 (2009)
21. Tun, T.T., Yu, Y., Laney, R., Nuseibeh, B.: Early identification of problem interactions: A tool-supported approach. In: Glinz, M., Heymans, P. (eds.) REFSQ 2009. LNCS, vol. 5512, pp. 74–88. Springer, Heidelberg (2009)
22. Turing, A.M.: Computability and lambda-definability. J. Symb. Log. 2(4), 153–163 (1937)
23. Wang, Y., McIlraith, S.A., Yu, Y., Mylopoulos, J.: Monitoring and diagnosing software requirements. Autom. Softw. Eng. 16(1), 3–35 (2009)
24. Yu, E.: Modelling strategic relationships for process reengineering. University of Toronto Toronto, Ont., Canada (1995)
25. Yu, Y., Lin, Y., Hu, Z., Hidaka, S., Kato, H., Montrieux, L.: Maintaining invariant traceability through bidirectional transformations. In: Proc. 34th International Conference on Software Engineering (ICSE 2012). ACM/IEEE, Zurich (June 2012)
26. Yu, Y., Bandara, A., Tun, T.T., Nuseibeh, B.: Towards learning to detect meaningful changes in software. In: Proceedings of the International Workshop on Machine Learning Technologies in Software Engineering, MALETS 2011, pp. 51–54. ACM, New York (2011), http://doi.acm.org/10.1145/2070821.2070828
27. Yu, Y., Jürjens, J., Mylopoulos, J.: Traceability for the maintenance of secure software. In: ICSM, pp. 297–306. IEEE (2008)
28. Yu, Y., Jürjens, J., Schreck, J.: Tools for traceability in secure software development. In: ASE, pp. 503–504. IEEE (2008)
29. Yu, Y., Tun, T.T., Nuseibeh, B.: Specifying and detecting meaningful changes in programs. In: 26th IEEE/ACM International Conference on Automated Software Engineering, pp. 273–282 (November 2011), http://oro.open.ac.uk/29450/

Research Challenges for Business Process Models at Run-Time

David Redlich[1,2], Gordon Blair[2], Awais Rashid[2], Thomas Molka[1,3], and Wasif Gilani[1]

[1] SAP Research Center Belfast, United Kingdom
{david.redlich,thomas.molka,wasif.gilani}@sap.com
[2] Lancaster University, United Kingdom
{gordon,marash}@comp.lancs.ac.uk
[3] University of Manchester, United Kingdom

Abstract. Today's fast and competitive markets require businesses to react faster to changes in its environment, and sometimes even before the changes actually happen. Changes can occur on almost every level, e.g. change in demand of customers, change of law, or change of the corporate strategy. Not adapting to these changes can result in financial and legal consequences for any business organisation. IT-controlled business processes are essential parts of modern organisations which motivates why business processes are required to efficiently adapt to these changes in a quick and flexible way. This requirement suggests a more dynamic handling of business processes and their models, moving from design-time business process models to run-time business process models. One general approach to address this problem is provided by the community of *models@run.time*, in which models reflect the system's current state at any point in time and allow immediate reasoning and adaptation mechanisms. This paper examines the potential role of business process models at run-time by: (1) discussing the state-of the art of both, business process modelling and models@run.time, (2) reflecting on the nature of business processes at run-time, and (3) most importantly, highlighting key research challenges that need addressing to make this step.

Keywords: run-time models, business process models, business process management, adaptive systems, business process optimisation.

1 Motivation

Business processes and business process models play a central role in modern businesses. In the early years of computer-aided management of business processes it was assumed that business processes do not change frequently during their execution. While this might be true for static processes, e.g. at the strategic level, less rigid processes, mostly found on the operational level, can be the subject of frequent changes. Processes of the latter type might need to adapt to dynamic changes [44] in environment (e.g., lack of available resources) or in flow

N. Bencomo et al. (Eds.): Models@run.time, LNCS 8378, pp. 208–236, 2014.

of work (e.g. introduction of a new activity). In fact, today's businesses have to act in a highly competitive environment which comes with strict requirements with regards to fast adaptations and optimisation. If changes in the environment happen a business has to act accordingly and potentially also adapt their core business processes to stay competitive or even outmatch their competitors. One example is a hospital, in which, based on the qualifications of the current staff and demand of the patients, the treatment process has to be adapted in case of a sudden virus outbreak. Another example is the dynamic field of security, almost daily new threats arise and an organisation has to be prepared in order to protect its confidential assets.

As business processes are ultimately driving today's modern organisations they are likely to change and adapt at increasing speed. A late action can result in a Service Level Agreement (SLA) violation, leading to financial and legal consequences. To prevent this from happening businesses have to deal with the following two general challenges[1]:

- **Need to adapt to changing demands:** A business organisation and its processes have to be flexible and continuously adapt to changing demands exposed to by internal or external sources. Adaptations need to be accurate and reliable in order to actually improve the current situation.
- **Need to shorten the business process life cycle:** The process of designing, configuring, deploying, and analysing a business process [54] should become further simplified, i.e. more automated.

Hence, a more dynamic handling of business processes is desirable, moving from design-time business process models to run-time business process models. One approach to address this problem is provided by the community of models@run.time, in which models reflect the system's current status at any point in time and allow immediate reasoning and adaption mechanisms. This paper is a first attempt to raise the abstraction level of models@run.time to the domain of business processes. This will, for one, contribute to research in models@run.time by providing a valid use-case as well as further requirements for models@run.time of a high abstraction level and, secondly, help to address the general challenges of business adaptation and automation.

The remainder of this paper is structured as follows: In Section 2 background information of the business process management domain necessary for the understanding of this paper is summarised. In Section 3 the state of the art with regards to the topic of business process models at run-time and the general challenges identified earlier is reviewed: business process modelling standards, business process adaptation, and models at run-time. Section 4 presents the three main research challenges that arise from raising the abstraction level of run-time models to the domain of business processes. These challenges are then individually discussed in the following three sections, each challenge comprising related work and first findings. We conclude with a summary and outlook in Section 8.

---

[1] These two relevant challenges have been extracted from a set of challenges for modern businesses identified by Simchi-Levi et al. in [52].

2   Background: Business Process Management

Processes accompany every human venture, from simply booking a holiday to manufacturing a car. In a similar way a business organisation is driven by its so-called "business processes": In order to achieve an organisation's objectives, tasks are usually carried out in certain ways, i.e. workflows are defined to express activities, the associated roles to perform them, and their order of execution. In [17] business processes are defined as *"...a series or network of value-added activities, performed by their relevant roles or collaborators, to purposefully achieve the common business goal."* Prominent examples of business processes are Order-to-Cash, Accounts Receivable, or Procure-to-Pay. Because of their central role in a business organisation they are considered to be *"...the most valuable corporate asset"* [1].

In order to deal with increasing complexity and respond to the arising importance of business processes, Information Technology (IT) was harnessed to manage business processes. This development lead to the rise of Business Process Management (BPM), as an IT-related discipline. In fact, BPM is a cross-discipline subject of "theory in practice" adopting a variety of paradigms and methodologies from computer science, management theory, philosophy, mathematics, and linguistic, just to name a few [17]. Perhaps because of its cross-disciplinary nature, even after a history of three decades, there are many duplicate, and contradictory publications trying to clarify definition and scope of basic BPM terminology [17], e.g. business process vs. workflow, BPM vs. Workflow Management (WfM) vs. Business Process Reengineering (BPR).

However, *Business Process Management* (BPM) is considered to be the next step after the workflow wave of the nineties [54]. Therefore, it is appropriate to use workflow terminology to define BPM. A *Workflow Management System* (WfMS) is defined as: *"A system that defines, creates and manages the execution of workflows through the use of software, running on one or more workflow engines, which is able to interpret the process definition, interact with workflow participants and, where required, invoke the use of IT tools and applications."* [19]. Based on that BPM is defined as follows: *"Supporting business processes using methods, techniques, and software to design, enact, control, and analyze operational processes involving humans, organizations, applications, documents, and other sources of information."* [54]. Software systems that support the management of operational business processes are called Business Process Management Systems or Business Process Management Suites (BPMS's) [18]. Although many other definitions of BPM exist, they are in most cases wrapped around *Workflow Management*(WfM).

In BPM a *process type* is a particular type of process with a defined business goal, e.g. Order-to-Cash. A process type is represented by a particular *process schema* which is captured in a *business process model* specifying business process aspects like activities, ordering, resources. A process type may be represented by more than one process schema expressing different versions or evolution steps of this type. Furthermore, a *process instance* is defined as a particular occurrence of the business process, i.e. a particular sequence of executed activities in order to process a *work item.*

Part of the complete BPM definition is the BPM lifecycle. Here that of prominent BPM researcher van der Aalst et al. is adopted. It originates from the standard development life cycle and consists of 4 stages (see Figure 1) [54]:

1. **Process Design** - In this stage, business processes are modelled for the BPMS.
2. **System Configuration** - This stage configures the BPMS and the underlying system infrastructure (e.g., synchronisation of roles).
3. **Process Enactment** - The modelled business processes are deployed and executed in a BPMS.
4. **Diagnosis** - With analysis and monitoring tools, the BPM analyst can identify bottlenecks and improve the business processes.

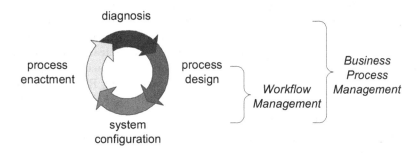

Fig. 1. BPM life cycle: Workflow Management vs. Business Process Management [54]

The viewpoint of Aalst et al. is that WfM covers only process design, system configuration, and process enactment, but BPM also includes the diagnosis phase to complete the BPM lifecycle [54]. This viewpoint makes WfM a logical subset of BPM. According to [17] "*...many BPMS are still very much workflow management systems (WfMS) and have not yet matured in the support of the BPM diagnosis.*" However, recently the diagnosis phase started to gain more attention which is reflected in the high number of publications in the sub-topics of Business Process Analysis (BPA) and Business Activity Monitoring (BAM).

A more industry-based viewpoint on BPM and WfM is provided by Gartner [14]: "*Business process management (BPM) is a process-oriented management discipline. It is not a technology. Workflow is a flow management technology found in business process management suites (BPMSs) and other product categories.*" Here BPM is a management discipline which is supported by WfM as a technology.

To put BPM terminology into one coherent picture, understanding the nested relationship of BPM theory (e.g., Pi Calculus [24] and Petri Nets [36]), BPM standards (e.g., Business Process Model and Notation (BPMN) [31] or Business Process Execution Language (BPEL) [28]), and BPM systems (e.g. SAP Netweaver BPM [64] or Intalio BPMS Designer [15]) is of essence: BPM standards are based on established BPM theory and eventually adopted into software, i.e. BPMSs [18].

3   State of the Art

To address the topic of business process models at run-time and its associated general challenges (see Section 1), in the following sections state of the art is surveyed for the topics: (1) business process modelling standards, (2) business process adaptation, and (3) general models at run-time.

3.1   Business Process Modelling Standards

The previously mentioned challenges are part of a set of general challenges that are meant to be addressed by BPM standards. At the moment there are more than 10 formal groups creating BPM standards [66], many of them dedicated to definitions for business process modelling [13]. In order to get an overview about the state of the art for business process modelling standards it makes sense to categorise them into groups with similar functions and characteristics [18]. Many of the standards address at least one of the phases of the BPM life cycle. For this reason Ko et al. suggest a separation of features found in existing standards into four different types of standards [18]:

1. **Graphical Standards** allow users to express information flow, decision points, and roles for business processes in a diagrammatic way. Standards of this type correspond to the design phase of the BPM life cycle and are usually the easiest to understand, i.e. most human-readable. Prominent examples of graphical standards are Business Process Model and Notation (BPMN) [31], Event-driven Process Chains (EPC) [48], and activity diagrams of Unified Modelling Language (UML) [33].
2. **Execution Standards** are code-like and enable business processes to be deployed in a BPMS. Standards of this type correspond to the enactment phase of the BPM lifecycle. The most prominent example is Business Process Execution Language (BPEL) (sometimes also called Web Service Business Execution Language (WS-BPEL)) [28].
3. **Interchange Standards** are used to translate graphical standards to execution standards and exchange business process models between BPMS's [23]. One of the reasons these standards became necessary was the fragmented BPM landscape. Two prominent examples of interchange standards exist: Business Process Definition Metamodel (BPDM) [32] and XML Process Definition Language (XPDL) [65].
4. **Diagnosis Standards** provide monitoring capabilities. These standards are to support audit trails, real-time business process information, trend analysis, bottleneck identification, etc. Examples are initiatives of Object Management Group: Business Process Runtime Interface (BPRI) [30] and Business

Process Query Language (BPQL) [29]. Though, both of the projects failed to produce a standard (yet).

Most of the existing standards dealing with modelling languages can be assigned to one of these types. Of course, this a simplified view and there exist some exceptions which can be assigned to more than just one, e.g. Yet Another Workflow Language (YAWL) [57] can be regarded as graphical and execution standard, or BPEL which can have a graphical representation, too.

Many standards already exist (perhaps too many) which address specific phases of the BPM life cycle. However, important is the relation to the system with regards to their time of validity. In practice, two types of business process models with regards to their time of validity could be identified (see Figure 2):

- **A-priori model** - Business process models at design-time: In this case business processes are documented *before* execution to define the execution of workflows in an organisation. This is either done informally via a document listing and describing the steps and their execution order or they are modelled via design-time languages. The most prominent business process model languages were developed to build design-time models, and focus on aspects like interoperability, or being a basis for reliable communication between different stakeholders [8]. Basically, every language that addresses the enactment phase or one of the preceding is considered a-priori model, e.g. BPMN or BPEL.

- **A-posteriori model** - In practice business process models are often extracted *after* execution to reflect the real execution of a process as part of the diagnosis phase of the BPM life cycle. This static a-posteriori analysis of business processes based on event logs is called process mining [59] or in the case of a performance analysis during run-time Business Activity Monitoring (BAM). A-posteriori models in the sense of process mining usually conform to languages of BPM theory, e.g. Petri-Nets [56]. In the case of recent BAM solutions, special modelling languages that address run-time challenges of the diagnosis phase, e.g. need for notification when detecting alarming behaviour, are common. One example for such a modelling language is presented by Friedenstab et al. [10]: it proposes an extension for

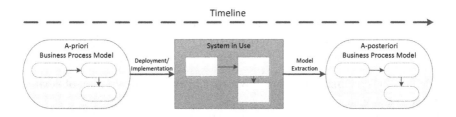

Fig. 2. Common Kinds of Business Process Models

BPMN to express process performance metrics. Both approaches, model extraction via BAM or via process mining, are considered run-time analyses in [59].

At the moment there is a shift towards a process diagnosis at run-time noticeable which is reflected in an increasing number of publications detailing approaches about how to make modelling of BAM more automated or even part of the business process modelling, e.g. [10,34,63,26,21]. In some cases even simple business process adaptation due to the monitoring results can be modelled. However, all of these approaches have limitations, one of which is that they are very much restricted to the purpose of traditional BAM: monitoring of Process Performance Indicators (PPIs) and Key Performance Indicators (KPIs) which are duration or frequency measures or aggregations of them.

3.2   Business Process Adaptation

Business processes need to be able to adapt to dynamic changes [44] in environment, e.g. because of a lack of available resources, or in flow of work, e.g. introduction of a new step. For instance, in domains like health care, Customer Relationship Management (CRM), or customised product manufacturing are process adaptations necessary or desirable to address changing demands.

In recent literature two different types of adaptation to dynamic changes could be identified: (1) *build-time flexibility*, i.e. the ability to pre-model flexible execution behaviour, and (2) *run-time flexibility*, i.e. in which an adaptation at run-time in the sense of exception handling or process evolution is carried out. In both cases the challenge is to balance flexibility and control [46].

Build-time flexibility is about leaving parts of the business process unspecified at design-time, i.e. the flexibility is modelled into the business process, and the missing information is added at run-time according to pre-specified constraints or rules. Different approaches to achieve this type of flexibility are by applying either general declarative processes [60,35], advanced modelling [53] or late-binding [46]. Pioneers of the more prominent latter approach are Sadiq et al. who introduced so called "pockets of flexibility" for workflow specifications [46]. The introduced workflow specification consists of [45]:

- core process consisting of pre-defined activities,
- pockets of flexibility within the process which in turn consist of
  - set of process elements, which can be a single activity or a sub-process,
  - set of constraints for concretising the pocket with a valid composition of process elements.

The definition is recursive and thus supports a hierarchical definition of flexibility pockets.

The other type of handling dynamic change: run-time flexibility, is about permanently or temporarily adapting the business process model at run-time. Permanent adaptation in the sense of process evolution is carried out by process schema changes on the process type level and supported by adaptive process languages [40]. Temporary adaptations in the sense of ad-hoc changes is carried out on the process instance level and supported by exception- or case-handling [58].

For both types of flexibility, run-time and build-time, 18 change patterns[2] have been identified in [62] to facilitate formal validation for different adaptation approaches. The identified change patterns comprise a set of common process changes that could be applied to a business process. Though, all changes should be generally supported not all of them leave the business process after application in a valid state, e.g. removal of an activity can lead to a run-time error due to missing data. Hence, a number of changes is usually applied simultaneously, which emphasises the important challenge of change validation in the area of process adaptation, which is discussed in further detail in Section 6.2.

So far research in the area of process adaptation mostly focuses on the challenges of *how* adaptations can be carried out (modification policies) and *which* adaptations can be carried out (validation), but not so much on the challenge of *what* adaptation *should* be carried out (optimisation). The common constraint-based reasoning approaches with distinct adaptation solutions are limited with regards to the optimisation potential of business processes. A first practical approach which addresses automated process optimisation can be found in [49] where a business process optimisation loop including simulation as a mean for performance parameter computation and process adaptation is proposed. In this solution a simulation engine is included into the monitoring process with the help of which optimal solutions for a process change are determined. The business process is automatically adapted according to the suggestion. Although an evaluation has been carried out it seems that this work is still in a proof of concept stage as important definitions, e.g. for modification policies which are further discussed in Section 6.2, are missing.

3.3 Generalising Models at Run-Time

In Model-Driven Engineering (MDE), models are abstractions or reduced representations of a system. The combination of principles from MDE and reflective systems build the foundations of models@run.time. Here, models reflect the system's current status at *any* point in time as opposed to differentiate between a-priori and a-posteriori models. More specifically, a model at runtime (M@RT) *"... is a causal connected self-representation of the associated system that emphasises the structure, behaviour, or goals of the system from a problem space perspective"* [2]. Run-time models are used in different domains and serve different purposes, i.e. are problem oriented. Depending on the model's purpose is its properties. Still, similarities can be found that are more or less existent in most of the run-time models.

One approach of classifying model elements of M@RT is presented in [4] in which an analysis of model dynamics and executability has been carried out.

---

[2] 14 for run-time flexibility and 4 for build-time flexibility.

Therein the following classification of elements of *executable* run-time models has been identified:

- Definition part: the static part of the model which is defined at design-time
- Situation part: describing the dynamic state of a system during execution
- Execution part: specifying the transitions from one state to another

Because of the classification's focus on executable models it does not fully apply to *general* run-time models [20], i.e. not every run-time model is an executable model: E.g. run-time models with the purpose of monitoring do not necessarily have to have a definition part; some are built completely at run-time (e.g. by data mining algorithms). The inapplicability for general run-time models of this element classification motivated Lehmann et al. [20] to focus on classifying run-time model elements based on the causal connections of the model. The causal connections in a M@RT are either of a descriptive or prescriptive nature [51]:

- A model is descriptive if all statements made in the model are true for the System Under Study (SUS), i.e. every relevant change of the system is captured in the descriptive part of a run-time model.
- A specific SUS is considered valid relative to a prescriptive model if no statement in the model is false for the SUS, i.e. the space of possible system states is defined by the prescriptive part of a run-time model.

In general, the specification ratios of descriptive and prescriptive parts in a run-time model differ dependent on its purpose. That is, a M@RT that focuses, for instance, on monitoring has a strong focus on descriptive parts (e.g. [47]) and a M@RT that focuses on executability has a dominating prescriptive role (e.g. [27]). In addition to the prescriptive and descriptive parts of the model, Lehmann at. al identified that valid model modifications for both, descriptive and prescriptive, and the actual information flow of the causal connection are part of a general run-time model, too. The resulting classification to define elements of meta-models for general run-time models is the following [20]:

- prescriptive part - how the model should be
- descriptive part - state of the SUS at run-time
- valid modifications of descriptive part during run-time
- valid modifications of prescriptive part during run-time
- causal connections - modelling the information flow between the model and its SUS

The classification of elements for run-time models by Lehmann et al. [20] is shown in an example in Figure 3. Assuming there is only a finite number of states the system can be in then the prescriptive part would reflect all these states and the descriptive part would consist of the single state the system is in at the moment. The valid modifications of the descriptive part would determine the transition from one state to another, it represents the execution logic of the system. Additionally, through the notion of modifications of the prescriptive part the run-time model would be available from within the run-time model itself,

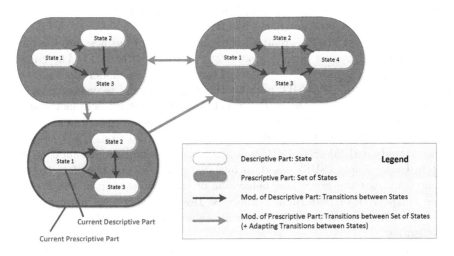

Fig. 3. Descriptive vs. Prescriptive Parts

i.e. be self-representative. Models that have the properties of self-representation and causal connection are called reflective [7]. However, per definition a run-time model does not necessarily has to have the property of self-representation, e.g. monitoring models are causally connected to the system sufficient for their purpose without having the ability to change the system. Plus, as pointed out earlier, the ratio of prescriptive and descriptive parts are dependent on the purpose of the model: For instance, prescriptive parts of a monitoring M@RT can be descriptive in a M@RT for dynamic adaptation.

However, there is one general issue that makes this classification only partly suitable for a general M@RT: The classification captures the self-representation property only partly because valid modifications for the descriptive parts should be able to change at run-time as well in order to support full self-representation. Assuming we are adding a state to the prescriptive part of the model, we would also have to define transitions describing how to reach this state (see Figure 3), i.e. add valid modifications of the descriptive part. We argue that the logical adaptation of the classification to overcome this issue is to declare the valid modifications of the descriptive part to be a part of the prescriptive part of the model. A good example of this fact are business processes models: They are generally prescriptive but also already define a workflow, i.e. the state transitions of the system.

3.4   Summary

As identified in Section 3.1 common business process model languages focus mostly on design-time aspects like interoperability, or being a basis for reliable communication between different stakeholders. For this reason important run-time aspects, like dimensions of change, are either only insufficiently supported or not regarded at all. A simple example is that simple state of a process instance cannot be expressed with languages like BPMN.

If the concepts of M@RT are applied to the domain of business process models the result is business process models at run-time (BPM@RT). The current classification into a-priori and a-posteriori business process models does not support the purpose of BPM@RT because this type of model is neither provided *before* nor extracted *after* the system was in use. A BPM@RT is in fact a model causally connected *while* the system is in use and therefore represents a new type of model. Technically, a performance model derived from BAM is for instance already a BPM@RT, i.e. it is a process performance representation of a System Under Study (SUS) based on business processes and therefore to some extent emphases the goals and behaviour of the processes from the problem space perspective of performance analysis. However, there are more perspectives on business processes than performance analysis, e.g. path prediction and optimisation.

Also, a number of adaptation approaches presented in Section 3.2 can be considered as causally connected business process models at run-time, e.g. [40,46], as they capture the current state and/or allow for run-time adaptations. However, automated optimisation of business processes is by neither of the reviewed approaches supported and stays a current challenge that needs to be addressed. Only one very initial optimisation approach [49] could be identified in which several adaptation concerns have not yet been addressed.

We generally agree with the notion of business process models being handled at run-time to sufficiently address the need for adapting to changing demands and for shorter BPM life cycles. But the current state of the industry in which business process models are mostly regarded as either a-priori or a-posteriori models is too static and does not fully meet the requirements of systems in which business processes are highly volatile with possible changes over time. In some cases, however, business process models at run-time already exist, but do neither fully leverage model driven concepts nor support important problems like business process optimisation.

4   Research Challenges

Through the application of principles of the models@run.time discipline we certainly expect the view on business process management to become more structured and thus promotes a much needed separation of concerns. The assumption is that if the abstraction level of models@run.time can be raised to the domain of business processes, this can make business process management more automated and business processes more flexible and easier to adapt. Future research in this area will provide valuable contributions to areas of BPM and M@RT alike.

In an attempt to generalise future research challenges we identified topics that have to be further addressed and are subject of the remainder of this paper. The topics are conceptually depicted in Figure 4 and further described in the following list:

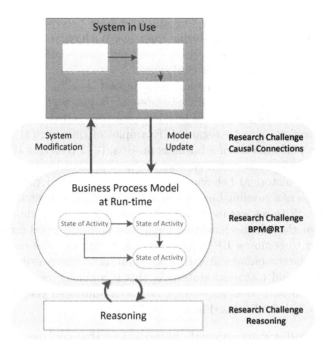

Fig. 4. Challenges for Run-time Business Process Models

1. **Run-Time Characteristics of BPM@RT:** First of all, BPM@RT has to deal with additional concerns as opposed to common business process models, such as capturing the current status information of the SUS's processes or the current performance of the process/system, depending on the problem space of the run-time model. Most business process models are a-posteriori models that only capture prescriptive information and this is why they need to be extended by certain run-time characteristics. One major challenge will therefore be to identify these run-time characteristics and elaborate a complete specification of a BPM@RT. A special emphasis has to be put on the dimensions of change the BPM@RT has to be able to express. The classifications of elements for general characteristics of run-time models reviewed in Section 3.3 is a good starting point to determine necessary parts for business process models at run-time. A review of related work and initial findings for this challenge are discussed in Section 5.

2. **Causal Connections between BPM@RT and the Associated System:** A second step towards BPM@RT is the identification of existing causal connections between the business process model and the SUS. Causal connections are either applied in the form of *Model Updates*, i.e. if the SUS changed the model has to be updated accordingly, or in the form of *System Modification*, i.e. the SUS has to be modified according to the associated model (see Figure 4). Due to the abstract nature of business process models this problem is particularly challenging as stronger requirements for the

causal connections between system and model are necessary, e.g. policies of how a BPMS can be updated during run-time. With regards to this challenge related work is reviewed in Section 6 and put into relation to the findings for the run-time characteristic challenge.

3. **Reasoning:** Models@run.time has been defined as a *"... causally connected self-representation of the associated system ... from a problem space perspective."* [2]. The problem space of business processes is diverse and dependent on what problem is to be regarded. Examples of this are: (1) Determining the current performance of a business process, (2) Predicting the future behaviour or performance of a current business process based on its current state and its historical behaviour and performance, and (3) Optimisation and adaption of a running business process according to given objectives and constraints. With respect to the actual problem in consideration appropriate reasoning methodologies have to be analysed and developed for BPM@RT. As opposed to common BPM reasoning methodologies like process mining and BAM, the reasoning will not be based on state change events but on the current state and historical states. As this is a change of paradigm which has, to the authors' best knowledge, not been addressed yet, this challenge can only be briefly discussed in Section 7.

After intensive literature review the authors claim that applying principles and theory of models@run.time to BPM has not yet been carried out to this extent. The expectation is to unify the BPM approaches towards the models@run.time paradigm, i.e. having a model express the current state and its history which is the basis of reasoning algorithms that can in turn change the model and eventually the system. Further research following this approach can initiate a shift from separate tools for modelling, execution, and diagnosis towards one framework comprising all of them. Already now the shift towards combining phases of the BPM life cycle are addressed by some approaches in industry (e.g., the existence of interchange standards to transform design models into execution models = design + enactment) and research (BAM solutions that can influence the business process execution = enactment + diagnosis).

Three different challenges towards BPM@RT have been identified: (1) Identifying characteristics for BPM@RT, (2) Identifying requirements for the causal connections between system and models, and (3) Reasoning upon BPM@RT. In the next three sections these challenges are individually discussed in further detail. That includes review of related work if available, first findings, and proposed next steps.

5   Research Challenge: Run-Time Characteristics of BPM@RT

A language for BPM@RT has to support specific run-time characteristics in order to deal with the requirements of a run-time model. The classifications of elements for general characteristics of run-time models, reviewed in Section 3.3, is a good entry point to define requirements for such a language. As pointed out in that section, the ratio of prescriptive and descriptive parts are dependent on the purpose of the model, e.g. monitoring M@RT vs. execution M@RT. But not only the ratio of these parts can be different also the run-time aspect, prescriptive or descriptive, can vary for the same model element types depending on the purpose. That is, an element type, e.g. an activity, can be of a prescriptive nature in one BPM@RT, e.g. execution standards like BPEL, but of a descriptive nature in another BPM@RT, e.g. a run-time model extracted via process mining. Though, in both cases it is important that changes on the activity level can be captured. Hence, a special emphasis has to be put on the dimensions of change a BPM@RT has to be able to express. This is discussed in the remainder of this section, surveying related literature that deals with process flexibility.

5.1   State of the Art: Process Flexibility

An extensive taxonomy for dimensions of process flexibility is presented in [50]:

1. *Flexibility by design* is the ability to model alternative execution paths within the process definition at design-time. Dependent on the circumstances, the most appropriate execution path for a process instance can be chosen at run-time. This dimension is supported by almost any business process modelling language to some extent.
2. *Flexibility by deviation* is the ability for a process instance to deviate at run-time from the prescribed execution path of the business process model. The deviation does not allow for changes in the process definition, i.e. the business process model.
3. *Flexibility by underspecification* is the ability to execute an only partially defined business process at run-time. The full specification of the model is made at run-time and can be unique for each process instance.
4. *Flexibility by momentary change* is the ability to modify the execution of one or more selected process instances. This change is performed at the process instance level and does not affect any future instances.
5. *Flexibility by permanent change* is the ability to modify business process model at run-time such that the process definition is permanently modified. All currently executing process instances need to be transfered to the new process definition.

Whereas the first three dimensions leave the prescriptive part of the business process model unchanged, the last two encompass modifications in the prescriptive part of the business process model (either momentarily or permanently) at run-time. We can find that most of the flexibility dimensions of this taxonomy correspond to adaptation approaches presented in Section 3.2: Item 2 from the list above corresponds to exception handling approaches, item 3 corresponds to late-binding/pockets of flexibility, item 4 corresponds to case-handling, and item 5 corresponds to adaptive processes.

Another similar differentiation can be found in [46], in which dimensions of change for workflows are defined. Note, that the terminology in the following approach is a little contradictory to the terminology used in the first approach. Some terms like "flexibility" and "change" have now a slightly different meaning. The classification of change dimensions for workflows is [46]:

1. *Flexibility* is the ability of the workflow process to execute on the basis of an incomplete specified model, where the full specification of the model is made at runtime. This dimension of change is the equivalent of *flexibility by underspecification* of the previous taxonomy.
2. *Adaptability* is the ability of the workflow processes to react to exceptional circumstances. These exceptional circumstances generally effect one or a few instances. This dimension of change is comparable to *flexibility of momentary change* or *flexibility of deviation* of the previous taxonomy dependent on if the process definition is momentarily adapted or not.
3. *Dynamism* is the ability of the workflow process to change when the business process evolves. This evolution may be slight as for process improvements, or drastic as for process innovation or process reengineering. Compared to the previous taxonomy this dimension is equivalent to *flexibility of permanent change*.

5.2   Identifying Run-Time Characteristics for BPM@RT

Both approaches capture dimensions of change that are either defined at design-time or at run-time. Of importance for the dimensions of change with regards to BPM@RT is, however, the associated abstraction level of the change, i.e. the granularity of a change. There are two abstraction levels of change that can be identified in both: (1) The change of the execution path of a process instance, in the remainder called *Variability*, and (2) the change of a complete business process definition, in the remainder called *Dynamism*. Due to the focus of both approaches on process change, one abstraction level of change has not been regarded, yet: the fine-granular state change in a process instance, in the remainder called *Reflectivity*. We argue that a language for BPM@RT needs to be able to support these three dimensions of change (see Figure 5) in order support any business process related purpose from business process monitoring to dynamic process optimisation of business processes.

The first conclusion to be drawn after identifying these three different dimensions of change is that some business process models already have the properties of adaptive models at run-time: Business process models that are executable and monitor the state of the system, e.g. certain workflow models like ADEPT [40], are adaptive models at run-time for *process instances*. That means in particular, that the prescriptive part specifies the possible states and transitions of one process instance, the descriptive part describes the current state in the process instance, and the valid modifications of the prescriptive parts are the shifts of execution paths for the process instance dependent on the circumstances. This is shown in Figure 6.

This is a good example to show how important the abstraction level of change is, i.e. in terms of dynamic adaptation: on what level do we capture change

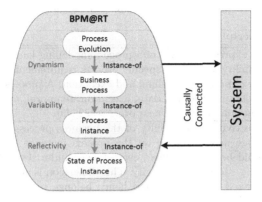

Fig. 5. Different Levels of State and State Change in BPM@RT

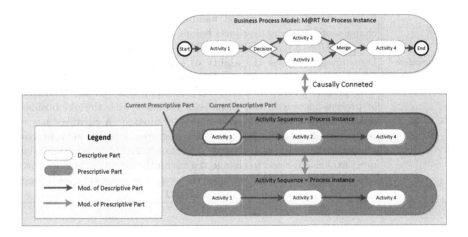

Fig. 6. Business Process Model as Process Instance Model at Run-time

of the system and on what level do we want to deploy change to the system. With regards to general BPM@RT, the requirements are to be able to capture and propagate change on the levels of reflectivity, flexibility, and dynamism. In addition to the desired change dimension of a BPM@RT the model also has to support standard business process modelling capabilities which is why the requirement of expressibility is essential, as well. A language to model BPM@RT has to support the requirements listed in Table 1.

Note, that some types of change cannot be assigned to one single level of change, e.g. the specification of language X might already allow to model a "Resource Change" but the specification of language Y does not support that notion. In that case, "Resource Change" is part of the variability dimension for X but part of the dynamism dimension for Y.

Table 1. Requirements for business process models at run-time

Requirement	Description
Expressibility	The expressive power of a process modelling language is governed by its ability to express specific process requirements reflecting the purpose of process modelling and execution. A process model is required to contain structure, data, execution, temporal, and transactional information of the business process [22][43].
Reflectivity	Reflectivity is the ability of the business process model to represent change in the system on the process instance level, i.e. the model should be able to reflect every fine-granular state the system can be in, e.g. state of the activity. This dimension is almost exclusively only triggered by the SUS and hence belongs to the descriptive part in most BPM@RTs.
Variability	Variability is the ability of a business process model to handle change on the business process level, i.e. it has the capabilities to model adaptations for process instances according to the desired behaviour, e.g. via a decision element, or according to exceptional but tolerated behaviour e.g. via exception handling. Depending on the purpose, changes of the variability level belong either to the descriptive or to the prescriptive part of the BPM@RT or to both.
Dynamism	Dynamism describes the ability of a business process model to be adapted at run-time according to changed circumstances. This business process evolution entails special challenges for the transition of process instances that have been initiated with the old business process generation but have not yet terminated. A Strategy has to be defined how these instances are migrated into the new process schema [50], which is discussed in Section 6.2. This dimension is almost exclusively used to change the currently executing business process model which in turn modifies the system in use and hence belongs to the prescriptive part of the BPM@RT.

As a next step towards BPM@RT we propose to check existing business process modelling languages like BPMN, BPEL, EPC, ADEPT, and YAWL against these requirements. Whereas most of them support the variability requirement to some extent, the other two dimensions of change, dynamism and reflectivity, are expected to be less supported. In case none of the existing solutions prove expressive enough an extension of the closest match or a new BPM@RT has to be specified. A formal validation of the resulting modelling language can be carried out based on general business process patterns [55] and business process change patterns [62].

6   Research Challenge: Causal Connections

In Section 3.3 we have distinguished between two different kinds of causal connections: (1) *model update* which alters the descriptive part of a model, and (2) system modification which has to be performed if the prescriptive part of the model has been updated. In this section we take both causal connections under examination with regards to business process models and survey existing methodologies, respectively.

6.1 Model Update

The focus of this section lies on descriptive parts of a BPM@RT, i.e. the propagation of system changes to the model. This action is called model update. The basic task of a model update is to make sure that the current state from a problem space perspective of the SUS is reflected in the corresponding BPM@RT at any point in time. The assumption is that every single change in the SUS is represented as an event e_n which triggers a transition of an old $BPM@RT_{n-1}$ into an updated $BPM@RT_n$. This means a BPM@RT is built incrementally as conceptually shown in Op_1.

$$(Op_1) \quad e_n + BPM@RT_{n-1} \stackrel{ModelUpdate}{\rightarrow} BPM@RT_n$$

However, the common approach of extracting a-posteriori business process model information is called process mining and operates in a different way: The input is a complete event set $e_1, e_2, ..., e_n$ from which the business process model $BPModel_n$ is determined as shown in Op_2.

$$(Op_2) \quad (e_1, e_2, ..., e_n) \stackrel{ProcessMining}{\rightarrow} BPModel_n$$

The traditional and static process mining approach of Op_2 stands in contrast to the process model update approach and is not appropriately supporting the run-time characteristic of M@RT. This is why the process model update operation Op_1 has to be addressed by investigating suitable, incrementally operating algorithms for dynamic process mining.

In general a dynamic descriptive M@RT in the business process domain, e.g. process performance model, is causally connected with the BPMS through an event stream. Events indicating a change in the system are processed, aggregated and eventually trigger an update of the descriptive BPM@RT. This approach is called Business Activity Monitoring (BAM) (see Section 3.1) and is achieved through the application of Complex Event Processing (CEP) technologies. Existing BAM solutions mostly focus on monitoring key performance indicators on the business process level, e.g. [16,39,10]. As identified in the previous section, this is, however, only one abstraction level on which dynamic model updates can be triggered. With respect to the classification of abstraction levels of change, three different update types exist which are depicted in Figure 7 and described in the following list:

- **Dynamic Process Mining** is the discipline of updating model information on the business process level at run-time, i.e. detecting changes in the variability dimension. Many BAM solutions operate on that dimension of change, i.e. extract the performance of a business process model at run-time. It corresponds to the traditional a-posteriori process mining discipline

226   D. Redlich et al.

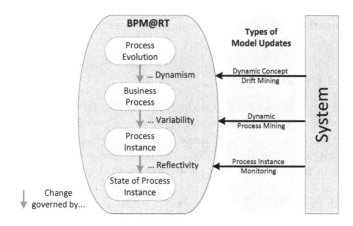

Fig. 7. Different types of model updates dependent on the level of change they are capturing

which is concerned with the extraction of knowledge about a business process based on its event logs [56]. Process mining approaches provide insight into a number of different perspectives: control-flow (called process discovered), performance, data, and organisation. Whereas BAM approaches address the performance perspective at run-time, development of solutions for dynamically mining knowledge about the other perspectives at run-time is, to the authors' best knowledge, still an open research challenge.

– **Process Instance Monitoring** is the discipline of updating model information on the process instance level at run-time, i.e. detecting changes in the reflectivity dimension. This represents capturing fine-granular atomic changes on the execution level, e.g. that an activity has been completed, and based on that updating the model to the current state of the instance. Some workflow and business process languages and their corresponding WfMS's and BPMS's already support the capturing and representation of that dimension of change at run-time, e.g. [40].

– **Dynamic Concept Drift Mining** is the discipline of updating model information on the process evolution level at run-time, i.e. detecting changes in the dynamism dimension. If the process gradually or suddenly evolves into another schema this has to be updated in the model. This corresponds to the traditional a-posteriori concept drift mining in processes [3], which to authors' best knowledge has not yet been approached in a dynamic way at run-time.

All three of these update types are event-based and should operate based on dynamic algorithms in the fashion of Op_1 as opposed to their static a-posteriori counter parts, i.e. concept drift mining and process mining. The common basis for model updates at run-time in the domain of BPM is through processing the event stream which is a standard interface of modern BPMS, e.g. SAP Netweaver BPM [64]. However, this stream contains change events of the lowest possible dimension: the fine-granular state changes of the system. As there are no other generalised hooks available for changes of both other dimensions, dynamism and variability, have to be detected based on these low-level events.

6.2   System Modification

Since business process designers are not capable of anticipating all possible cases, exceptions, and events beforehand, the run-time system may not have sufficient knowledge to handle these situations and an adapted business process model might have to be redeployed. State of the art for business process adaptation with regards to existing approaches (build-time flexibility vs. run-time flexibility) has already been presented in Section 3.2. System modification is the action that has to be performed if the prescriptive part of the deployed business process model has been adapted at run-time.

Generally, business process models are abstract workflows where the abstraction level correlates to the type of causal connections between business process model and SUS, i.e. the higher the abstraction level of the business process model the more manual effort is potentially needed to execute an adaptation. In terms of the application of a system modification this means that with a high abstraction level it becomes more difficult to perform a system modification on the basis of the prescriptive part of the BPM@RT in an automated way. Common practice is that a graphical standard (e.g. BPMN) is used to design the business process model [change], then an interchange standard (e.g. BPDM) is utilised to transform that into an execution standard (e.g. BPEL) which is then executed and monitored. The actual modification of the system based on model adaptations is in the prominent BPMS not supported. Even though, there have been approaches to deal with adaptations for business processes as presented in Section 3.2, e.g. by build-time flexibility [25,60,35,53,46] or run-time flexibility [40,58], the actual system modification in an automated way remains to be generally very difficult to execute due to the high abstraction level of business processes.

One challenge that needs addressing to enable automation of system modification is the *validation* of the change that is to be applied to the system. In [40] a conceptual and operational framework is proposed that can reason about the correctness of a requested change to handle dynamic structural adaptations of workflows. At the core of this framework is a conceptual graphical workflow model (ADEPT) based upon which a complete and minimal set of change operations (ADEPT$_{flex}$) is defined, e.g. dynamic insertions/deletion of activities, or changing activity sequence. These operations allow for modifying the structure while preserving correctness and consistency of the system. With the help of formal constraints for state, flow of data, and flow of control, changes can be rejected if they can potentially lead to an invalid state of the system. This solution provides only a minimal set of changes with strict constraints to ensure that no invalid state can be reached. A more coarse-grained view on these changes can help to reduce or relax these constraints, i.e. grouping changes instead of regarding every change as an atomic modification action. For instance, assuming two previously sequential activities are to become parallel, the constraints for this coarse-grained modification would be less strong than the constraints of the sub-modifications, deletion and parallel insertion, regarded individually. Weber et al. [62] identified 18 change patterns based on 157 real-life business processes from the domains of health care and automotive. 14 of these are adaptation patterns of different granularity, e.g. insert process fragment, delete process fragment, swap process fragments, parallelise activities, and embed process fragment in loop. The identified changes only consider the control-flow perspective and would have to be extended by patterns for the other perspectives, e.g. reallocation of resources.

However, if more complex changes, e.g. to split or parallelise activities, are requested *modification policies* have to be in place to ensure that the run-time system continues to operate in the expected manner. Modification policies specify how the transition from one business process to another is carried out [44]. These policies are important with respect to the still active process instances of the outdated business process and describe how to deal with them. Example policies are *Flush*, which allows all current instances to complete according to the old process model, *Abort*, which aborts all active process instances, and *Migrate*, which maps the state of active process instances to the new model. The last option is only applicable if additional migration constraints can be met, i.e. the migration into a valid instance is possible. Modification policies are discussed in more detail by Sadiq [44] and Schonenberg et al. [50].

In conclusion, due to the usually high abstraction level of business processes both causal connections, model update and system modification, pose difficult challenges. In the case of model updates for BPM@RT especially the dynamic update algorithms for the higher levels of change, dynamism and variability, are highlighted challenges for the future. In the case of system modification, determining patterns of change for different perspectives of business process models, e.g. resource and organisation perspective, will be a challenging task in the future.

7   Research Challenge: Reasoning on Run-Time Business Process Models

Reasoning is the action of drawing conclusions from available facts or statements. We understand reasoning as a discipline not only based on logic but also achieved by, for instance, statistical reasoning techniques, e.g. computation of key performance indicators. With regards to the actual problem in consideration appropriate reasoning methodologies can strongly vary in terms of input, applied techniques, and resulting output. In the remainder we summarise existing work in the domains of BPM and models@run.time with regards to these aspects and relate it to the concept presented in Section 4.

7.1 Input Information for Reasoning on BPM@RT

As opposed to traditional BPM reasoning methodologies like process mining and BAM, the reasoning in the proposed setup (see Figure 4) will not be based on *state change events* but on run-time business process models which capture the *current state* and *historical states* of the system. In the following listing both information types are described in further detail:

- *Current state information* comprises the descriptive parts of the BPM@RT representing the state of the BPMS on all three identified dimensions of change: reflectivity (i.e., the current state of an active process instance), variability (i.e., the current state of the business process, comprising all states of the active process instances), and dynamism (i.e., the current state of the process evolution, representing the current business process schema in use). Usually, at most two of the change dimensions are captured in current BPM@RT as they serve a specific purpose, e.g. BAM solutions capturing performance information on the reflectivity and/or variability level [16,38]. However, we propose to separate the concerns of capturing and reasoning: capturing the general state of the SUS on all three dimensions and apply the purpose-oriented reasoning based on this information.
- *Historic state information* comprises all past states the SUS has been in and their associated time spans. State changes happen with different frequency, ranging from a high frequency on the reflectivity dimension to a rather low frequency at the dynamism dimension. However, for elaborate reasoning techniques, e.g. simulation, it is a requirement to take the past states into consideration to achieve meaningful results. Hence, a general-purpose BPM@RT captures not only the current state on all three levels it also has a record of all the past states on these levels.

With these two types simple reasoning can already be applied, e.g. performance analysis, trend analysis, or path prediction. In terms of more elaborate reasoning additional *adaption information*, i.e. constraints, rules, and variants [9], which is usually defined at design time are necessary. These aspects would then belong to the prescriptive part of the BPM@RT and are dependent on which level of change the reasoning is considering. In our proposed setup this adaptation information is associated with the highest level of change abstraction: dynamism, i.e. changing the deployed business process models at run-time.

Note, that in literature for some analysis techniques (e.g., business process simulation [42,61]) an additional input data type is required: *design information*, which contains business process design information, e.g. control- and data-flow [42]. This type of information is in our point of view already captured in the current state information as all three change dimensions are to be captured, including the current business process schema (as a state).

7.2 Analysis Types for Reasoning on BPM@RT

In the following we discuss three analysis types that we consider important in terms of reasoning on BPM@RT: decision support, adaptation, and optimisation.

Decision Support. are analyses supporting the business analyst in making decisions about the business process through providing him with additional computed information of diverse nature, e.g. performance of the business process or involved resources. This information enables the analyst to obtain more insight into the process execution and its environment and react if an adaptation or exceptional interference becomes necessary, reallocation of resources. Examples of these analyses are *what-if analysis* [12], *performance monitoring* [16], *performance prediction* [38], *path prediction* [6], *sensitivity analysis* [11], and *bottleneck detection* [41]. Traditionally, in the BPM domain two basic types of analysis techniques are utilised to extract additional information from low-level data, i.e. event logs:

- *Analytical techniques* are based on mathematical methods and models to directly obtain information from the given data, e.g. FMC-QE [37]. Generally speaking, the biggest advantage is that instant results can be computed, which is why analytical techniques are preferably used in high-level analyses like optimisation were thousands of different cases have to be analysed as fast as possible. Disadvantages are that they typically are only simplified approximations (e.g., conditional loop behaviour hard to be represented by a formula [37]), impose additional constraints and are difficult to use [5].
- *Simulation* "... attempts to mimic real-life or hypothetical behaviour" [61]. It is considered to be versatile, impose only a few constraints, and produce results that similarly interpreted as the ones of the simulated system [61]. This is why simulation is one of the most established techniques in the domain of BPM supported by many tools. Most of these tools, however, focus on analysing rather abstract *steady-state* situations which are simplified models and less suitable run-time decision support [42]. To achieve more accurate results a *transient* analysis, where the current state is the starting point for an analysis is preferred [42]. This notion is fully supported by the BPM@RT approach. The biggest disadvantage of simulations is that they are time consuming and not very scalable: size of the business process, time to simulate, and average instance occurrence similarly have a linear influence on the execution time of the simulation. Additionally, as heuristic approach simulations even have to be executed several times to gain a certain confidence about the results.

Adaptation Reasoning. The challenge of reasoning is the connection between the descriptive and the prescriptive part of a M@RT and triggers possible system adaptations caused by an environment change. According to Fleurey et al. adaptation reasoning requires the following types of input [9]:

- *Context* which abstractly captures all the descriptive information, including current state and historical states. Traditional approaches however, only consider the current state to be important for an ad-hoc adaptation. Computed high-level information in the sense of the previously discussed decision support, e.g. performance information, can be part of the context and help determining the adaptation.

- *Variants* describe the flexibility of the run-time model or system, i.e. what adaptations are possible. Variants are of a prescriptive nature and belong to the adaptation information, introduced earlier. In the domain of BPM variants are, for instance, inserting a new activity, and reallocation of resources.
- *Constraints* specify restrictions on the variants and hence reduce the problem space. Constraints are extending the prescriptive part of a BPM@RT and also belong to the adaptation information. Examples for adaptation constraints can be state dependent, e.g. an activity can only be duplicated if it is not active at the moment, or state independent, e.g. an activity can only be allocated to a resource which can fulfill that role.
- *Rules* define how model and system should adapt to the change in the environment. These rules are in practice relations between the current state and the possible variants [9]. They extend the prescriptive part and belong to the adaptation information. One example is $\forall r \in Resources$: IF $utilisation(r) > 0.8$ THEN $multiplicity(r) \leftarrow multiplicity(r) + 1$.

The reasoning framework processes makes a decision based on the current context, variants, constraints, and rules at run-time. The output of the reasoning framework is an adaptation that matches the rules based on variants as well as context and satisfies the dependency constraints.

Optimisation. The reasoning based on rules and logic as proposed by [9] and introduced in the previous paragraph requires very good knowledge about the business process and about its possible adaptations. A more flexible approach is optimisation, an analysis which is driven by a fitness function. With the help of this function variants within the constraints can be rated and the one with the highest rating is considered to be the optimum. An optimisation is about finding the best solution for a given environment, i.e. technically it is not a subset of adaptation, but can be utilised to replace the adaptation reasoning via rules/logic. Alternatively, an optimisation function could be part of the rules but then all variants would have to be analysed. This is not suitable for a large number of variants. Well known optimisation techniques can be found in the areas of artificial intelligence, e.g. evolutionary/genetic algorithms, and mathematics, e.g. numerical algorithms. Note, that if an heuristic approach is utilised, a continuous swapping between localoptima is possible. This is a very undesired effect.

In BPM only one initial approach for optimisation is known by the authors which was discussed in Section 3.2. Here the future performance of every business process variant, which was computed via using simulation, represents the fitness function for the optimisation [49].

In conclusion, traditional reasoning in BPM is mostly based on the analysis of state transition events, especially in the very prominent area of decision support. With introducing the concepts of models@run.time a shift towards reasoning on current and historic states is motivated and has to be further investigated.

Adaptation reasoning is already well researched, its major limitation being the lack of applicability of current solutions in the industry, i.e. a challenge is how an adaptation can be modelled in an easier way. Additionally, in this section we did not distinguish between online or offline reasoning, i.e. static reasoning solutions have to be transformed if they are to be used at run-time.

8   Conclusion

Adapting to changing demands and shortening the business process lifecycle are prominent challenges in the domain of business process management. This paper motivates that a more dynamic handling of business processes is desirable, moving from design-time business process models to run-time business process models. We argue that a promising approach to address these challenges is provided by the community of models@run.time, in which causally connected models reflect the system's current state at any point in time and allow immediate reasoning and adaption mechanisms. This paper is a first attempt to raise the abstraction level of models@run.time to the domain of business processes, i.e. leveraging principles and concepts of the M@RT discipline to address the challenges of business adaptation and automation. With that it aims to unify BPM solutions towards a general models@run.time paradigm, i.e. having a model express the current state and its history which is the basis of reasoning algorithms that can in turn change the model and eventually the system. In order to generalise future research challenges three topics were highlighted that need further addressing:

1. Run-time characteristics of BPM@RT
2. Causal connections between BPM@RT and the associated system
3. Reasoning on BPM@RT

Each of these topics have been discussed in more detail individually, including review of related work, first findings, and proposed next steps. A number of resulting and more specific research challenges that need to be addressed have been identified and discussed: dimensions of change for BPM@RT, model update methodologies, modification types, modification policies, and business process optimisation. In the case of dimensions of change for BPM@RT, a first step has been taken by specifying the three different levels of business processes in which change can happen: dynamism, variability, and reflectivity.

Concluding, raising the abstraction level to the domain of BPM will provide contributions to the area of models@run.time generally, and for other M@RT at a similarly high abstraction level in particular. Furthermore, work in the area of BPM@RT will provide a valid use-case for M@RT and help to address the general challenges of business adaptation and automation.

References

1. von Ammon, R., Ertlmaier, T., Etzion, O., Kofman, A., Paulus, T.: Integrating Complex Events for Collaborating and Dynamically Changing Business Processes. In: Dan, A., Gittler, F., Toumani, F. (eds.) ICSOC/ServiceWave 2009. LNCS, vol. 6275, pp. 370–384. Springer, Heidelberg (2010)
2. Blair, G., Bencomo, N., France, R.B.: Models@run.time. Computer 42(10), 22–27 (2009)
3. Bose, R.P.J.C., van der Aalst, W.M.P., Žliobaitė, I.e., Pechenizkiy, M.: Handling concept drift in process mining. In: Mouratidis, H., Rolland, C. (eds.) CAiSE 2011. LNCS, vol. 6741, pp. 391–405. Springer, Heidelberg (2011)
4. Breton, B., Bézivin, J.: Towards an understanding of model executability. In: Proc. of the International Conference on Formal Ontology in Information Systems (2001)
5. Buzacott, J.: Commonalities in Reengineerd Business Processes: Models and Issues. Management Science 2(5), 768–782 (1996)
6. Cardoso, J., Lenic, M.: Web process and workflow path mining using the Multi-method approach. IJBIDM 2006 1(3), 304–328 (2006)
7. Cheng, B.H.C., et al.: Software Engineering for Self-Adaptive Systems: A Research Roadmap. In: Cheng, B.H.C., de Lemos, R., Giese, H., Inverardi, P., Magee, J. (eds.) Self-Adaptive Systems. LNCS, vol. 5525, pp. 1–26. Springer, Heidelberg (2009)
8. Dehnert, J., Van Der Aalst, W.: Bridging The Gap Between Business Models and Workflow Specifications. Int. J. Cooperative Inf. Syst. 13, 289–332 (2004)
9. Fleurey, F., Dehlen, V., Bencomo, N., Morin, B., Jézéquel, J.-M.: Modeling and validating dynamic adaptation. In: 3rd Int. Workshop on Models@run.time (2008)
10. Friedenstab, J.-P., Janiesch, C., Matzner, M., Müller, O.: Extending BPMN for Business Activity Monitoring. In: Proceedings of 45th Hawaii International International Conference on Systems Science, pp. 4158–4167. IEEE (2012)
11. Fritzsche, M.: PhD Thesis - Performance related Decision Support for Process Modelling. School of Electronics, Electrical Engineering and Computer Science, Queens University Belfast (2010)
12. Fritzsche, M., Johannes, J., Cech, S., Gilani, W.: MDPE Workbench - A Solution for Performance Related Decision Support. In: Proceedings of the Business Process Management Demonstration Track, vol. 489 (2009)
13. Ghalimi and D. McGoveran, D.: Standards and BPM. bpm.com (2005)
14. Hill, J.B., Pezzini, M., Natis, Y.V.: Findings: Confusion remains regarding BPM terminologies. ID no. G00155817. Gartner Research (2008)
15. Intalio. BPMS designer, http://www.intalio.com/products/designer/ (accessed October 13, 2012)
16. Janiesch, C., Matzner, M., Müller, M., Vollmer, R., Becker, J.: Slipstream: architecture options for real-time process analytics. In: Chu, W., Wong, W., Palakal, M., Hung, C. (eds.) Proceedings of the 2011 ACM Symposium on Applied Computing (SAC). ACM (2011)
17. Ko, R.K.L.: A computer scientist's introductory guide to business process management (BPM). Crossroads Journal (2009)
18. Ko, R.K.L., Lee, S.S.G., Lee, E.W.: Business process management (BPM) standards: A survey. Business Process Management Journal 15(5), 744–791 (2009)
19. Lawrence, P.: Workflow Handbook 1997, Workflow Management Coalition. John Wiley and Sons, NY (1997)

20. Lehmann, G., Blumendorf, M., Trollmann, F., Albayrak, S.: Meta-modeling Runtime Models. In: MODELS Workshops 2010, pp. 209–223 (2010)

21. Liu, R., Nigam, A., Jeng, J., Shieh, C.-R.: Integrated Modeling of Performance Monitoring with Business Artifacts. In: Proceedings of 7th IEEE International Conference on e-Business Engineering (ICEBE), pp. 64–71 (2010)

22. Lu, R., Shazia, S.: A survey of comparative business process modeling approaches. In: Abramowicz, W. (ed.) BIS 2007. LNCS, vol. 4439, pp. 82–94. Springer, Heidelberg (2007)

23. Mendling, J., Neumann, G.: A Comparison of XML Interchange Formats for Business Process Modelling. In: Workflow Handbook (2005)

24. Milner, R.: Communicating and Mobile Systems: The Pi Calculus. Cambridge University Press (1999)

25. Modafferi, S., Mussi, E., Pernici, B.: SH-BPEL: A self-healing plug-in for Ws-BPEL engines. In: MW4SOC 2006, vol. 184, pp. 48–53 (2006)

26. Momm, C., Malec, R., Abeck, S.: Towards a Model-driven development of monitored processes. In: Proceedings of the 8th Internationale Tagung Wirtschaftsinformatik, pp. 319–336 (2007)

27. Muller, P., Fleurey, F., J'ez'equel, J.: Weaving executability into objectoriented meta-languages. In: Proc. of the 8th International Conference on Model-Driven Engineering Languages and Systems (2005)

28. OASIS: Web Services Business Process Execution Language Version 2.0 (2007), http://docs.oasis-open.org/wsbpel/2.0/wsbpel-v2.0.pdf

29. Object Management Group Inc: BPMN and Business Process Management - Introduction to the New Business Process Modeling Standard (2003), http://www.omg.org/bpmn/Documents/6AD5D16960.BPMN_and_BPM.pdf

30. Object Management Group Inc: The OMG Business Process Related Standards (2007), http://bpmfocus.pbworks.com/f/BPM+Standards+At+The+OMG+-+July+07.pdf

31. Object Management Group Inc: Business Process Model and Notation (BPMN) Specification 2.0 (2011), http://www.omg.org/spec/BPMN/2.0/PDF.formal/2011-01-03

32. Object Management Group Inc: Business Process Definition MetaModel - Volume I: Common Infrastructure (2008), http://www.omg.org/spec/BPDM/1.0./formal/2008-11-03

33. Object Management Group Inc: Unified Modeling Language 2.0: Superstructure (2005), http://www.omg.org/spec/UML/2.0/Superstructure/PDF.formal/05-07-04,

34. del-Río-Ortega, A., Resinas, M., Ruiz-Cortés, A.: Defining Process Performance Indicators: An Ontological Approach. In: Meersman, R., Dillon, T., Herrero, P. (eds.) OTM 2010, Part I. LNCS, vol. 6426, pp. 555–572. Springer, Heidelberg (2010)

35. Pesic, M., Schonenberg, M.H., Sidorova, N., van der Aalst, W.M.P.: Constraint-Based Workflow Models: Change Made Easy. In: Meersman, R., Tari, Z. (eds.) OTM 2007, Part I. LNCS, vol. 4803, pp. 77–94. Springer, Heidelberg (2007)

36. Petri, C.A.: Kommunikation mit Automaten. PhD thesis. Rheinisch-Westfälisches Institut f. Instrumentelle Mathematik (1962)

37. Porzucek, T., Kluth, S., Fritzsche, M., Redlich, D.: Combination of a Discrete Event Simulation and an Analytical Performance Analysis through Model-Transformations. In: IEEE ECBS 2010, pp. 183–192 (2010)

38. Redlich, D., Gilani, W.: Event-Driven Process-Centric Performance Prediction via Simulation. In: Daniel, F., Barkaoui, K., Dustdar, S. (eds.) BPM Workshops 2011, Part I. LNBIP, vol. 99, pp. 473–478. Springer, Heidelberg (2012)
39. Redlich, D., Platz, S., Molka, T., Gilani, W., Winkler, U.: MDE in Practice: Process-centric Performance Prediction via Simulation in Real-time. In: Störrle, H., et al. (eds.) Joint Proceedings of co-located Events at the 8th European Conference on Modelling Foundations and Applications, pp. 336–339 (2012)
40. Reichert, M., Dadam, P.: ADEPT flex - Supporting Dynamic Changes of Workflows Without Loosing Control. Journal of Intelligent Information Systems, vol 10, 93–129 (1998)
41. Roser, C., Nakano, M., Tanaka, M.: A practical bottleneck detection method. In: Proceedings of the 33nd Conference on Winter Simulation, pp. 949–953 (2001)
42. Rozinat, A., Wynn, M.T., van der Aalst, W.M.P., ter Hofstede, A.H.M., Fidge, C.J.: Workflow Simulation for Operational Decision Support Using Design, Historic and State Information. In: Dumas, M., Reichert, M., Shan, M.-C. (eds.) BPM 2008. LNCS, vol. 5240, pp. 196–211. Springer, Heidelberg (2008)
43. Sadiq, W., Orlowska, M.: On Capturing Process Requirements of Workflow Based Business Information System. In: Proceedings of 3rd International Conference on Business Information Systems (1999)
44. Sadiq, S.: Handling Dynamic Schema Change in Process Models. In: Proceedings of the Australasian Database Conference. IEEE (2000)
45. Sadiq, S., Orlowska, M., Sadiq, W.: Specification and validation of process constraints for flexible workflows. In Inf. Syst. Journal 30(5), 349–378 (2005)
46. Sadiq, S.K., Sadiq, W., Orlowska, M.E.: Pockets of flexibility in workflow specification. In: Kunii, H.S., Jajodia, S., Sølvberg, A. (eds.) ER 2001. LNCS, vol. 2224, pp. 513–526. Springer, Heidelberg (2001)
47. Sanchez, M., Barrero, I., Villalobos, J., Deridder, D.: An execution platform for extensible runtime models. In: 3rd Int. Workshop on Models@run.time (2008)
48. Scheer, I.D.S.: ARIS (Architecture of integrated Information Systems) (1992)
49. Solomon, A., Litoiu, M., Lau, A.: Business Process Adaptation on a Tracked Simulation Model. In: ACM IBM Center for Advanced Studies Conference (2010)
50. Schonenberg, H., Mans, R., Russell, N., Mulyar, N., Van Der Aalst, W.: Towards a taxonomy of process flexibility (extended version). BPM Center Report BPM-07-11 (2007)
51. Seidewitz, E.: What models means. IEEE Software 20(5), 26–32 (2003)
52. Simchi-Levi, D., Simchi-Levi, E., Kaminsky, P.: Designing and managing the supply chain: Concepts, strategies, and cases. McGraw-Hill United-States (1999)
53. van der Aalst, W.M.P., Barros, A.P., ter Hofstede, A.H.M., Kiepuszewski, B.: Advanced workflow patterns. In: Scheuermann, P., Etzion, O. (eds.) CoopIS 2000. LNCS, vol. 1901, pp. 18–29. Springer, Heidelberg (2000)
54. van der Aalst, W.M.P., ter Hofstede, A.H.M., Weske, M.: Business process management: A survey. In: van der Aalst, W.M.P., Weske, M. (eds.) BPM 2003. LNCS, vol. 2678, pp. 1–12. Springer, Heidelberg (2003)
55. Van Der Aalst, W., Ter Hofstede, A., Kiepuszewski, B., Barros, A.: WorkflowPatterns. Distributed and Parallel Databases 14(1), 5–51 (2003)
56. Van Der Aalst, W., Weijters, A.: Process mining: A research agenda. Comput. Ind. 53(3), 231–244 (2004)
57. Van Der Aalst, W., Ter Hofstede, A.: YAWL: Yet Another Workflow Language (2003)

58. Van Der Aalst, W., Weske, M., Grünbauer, D.: Case Handling: A New Paradigm for Business Process Support. Data and Knowledge Engineering 53(2), 129–162 (2005)
59. Van Der Aalst, W.: Trends in business process analysis - from verification to process mining. In: Cardoso, J., Cordeiro, J., Filipe, J. (eds.) ICEIS 2007 - Proceedings of the Ninth International Conference on Enterprise Information Systems, ICEIS 2007, pp. 5–9 (2007)
60. Van Der Aalst, W., Pesic, M., Schonenberg, H.: Declarative workflows: Balancing between flexibility and support. Computer Science - Research and Development 23(2), 99–113 (2009)
61. van der Aalst, W.M.P.: Business Process Simulation Revisited. In: Barjis, J. (ed.) EOMAS 2010. LNBIP, vol. 63, pp. 1–14. Springer, Heidelberg (2010)
62. Weber, B., Reichert, M., Rinderle-Ma, S.: Change patterns and change support features - Enhancing flexibility in process-aware information systems. Data and Knowledge Engineering, vol 66(3), 438–466 (2008)
63. Wetzstein, B., Ma, Z., Leymann, F.: Towards Measuring Key Performance Indicators of Semantic Business Processes. In: Abramowicz, W., Fensel, D. (eds.) BIS 2008. LNBIP, vol. 7(7), pp. 227–238. Springer, Heidelberg (1974)
64. Woods, D., Word, J.: SAP Netweaver for Dummies. Wiley, NJ (2004)
65. Workflow Management Coalition: XML Process Definition Language (XMDL) 2.2, http://www.xpdl.org/ (accessed October 13, 2012)
66. Zur Muehlen, M.: Tutorial - Business process management standards. In: Proceedings of the 5th International Conference on Business Process Management (2007)

Fine-Grained Semi-automated
Runtime Evolution

Walter Cazzola[1], Nicole Alicia Rossini[1],
Phillipa Bennett[2], Sai Pradeep Mandalaparty[2], and Robert France[2]

[1] Computer Science Department, Università degli Studi di Milano, Italy
[2] Computer Science Department, Colorado State University, USA

Abstract. Modern software systems that play critical roles in society
are often required to change at runtime so that they can continuously
provide essential services in the dynamic environments they operate in.
Updating open, distributed software systems at runtime is very challenging. Using runtime models as an interface for updating software at
runtime can help developers manage the complexity of updating software
while it is executing. In this chapter we describe an approach to updating
Java software at runtime through the use of runtime models consisting of
UML class and sequence diagrams. Changes to models are transformed
to changes on Java source code, which is then propagated to the runtime
system using the JavAdaptor technology. In particular, the presented
approach permits in-the-small software changes, i.e., changes at the code
statement level, as opposed to in-the-large changes, i.e., changes at the
component level. We present a case study that demonstrates the major aspects of the approach and its use. We also give the results of a
preliminary evaluation of the approach.

1   Motivation

The ability to perform updates on running systems is a requirement for many
modern software systems that play critical roles in society. Emerging cyberphys-
ical systems such as smart grids, next-generation air-traffic control systems, and
intelligent transportation systems must be updated while running if they are to
continue to perform effectively in dynamically changing environments. Shutting
down these systems to make a change is often not an option because loss or
interruption of provided services could have a detrimental effect on the parts of
society that rely on the services. Updating software at runtime is challenging
and models that provide effective abstractions of runtime phenomenon can be
used to manage the complexity [1].

Research on Models@RunTime (M@RT) is concerned with how abstractions
of software implementations can be used at runtime to manage the complexity
of making changes to software at runtime [1]. Current M@RT work tends to
focus on how models can be used to support runtime adaptation in autonomous
systems (i.e., in self-* systems) [17,11]. While M@RT research is dominated by
work in the self-adaptation area, runtime models can be used to support other

N. Bencomo et al. (Eds.): Models@run.time, LNCS 8378, pp. 237–258, 2014.

forms of runtime system evolution. In particular, runtime models can be interfaces used by change agents for effecting changes on a software system while it is executing [7]. A change agent can be human or a software mechanism. For example, a developer can modify a runtime model consisting of sequence diagrams to describe changes in how objects will interact, or modify a class diagram describing the structure of runtime objects to describe changes in object attributes and references.

Runtime models can potentially be used to present the aspects of a running system that can be changed using abstractions that are understandable by a developer and that can be conveniently processed by a software change mechanism [7]. In many model-based self-adaptation approaches (e.g., see [4,8]) the models present the running system as a configuration of runtime components, and adaptation is often restricted to changes that can be effected by reconfiguring the component structure. We consider these approaches to be course-grained because changes are restricted to adding and removing components and links between components. More fine-grained evolution of a running system is limited by a lack of support in mainstream program development technologies (e.g., C/C++, C#, Java technologies) for dynamic update actions that involve dynamic object schema changes. For example, substitution of an object of a class by a corresponding object of the modified class during execution is typically treated as type mismatch and thus is not allowed in mainstream technologies.

In this contribution we describe a M@RT approach that supports runtime updates of Java programs by developers. In the approach, runtime models consisting of class and sequence diagrams describe the aspects of the runtime structure and behavior that can be modified by a developer at runtime. Changes in the runtime models are formally related to changes in the running system, and thus changes to the models can be propagated to changes in the running system. This use of runtime models requires more fine-grained descriptions of changes than those typically used to support self-reconfiguration of running systems. In the proposed approach, JavAdaptor [15], a tool that provides support for performing dynamic update of Java programs at runtime, provides the required fine-grained code changing facilities. Changes to the models are transformed to changes in the Java source code which are then effected on the running system using JavAdaptor.

We illustrate the approach using a railway simulation software system that undergoes two changes: one is the introduction of a realization of the strategy design pattern that is intended to make the original design more flexible, and the second change exploits the new flexible design to introduce a new type of train that is handled differently in the system.

In Sect. 2 we give an overview of how runtime updates are performed using the approach. A more detailed account of the model change operators and their mappings to code level change operators is given in Sect. 3 and 4 respectively. A demonstration case study is provided in Sect. 5, and results from an initial evaluation of the approach are described in Sect. 6. Related work is presented in Sect. 7, and we conclude with a discussion on further work in Sect. 8.

2   Overview of the Approach

In the JavAdaptor [15] approach to updating programs at runtime, the Java source code is the interface for changing the running program. The *fine grained adaptation* (FiGA) approach extends the JavAdaptor approach by providing support for the use of models as the primary means for modifying the runtime behavior of the program. The FiGA approach provides models that capture different aspects of a running program. Developers are restricted to performing only those changes that are possible using the abstractions provided by the models. In the current version of the approach, class and sequence diagrams provide the interface through which developers express changes on the running program. A developer uses the class diagrams to express changes on class structures (e.g., addition or removal of attributes or associations). Sequence diagrams are used to express changes in how objects interact. In future work we will extend this approach to include models that capture other aspects of a running program that can be changed by a developer (e.g., use of state diagrams to describe how objects react to input events and activity diagrams to provide a finer-grained view on the semantics of the running system).

A developer using the FiGA approach makes changes to the running system by performing a sequence of changes on the models. Each model change is performed by the developer applying a change operator. Each application of a change operator corresponds to a well-defined set of syntactic changes at the source code level. It is important to note that the application of a change operator on the model can leave the model inconsistent (e.g., removing a class from the class diagram does not automatically result in the removal of all its object interactions from the sequence diagrams). In addition, syntactic code changes that correspond to the application of a single model change operator may not produce source code that is compilable or executable. Only after a developer applies a consistent sequence of change operators to a model (i.e., a sequence of changes that results in a new consistent model) can the runtime updating mechanism be used to produce the new source code. The updating mechanism performs source code level changes that correspond to the model change operators in the order they are applied on the model to produce a new compilable code version. If compilation is successful, the result is fed into the JavAdaptor tool that performs the changes on the running program. The modified source code becomes the new baseline source code for the modified running program and is used to generate the models used by developers to perform future changes. We use a tool called ReverseЯ [2] to produce models from the source code.

The FiGA approach is illustrated in Fig. 1. In the figure, Model M_0 is the interface for the running program produced using the source code S_0. A developer modifies M_0 by applying a sequence of model operators $\gamma_1, \gamma_2, \ldots, \gamma_n$ to produce a new model M_1 that describes the changed program. The model operators correspond to source code changes, that, when applied in the order in which the model operators are applied, produces the modified compilable source code S_1. The source code S_1 is then compiled and used to change the running

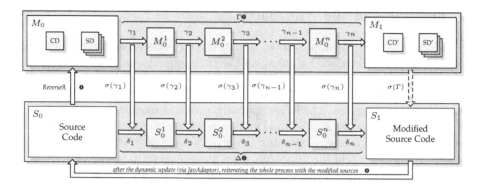

Fig. 1. Overview of the FiGA Approach

program using JavAdaptor. In the remainder of this section we describe the process for updating a running Java program using the FiGA approach:

Step 1: Generating Models from the Source Code. Models can be used to present aspects of a software program that can be changed in a manner that shields a developer from extraneous details in the source code, and thus helps developers better focus their development effort. A tool (ReverseЯ [2]) is used to reverse engineer the baseline source code to produce a model. This ensures that the model is a faithful representation of the running program. The approach is thus feasible when a design model is not available. In the FiGA approach, models are generated even when an initial design model is available at the time the running program is first started. This helps to overcome the well-known drift problem that occurs during development when design models are not properly synchronized with code changes. The use of models that are not consistent with the running code would jeopardize the feasibility of the FiGA approach.

Currently, the reverse engineering tool generates class diagrams to capture the structural aspects of the system, and sequence diagrams to capture the runtime interactions between different modules of the program. The sequence diagrams generated via reverse engineering contain not only method names and parameters, but also descriptions of method bodies. ReverseЯ is a Java tool which is based on @Java[1] a modified version of the Java language where the user can annotate blocks of code. This annotation extension is exploited in ReverseЯ by defining a set of @Java annotation that are specific to the needs of ReverseЯ. Specifically, these annotations contain meta-data used for generating the diagrams. ReverseЯ takes as input a set of compiled classes and a configuration file and produces as final output an IBM Rational Architect diagram file.

Step 2: Changing the Models. Rather than produce a new model in one monolithic step, a developer using the FiGA approach will apply model change operators that perform small model changes. Dividing a monolithic change into

---

[1] http://cazzola.di.unimi.it/atjava.html

smaller steps is advantageous for debugging and dependency analysis purposes, and it also provides a convenient way to automatically link model changes to source code changes. A change operator γ_i invoked by a developer on a current model corresponds to a well-defined change at the source code level, as we will see in Sect. 4. Currently, the structural changes are specified by modifying the class diagram. For example, FiGA provides change operators for adding a new class, adding new data members to a class, and so on. Changes to sequence diagrams correspond to changes in how parts of a program interact, for example, changing a method call in an object so that it calls another method defined in another object (e.g., this can be done in conjunction with a structural change in which a method is moved from one class to another). Complex changes could be defined as combinations of change operators on both sequence and class diagrams. For example, describing an extrude method refactoring, which involves creating a new method using part of an existing method, can be described as a combination of change operators on the class diagram and change operators on the sequence diagram. The change operators are described in Sect. 3.

Step 3: Relating Model Changes to Source Code Changes. Each model change operator (that is, each γ_i operation applied by the developer) is designed to correspond to a well-defined change at the source code level, represented by δ_i in Fig. 1. We use a mapping function σ to map each model change, γ_i, to a source code change, δ_i. The application of the σ mapping to the sequence of model changes (Γ) results in a corresponding sequence of code changes (Δ). That is, given

$$\delta_i = \sigma(\gamma_i)$$

and

$$\Gamma = \gamma_1 \boxplus \gamma_2 \boxplus \cdots \boxplus \gamma_n \tag{1}$$
$$\Delta = \delta_1 \boxplus \delta_2 \boxplus \cdots \boxplus \delta_n \tag{2}$$

where $\boxplus$ is the *change sequencing operator*, we have

$$\delta_1 \boxplus \delta_2 \boxplus \cdots \boxplus \delta_n = \sigma(\gamma_1) \boxplus \sigma(\gamma_2) \boxplus \cdots \boxplus \sigma(\gamma_n) \equiv \sigma(\Gamma) = \Delta.$$

The σ mapping is described in Sect. 4.

Step 4: Effecting the Changes on the Running Program. As mentioned in the previous steps, the model change is done in small steps where each change γ_i is mapped through σ to the corresponding code change δ_i. The FiGA tool internally records the order of model changes (Γ) and once the developer indicates that the model changes are ready to be deployed the tool triggers a series of source code changes corresponding to Δ. The modified source code is then compiled by javac and the modified .class files are input to JavAdaptor, which propagates the changes to the runtime program. Fig. 2 illustrates this workflow.

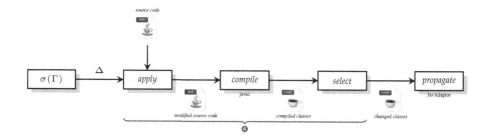

Fig. 2. The FiGA Process

Step 5: Reiterating the Process. The above process is repeated if a change to the updated software is required, that is, ReverseЯ is used to generate a new set of models from the modified source code, and these models become the interface used by developers to make changes to the running system.

3   Operators for Model Adaptation

In this section we describe the basic model change operators supported by our approach. These operators embody well-defined semantics for specific forms of UML diagram changes, and thus they provide the means to map model changes to code changes. It is important to note that when a user changes a UML diagram using a diagram editor the corresponding applications of basic change operators are inferred by the IDE. Moreover, the IDE provides the users with more complex operators built up from the basic change operators, for example, operators for cascading removal of elements.

Given a set of UML diagrams, M_0, representing the running system, we apply a sequence of operations Γ and produce a new set of UML diagrams M_1, i.e.,

$$\Gamma = \{\gamma_1, \gamma_2, \gamma_3, \ldots, \gamma_n\} \text{ such that } M_0 \boxplus \Gamma = M_1.$$

Since models M_0 and M_1 must be consistent, Γ must be a sequence of operations which transforms a consistent set of diagrams to another consistent set of diagrams when applied in the given order. However this condition may not hold for all the intermediate steps M_0^i obtained by applying γ_i on M_0^{i-1}. Each γ_i is an elementary step that changes only one aspect of a model, so there is no guarantee that the result will be consistent at each (intermediate) step. Only Γ is required to preserve the consistency of the model.

In the remainder of this section we describe the syntax and effect of the γ_i operators. For the sake of brevity we describe only the core set of operators. As mentioned in Sect. 2, we use only class and sequence diagrams in the approach, so only operators for these diagrams are described here.

Table 1. Class diagram change operators

Operator	Specifies into	Description
$\oplus_{cd}$	$\oplus_{class}$ $\oplus_{interface}$ $\oplus_{field}$ $\oplus_{constructor}$ $\oplus_{method}$	*These operators add elements of a particular type to a class diagram.* *The arguments of an $\oplus$ operator is determined by the type of element to be added and can include element name, visibility level, abstract[?] static[?], type, return type, containing class*
$\ominus_{cd}$	$\ominus_{class}$ $\ominus_{interface}$ $\ominus_{field}$ $\ominus_{constructor}$ $\ominus_{method}$	*These operators remove elements of a particular type from a class diagram.* *Cascading removal is not supported. Each operator removes only the given element. The application layer can provide cascading operations for the user.*
$\triangleright$	—	*This operator adds a generalization relationship.* *It does not add inherited methods.*
$\not\triangleright$	—	*This operator removes a generalization relationship.* *It does not remove inherited methods.*

Class Diagram Change Operators. Operators for class diagrams work on class diagram entities: classes, interfaces, fields, constructors and methods. The approach currently provides basic operators for adding and removing (1) classifiers (interfaces, classes) and their properties, and (2) generalization relationships between classes. Table 1 lists the core class diagram change operators.

The set of add operators, $\oplus_{cd}$, contains operators for adding elements of a particular type to a class diagram. For example, $\oplus_{class}$ adds a class to a class diagram, while $\oplus_{field}$ adds an attribute to a given class. Similarly, the set of remove operators, $\ominus_{cd}$, contains operators for removing classes ($\ominus_{class}$), interfaces ($\ominus_{interface}$), fields ($\ominus_{field}$), constructors ($\ominus_{constructor}$), and methods ($\ominus_{method}$). The operator $\triangleright$ adds a generalization relation between two containers, while the operator $\not\triangleright$ removes an existing generalization relationship between containers.

Sequence Diagram Change Operators. The sequence diagram elements that can be changed in our approach are lifelines and messages. Given that the approach is Java-specific, the sequence diagrams supported by the approach consist only of synchronous and create messages[2].

As with class diagrams, we have a set of adding operators $\oplus_{sd}$ for sequence diagram elements ($\oplus_{lifeline}$ and $\oplus_{message}$) and a corresponding set of removal operators $\ominus_{sd}$ ($\ominus_{lifeline}$ and $\ominus_{message}$). Table 2 lists the core sequence diagram change operators.

---

[2] The start() message that activates a thread could be considered as an exception but we deal with it as with a call to a constructor.

Table 2. Sequence diagram change operators

Operator	Specifies into	Description
$\oplus_{sd}$	$\oplus_{\text{lifeline}}$ $\oplus_{\text{message}}$	*Add element.* *Lifelines can refer to class or to single objects. Messages* *can be creation or synchronous. Other parameters can be:* *element name, message position, lifeline type.*
$\ominus_{sd}$	$\ominus_{\text{lifeline}}$ $\ominus_{\text{message}}$	*Remove element.* *It does not act as a cascade operator. Each element must* *be removed explicitly. The application layer can provide* *cascading operations for the user.*

More complex operators can be built up from basic class and sequence diagram change operators. For example, a replace operator can be obtained by removing the old element using basic remove operators and by adding the new one using a basic add operator. Some minor aspects, such as the initialization of static fields, are currently not handled and will be added in a future version of the work.

Precedence Among Operators. We impose constraints on the order in which the different kinds of change operators can be applied to ensure that model changes produce consistent models. While the constraints do not guarantee that the changes produce programs that satisfy the programmer's goals, they do ensure that the class and sequence diagrams are internally consistent and consistent with each other. Model change operators are ordered as follows to ensure consistency:

1. **Add new classifiers ($\oplus_{\text{interface}}$ and $\oplus_{\text{class}}$):** All new interfaces and classes are added first because they are the containers to which subsequent new classifier parts are added (e.g., methods, attributes), and sequence diagrams may need to reference these new classifiers (e.g., via new lifelines).
2. **Add elements to new classifiers ($\oplus_{\text{field}}$, $\oplus_{\text{constructor}}$, $\oplus_{\text{method}}$):** Elements are added to the containers produced in the previous step, and to already existing classifiers.
3. **Remove generalizations that are targeted for change ($\not\triangleright$):** If a generalization relationship is to be changed, the old generalization is removed before adding the new one. This helps to avoid situations where a user wants to change a generalization between a subclass *Sub* and a superclass *Super* to one between *Sub* and another superclass *Sup2*, and first adds the new generalization, but then forgets to remove the original generalization between *Sub* and *Super*. That is, this ordering helps avoid changes that result in multiple inheritance structures not supported by Java.
4. **Add new generalizations ($\triangleright$):** New generalizations are added after target generalizations are removed.
5. **Change sequence diagrams ($\oplus_{sd}$, $\ominus_{sd}$):** When all the above changes are made to class diagrams, changes can proceed on the sequence diagrams. These changes are ordered as follows:

(a) Add new lifelines ($\oplus_{\text{lifeline}}$) to sequence diagrams first.

(b) Add new messages ($\oplus_{\text{message}}$) to sequence diagrams. The create messages have a higher precedence than the synchronous messages. Note that messages have a progressive numeration that is unique for each sequence diagram. This facilitates easier addition of new messages.

(c) Remove messages ($\ominus_{\text{message}}$) from the sequence diagrams; similarly to $\oplus_{\text{message}}$ but synchronous messages are deleted before the creational ones.

(d) Remove lifelines ($\ominus_{\text{lifeline}}$) from sequence diagrams.

6. **Remove elements from class diagrams ($\ominus_{\textbf{cd}}$):** all class diagram removal operators are applied last. Each operator first checks that the element to be removed is not referenced elsewhere in the class or sequence diagrams.

Note that removal operations are all made at the end of the process and that operators for sequence diagrams are carried out after all additions are made to class diagrams. By doing this, we guarantee that methods exist before messages are added and that messages are removed before removing methods, that is, $\oplus_{cd}$ operators are performed first and $\ominus_{cd}$ operations performed last.

4   Mapping between Code and Model

The operators defined in the previous section correspond to well-defined changes at the source code level. In this section we describe the morphism σ that maps each model level change, γ_i, to a corresponding source code level change, δ_i.

Mappings for Class Diagram Operators. Class diagrams are used to describe the static class structure of programs in a straightforward manner (each program class corresponds to a single class in the diagram), hence σ provides a one to one mapping between the class diagram changes described in the previous section and changes to (source) code structures. These mappings are straightforward, and thus we only use an example here to illustrate the mappings.

Class diagram mappings example. Figure 3 shows changes made to a class diagram of a program. Initially, the program has only a single class: ClassA. The user then decides to modify the program by adding a new class, called NewClassB with a field and a method. This results in a sequence of three basic changes to the model: (1) add an empty class, (2) add the field, and (3) add the method. Finally, the user reorganizes the class hierarchy by making NewClassB a subclass of ClassA. These changes are realized at the code level by the following sequence of operations:

1. $\oplus_{\text{class}}$(NewClassB, **public**): add new **public** class with name NewClassB (see Fig. 3(b))

2. $\oplus_{\text{field}}$(field1, **private**, Object, NewClassB): add a **private** field inside class NewClassB (see Fig. 3(c))

3. $\oplus_{\text{method}}$(method1, **public**, **void**, NewClassB): add a **public** method, with return type **void**, inside class NewClassB (see Fig. 3(d))

(a) Original system

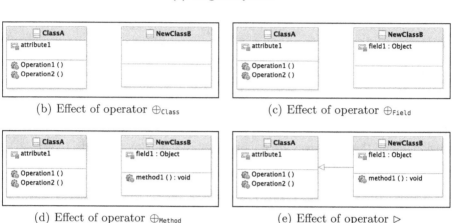

(b) Effect of operator $\oplus_{class}$

(c) Effect of operator $\oplus_{Field}$

(d) Effect of operator $\oplus_{Method}$

(e) Effect of operator $\triangleright$

Fig. 3. Class diagram example: evolution of the models

4. $\triangleright$(NewClassB, ClassA): make NewClassB a subclass of ClassA (see Fig. 3(e))

The effect on the code is illustrated in Fig. 4. In the first step, the operator $\oplus_{class}$ creates an empty class at the model level, and thus $\sigma(\oplus_{class})$ will produce an empty class declaration, with name NewClassB and **public** visibility. In the second step, $\oplus_{field}$ adds a new field to the diagram, and thus $\sigma(\oplus_{field})$ adds a line inside the newly created class declaration with the field declaration. Since in Java the field position in a class declaration is irrelevant, the new fields are always introduced at the top of the class body as in Fig. 4(b). In the third step, the mapping $\sigma(\oplus_{method})$ has the effect of adding a method signature with an empty body to NewClassB (see Fig. 4(c)). The position of method declarations inside a class is also irrelevant, so they are added at the bottom of all existing code in order to preserve readability. Finally, the operator $\triangleright$ is used to create the inheritance relationship between ClassA and ClassNewB. The corresponding code change $\sigma(\triangleright)$ adds the **extends** clause to the class declaration (see Fig. 4(d)). If the second parameter given is an interface then $\sigma(\triangleright)$ adds the **implements** clause.

The mapping for the $\ominus_{cd}$ operator works in a similar way. $\sigma(\ominus_{cd})$ simply removes the portion of code where the corresponding entity is declared. The remove operator is not a cascading operator, and thus to perform correct removal it is necessary to explicitly remove all the element contained in the one that is being removed before its effective removal. For example, to remove a class

```
public class NewClassB {



}
```
(a) Created the empty NewClassB.

```
public class NewClassB {
    private Object field1;

}
```
(b) Added the new field.

```
public class NewClassB {
    private Object field1;
    public void method1(){}
}
```
(c) Added the new method.

```
public class NewClassB extends ClassA {
    private Object field1;
    public void method1(){}
}
```
(d) Changed the inheritance hierarchy.

Fig. 4. Class Diagram example: changes impact on sources

the user should remove all its methods and fields before applying the operator for removing the class itself. Likewise $\sigma(\not\triangleright)$ removes either the **extends** or the **implements** clause.

Mappings for Sequence Diagram Operators. Mapping sequence diagram changes to code changes is more complex. This is because sequence diagrams describe dynamic aspects of a program that are sometimes not directly reflected in source code. Moreover a sequence diagram does not represent a complete description of behavior; it typically represents a set of behavioral scenarios and thus is an incomplete view of behavior. For this reason, not all changes to a sequence diagram will produce a corresponding change at the code level. For example, adding a lifeline to a sequence diagram may not produce a resulting change in the code if the class of the object already exists in the original program. Figure 5(b) illustrates the effect of an application of the $\oplus_{\texttt{lifeline}}$ operator on the model in Fig. 5(a). Adding a lifeline means that another object (not necessarily a new object) is part of the message exchange sequence. Only the objects which interact with the new lifeline need a reference to the object, but the kind of reference (instance of an association or a more dynamic dependency) cannot be deduced simply by looking only at the *add new lifeline* change. The kind of reference must be deduced by examining previous changes to the class diagrams (e.g., to add a field that contains a reference to the object represented by the lifeline) or from the introduction of a create message (a call to the constructor to create an object represented by the new lifeline). In these cases, adding the lifeline has no effect on the code.

Adding a message to a sequence diagram is another matter. Generally speaking, a message is a method call that needs to be added inside the method body. $\oplus_{\texttt{message}}$ has two different mappings depending on the kind of the added message: *create* or *synchronous*. In the case of a creation ($\oplus_{\texttt{message}}(\texttt{create}, ...)$), the message represents a constructor call. At the code level, $\sigma(\oplus_{\texttt{message}}(\texttt{create}, ...))$ adds a call to the constructor of the class of the created lifeline (object) into the method body executed in the source lifeline. Figure 5(c) illustrates the situation at the model level. As shown in Fig. 6, we can get the desired behavior in two ways: either by adding a field to the class or declaring a local variable, and then instantiate the field or variable with a reference to the new object in the method `m0()`. The choice between the two depends on what operations preceded this change: in the former case, due to the imposed order (see Sect. 3) a new field with that name was already added in the class diagram. As a rule, we store the new object into a field if there is a field of a compatible type and with the same name as the new object, otherwise a new local variables is declared (and named after the corresponding lifeline name), and the new object assigned to it. Note that, in this case, a call to the constructor could be added anywhere inside the body of method `m0()`, except within loops and conditionals, as long as it respects the ordering of other message exchanges shown in the sequence diagram. Since the sequence diagram shows no other exchanges in `m0()` the create message can be placed anywhere in the body of `m0()`. The decision to add the call as the first instruction was made simply for convenience.

A special case occurs when objects are stored in the variables representing the passed parameters. If we have a method **void** `method(String parameter1){..}` the user could decide to reuse the variable `parameter1` to store a new object. Given a message label containing parameters name (`parameter1 = ` **new** ` String()`) we treat the parameters like any other already declared local variable, trusting the developer to name the parameters appropriately.

As an example of how the addition of a synchronous message is added, consider the situation described in Fig. 5(d) where a new method call to the method `m1()` is added to the sequence diagram in Fig. 5(c). The method `m1()` must exist in class `ClassB`, and since `ClassA` will use `objectB` it is up to the user to guarantee its existence. In this example, the code to add is `objectB.m1()` and from the sequence diagram we can determine that it must be added in the body of `m0()` in any position, after **new** `ClassB()`. If a finer positioning mechanism is desired, it is possible to look at the method body that is included in the sequence diagram by our reverse engineering tool as a UML comment and specify after which statement the new code is to be inserted.

In a more general case, the new message will be inserted between two messages, so it is necessary to look at only the portion between the two method calls. Our planned work on extending the approach to include activity diagrams will make this step unnecessary, because a fine grain addition could be done directly on the complete descriptions of method bodies provided by activity diagrams.

Changes effected by $\ominus_{lifeline}$ do not affect the code. The removal of a lifeline from a sequence diagram means that the object represented by the lifeline ceases to participate in the interaction described by the sequence diagram. This does not mean that the object should be removed from the system.

The $\ominus_{message}$ causes the deletion of a single line of code: the one which contains the method or constructor call described by the exchanged message from the method body referred from the source object lifeline. Note that the call is uniquely determined by its position inside the sequence diagram.

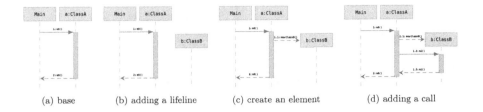

| (a) base | (b) adding a lifeline | (c) create an element | (d) adding a call |

Fig. 5. An example of sequence diagrama manipulation

```
public class ClassA {
    private ClassB objectB;
    public void m0() {
        objectB = new ClassB();
        stmt1;
        stmt2;
        ...
        stmtn;
    }
}
```

```
public class ClassA {

    public void m0() {
        ClassB objectB = new ClassB();
        stmt1;
        stmt2;
        ...
        stmtn;
    }
}
```

(a) initializing a field.   (b) initializing a local variable.

Fig. 6. Example of code affection ambiguity due to a new creation message

5   Case Study

The case study we use to illustrate the approach is a Train Management System (TMS) that is responsible for tracking trains driven by humans and for controlling the traffic signals that determine whether a train should stop or proceed. Stopping such a system to make an update is often not desirable because this would mean that all train activity on the system would have to be halted since it cannot be monitored and controlled.

To demonstrate the FIGA approach, we implemented the TMS and integrated it with a Railway Simulator (RS) representing a real world situation in which the TMS is used. The railway system monitored by the TMS is a network of routes connecting stations (each route has a start and end station). Each route uni-directional and is divided into uniquely identified segments. Each segment has a sensor for detecting a train leaving the segment, and a traffic light that indicates whether a train is allowed to move to the next segment or not. The RS initializes and moves trains through the system. Each train entering the system must submit journey that is validated and stored in the TMS. The RS tells the TMS when trains move by simulating the triggering of sensors, and the TMS in turn tells the RS when to toggle the traffic lights in the segments. In the initial version of the system all trains are passenger trains.

Requested evolution. In the case study scenario, the company that manages the railway system decides to expand its system to support monitoring of freight trains that require special treatment, for example, trains that carry hazardous

(a) original class diagram.   (b) class diagram with strategy pattern.

Fig. 7. TMS class diagram, before/after the strategy pattern reorganization

materials (referred to as *hazardous train*). When transporting hazardous materials, special security rules must be enforced and the TMS must be updated accordingly. The TMS must be able to distinguish these trains from other trains, and must enforce traffic light control policies that are specific to hazardous trains (e.g., a policy can require that no other trains must be on the same route as a hazardous train). The system manager responsible for managing this update decides that the update will be performed as two updates. The first update aims to improve the TMS architecture to make it easier to add a new type of train that requires special light control policies. Specifically, this first adaptation involves implementing an instance of the strategy pattern in the TMS software to make it easier to add new traffic light rules (strategies). The second update is concerned with introducing hazardous trains and their associated rules to the more flexible TMS produced by the first update.

We will provide details here for only the first update; the incorporation of the strategy pattern instance in the initial TMS. The second update does not provide any interesting new insights.

Figure 7(a) shows the class diagram for the initial version of the TMS and Fig. 7(b) shows the modified class diagram. This update changes only the `Message` class, which represents the evaluator for the messages the TMS receives from the RS. In the initial version `Message` implements the `Runnable` interface. When a message is received the computation is threaded to evaluate it. In the first version only two kind of messages can be received: the journey authorization request and the notification of the train position from the segments sensors. `Message` has methods to handle these messages and uses (an **if** statement) to determine which method to execute on receiving a message. In the new version, `Message` is an abstract class, subclassed as many times as the supported kinds of messages. Each subclass implements a method to evaluate the corresponding message and the selection is accomplished using polymorphism. `Message` is also a factory that creates a subclass instance representing the received message.

The main changes between the two class diagrams are the following: (1) new subclasses that extend `Message`, (2) methods belonging to `Message` are moved to the new subclasses, (3) constructors are made private and (4) new `Message` object can be created only through a static method in `Message`. The following is an excerpt of the operations that have to be applied to go from the class diagram in Fig. 7(a) to the one in Fig. 7(b).

- $\oplus_{\text{class}}$(EnteringStationMessage, **public**)
- $\oplus_{\text{class}}$(SensorMessage, **public**)
- $\oplus_{\text{class}}$(JourneyMessage, **public**)
- $\triangleright$(EnteringStationMessage, Message)
- $\triangleright$(SensorMessage, Message)
- $\triangleright$(JourneyMessage, Message)
- $\oplus_{\text{method}}$(**public**, **static**, Message, {String}, Message)
- $\oplus_{\text{constructor}}$(**protected**, {String[]}, EnteringStationMessage)
- $\oplus_{\text{constructor}}$(**protected**, {String[]}, SensorMessage)
- $\oplus_{\text{constructor}}$(**protected**, {String[]}, JourneyMessage)
- $\oplus_{\text{method}}$(run, **public**, **void**, {}, EnteringStationMessage)
- $\oplus_{\text{method}}$(correctPlatform, **public**, String, {String,String}, EnteringStationMessage)
- $\oplus_{\text{method}}$(letTrainLeaveStation, **public**, String, {String}, EnteringStationMessage)
- $\oplus_{\text{method}}$(run, **public**, **void**, {}, SensorMessage)
- $\oplus_{\text{method}}$(checkIfRunaway, **public**, **boolean**, {String, String}, SensorMessage)
- $\oplus_{\text{method}}$(updateSystemTime, **public**, **void**, {**int**}, SensorMessage)
- $\oplus_{\text{method}}$(updateTrainPosition, **public**, String[], {String,String,**int**}, SensorMessage)
- $\oplus_{\text{method}}$(run, **public**, **void**, {}, JourneyMessage)
- ...[3]
- $\ominus_{\text{method}}$(authorizeJourney, Message)
- $\ominus_{\text{method}}$(changeSegmentState, Message)
- $\ominus_{\text{method}}$(checkIfRunaway, Message)
- $\ominus_{\text{method}}$(correctPlatform, Message)
- $\ominus_{\text{method}}$(letTrainLeaveStation, Message)
- $\ominus_{\text{method}}$(updateTrainPosition, Message)
- $\ominus_{\text{method}}$(interpretMessage, Message)
- $\ominus_{\text{method}}$(updateSystemTime, Message)

The major changes on the sequence diagram involve message identification and evaluation (Fig. 8). In the initial sequence diagram, the RailwayIn class, which is the class that receives the messages, directly creates a Message object. In the modified sequence diagram a static method (getMessage(String)) is to be used instead. This method will call the correct constructor to deal with the subclass instances. Therefore the object that is now being passed to Thread is not a Message object anymore, but an instance of one of its child classes (see Fig. 8(b)). The entire sequence diagram must change: Methods that were in the Message class now are in the child JourneyMessage class; and validateJourney(), addTrain(t), sendMessage(output) must now be called from the journeyMessage:JourneyMessage lifeline and their old invocation must be deleted.

The following is an excerpt of the operations that have to be applied to go from the sequence diagram in Fig. 8(a) to the one in Fig. 8(b).

1. $\oplus_{\text{lifeline}}$(journeyMessage:JourneyMessage)
2. $\oplus_{\text{message}}$(synchronous, 5, RailwayIn, Message, Message m2 = getMessage(m), 33)
3. $\oplus_{\text{message}}$(create, 5.1, Message, JourneyMessage, inside(5), **new** JourneyMessage(m), 208)

---

[3] Following the precedence rules given in Sect. 3 the operations on sequence diagrams are interleaved with those on class diagrams. For sake of comprehension we will present the operations on sequence diagrams later.

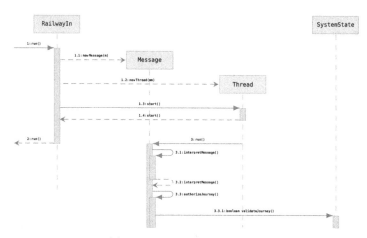

(a) original sequence diagram

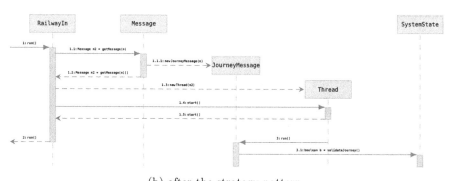

(b) after the strategy pattern

Fig. 8. The sequence diagram describing the run method of `RailwayIn`

4. $\oplus_{message}$(create, 6, RailwayIn, Thread, after(5), **new** Thread(m2), 34)
5. $\oplus_{message}$(synchronous, 7, RailwayIn, Thread, after(6), start(), 35)
6. $\oplus_{message}$(synchronous, 8, Thread, JourneyMessage, after(7), run(), 23)
7. $\oplus_{message}$(synchronous, 8.1, JourneyMessage, SystemState, inside(8),
   boolean b = validateJourney(), 27)
8. $\oplus_{message}$(synchronous, 8.2, JourneyMessage, SystemState, after(8.1), addTrain(t), 33)
9. $\oplus_{message}$(synchronous, 8.3, JourneyMessage, RailwayOut, after(8.2),
   sendMessage(output), 49)
10. $\ominus_{message}$(synchronous, 3.1.3.3, 144)
11. $\ominus_{message}$(synchronous, 3.1.3.2, 140)
12. $\ominus_{message}$(synchronous, 3.1.3.1, 137)
13. $\ominus_{message}$(synchronous, 3.1.3, 130)
14. $\ominus_{message}$(synchronous, 3.1.1, 114)
15. $\ominus_{message}$(synchronous, 2, 32)
16. $\ominus_{message}$(synchronous, 1, 31)

The $\oplus_{message}$ operator takes many arguments, if we consider the seventh operation in the previous list as an example, its argument reads as follows: "inserts a new synchronous message marked with ID 8.1 exchanged from `JourneyMessage` to `SystemState`, this call is inside message 8 and is performed by the code «**boolean** b = validateJourney()» that has to be inserted at line 27". The message IDs are provided, in sequential order, by the IBM's Rational Software Architect when the changes are given, and they refer to the graphical representation of the UML diagram (see Fig. 8). The line number indicating where to insert the call, is given here as an absolute number, but it is actually computed based on the portion of code shown to the user and a point&click mechanism is used to show where the code should be inserted.

We now present how changes to the sequence diagram affect the class `RailwayIn`. Figure 9 shows how the changes step by step. First, we add the new method call to the original code (Fig. 9(b)). This is a call to a static method and its return value is stored in a local variable (operation 2). Such an addition is done at line 33, but note that numbering is just a convention we use in the explanation: all the positioning inside the code is relative to the piece of code shown in the annotation and recalculated every time. Recall that the operations are not written by the user but they are the result of the changes done to the diagrams, and the line of code are adjusted accordingly. After this, the effect of operations 4 and 5 is to add the code to create (Fig. 9(c) at line 34) and then start the thread (Fig. 9(d) at line 35). At last, the operations 15 and 16 remove the obsolete code: the old thread creation/activation (Fig. 9(e) at line 32) and the message creation (Fig. 9(f) at line 31).

6   Discussion

In the FiGA approach, developers update a running system by modifying generated UML class and sequence diagrams. Empirical results [5] provide some evidence that the use UML during software maintenance and evolution enhances a developers ability to correctly implement changes when developers are not familiar with the system. Using UML models as the primary means to update running code can help by presenting runtime information in modeling languages that developers are more familiar with, while shielding developers from extraneous source code details.

The FiGA approach further reduce the time to effect changes, by automating the propagation of the changes to the running code. In a context where an application needs to be updated as quickly as possible,the FiGA approach allows a developer to focus on planning tyne changes via the models with the awareness that the changes on the sources will be automatically performed in a consistent manner.

To support automatic propagation of model changes to the source code, the abstraction gap between code and models has to be bridged [2,19] This issue is addressed in FiGA by generating UML diagrams from source code that includes specific meta-data (Java annotations) that is maintained by the system during evolution. This tight link between the models and the code supports their co-evolution.

```
30 for (String m: msg.split("!")) {
31     Message mm = new Message(m);
32     new Thread(mm).start();
33
34
35
36 }
```

(a) original code.

```
30 for (String m: msg.split("!")) {
31     Message mm = new Message(m);
32     new Thread(mm).start();
33     Message m2 = Message.getMessage(m);
34
35
36 }
```

(b) adding a call to getMessage.

```
30 for (String m: msg.split("!")) {
31     Message mm = new Message(m);
32     new Thread(mm).start();
33     Message m2 = Message.getMessage(m);
34     Thread t2 = new Thread(m2);
35
36 }
```

(c) creating a new thread.

```
30 for (String m: msg.split("!")) {
31     Message mm = new Message(m);
32     new Thread(mm).start();
33     Message m2 = Message.getMessage(m);
34     Thread t2 = new Thread(m2);
35     t2.start();
36 }
```

(d) activating the new thread.

```
30 for (String m: msg.split("!")) {
31     Message mm = new Message(m);
32     new Thread(mm).start();
33     Message m2 = Message.getMessage(m);
34     Thread t2 = new Thread(m2);
35     t2.start();
36 }
```

(e) removing the other thread.

```
30 for (String m: msg.split("!")) {
31     Message mm = new Message(m);
32
33     Message m2 = Message.getMessage(m);
34     Thread t2 = new Thread(m2);
35     t2.start();
36 }
```

(f) removing the Message creation.

Fig. 9. Changes in RailwayIn

To make the FiGA approach usable, we provide an IDE that acts an intermediate layer between the developer and the runtime updating system. The IDE aims to provide a convenient interface for describing model changes and for automatically propagating those changes to the runtime updating system. The IDE presents a developer with a set of diagrams and all the operations he can performs on the diagrams (see Sect. 3). The IDE also takes care of converting a developer's changes to a model to function calls that mirror the operator definitions.

Another factor which reduces the complexity of the update is the use of JavAdaptor [15] as a reloading mechanism during system execution. Many published approaches (e.g., see [22]) focus on the definition of states in which the application can safely migrate from its original form to its evolved one. This is not a concern in FiGA because it relies on JavAdaptor to replace each class while keeping its state intact; no data is lost and each object in the new version immediately starts running with its old state. JavAdaptor also determines when to freeze the class for the reloading operation. The new version of JavAdaptor (more advanced than the one described in [15]) is also able to safely handle the reloading operation in a multi-threaded environment. Constraints on *when* to update the application are thus looser in FiGA.

Constraints on what to replace are also loosened in FiGA. In many cases, software needs to evolve because the context in which it operates changes, thus leading to different requirements for the application. Software evolution is thus as predictable as the context in which it runs in, and thus one can anticipate that there will be some unforeseen evolution. From the programmer's point of view this means that any part of the software might need to be changed. FiGA supports this type of unforeseen evolution through the generation of detailed diagrams for any part of the software. Furthermore some changes might affect only a small portion of the software. In [3] a case study is presented in which the requested change involved adding a time constraint for an online order. While the impact of the change on the models was relatively small, at the code level it involved adding **if** statements in many places and providing an orderExpired mechanism that could be implemented as a Java exception. FiGA allows one to apply fine-grained code changes (at the source code line level) and change only the affected classes in the running system. In other approaches, this would required larger-grained changes involving replacing a whole module or component (e.g., see [13,16]).

FiGA is code-centric. As the evolution process needs to end with the production of running code, our research effort focused on meeting the need for fast deployment of runtime changes described in terms of models.Having said that, the current version of the approach does have limitations. The UML diagrams do not provide all necessary information to deal with every kind of fine-grained update. For example, the addition and the removal of conditional jump structures are currently not supported. Given that the current version was developed more as a proof of concept, one can expect that there will be limitations. We are currently working on addressing these limitations by considering how other types of UML diagrams, for example, activity diagrams, can be included in FiGA.

7   Related Work

Architecture-based software adaptation approaches focus on supporting automated coarse-grained reconfiguration of software structure at runtime (for example, see [6,8,9,12,13,21]. In these approaches, the running system is structured to facilitate the use of component-based runtime models that are causally connected to the running system. Each component is a coarse-grained abstraction that represents a logically encapsulated part of the running system. Runtime modifications are restricted to adding and removing components and links between components. The approach described in this chapter provides support for finer-grained modifications at the Java program class level. Unlike the architecture-based approaches, our fine-grained approach does not constrain the structure of Java programs that can undergo runtime modifications. On the other hand, our approach currently supports manual changes, that is, humans manually modify the runtime models rather than the system itself. We will investigate how the approach can be extended to support self-adaptation.

Research on dynamic software updates (e.g., see [10,14,20,18]) aims to produce mechanisms that allow developers to change a running system without stopping and restarting the running system. Code level changes are submitted to these mechanisms, which are then effected on running systems. JavAdaptor [15] is one such mechanisms that supports a finer granularity of changes.

Unlike other work on dynamic software updates, FiGA, which is built on top of JavAdaptor, focuses on using models to raise the level of abstraction at which changes are presented to the running system. We are not aware of any dynamic update mechanism that uses models as an interface for making changes to a running system.

Our approach requires mechanisms that generate models that faithfully abstract over the aspects of a running system that are subject to change. In our approach we specifically require mechanisms that generate class and sequence diagrams from the current source Java program. Tools such as IBM's Software Architect[4], VisualParadigm[5] and ArgoUML[6] can be used to generate class and sequence diagrams from Java code. Integrating these complex tools into a runtime update environment can be challenging. In our work we chose to use ReverseЯ because we had full access to its implementation and could thus more easily integrate it with our software updating mechanism, and since it is based on Java annotations it can be smoothly integrated in the running system.

8   Conclusion

In this paper, we presented a model based approach to fine-grained updating of running software. UML diagrams of the running application are the model@runtime. These models are used by developers to describe desired changes on the running system in terms of model changes that are transformed to source ode changes. In this way is possible to co-evolve the model and the source code. The source code changes are then applied to the running application through the JavAdaptor framework [15], without the need to stop the running system.

The approach does not make any assumptions about the changes that might occur nor about which part of the program the changes affect. The only restriction is on the kinds of models currently supported (class and sequence diagrams), and therefore on the kind of changes that can be described. The current version of FiGA was developed to demonstrate the feasibility of the approach, and thus the types of models is restricted. However in the future plans we will develop support for a wider range of UML diagrams.

References

1. Blair, G.S., Bencomo, N., France, R.B.: Models@run.time. IEEE Computer 42(10), 22–27 (2009)
2. Cazzola, W., Pini, S., Ghoneim, A., Saake, G.: Co-Evolving Application Code and Design Models by Exploiting Meta-Data. In: Proceedings of the 12th Annual ACM Symposium on Applied Computing (SAC 2007), Seoul, South Korea, March 11–15, pp. 1275–1279. ACM Press (2007)

---

[4] http://www.ibm.com/developerworks/rational/library/08/0610_xu-wood/
[5] http://www.visual-paradigm.com/product/vpuml/tutorials/seqrev.jsp
[6] http://argouml-users.net/index.php?title=Java_Sequence_Diagram_Reverse_Engineering

3. Chechik, M., Lai, W., Nejati, S., Cabot, J., Diskin, Z., Easterbrook, S., Sabetzadeh, M., Salay, R.: Relationship-Based Change Propagation: A Case Study. In: Proceedings of the ICSE Workshop on Modeling in Software Engineering (MiSE 2009), Vancouver, Canada, pp. 7–12. IEEE (May 2009)
4. Costa-Soria, C., Hervás-Muñoz, D., Pérez Benedí, J., Carsí Cubel, J.A.: A Reflective Approach for Supporting the Dynamic Evolution of Component Types. In: Proceedings of the 14th IEEE International Conference on Engineering of Complex Computer Systems (ICECCS 2009), pp. 301–310, Potsdam, Germany (June 2009)
5. Dzidek, W.J., Arisholm, E., Briand, L.C.: A Realistic Empirical Evaluation of the Costs and Benefits of UML in Software Maintenance. IEEE Transactions on Software Engineering 34(3), 407–432 (2008)
6. Floch, J., Hallsteinsen, S., Stav, E., Eliassen, F., Lund, K., Gjørven, E.: Beyond Design Time: Using Architecture Models for Runtime Adaptability. IEEE Software 23(2), 62–70 (2006)
7. France, R.B., Rumpe, B.: Model-Driven Development of Complex Software: A Research Roadmap. In: Briand, L.C., Wolf, A.L. (eds.) Proceedings of Future of Software Engineering (FoSE 2007), Minneapolis, MN, USA, pp. 37–54. IEEE Computer Society (May 2007)
8. Garlan, D., Cheng, S.-W., Huang, A.-C., Schmerl, B., Steenkiste, P.: Rainbow: Architecture-Based Self Adaptation with Reusable Infrastructure. IEEE Computer 37(10), 46–54 (2004)
9. Georgas, J.C., van der Hoek, A., Taylor, R.N.: Using Architectural Models to Manage and Visualize Runtime Adaptation. IEEE Computer 42(10), 52–60 (2009)
10. Hicks, M., Nettles, S.: Dynamic Software Updating. ACM Transaction on Programming Languages and Systems 27(6), 1049–1096 (2005)
11. Kramer, J., Magee, J.: Self-Managed Systems: an Architectural Challenge. In: Briand, L.C., Wolf, A.L. (eds.) Proceedings of 29th International Conference on Software Engineering (ICSE 2007): Future of Software Engineering (FoSE 2007), Minneapolis, MN, USA, pp. 259–268. IEEE Computer Society (May 2007)
12. Morin, B., Barais, O., Jézéquel, J.-M., Fleurey, F., Solberg, A.: Models@ Run.time to Support Dynamic Adaptation. IEEE Computer 42(10), 44–51 (2009)
13. Oreizy, P., Medvidovic, N., Taylor, R.N.: Architecture-Based Runtime Software Evolution. In: Proceedings of the 20th International Conference on Software Engineering (ICSE 1998), Kyoto, Japan, pp. 177–186. IEEE Computer Society (1998)
14. Orso, A., Rao, A., Harrold, M.J.: A Technique for Dynamic Updating of Java Software. In: Proceedings of the International Conference on Software Maintenance (ICSM 2002), Montréal, Canada, pp. 649–658. IEEE Press (October 2002)
15. Pukall, M., Kästner, C., Cazzola, W., Götz, S., Grebhahn, A., Schöter, R., Saake, G.: JavAdaptor — Flexible Runtime Updates of Java Applications. Software— Practice and Experience 43(2), 153–185 (2013)
16. Sadjadi, S.M., McKinley, P.K.: ACT: An Adaptive CORBA Template to Support Unanticipated Adaptation. In: Proceedings of the 24th International Conference on Distributed Computing Systems (ICDCS 2004), Tokyo, Japan, pp. 74–83. IEEE Computer Society (March 2004)
17. Salehie, M., Tahvildari, L.: Self-Adaptive Software: Landscape and Research Challenges. ACM Transactions on Autonomous and Adaptive Systems 14, 14:1–14:42 (2009)
18. Stoyle, G., Hicks, M., Bierman, G., Sewell, P., Neamtiu, I.: Mutatis Mutandis: Safe and Predictable Dynamic Software Updating. ACM Transaction on Programming Languages and Systems 29(4) (August 2007)

19. Ubayashi, N., Akatoki, H., Nomura, J.: Pointcut-based Architectural Interface for Bridging a Gap between Design and Implementation. In: Oriol, M., Cazzola, W., Chiba, S., Saake, G. (eds.) Proceedings of the 6th ECOOP Workshop on Reflection, AOP and Meta-Data for Software Evolution (RAM-SE 2009), Genoa, Italy (July 2009)
20. Čech Previtali, S., Gross, T.: Dynamic Updating of Software Systems Based on Aspects. In: Proceedings of the 22nd IEEE International Conference on Software Maintenance (ICSM 2006), Philadelphia, USA, pp. 83–92 (September 2006)
21. Vogel, T., Giese, H.: Adaptation and Abstract Runtime Models. In: Proceedings of the ICSE Workshop on Software Engineering for Adaptive and Self-Managing Systems (SEAMS 2010), Cape Town, South Africa, pp. 39–48. ACM (May 2010)
22. Zhang, J., Cheng, B.H.C.: Model-Based Development of Dynamically Adaptive Software. In: Proceedings of the 28th International Conference on Software Engineering (ICSE 2006), Shanghai, China, pp. 371–380. ACM (May 2006)

Evolution as «Reflections on the Design»

Walter Cazzola

Computer Science Department
Università degli Studi di Milano
cazzola@di.unimi.it

Abstract. No system escapes from the need of evolving either to fix bugs, to be reconfigured or to add new features. To evolve becomes particularly problematic when the system to evolve cannot be stopped.

Traditionally the evolution of a continuously running system is tackled on by calculating all the possible evolutions in advance and coding them in the artifact itself. This approach gives origin to the *code pollution phenomenon* where the code is polluted by code that could never be applied. The approach has the following defects: i) code bloating, ii) it is impossible to predict any possible change and iii) the code becomes hard to read and maintain.

Computational reflection by definition allows an artifact to introspect and to intercede on its own structure and behavior endowing, therefore, a reflective artifact with (potentially) the ability of self-evolving. Furthermore, to deal with the evolution as a nonfunctional concern can limit the *code pollution* phenomenon.

To bring the design information (model and/or architecture) at runtime provides the artifact with a basic knowledge about itself to reflect on when a change is necessary and on how to deploy it. The availability of such a knowledge at run-time enables the designer of postponing the planning and the coding of the evolution to when and only when really necessary. Reflection permits to separate the evolution from the artifact and the design information allows a (semi-)automatic planning of how the artifact should evolve when necessary.

In this contribution, we overview the role that reflection and design information have in the development of self-evolving artifacts. Moreover, we summarize the lesson learned as a high-level reflective architecture to support dynamic self-evolution in various contexts and we show how some of the existing frameworks adhere to such an architecture and how the kind of evolution affects their structure.

Keywords: Reflection, Software Evolution, Design Information.

1 Introduction

All software systems are subject to evolution, they evolve over time as new requirements emerge, or bug fixing is necessary. Lehman *et al.* [51] pointed out that up to 80% of the system lifetime is spent on maintenance and evolution activities. A program that is useful in a real-world environment necessarily must change or

N. Bencomo et al. (Eds.): Models@run.time, LNCS 8378, pp. 259–278, 2014.

it will become progressively less useful in that environment [49]. Continuously running systems do not escape this law.

The common sense will let us consider that a well-planned evolution should pass through the evolution of system design information and then through the propagation of such changes to the implementation. This approach should be the most natural and intuitive to use (because it adopts the same mechanisms adopted during the development phase) and it should produce the best results (because each evolutionary step is planned and documented before its deployment) and the general quality of the code will not decline (as stated by the 7th law of software evolution [50]). Recently, this feeling has also been supported by empirical experiments [33].

Unfortunately, this approach requires more time than to directly modify the code itself and, in principle, needs to be planned off-line. Despite its benefits, it is in contrast with the urgency often required by the change (e.g., to fix a bug in a critical system or to enhance an application with rough competitors) and badly fits with the unstoppable characteristic of the continuously running systems since design information is not accessible from the artifact during its execution and its code is loosely coupled to its design hindering any automatic form of evolution based on it.

Moreover, to plan the evolution on the design information could be hard or inapplicable at all when involves critical, non-stopping and/or a distributed systems. In this case, to stop the application implies an unacceptable denial of service or the coordination of several sites potentially spread all around the world and not necessarily accessible. Normally, the evolution of critical, distributed and/or continuously running systems is emulated by directly enriching the original design information (and consequently code) with aspects concerning possible evolutions selected by conditional expressions. This approach has several drawbacks:

- all possible evolutions are not always predictable *a priori*;
- system design information and code are *polluted* by details related to the evolutionary design;
- code and model pollution hinders maintenance and reduces possibility of reuse.

Clearly, this cannot be the ultimate solution to the problem of promptly evolving a system without interruptions in the service provision. Rather, *the promptness of action could be granted if the system itself should be able to plan and realize its own evolution.*

Software evolution is an aspect orthogonal to (current) system behavior that crosscuts both artifact code and design; hence it should be subject to be developed as a separate concern (*separation of concerns* [40]). Separating evolution from the rest of a system is worthwhile, because evolution is made independent of the evolving system and the abovementioned problems are avoided. Design information will not be polluted by non pertinent details and will exclusively represent current system functionality without patches. This leads to a simpler and cleaner implementation that can be more easily maintained and analyzed without discriminating between what is and what could be the artifact structure and behavior. Evolution is clearly modeled separately from the artifact and can be defined or extended on demand rendering useless to predict all the possible evolutions in advance.

Reflection [52] is one of the mechanisms that easily permits to separate cross-cutting concerns and to get self-aware artifacts. Reflective systems have the capability to reason about and act on their own behavior and structure so that they could be able to decide how to evolve and apply the necessary steps and face their own evolution.

In the rest of the contribution we will explore how reflection can cope with design information to develop a self evolvable system that can operate without human interference. In Sect. 2 we give an overview of the reflective architecture of a self-evolving system; in Sect. 3 we will explore the role of design information in the generic reflective architecture and the impact that different kinds of design information have on the approach to self-evolution; whereas in Sect. 4 we explore how to model a system that can autonomously evolve itself. Finally in Sect. 5 we will have some discussions on the topic and draw our conclusions.

2   Evolution and Reflection

2.1   Computational Reflection

Computational reflection (or *reflection* for short) is defined as the activity performed by an agent when doing computations about itself [52]. This activity involves two aspects: *introspection* and *intercession*. Bobrow et al. [9] define these two terms as follows:

> *Introspection is the ability of a program to observe and therefore reason about its own state. Intercession is the ability for a program to modify its own execution state, or alter its own interpretation or meaning.*

Reflection applies quite naturally to the object-oriented paradigm [34,52]. Just as objects in the conventional object-oriented paradigm are representations of *real world* entities, objects can themselves be represented by other objects, usually referred to as *meta-objects*. Computation done by meta-objects is for the purpose of observing and modifying the objects they represent, called *referents*. Meta-computation is often performed by meta-objects by *trapping* the normal computation of their referents. In other words, an action of the referent is trapped by the meta-object, which performs a computation either replacing or encapsulating the referent's action. Of course, meta-objects themselves can be manipulated by meta-meta-objects, and so on. Thus, a reflective system can be structured in multiple levels, constituting a *reflective tower*. Base-level objects (termed *base-objects*) perform computations on the entities of the application domain. Objects in the other levels (termed *meta-levels*) perform computations on the objects residing in the lower levels. The interface between adjacent levels in the reflective tower is usually termed as *meta-object protocol* [45].

Reification is an essential capability of all reflective models. Each level of the reflective tower maintains a set of data structures representing (*reifying*) lower level computation. Such data structures comprising a reification must be *causally connected* to the aspect(s) of the system being reified. All changes to the reification are reflected in the system (*shift-down action*), and vice versa (*shift-up action*). More details can be read on [14].

2.2 Evolution as a Crosscutting Concern

Any kind of software evolution consists of a modification to a software artifact to correct, adapt or extend its functionality. The evolution normally affects all the aspects of the software artifact (that is, model and code) but specially impacts on its implementation. Independently of the reason, the act of evolving a software artifact can be traced back to a bunch of pieces of code of varying size (few code lines or whole classes) that should be intertwined with and potentially scattered around the code of the software artifact. The extent of the evolution determines the need of applying it to all the development phases from the design to the documentation. In any case, when applying such modifications to existing software, the change rarely is localized and confined in a single point or area but involves several components; so it is fairly evident that the code that should be added and the code that should be replaced/removed is *tangled to* and *scattered around* the remaining code.

From the point of view of the artifact development, the code necessary to evolve the software artifact or better the software evolvability is nonfunctional to satisfy the original requirements of the artifact. The software evolvability regards features or extensions that are not included at the design time (because it implements an unpredicted feature or it solves a problem not known at design-time) or patches to bugs that are not discovered earlier. If you consider the time as a dimension, the software evolvability is a concern that exists over a limited period of time (not necessarily from the beginning nor to the end) that will be absorbed by other concerns when applied. For example, let us consider a bank system artifact —with logging and many other concerns— and after a long uptime the system administrator decides to add an extra monitor to the available hardware in order to show the logging in real-time to the clerks and the bank responsible besides the normal logging activity. This kind of new requirement is difficult to anticipate or at least it could be economically disadvantageous to consider it at design-time and thence the code to support it will only be introduced when necessary. The evolution concern is just a special facet of the logging concern and it will lose its identity in favor of it once deployed.

On the other hand, the evolution of a continuously running system is traditionally tackled on by predicting all the possible evolutions and hardwiring them in the artifact itself. This approach gives origin to the *code pollution phenomenon* where the code of the artifact is polluted by code that could never be applied. Moreover, the approach shows the following defects: i) code bloating, ii) it is impossible to predict any possible change and iii) the code becomes hard to read and maintain. In this case, in spite of its defects, the evolution concern will live together with all the other concerns for the whole artifact execution. The software artifact evolves without changing its structure; simply the "pollution" will be no more taking an active role in the artifact execution, i.e., when the need for a specific evolution predicted by the extra code in the software artifact raises the corresponding code will become reachable.

Since the beginning, we are used to think about reflection as the perfect mechanism to separate nonfunctional and crosscutting concerns —i.e., concerns that do not contribute to the artifact main functionality and whose implementation is tangled with such an implementation— from the rest of the artifact [40]. This is particularly true when we are speaking about separating a clearly defined feature whose implementation can be easily identified as in the case of logging and authentication but the truthfulness of such a statement is arguable when these characteristics are not present at design-time or are difficult to grasp as when the feature implementation is scattered in distributed components whose code could be inaccessible or when it should be part of a continuously running system. Let us consider the bank system example again, the logging and all the other "standard" concerns can be easily detected and separately modularize with a clear interface but, above all, it is easy to reflectively reassemble them together to form the original artifact. This is mainly due to the presence of a clear interface that can be used to couple different concerns. On the contrary, the proposed extension to the logging system lacks of these characteristics (cf. with the example in [18]); it is just a bunch of lines of code without a usable interface that should integrate or substitute code in another concern. Mostly all the reflective approaches (but also the aspect-oriented approaches) have a granularity at method level [14] whereas the evolutionary concerns need a finer granularity in order to be applied. It should be fairly evident that the capability to evolve and any particular evolution —especially in the case of the evolution of continuously running systems— are clearly nonfunctional and crosscutting concerns [16, 54, 56]. The code necessary to evolve an artifact cannot contribute to implement its basic functionality until the urgency for the evolution comes up. Moreover the evolution of a continuously running system hardly can be prepared in advance but need to be decided according to the (sudden and unexpected) risen necessity and the decision must be immediate due to the urgency often required by the evolution, e.g., to reconfigure a urban traffic control system to face a traffic jam [17, 67]. Due to the previous considerations it is still more natural to think about the evolution as something to add when necessary and to be kept separate from the core of the artifact.

2.3   Reflecting on the Design Information

Normally, the evolutionary process is supported by human operators (programmers, designers or system administrators) but to grant a timely and responsive assistance, especially to non stopping systems, it is necessary to imbue the software artifact with the ability of autonomously tackling the situation, i.e., the software artifact must be able to work out how to evolve from its current state. The evolutionary process starts from analysis of the situation and of the artifact state to determine how to face the issue and then uses the analysis result to decide how to proceed. To this respect, the artifact needs to introspect into its state and structure and to know how to decide the correct strategy to tackle the risen issue; this means to select one among several prearranged strategies and to evolve it to fit the problem or (more difficult) to define a new strategy to fix it.

Reflection helps to introspect and to apply the strategy but it is grounded on the artifact code and provides a limited view on the artifact behavior. But —as previously stated—, a correct evolutionary strategy can be decided only if the whole artifact architecture and behavior is known and taken in consideration: evolution impact is not limited to the part of the artifact responsible of the issue rather it affects several other non necessarily correlated parts [7] and often unimaginable from looking at the code, e.g., you cannot close a road for maintenance without considering the traffic flow through such a road and without changing the direction of the incident roads to avoid further disruptions.

Design information —when consistent with the implementation— provides an accurate snapshot of the artifact structure and behavior. The artifact design information abstracts from the code —that is, a very local and concrete view— giving a *global view* of the whole system —that is, the abstraction immediately shows which part of the artifact is in charge of which feature *without* looking at the code details. To complete the previous short example about the road maintenance and to assimilate the previous statement look at [17] where the deployment diagram for the urban traffic control system immediately shows which roads are interested by the closing of another road without browsing the code and without asking each road object for its neighbors. As stated in [18], design information summarizes the overall knowledge about the artifact in a handy form that is suited to plan the evolution.

Design information as a knowledge base for planning the evolution is not a *panacea* for automating the evolutionary process but it can be considered as a step towards a self-evolving software system. Reflection traditionally works at code level so it is necessary to extend the reflection to deal with the design information as application domain, similarly to [22] (software architecture) and [16] (UML models) and to causally connect the design information to the code to avoid the *design/implementation gap* [19,68]. In this way, reflective introspection and intercession apply to the artifact design information that can be used by the artifact to autonomously plan how to evolve and the causal connection relationship will deploy the evolution when necessary; the shift-down operation will take care of coordinating the changes and to avoid inconsistencies.

2.4 Self-evolving Architecture

Summarizing the previous considerations and according to several other works on the topic (such as [1,8,27,46]), the adoption of a reflective architecture based on design-information enables a software artifact with the ability of *autonomously* evolving (self-evolving for short). Reflection permits to postpone the planning and coding of the evolution from design to run-time since the changes can be reflectively (either via code injection, callbacks or controlled executions) applied during the execution rather than simply activated if predicted during the development. Moreover to grant the entity supervising the evolution with a global knowledge of the artifact behavior and structure, the reflection should shift its application domain from code to design information (to plan the evolution) and back (to deploy the planned evolution on the artifact).

Several reflective frameworks [8, 16, 22, 25, 31, 36, 46] supporting self-evolution and models@runtime have been developed over the last 15 years. They differ on the realization and in what they can do as we will show in the next section but they share a reflective nature, the use of design information (meta-models, software architectures, UML diagrams and so on) to plan the evolution and a *control loop* (monitor-plan-execute) that follows the vision given in [44] and [30]. Notwithstanding the similarity in their approaches they lack of a common terminology. In the rest of the paper, we will try to abstract their reflective architecture and to draft such a common terminology.

A reflective architecture for self-evolution will be logically structured in two levels: the artifact prone to evolve will run in the base-level whereas the artifact in the meta-level will take care of the evolution of the base-level artifact. The *reification* will be bound to the design information of the base-level rather than to its code. An *evolutionary engine* in the meta-level will use such a reification to plan how to evolve the base-level artifact. Such a reflective architecture is completed by a pool of *reflectors*. These components take care of realizing the reflective behavior of the whole framework realizing the shift-up and -down operations and keeping the causal connection between the artifact in the base-level and its representative (the reification). These components have also to deal with the particular application domain binding the code to the design information. Due to the well-known gap between design and implementation [19, 68] to work out an evolutionary plan from the artifact design information and apply it to the artifact code will be challenging; [17] shows an attempt about how to put in correspondence design information and code, i.e., how to implement the causal connection in this reflective architecture.

The evolutionary engine is in charge of evolving the base-level artifact when a settled event occurs. The engine works on the artifact's reification to preserve the base-level consistency in case of badly engineered or untimely evolution. The reflectors reify the base-level design information into the reification and deal with the issue of providing a corresponding run-time representative for them. Moreover, the engine has two kinds of cooperating components: *planners* and *actuators*. The multiplicity of components of the evolutionary engine depends on the granularity of the evolutionary actions: each aspect of the system could be handled by a different component. As the names suggest, the planners are in charge of planning the evolution whereas the actuators put the planned evolution into practice.

Planners plan the evolution on the reification supported by an *evolutionary knowledge base* when a settled event occurs. The evolutionary knowledge base contains strategies, i.e., predetermined solutions to situations that could happen; the knowledge base can be fixed, augmentable with the strategies derived by the

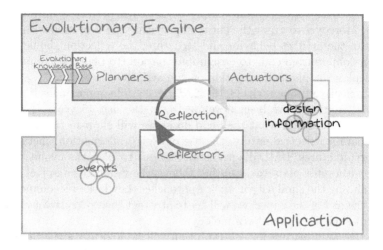

Fig. 1. Architecture for a Self-Evolving Artifact

planners and/or dynamically enrichable by a human operator. The events could be related to the state and the structure of the base-level artifact (e.g., when an urban traffic control system detects a traffic jam) or completely unrelated (e.g., time-based events: at every hour, at noon, ...). In both cases the evolutionary engine has to monitor the base-level artifact and to trigger the planners when it detects a settled event. Actuators cooperate with planners to render effective the planned evolution: they apply the strategy decided by the planners to the reification validating the consistency of the result before asking the reflectors for reflecting the changes back to the base-level.

Fig. 1 depicts the described reflective architecture. In [15] the generic architecture is described through a pattern family capturing its behavior. Changing the perspective, the described reflective architecture is a generic architecture for providing a software artifact with the ability of autonomously evolving. It describes the main components of the framework and how they interact to achieve the artifact evolution. To some extent it depicts a pattern which should match mostly every approach to self-evolution. This pattern describes in-the-large how to achieve the evolution, which components are involved and in which role but does not detail how the single components (especially planners and actuators) are implemented or how their strategies are extracted from the design information such details will change from approach to approach as we will show in the next. Moreover, the use of reflection permits to move the artifact prone to be evolved out of the *monitor-plan-execute* control loop in favor of using a representative (the reification, i.e., the design information) to guarantee a safe planning and deployment of the evolution.

In spite of the fact that the described architecture is just a *logical architectural pattern* describing the architecture and the basic behavior that an artifact able to autonomously evolve should have, we want to stress that the evolutionary engine can be realized in a monolithic way as well as in a decentralized way: each planner, actuator and reflector can run on a different host machine and can coordinate the evolution of a monolithic/distributed software artifact (that is, the architecture is intrinsically distributed). Of course a decentralized management of the evolution will need an higher and tighter coordination among the components in the reflective framework. Speaking about decentralized management of the evolution, the real challenge is represented by the possibility of automatically scale up a centralized self-evolving artifact to seamlessly work in a distributed environment. In particular the planned evolution could affect several distributed components (the change affects components potentially running on different host machines) and therefore the change could be realized by several different actuators/reflectors to reduce the time necessary to update the artifact; this points out the possibility of enabling the framework with the capacity of parallelizing the evolutionary plan, job not easy to face especially without the help of a human operator.

3   Reflecting on the Existing

The architecture for self-evolution described in Sect. 2.3 has a reflective nature, implements the monitor-plan-execute control-loop [44] and exploits models at run-time to provide the artifact (running in the base-level) with the capability of autonomously planning and actuating its own evolution. Such an architecture directly descends from the architectures of several frameworks available in the literature and intend to provide a common terminology. In general, such an architecture describes which components should be present and which role they would play but it does not describe how they realize such a role that depends on the adopted approach and which kind of evolution could be achieved. The *granularity* of the change permits also to classify the existing approaches with respect to the extent of the evolution.

According to [11], the *granularity of the change* is the dimension of the evolution that affects more the self-evolution approaches. To tackle on such a variability it is necessary to have a similar variability also in the used design information. For example, (self-)configuring [66] takes place at component level, the system architecture changes (added/removed components or rearranged connections) to face the requested reconfiguration. To plan its own reconfiguration, the artifact must reason and act *in-the-large*[1] i.e., on how the components interact rather than on how they work.

In the next, we will explore how such a variability is tackled by the approaches in the literature case by case and we will classify them according to the results of the analysis. In particular, we focus our efforts on the following two cases of self-evolution (the former has been described in [66]):

---

[1] After [29] we use the term *in-the-large* in contrast to *in-the-small* to put in evidence the necessary granularity and abstraction level.

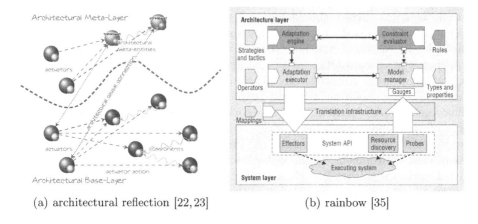

(a) architectural reflection [22, 23]   (b) rainbow [35]

Fig. 2. Architecture of some self-configuring approaches

- a *self-configuring* artifact can add, remove and substitute its components and change how they interact but cannot change how the single (or group of) component(s) behaves (to some extent we can call it *evolution in-the-large*); and
- a *self-adjusting* artifact can modify the behavior of each of its components by changing their code (to some extent we can call it *evolution in-the-small*).

3.1   Self-configuring: Reflecting on the Architecture

Several definitions for software architecture are available[2] but the one that better fits our needs is:

> Software Architectures deal with the design and implementation of the high-level structure of the software. It is the result of assembling a certain number of architectural elements in some well-chosen forms to satisfy the major functionality and performance requirements such as scalability and availability. Software architecture deals with abstraction, with decomposition and composition, with style and aesthetics [48].

Software architectures provide a global view of how artifact components fit together neglecting to detail what every component does, that is, they describe the artifact *in-the-large* rather than *in-the-small* [29]. The software architecture higher abstraction explicits a link to components and connectors as a whole rather than to their implementation; this helps to plan the artifact reconfiguration [53, 55] but hinders a deeper evolution involving changes to the code. Software architectures were designed to support component-programming (i.e., programming-in-the-large) so an explicit link between code and architecture is missing and code changes driven by the architecture could result impossible.

---

[2] Give a look at http://www.sei.cmu.edu/architecture/start/glossary/index.cfm to get a grasp.

In the years a plethora of approaches that support self-configuring through design information manipulation have been explored, e.g., architectural reflection [22, 23, 64], Rainbow [35, 36], and MUSIC [65].

Architectural Reflection [22, 23] exploits the artifact software architecture as the application domain for reflective activities; all the reflective concepts have been moved from the code to the architectural domain. The software architecture is reified, decomposed into topology and strategy and manipulated, respectively, by two meta-level components, called *topologist* and *strategist*. The software architecture reification renders the artifact architecture explicit and observable and the system controllable through its architecture. The topologist and the strategist plan and force the artifact reconfiguration through the manipulation of the (reified) software architecture; a specific actuator is used to reflect the change on the system. Mapping the terminology used by this architecture (depicted in Fig. 2(a)) on the one used in Sect. 2.4: the topologist and the strategist are two kind of planners, each of them cooperates with their own actuator; both planning and validating the evolution on the artifact software architecture as design information.

The Rainbow framework [35, 36] adopts an architecture-based approach as well. It provides reusable infrastructure together with mechanisms for specializing that infrastructure to the needs of specific systems. The Rainbow framework includes an artifact architectural model in its run-time system. In particular, developers of self-configuring capabilities use a system software architectural model to monitor and reason about the system (to some extent a reflective system whose application domain is the artifact software architecture). The Rainbow control loop for self-reconfiguration passes through the following steps (look at Fig. 2(b)): i) a *model manager* handles and provides access to the artifact architectural model; ii) a *constraint evaluator* checks the model periodically and ask for evolution when a constraint violation occurs; then iii) an *adaptation engine* determines the course of action and carries out the necessary evolution; finally iv) an *adaptation executor* triggers the *effectors* to reflect the changes on the artifact. In this case, the model manager together with the adaptation executor and the effectors play the role of reflectors whereas the adaptation engine and the constraint evaluator play the role of the evolutionary engine.

The MUSIC framework [65] defines an evolution middleware that exploits a *quality-of-service* (QoS) *aware* model for planning the evolution. All the possible changes are at component-level and are related to the configuration of how these components compose, called *component realizations*. A component realization implements the *ports* the components use to collaborate and can be used in a specific *roles* if the ports match. The model is represented by plans and each plan reflect a component realization. Planning refers to the process of selecting the components that configure the artifact to provide the best possible utility to the end-user. The evolution process is mainly in charge of three components: the *adaptation controller*, the *adaptation reasoner* and the *configuration executor* that respectively play the role of *actuator*, *planner* and *reflector* in our architecture.

In this particular approach the design information is scattered inside the plans together with the evolutionary strategies.

Several other self-configuring approaches (such as TranSAT [3, 4], RSA [39], PRISMA [24, 25], ArchStudio [59], K-Components Architecture [31, 32] and Dellarocas *et al.* [28]) reflectively exploit software architecture to plan and realize the artifact reconfiguration but since to report their analysis will not add much more to the discussion and due to space limitation we are not describing them all in detail.

3.2   Self-adjusting: Reflecting on the Model

Configuration works at component level by adding, removing or substituting components and/or rearranging their connections; all information provided by the artifact software architecture that can be used to plan the artifact self-configuration. In general evolution also includes bugs fixing and extending/changing already implemented code; this kind of evolution is hard to be planned on the artifact software architecture since it provides a coarse grain view (at component level) of the artifact behavior and the details necessary to deal with this kind of evolution are removed by the abstraction process. In general any kind of design information gives an abstract view on the software artifact it represents, at least, a view more abstract than the code itself; this characteristic hinders the use of design information to plan this kind of evolution. In this case, the design information should represent the artifact *in-the-small* with a finer granularity and with a strong connection to the code as the UML models [10], but not only, do.

Self-Adjusting implies to adjust how the components work not just how they interact with other components (problem that can be faced through the manipulation of configuration files) that means to alter their implementation. To plan an evolution that goes so deepen in the artifact code poses some new challenges:

- how to modify the code during its execution (several tools, —as JavAdaptor [61, 62], Javeleon [38] and jRebel [41]– and some JVM extensions —as Java hotspot and the Wurthinger *et al.*'s work [69]— help with this issue);
- how to associate the design information to the running code (normally models and code are statically coupled and the generation of the new code is model-driven);
- how to face the natural gap between code and design information especially in case of evolution [19, 68].

These additional challenges have rendered less appealing to perform dynamic self-adjusting and, therefore, few attempts can be found in the literature; most of them exploit the model driven engineering [43] methodology where models have a proactive role and are used to generate the artifact itself, e.g., WEAVR [26] and the Adaptive Object Model Architecture [70]; in the next we will neglect to analyze these approaches since they have a different perspective: the artifact is generated from the design information rather than simply used as a source of information to drive the change of the existing code.

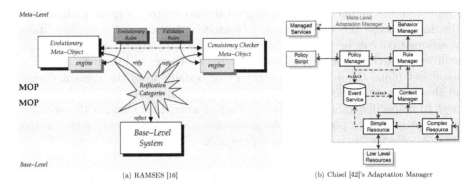

(a) RAMSES [16]   (b) Chisel [42]'s Adaptation Manager

Fig. 3. Architecture of some self-adjusting approaches

RAMSES (Reflective and Adaptive Middleware for Software Evolution of Systems) [16] is a reflective framework that provides an artifact with the capability of dynamically self-adjusting. The framework has two logic levels (as sketched in Fig. 3(a)): the artifact prone to be adjusted runs in the base-level whereas in the meta-level a couple of meta-objects (the *evolutionary* and *consistency checker* meta-objects) take care of planning and validating the artifact evolution. The work of both such meta-objects is supported by dedicated engines that applies validation and evolutionary rules (ruby scripts) to the artifact reification when triggered by the meta-objects. The base-level models are reified in the meta-level as XMI [58] schema and the changes are reflected back on the artifact through techniques of code instrumentation [61–63]. In this case, the evolutionary and validation rules are respectively the knowledge base used by the planners, i.e., the evolutionary meta-objects and by the actuators, i.e., the consistency checker meta-objects, the whole meta-level corresponds to the evolutionary engine. Similar concepts are used in the FiGA architecture [20, 21].

Chisel [42] is an open framework for self-adjusting of services using reflection in a policy-driven, context-aware manner. The system is based on decomposing the particular aspects of a service object that do not provide its core functionality into multiple possible behaviors. As the execution environment, user context and artifact context change, the service object will be adjusted to use a different behaviors, driven by a human-readable declarative adaptation policy script. The Chisel framework has a *meta-level adaptation manager* (depicted in Fig. 3(b)) that coordinates the whole adjusting process by monitoring the artifact execution environment, by planning the adjustment via a set of *adaptation policies* and by extracting (reifying) the *meta-types* from the running artifact and reflecting the adjustment. In the Chisel framework the meta-level adaptation manager plays the role of evolutionary engine (including planners, actuators and reflectors), the adaptation policies are the evolutionary strategies and the meta-types plays the role of design information.

Genie [5, 6] is a reflective framework to support self-adjusting of a software artifact through its design information. Even if it adopts software architecture to represent the artifact in the meta-level it also enables a quite limited self-adjusting through the self-generation of models describing the artifact state transitions that can be used to change the artifact behavior. Genie framework monitors the artifact context, reifies the artifact software architecture, a specific component plans the adjustment strategy as a delta from the current design and the design that should be and finally passes the generated *reconfiguration script* to a specific component (named *configurator*) that changes the artifact. The script generator plays the role of planner whereas the configurator is the actuator/reflector of the architecture presented in Sect. 2.4.

4 A Model for a Self-evolving Artifact Should Be Self-evolving

An artifact able to evolve itself or at least the capability of evolving cannot be modeled with traditional design techniques, such as Petri nets, UML, and so on. To use the traditional design techniques has the evident drawback of i) polluting the artifact design information with details related to something not relevant at the moment and ii) propagating such a pollution to the code as well leading to a sort of domino effect that ends in code bloating. Unfortunately, these issues do not only render difficult to model the self-evolving artifact by using the traditional approaches but if done it also nullifies many of the benefits we got from designing the artifact: to distinguish among what is or is not part of the artifact complicates (sometimes it renders impossible) the model analysis and validation of some properties (e.g., quality of services and efficiency) especially over time, i.e., when some of the extra code will become effective.

Moreover, traditionally approaches to modeling do not consider the evolution as well; the artifact model is not affected by the artifact evolution and it tends to rapidly become obsolete and therefore useless for planning the successive evolutions of the artifact —this problem is known in literature as the *design/implementation gap* [19, 68].

It should be fairly evident that the design information used to plan the evolution (see Sect. 2.3 and Sect. 2.4) should not be polluted by the details related to the evolution itself since they are

- redundant — evolution is planned by the evolutionary engine exploiting such a model in its reasoning process;
- difficult to (automatically) separate from the relevant part of the model to have a clean view of the current situation; and
- difficult to be kept coherent with the artifact evolution (extra and complicate work for the planner)

From these considerations, the artifact design information should simply model the current version of the base-level artifact and it should be updated after the evolution or it should be generated out of the artifact code as in [37, 57] providing a very detailed view on the artifact code —in order to fill the design/implementation gap. In both cases some of the advantages and flexibility

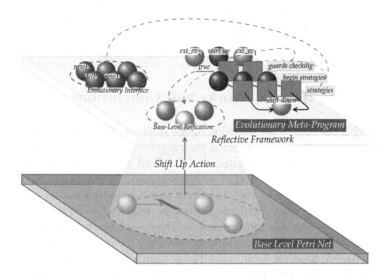

Fig. 4. Reflective Petri Net Model

provided by the approach are compromised: in the former case you have to (probably manually) update the model after the evolution; in the latter case the model could be too detailed and hinders any kind of evolution in-the-large as self-configuration. Therefore, design information suitable for the approach that allows to avoid such issues should be self-evolvable similarly to the artifact with the strategies to evolve the model separated from the model itself and dynamically enrichable.

A few attempts to model the self-evolvable capability separately of the rest of the artifact have been done: *reconfigurable nets* [2], *nets-within-nets* [12] and *reflective Petri nets* [13]. From the point of view of this work, even if all these approaches support the evolution of the artifact model only the reflective Petri nets provide a clear separation between the base-level model and the evolutionary strategies to keep clearly separated what the artifact is and what it could become.

A reflective Petri net (whose idea is shown in Fig. 4) is a high-level Petri net extension that permits to model a self-evolving artifact. The artifact current model defines the base-level model (a classic place/transition Petri net) whereas the evolutionary strategies applicable to the artifact define the meta-level model (each strategy is modeled by a Petri net). The base-level model is reified as a marking in the meta-level and a set of primitive operations (such as add a place or remove a transition) can be used to evolve the reification. The semantics of the reflective Petri nets will take care of keeping the base-level model and its reification consistent over time.

Reflective Petri nets respect the described criteria: i) they can model the base-level artifact separately from its evolution ii) the evolution can be applied similarly to the artifact and to its model iii) the model is always consistent with the modeled artifact. Using this approach to model the artifact provides the planners with design information that remains consistent after the evolution ready to be used for the next planning phase and a common set of strategies can be used by the reflectors to update both the model and the artifact.

5 Discussion, Related Works and Conclusions

Nowadays, with the increasing diffusion of the Internet, more and more artifacts need to continuously run and to provide their services without interruptions, e.g., air and urban traffic control systems, nuclear plant control systems, electronic shops and so on. To stop such a kind of systems could be mission critical but it also represents a disservice to the customers and a potential loss of money. Of course continuously running artifacts cannot be bug free or equipped with all the desired features over the long period, so they need to evolve exactly as the other artifacts do but with the constraint that they have to evolve *during* their execution, without disservices and possibly promptly and autonomously.

Such considerations drive forth to the need of self-evolving artifacts, that is, artifacts that can reason about themselves and, in case, can decide how to change their own behavior and structure and can deploy such a decision.

In the last few years a plethora of frameworks supporting self-evolution have been developed — [5,8,16,22,25,28,31,35,42,46] just to cite a few of them. Even if apparently all these frameworks differ, they share reflective nature, the use of design information (meta-models, software architectures, Petri nets, UML diagrams and so on) to plan the evolution and a *control loop* (monitor-plan-execute) that follows the vision given in [44] and [30]. The contribution of this chapter is to sort out this plethora of proposals and to give a common terminology for the different actors playing similar roles present in all the available frameworks; such a terminology can be logically summarized by Fig. 1.

A second consideration we have pointed out regards the granularity used for the artifact reification (that is, the kind of used design information); the granularity directly affects the kind of self-evolution that can be carried out. For example, software architecture well fits the self-configuration but are hard to use for self-adjusting due to their level of abstraction (software architectures describe the artifact in-the-large, self-adjusting can be considered a kind of evolution in-the-small since it affects the artifact code and not its configuration). Andersson *et al.* [1] do not consider this issue focusing their analysis on the software architectures but they agree on the poor expressiveness of the software architectures when used to describe the artifact in-the-small and suggest to fill the gap in the causal relationship implementation to support any kind of evolution (Sect. 5.1 of [1]). Instead we suggest to consider more appropriate representation models case by case. Nierstrasz *et al.* [57] support our idea of getting dynamic self-adjusting through a fine granularity model of the artifact by proposing to reify the artifact code into the corresponding abstract syntax tree (AST).

To finish we also gave some remarks about the characteristics the design information should have to be used as a knowledge base for planning the evolution without side-effects and complications. In short, they should be modeled keeping in consideration they could evolve but avoiding to be polluted by this knowledge. For example, reflective Petri nets [13] are structured to permit a clear separation of the current model from the strategies to evolve it and can be easily part of the evolutionary process. Perrouin *et al.* [60] do similar considerations even if they suggest to enable the (self-)evolution of the single component of the MAPE loop instead of imbuing the artifact model with this capability.

In the future we would like to widen our analysis including different flavors of (self-)evolutions, such as self-healing and self-optimizations, and different approaches to code adjusting as aspect-oriented and generative programming instead of reflection and finally to classify the existing architectures with respect to the model of adopted reflection.

Acknowledgment. The author would like to thank Sonia Pini and Ahmed Ghoneim that helped him in exploring the role of the design information in the evolution/co-evolution of a software system. Moreover, he wishes to thank Francesco Tisato and Massimo Ancona that introduced him to the problems of reflection and software evolution. The author wishes to thank the anonymous reviewers that with their insights helped a lot in improving this contribution.

References

1. Andersson, J., de Lemos, R., Malek, S., Weyns, D.: Reflecting on Self-Adaptive Software Systems. In: Proc. of SEAMS 2009, Vancouver, Canada, pp. 38–47 (May 2009)
2. Badouel, E., Oliver, J.: Reconfigurable Nets, a Class of High Level Petri Nets Supporting Dynamic Changes within Workflow Systems. RR PI-1163, IRISA (1998)
3. Barais, O., Cariou, E., Duchien, L., Pessemier, N., Seinturier,L.: TranSAT: A Framework for the specification of Software Architecture Evolution. In: Proc. of WCAT 2004, pp. 31–38, Oslo, Norway (June 2004)
4. Barais, O., Le Meur, A.-F., Duchien, L., Lawall, J.L.: Software Architecture Evolution. In: Software Evolution, pp. 233–262. Springer (2008)
5. Bencomo, N.: Supporting the Modelling and Generation of Reflective Middleware Families and Applications using Dynamic Variability. Phd thesis, Computing Department, Lancaster University, Lancaster, United Kingdom (March 2008)
6. Bencomo, N.: On the Use of Software Models during Software Execution. In: Proc. of MISE 2009, Vancouver, Canada (May 2009)
7. Black, S.: The Role of Ripple Effect in Software Evolution. In: Software Evolution and Feedback, ch. 12, pp. 249–268. John Wiley & Sons, Ltd. (June 2006)
8. Blair, G.S., Coulson, G., Blair, L., Duran-Limon, H., Grace, P., Moreira, R., Parlavantzas, N.: Reflection, Self-Awareness and Self-Healing in OpenORB. In: Proc. of WOSS 2002, Charleston, South Carolina, USA, pp. 9–14. ACM (November 2002)
9. Bobrow, D.G., Gabriel, R.G., White, J.L.: CLOS in Context - The Shape of the Design Space. In: OOP: The CLOS Perspective, pp. 29–61. MIT Press (1993)
10. Booch, G., Rumbaugh, J., Jacobson, I.: The Unified Modeling Language User Guide, 3rd edn. Object Technology Series. Addison-Wesley (February 1999)

11. Buckley, J., Mens, T., Zenger, M., Rashid, A., Kniesel, G.: Towards a Taxonomy of Software Change. J.of SW Maintenance and Evolution 17(5), 309–332 (2005)
12. Cabac, L., Duvigneau, M., Moldt, D., Rölke, H.: Modeling Dynamic Architectures Using Nets-Within-Nets. In: Ciardo, G., Darondeau, P. (eds.) ICATPN 2005. LNCS, vol. 3536, pp. 148–167. Springer, Heidelberg (2005)
13. Capra, L., Cazzola, W.: Self-Evolving Petri Nets. Journal of Universal Computer Science 13(13), 2002–2034 (2007)
14. Cazzola, W.: Evaluation of Object-Oriented Reflective Models. In: Proc. of EWROOPS 1998, Brussels, Belgium (July 1998)
15. Cazzola, W., Coplien, J.O., Ghoneim, A., Saake, G.: Framework Patterns for the Evolution of Nonstoppable Software Systems. In: Proc. of VikingPLoP 2002, Højstrupgård, Denmark, pp. 35–54. Microsoft Business Solutions (September 2002)
16. Cazzola, W., Ghoneim, A.: Software Evolution through Dynamic Adaptation of Its OO Design. In: Ryan, M.D., Meyer, J.-J.C., Ehrich, H.-D. (eds.) Objects, Agents, and Features. LNCS, vol. 2975, pp. 67–80. Springer, Heidelberg (2004)
17. Cazzola, W., Ghoneim, A., Saake, G.: System Evolution through Design Information Evolution: a Case Study. In: Proc. of IASSE 2004, pp. 145–150 (July 2004)
18. Cazzola, W., Pini, S., Ancona, M.: AOP for Software Evolution: A Design Oriented Approach. In: SAC 2005, Santa Fe, USA, pp. 1356–1360. ACM Press (March 2005)
19. Cazzola, W., Pini, S., Ghoneim, A., Saake,G.: Co-Evolving Application Code and Design Models by Exploiting Meta-Data. In: Proc. of SAC 2007, Seoul, South Korea, pp. 1275–1279. ACM Press (March 2007)
20. Cazzola, W., Rossini, N.A., Al-Refai, M., France, R.B.: Fine-Grained Software Evolution Using UML Activity and Class Models. In: Moreira, A., Schätz, B., Gray, J., Vallecillo, A., Clarke, P. (eds.) MODELS 2013. LNCS, vol. 8107, pp. 271–286. Springer, Heidelberg (2013)
21. Cazzola, W., Rossini, N.A., Bennett, P., Mandalaparty, S.P., France, R.: Fine-grained semi-automated runtime evolution. In: MoDELS@Run-Time, vol. 8378, pp. 225–246. Springer, Heidelberg (2014)
22. Cazzola, W., Savigni, A., Sosio, A., Tisato, F.: Architectural Reflection: Bridging the Gap Between a Running System and its Architectural Specification. In: Proc. of REF 1998, Firenze, Italia, pp. 12-1–12-6. IEEE (March 1998)
23. Cazzola, W., Savigni, A., Sosio, A., Tisato, F.: Rule-Based Strategic Reflection: Observing and Modifying Behaviour at the Architectural Level. In: Proc. of ASE 1999, Cocoa Beach, Florida, USA, pp. 263–266 (October 1999)
24. Costa-Soria, C.: Dynamic Evolution and Reconfiguration of Software Architectures through Aspects. Ph.D. Thesis, Universitat Politècnica de València (June 2011)
25. Costa-Soria, C., Hervás-Muñoz, D., Pérez Benedí, J., Carsí Cubel, J.Á.: A Reflective Approach for Supporting the Dynamic Evolution of Component Types. In: Proc. of ICECCS 2009, Potsdam, Germany, pp. 301–310 (June 2009)
26. Cottenier, T., van den Berg, A., Elrad, T.: Motorola WEAVR: Aspect Orientation and Model-Driven Engineering. J. of Object Technology 6(7), 51–88 (2007)
27. Coulson, G., Blair, G., Grace, P., Taiani, F., Joolia, A., Lee, K., Ueyama, J., Sivaharan, T.: A Generic Component Model for Building Systems Software. ACM Transactions on Computer Systems 26(1), 1–29 (2008)
28. Dellarocas, C., Klein, M., Shrobe, H.: An Architecture for Constructing Self-Evolving Software Systems. In: Proc. of IWSA 1998, USA, pp. 29–32 (November 1998)
29. DeRemer, F., Kron, H.H.: Programming-in-the-large versus Programming-in-the-small. IEEE Transactions on Software Engineering 2, 80–86 (1976)

30. Dobson, S.: Fulfilling the Vision of Autonomic Computing. IEEE Computer 43(1), 35–41 (2010)
31. Dowling, J., Cahill, V.: The K-Component Architecture Meta-model for Self-Adaptive Software. In: Matsuoka, S. (ed.) Reflection 2001. LNCS, vol. 2192, pp. 81–88. Springer, Heidelberg (2001)
32. Dowling, J., Schäfer, T., Cahill, V., Haraszti, P., Redmond, B.: Using Reflection to Support Dynamic Adaptation of System Software: A Case Study Driven Evaluation. In: Cazzola, W., Houmb, S.H., Tisato, F. (eds.) Reflection and Software Engineering. LNCS, vol. 1826, pp. 169–188. Springer, Heidelberg (2000)
33. Dzidek, W.J., Arisholm, E., Briand, L.C.: A Realistic Empirical Evaluation of the Costs and Benefits of UML in Software Maintenance. IEEE Transactions on Software Engineering 34(3), 407–432 (2008)
34. Ferber, J.: Computational Reflection in Class Based Object Oriented Languages. In: Proc. of OOPSLA 1989, pp. 317–326. ACM (October 1989)
35. Garlan, D., Cheng, S.-W., Huang, A.-C., Schmerl, B., Steenkiste, P.: Rainbow: Architecture-Based Self Adaptation with Reusable Infrastructure. IEEE Computer 37(10), 46–54 (2004)
36. Garlan, D., Schmerl, B., Cheng, S.-W.: Software Architecture-Based Self-Adaptation. In: Autonomic Computing and Networking, pp. 31–55. Springer (2009)
37. Goldsby, H.J., Cheng, B.H.C.: Automatically Generating Behavioral Models of Adaptive Systems to Address Uncertainty. In: Czarnecki, K., Ober, I., Bruel, J.-M., Uhl, A., Völter, M. (eds.) MODELS 2008. LNCS, vol. 5301, pp. 568–583. Springer, Heidelberg (2008)
38. Gregersen, A.R., Jørgensen, B.N.: Dynamic Update of Java Applications — Balancing Change Flexibility vs Programming Transparency. Journal of Software Maintenance and Evolution: Research and Practice 21(2), 81–112 (2009)
39. Huang, G., Mei, H., Yang, F.-Q.: Runtime Software Architecture Based on Reflective Middleware. Journal of Information Science 47(5), 555–576 (2004)
40. Hürsch, W., Videira Lopes, C.: Separation of Concerns. Technical Report NU-CCS-95-03, Northeastern University, Boston (February 1995)
41. Kabanov, J.: JRebel Tool Demo. ENTCS 264(4), 51–57 (2011)
42. Keeney, J., Cahill, V.: Chisel: A Policy-Driven, Context-Aware, Dynamic Adaptation Framework. In: Proc. of POLICY 2003, Como, Italy, pp. 3–14 (June 2003)
43. Caskurlu, B.: Model Driven Engineering. In: Butler, M., Petre, L., Sere, K. (eds.) IFM 2002. LNCS, vol. 2335, pp. 286–298. Springer, Heidelberg (2002)
44. Kephart, J.O., Chess, D.M.: The Vision of Autonomic Computing. IEEE Computer 36(1), 41–50 (2003)
45. Kiczales, G., des Rivières, J., Bobrow, D.G.: The Art of the Metaobject Protocol. MIT Press, Cambridge (1991)
46. Kon, F., Costa, F., Blair, G., Campbell, R.H.: The Case for Reflective Middleware. Commun. ACM 45(6), 33–38 (2002)
47. Kramer, J., Magee, J.: Self-Managed Systems: an Architectural Challenge. In: Proc. of FoSE 2007, Minneapolis, USA, pp. 259–268. IEEE (May 2007)
48. Kruchten, P.: The 4+1 View Model of Architecture. IEEE SW 12(6), 61–70 (1995)
49. Lehman, M.M.: Programs, Life Cycles, and Laws of Software Evolution. Proc. of the IEEE 68(9), 1060–1076 (1980); Special Issue on Software Engineering
50. Lehman, M.M.: Laws of Software Evolution Revisited. In: Montangero, C. (ed.) EWSPT 1996. LNCS, vol. 1149, pp. 108–124. Springer, Heidelberg (1996)
51. Lehman, M.M., Fernández-Ramil, J.C., Kahen, G.: A Paradigm for the Behavioural Modelling of Software Processes using System Dynamics. Technical Report 2001/8, Imperial College, London, United Kingdom (September 2001)

52. Maes, P.: Concepts and Experiments in Computational Reflection. In: Proc. of OOPSLA 1987, Orlando, USA, pp. 147–156. ACM (October 1987)
53. Magee, J., Kramer, J.: Self-Organising Software Architecture. In: Proc. of ISAW 1996, San Francisco, CA, USA, pp. 35–38. ACM (October 1996)
54. Mens, T., Wermelinger, M.: Separation of Concerns for Software Evolution. Journal of Maintenance and Evolution 14(5), 311–315 (2002)
55. Murphy, G.C.: Architecture for Evolution. In: Proc. of ISAW 1996, San Francisco, CA, USA, pp. 83–86. ACM (October 1996)
56. Nierstrasz, O., Achermann, F.: Supporting Compositional Styles for Software Evolution. In: Proc. of ISPSE 2000, Kanazawa, Japan, pp. 11–19 (November 2000)
57. Nierstrasz, O., Denker, M., Renggli, L.: Model-Centric, Context-Aware Software Adaptation. In: Cheng, B.H.C., de Lemos, R., Giese, H., Inverardi, P., Magee, J. (eds.) Software Engineering for Self-Adaptive Systems. LNCS, vol. 5525, pp. 128–145. Springer, Heidelberg (2009)
58. OMG. OMG-XML Metadata Interchange (XMI) Specification, v1.2. OMG Modeling and Metadata Specifications (January 2002), http://www.omg.org
59. Oreizy, P., Gorlick, M.M., Taylor, R.N., Heimbigner, D., Johnson, G., Medvidovic, N., Quilici, A., Rosenblum, D.S., Wolf, A.L.: An Architecture Based Approach to Self-Adaptive Software. IEEE Intelligent Systems, 54–62 (1999)
60. Perrouin, G., Morin, B., Chauvel, F., Fleurey, F., Klein, J., Traon, Y.L., Barais, O., Jézéquel, J.-M.: Towards Flexible Evolution of Dynamically Adaptive Systems. In: Proc. of ICSE 2012, Zürich, Switzerland, pp. 1353–1356. IEEE (June 2012)
61. Pukall, M., Grebhahn, A., Schröter, R., Kästner, C., Cazzola, W., Götz, S.: JavAdaptor: Unrestricted Dynamic Software Updates for Java. In: Proc. of ICSE 2011, Waikiki, Honolulu, Hawaii, pp. 989–991. IEEE (May 2011)
62. Pukall, M., Kästner, C., Cazzola, W., Götz, S., Grebhahn, A., Schöter, R., Saake, G.: JavAdaptor — Flexible Runtime Updates of Java Applications. Software—Practice and Experience 43(2), 153–185 (2013)
63. Pukall, M., Kästner, C., Saake, G.: Towards Unanticipated Runtime Adaptation of Java Applications. In: Proc. of APSEC 2008, Bejing, China, pp. 85–92. IEEE Computer Society (December 2008)
64. Rank, S.: Architectural Reflection for Software Evolution. In: Proc. of RAM-SE 2005, Glasgow, Scotland, pp. 53–58 (July 2005)
65. Rouvoy, R., Barone, P., Ding, Y., Eliassen, F., Hallsteinsen, S., Lorenzo, J., Mamelli, A., Scholz, U.: MUSIC: Middleware Support for Self-Adaptation in Ubiquitous and Service-Oriented Environments. In: Cheng, B.H.C., de Lemos, R., Giese, H., Inverardi, P., Magee, J. (eds.) Self-Adaptive Systems. LNCS, vol. 5525, pp. 164–182. Springer, Heidelberg (2009)
66. Salehie, M., Tahvildari, L.: Self-Adaptive Software: Landscape and Research Challenges. Trans. on Autonomous and Adaptive Systems 14, 14:1–14:42 (2009)
67. Savigni, A., Tisato, F.: Designing Traffic Control Systems. A Software Engineering Perspective. In: Proc. of Jubilee 2000 Conference, Roma, Italy (September 2000)
68. Ubayashi, N., Akatoki, H., Nomura, J.: Pointcut-based Architectural Interface for Bridging a Gap between Design and Implementation. In: Proc. of RAM-SE 2009, Genoa, Italy (July 2009)
69. Würthinger, T., Wimmer, C., Stadler, L.: Dynamic Code Evolution for Java. In: Proc. of PPPJ 2010, Vienna, Austria, pp. 10–19 (September 2010)
70. Yoder, J.W., Johnson, R.E.: The Adaptive Object-Model Architectural Style. In: Proc. of WICSA 2002, pp. 3–27. Kluwer (August 2002)

Safety Assurance of Open Adaptive Systems – A Survey

Mario Trapp and Daniel Schneider

Fraunhofer Institute for Experimental Software Engineering
Kaiserslautern, Germany
{mario.trapp,daniel.schneider}@iese.fraunhofer.de

Open adaptive systems are the basis for a promising new generation of embedded systems with huge economic potential. In many application domains, however, the systems are safety-critical and an appropriate safety assurance approach is still missing.

In recent years, models at runtime have emerged as a promising way to systematically engineer adaptive systems. This approach seems to provide the indispensable leverage for applying safety assurance techniques in adaptive systems. Therefore, this survey analyzes the state-of-the-art of models at runtime from a safety engineering point of view in order to assess the potential of this approach and to identify open gaps that have to be closed in future research to yield a safety assurance approach for open adaptive systems.

1   Introduction

The development of safety-critical embedded systems has to follow strict rules and a rigorous safety assurance case is required before a product can be introduced to the market. Developers therefore avoid using flexible and progressive concepts like dynamic adaptation in safety-critical contexts. Many safety standards such as IEC 61508[47] even prohibit the use of techniques like dynamic reconfiguration or self-healing.

Over the last decade, however, new applications have emerged, which are today often subsumed under the popular term cyber-physical systems. In some sense, cyber-physical systems are Open Adaptive Systems (OAS), i.e. systems of systems that dynamically connect to each other (openness) and adapt to a changing context at runtime (adaptive). Industry sees huge economic potential in such systems -particularly because their openness and adaptivity enables new kinds of promising applications in different application domains. Many application domains of cyber-physical systems, however, are safety-critical. This includes, for example, car2car scenarios, plug'n'play operating rooms, or collaborative autonomous mobile machines.

This means that two different worlds, which have intentionally been kept separate, have to grow together in the near future. Using the full potential of OAS without endangering a product's safety is therefore one of the primary challenges today. Regarding the state-of-the-art, however, there are only a few approaches that explicitly address the safety assurance of OAS. Whereas the adaptive systems community mostly considers safety as one of many quality properties, the safety engineering

N. Bencomo et al. (Eds.): Models@run.time, LNCS 8378, pp. 279–318, 2014.

community is still mainly concerned with design time variability, and only a few groups focus on the safety of Open Adaptive Systems. Therefore, safety could easily become a bottleneck preventing the successful transition of a promising idea into business success.

From a safety point of view, there are, in fact, a few approaches that could be extended to assure safety in OAS. For example, some groups are pursuing the idea of safety bags [47], which detect and handle failures at runtime. By this means, even failures that potentially result from system adaptations would be covered so that the system adaptation as such would not be the subject of safety assurance anymore. In practice, however, the effectiveness of such approaches is still very limited. A further alternative would be to assure safety completely at design time by predicting all possible system adaptations and covering the complete adaptation space already during safety assurance at development time. Such approaches could easily run into a state space explosion problem and for open systems in particular, the structure cannot be completely predicted at development time.

Therefore, this article focuses on alternative approaches enabling safety assurance at runtime. To this end, we particularly regard Models@Runtime, which have emerged as a possible means for the systematic development and runtime management of adaptive systems. It is our perception that Models@Runtime as a new paradigm could be an appropriate catalyst for accelerating progress in the safety assurance of OAS. In particular, they seem to provide an efficient basis for the safety assurance of Open Adaptive Systems: Models@Runtime provide a kind of formal basis for reasoning about the current system state at runtime, for reasoning about necessary adaptations, and for analyzing or predicting the consequences of possible system adaptations. This makes dynamic adaptation tractable, traceable and in some sense predictable. Therefore, having explicit Models@Runtime may provide the indispensable leverage needed for applying safety assurance techniques at runtime, hence bridging the gap between traditional adaptive systems and safety engineering research. At the same time, however, a Models@Runtime framework imposes additional complexity that potentially detriments the assurance of safety. As a consequence, it will be important to find the right balance between capabilities and complexity of the Models@Runtime framework on the one hand and the corresponding complexity and feasibility of the safety assurance on the other hand. Moreover, in order to be accepted, any safety assurance concept must still fit into the safety engineers' and certification bodies' views of the world.

Using conventional safety assurance approaches as a reference, however, would immediately lead to the result that dynamic adaptation must not be applied at all. In order to identify the current position and missing steps on the way to safety assurance in OAS, it is nonetheless necessary to know the target we want to reach. Therefore, we have to look ahead in order to get an idea of what such a safety assurance framework based on Models@Runtime could look like. To this end, we use an established, conventional safety engineering lifecycle as starting point which is introduced in Chapter 2. By applying the idea of Models@Runtime to the models and activities of the safety lifecycle we create a projection of a possible future safety assurance framework in Chapter 3. In a subsequent step, we analyze the state-of-the-art with respect to adequate starting points and building blocks for our envisioned future safety assurance framework. The state-of-the-art analysis will thereby be twofold. On the one hand, in Chapter 4, the state-of-the-art of the safety engineering community will be investigated with respect to promising approaches and concepts that might be employed in the context of the envisioned framework and runtime assurance measures. On the other hand, in Chapter 5, the same will be done for the adaptive systems community. In addition, for the adaptive systems community there will also a brief overview on current Models@Runtime approaches that might serve as a technological basis or starting point for the envisioned safety assurance approach. In Chapter 6.1 the state-of-the-art is then being categorized based on the different conceptual classes of safety assurance approaches that have been identified in the context of the envisioned framework. Based thereon, open gaps are pointed out and possible future research directions are devised in Chapter 6.2.

2   Safety Engineering for Traditional Embedded Systems

2.1   Safety Engineering in a Nut-Shell

The precise definition of a safety engineering lifecycle, and particularly of the terms used, depends on the concrete application domain. The principal idea, however, is similar across all safety-related application domains. For the sake of simplicity, we therefore use the terms as defined in the ISO 26262[55], which is the relevant safety standard for automotive systems. It is at the same time one of the most recent safety standards.

The overall goal of safety engineering is to ensure 'freedom from unacceptable risk'[55]. The term risk is defined as the 'combination of the probability of occurrence of harm and the severity of that harm'[55]. Usually, however, it is not possible to directly assess the harm that is potentially caused by a system. Instead, safety managers identify the hazards of a system, i.e., 'potential sources of harm'[55]. In many domains, this vague definition is further refined. In the automotive domain, for example, 'hazards shall be defined in the terms of conditions and events that can be observed at the vehicle level'[55]. Usually, harm is only caused when a hazard, a specific environmental situation, and a specific operation mode of the system coincide. This coincidence is called 'hazardous event'.

The identification of these hazardous events and the assessment of the associated risks is the first step in any safety engineering lifecycle, namely the 'hazard analysis and risk assessment (HRA)' as shown in Figure 1. This step is performed during the very early phases of the development process, at the latest when the system requirements are available.

As a result of this step, safety goals are defined as top-level safety requirements, which have to be incrementally refined during the safety engineering lifecycle. Usually, any safety requirement consists of a functional part and an associated integrity level. The functional part defines what the system must (not) do, whereas the integrity level defines the rigor demanded for the implementation of this requirement. The integrity level depends on the risk associated with the hazardous event, which is addressed by the safety goal. For example, ISO 26262 defines so-called automotive safety integrity levels (ASIL).

Once the safety goals have been defined, the system development continues through different phases like the definition of a network of functions, the system and software architecture, the design, and finally the implementation of the system. In the same way that the validation and verification of the system should run in parallel to the development, the subsequent steps in the safety engineering process should be performed in parallel as well (though this is often not the case in practice). To this end, the available development artifacts are used as input to safety analyses in order to identify potential causes of the identified system failures. A wide range of different analysis techniques is available. Failure Modes and Effects Analysis (FMEA) and Fault Tree Analysis (FTA) are certainly the most widely used safety analysis techniques in practice.

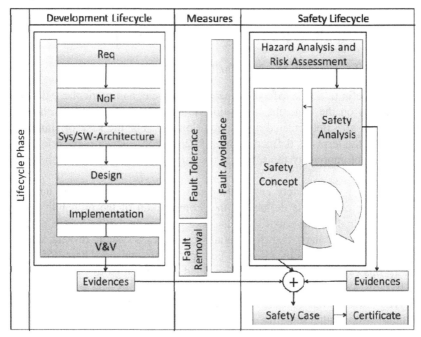

Fig. 1. Safety Engineering Lifecycle and possible countermeasures

Based on these results, a safety manager derives a safety concept. Following the idea of ISO 26262, a safety concept can be defined as a 'specification of the safety requirements, their allocation to architectural elements and their interaction necessary to achieve the safety goals, and information associated with these requirements. In the same way as the developers incrementally refine the system over the different development phases, the safety manager analyzes the refined development artifacts step by step and refines the safety concept accordingly.

The safety concept plays a very important role in safety engineering. It defines which countermeasures have to be applied and how the measures in combination shall ensure the safety goals. Following the definition of Avižienis et al. [21], there are three principal classes of countermeasures, as shown in the middle of Figure 1. Any measure available can be assigned to one of these classes. First of all, fault avoidance measures shall mitigate the creation of faults from the very beginning. This includes measures such as strict development processes or coding rules. Usually, however, it is not possible to avoid all kinds of faults using such measures. Therefore, it is additionally necessary to apply fault removal measures. This particularly includes validation and verification activities, which try to reveal and remove faults during the development phase. Since we cannot assume that these measures are sufficient to yield a fault-free system, it is also necessary to apply fault tolerance measures. Fault tolerance measures detect and handle errors at runtime in order to prevent system failures.

Finally the safety manager has to define a safety case, which forms the basis for certification. A safety case can be defined as an 'argument why an item is safe supported by evidence compiled from work products of all safety activities during the whole lifecycle.'[55]. Evidence might be anything supporting an argument in the safety case. Evidences of particular importance are the results of validation and verification activities as well as safety analysis results. Since a safety case compiles all evidences that are relevant for proving the system's safety, it is an efficient basis for safety certification.

2.2   Modular Certification

In most domains, safety managers follow a comparable approach to assure the functional safety of systems. Usually, however, the resulting safety certificate is valid for a specific system configuration only. Even a single change requires the system to be recertified. For example, in the avionics domain, even small system changes cause recertification costs approaching or even exceeding the original costs [73]. Considering that in the avionics domain 60%-70% of the overall development costs are caused by verification and certification activities, this leads to tremendous costs for recertification.

Consequently, in the last decade, safety research has focused on approaches called modular or incremental certification, as described in more detail in Chapter 4. As illustrated in Figure 2, the idea of modular certification is that the individual subsystems are modularly certified and provide a modular safety certificate. When the system is integrated, the certification effort shall be reduced to a composition of the subsystem certificates. In fact, most of the current approaches do not consider modular certificates, but modular safety cases, which have to be composed into a safety case for the overall system. The overall system certification is then a traditional, manual process based on the composed safety case.

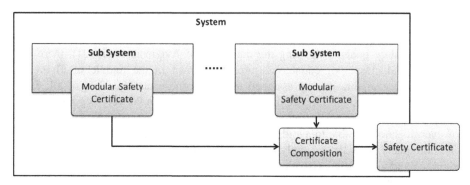

Fig. 2. Principal idea of modular certification

Nonetheless, this simplifies the certification process for complex systems, which are composed of various different systems purchased off-the-shelf or delivered by different suppliers. Even more importantly, such an approach simplifies recertification, since a change of a component only requires recertification of the changed component and re-composition of the overall system certificate.

Such an approach is obviously very interesting for the safety assurance of Open Adaptive Systems, which are subject to continuous changes at runtime. In practice, however, safety research is still dealing with different challenges raised by modular certification at development time.

3   Models@Runtime for Safety Assurance in Open Adaptive Systems

In modular certification, a safety expert assesses the integrated system. If we want to apply such concepts for Open Adaptive Systems, however, there will be no human expert to check the system's safety. Rather, the system must assure its own safety. This leads to a series of new challenges as to how the safety-relevant information can be formalized and utilized an adequate way. Considering that safety research is still solving the problems of modular certification, safety assurance in Open Adaptive Systems seems to be a very challenging endeavor. Extrapolating the current developments of safety engineering, it would take much too long until urgently required safety assurance approaches for Open Adaptive Systems would be available. In the same way as Open Adaptive Systems form a new paradigm in system development, there must be a change of paradigms in safety assurance as well.

Regarding the future safety assurance framework for OAS, we consequently pursued the idea of combining a typical safety assurance approach with the principle of Models@Runtime, as already motivated above. Starting from traditional techniques implies the additional benefit that a clear trace can be provided from conventional safety engineering to the future concepts supporting Open Adaptive Systems, which could facilitate the acceptance of the framework. In essence, we understand the conceptual safety assurance framework as a means to:

- Raise awareness within the research communities for the specific challenges of safety assurance in OAS
- Provide orientation for researchers by interconnecting different kinds of research into a bigger picture
- Provide clear interfaces for future research

In order to create the conceptual safety assurance framework, we incrementally project elements (i.e., typical safety models) of the safety engineering lifecycle to runtime. To do so, we start with SafetyCertificates@Runtime and extend the approach backward step by step along the safety engineering lifecycle. Shifting an element into runtime always implies that corresponding runtime mechanisms need to be established that operate on the element. These are required to automate the tasks that used to be conducted by safety experts. It is obvious that the earlier the shifted element is in the lifecycle, the more engineering activities need to be automated, the more intelligence is required at runtime – and the more difficult it will be for the approach to be realized and accepted.

In accordance with the above, we first describe the ideas of SafetyCertificates@Runtime (section 3.1), then SafetyCases@Runtime (section 3.2), followed by validation and verification of Models@Runtime (section 3.3), and finally Hazard Analysis and Risk Assessment@Runtime (section 3.4). These different options are evaluated in section 3.5 before section 3.6 shows a possible safety assurance framework integrating the different approaches. The framework will finally be the basis for assessing the state-of-the-art and assigning existing work and research directions to the different classes of the framework according to their respective suitability.

3.1   SafetyCertificates@Runtime

Following the idea described above, making safety certificates available at runtime is the first option. SafetyCertificates@Runtime contain all information that is necessary to identify which safety requirements are fulfilled with which integrity by the associated system. Just like conventional safety certificates, SafetyCertificates@Runtime do not contain any white-box information on how the system was realized to yield the certification. A clear advantage of such an approach is that the runtime models and their evaluation can be quite simple and efficient as, for instance, shown by the ConSert approach [70] [71] [76]. This would also imply that an overly complex Models@Runtime framework would not be required, thus alleviating the safety assurance of the framework itself.

Classification Criteria: SafetyCertificates@Runtime are modular certificates that can be interpreted, composed, and adapted at runtime. They are dynamically adapted to represent the safety state of the system at runtime. The certificates of subsystems can be composed at runtime in order to yield an overall safety approval for a given composition.

Using SafetyCertificates@Runtime, it is particularly possible to compose systems at runtime. As illustrated in Figure 3, the individual subsystems provide a runtime representation of the modular certificates (SafetyCertificate@Runtime). In order to assess the safety of the resulting system of systems, the single certificates have to be

composed. In order to yield such a Certificate@Runtime, the process is very similar
to modular certification. After the subsystem has been developed, it must undergo a
manual certification process at design time. Usually, however, the safety assurance of
a single subsystem at design time can only yield a conditional certificate, since the
certification is based on various assumptions. These assumptions might be concrete
demands on other subsystems. For example, there might be a demand that the failure
modes of a received signal must be mitigated by another subsystem according to a
specific safety integrity level. Other assumptions might consider the integration context in general, such as the maximal number of collaborating subsystems, the type and
quality of the communication system used, etc. Consequently, SafetyCertifi-
cates@Runtime often follow the idea of safety contracts defining a set of safety guarantees provided by the subsystem and a set of safety demands the subsystems require
to be fulfilled by the integration context. This means that they provide runtime information on which safety properties can be guaranteed by the system under the precondition that the defined demands are fulfilled. At runtime, the fulfillment of the demands is checked and the resulting guarantees are derived. Usually, however, safety is
not a completely modular property, i.e., the composition of safe components does not
necessarily lead to a safe composition, even though the safety demands are fulfilled.
Therefore, it is often necessary to perform additional checks in the integration context
at runtime (cf. section 5.1).

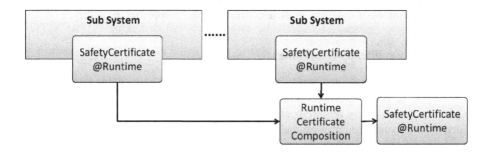

Fig. 3. SafetyCertificates@Runtime enable dynamic system composition

When subsystems are composed at runtime, it is possible to compose the Certifi-
cates@Runtime as well. To this end, the conditions defined in the runtime certificates
must be checked. In the simplest approach, a system of systems is considered safe if
all preconditions of all conditional certificates are true. Otherwise, the system of system must not be used. In most cases, however, the certificates of the single subsystems are not harmonized with each other. So it is very unlikely that there will be a
safe match at all. In fact, such an approach is only reasonable if it is possible to adapt
the Certificate@Runtime to the current integration context.

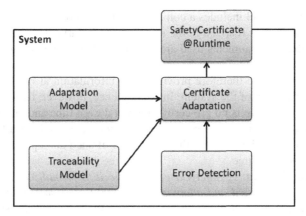

Fig. 4. Runtime adaptation of certificates provides more flexibility

Actually, the possibilities of how a runtime certificate could adapt are as versatile as adaptation in general. There could be different pre-defined variants that are dynamically selected in a given context. Or there could be more sophisticated and flexible adaptations of the certificate. From a safety point of view, however, predictable, traceable, or even provable solutions are more likely to be accepted. Some ideas are illustrated in Figure 4. If we assume, for example, that there is an adaptation model defining how the system adapts in certain situations, this information could also be used to adapt the certificate.

Alternatively or additionally, a traceability model could be used to identify those elements that are affected by system adaptations and to derive necessary certificate adaptations. In fact, traceability Models@Runtime might play an important role for the safety assurance of OAS. An efficient impact analysis is of utmost importance in traditional safety engineering in order to identify necessary changes and thus reduce the revalidation effort. As long as the effects of adaptations can be traced back to anticipated classes of system changes, even complex system adaptations could be handled by simple variants in the SafetyModel@Runtime.

As a further extension, it could be possible to use error detection mechanisms to adjust the runtime certificates using up-to-date runtime error information.

Usually, the adaptation goal for the certificates is to provide the best possible guarantees in the given context. The context, in turn, is usually given by the set of externally fulfilled safety demands and the internal state of the system.

3.2 SafetyCases@Runtime

The more adaptive a system is, the more difficult it is to consider all the different adaptations in a Certificate@Runtime. This particularly increases the effort at design time since the complete adaptation space must be considered in the certification process. Alternatively, it could therefore be another option to provide SafetyCases@Runtime. Safety cases are direct input to certification. In contrast to certificates, however, they include the complete argument of why a system is considered safe.

A good safety case model includes a complete breakdown of top-level safety goals to the detailed requirements realized in the system. And it particularly includes the evidence proving that the arguments used are sound and that the requirements have been fulfilled.

SafetyCases@Runtime therefore provide more information at runtime and enable more flexible adaptation of the system. In consequence, however, they are more complex to handle, since there is no pre-certification at design time and all the steps from a safety case to certification have to be shifted to runtime as well. As a further consequence, this will most likely reduce the acceptance of such an approach compared to SafetyCertificates@Runtime.

Classification Criteria*: A SafetyCase@Runtime is a formalized, modular safety case that can be interpreted and adapted at runtime. Based on the interpretation, it can be dynamically checked to which extent the safety goals of subsystems are met. With adaptation, the line argument can be adjusted to system adaptations. In addition, the revalidation of evidences at runtime must be supported in case system adaptations lead to the invalidation of evidences.*

As shown in Figure 5, SafetyCases@Runtime extend the idea of SafetyCertificates@Runtime. Instead of explicitly defining the adaptation of the certificates, it is possible to describe the adaptation of the safety cases and use the SafetyCases@Runtime to adapt the safety certificates automatically.

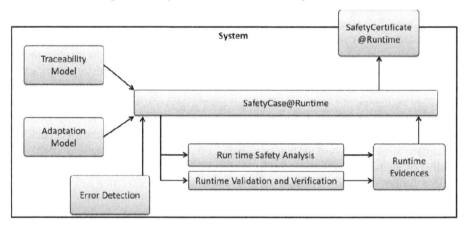

Fig. 5. Conceptual model of how safety cases could be used at runtime

A certificate certifies that certain safety guarantees are fulfilled. The safety case models the argument of why these guarantees are fulfilled. If a safety case is adapted at runtime, the resulting argumentation should enable the system to conclude autonomously which safety guarantees can still be provided at which integrity level.

A basic element of safety cases are evidences, which are, for example, verification and validation results or the results of safety analyses. By shifting safety cases to runtime, it is possible to adapt (1) the argumentation and/or (2) the evidences to the currently given context. As regards the adaptation of the argumentation, a very straightforward solution would be to include different variants of the argumentation.

In more complex versions, more intelligence might be integrated that is able to derive new lines of argumentation.

With regard to the evidences, it is necessary to attach constraints to the evidences used in the safety case. At runtime it is then necessary to evaluate whether or not these constraints are still fulfilled. If not, there are basically two combinable options. First, it is possible to find an alternative argumentation based on the remaining valid evidences – including argumentations that potentially require a reduction of the safety guarantees that can be provided in the given context. A second option would be the revalidation of evidences. This requires the capability to re-perform safety analyses as well as validation and verification activities at runtime. For SafetyCases@Runtime, let us assume that this revalidation is limited to repeating the checks defined at design time in order to provide the evidence. This presumes that the system adaptation does not lead to a change of requirements or a change of the system's interface.

If the respective pass-criteria are met, the newly created evidence can replace the invalidated original evidence and be integrated into a new argumentation. Otherwise, the evidence remains invalid and the system must either find an alternative line of argumentation or invalidate the affected safety goals.

3.3   V&V-Models@Runtime

SafetyCases@Runtime already provide a very flexible means for safety assurance at runtime. Some system adaptations, however, might require a new set of verification and validation checks to provide the evidence required for the argument. Moreover, it might be desirable to be able to remove the faults identified during runtime V&V instead of being limited to only checking the pass-criteria.

For the former aspect, it is necessary to additionally enable the system to define verification and validation suites autonomously. Realizing the latter aspect even requires systems that are able to localize the causing faults, and to isolate or even remove them. Considering how difficult this step easily becomes for developers at design time, it is obviously a very challenging task to shift these activities to runtime.

Classification Criteria: V&V-Models@Runtime presume that all models that are necessary to perform validation and verification activities (e.g., test cases, pass/fail-criteria etc.) can be interpreted and adapted at runtime in order to create new evidences after system adaptations.

3.4   Hazard Analysis and Risk Assessment@Runtime (HRA@Runtime)

In the previous alternatives, we assume that the requirements and the resulting safety goals are not adapted. As a consequence, it has only been necessary to adapt the argumentation that the safety goals are still met in spite of system adaptations based on the safety case and the evidences created at runtime. Some adaptation approaches, however, also consider a change of requirements at runtime. If we apply the safety lifecycle to the idea of Models@Runtime, this means that we require a hazard and risk analysis at runtime, i.e. that the system must adapt and extend the hazard and risk analysis and potentially have to adapt and extend the set of safety goals. By doing so, the complete existing argumentation for a changed safety goal might be invalidated. For new safety goals, an argumentation is completely missing. On the one hand, this type of runtime assurance certainly provides the highest possible flexibility. On the other hand, however, it requires very intelligent mechanisms for defining a safety argumentation and generating the necessary evidence autonomously at runtime.

Classification Criteria: *HRA@Runtime implies that a hazard and risk analysis model can be interpreted and adapted at runtime. This includes the identification of new hazards and the reassessment of existing hazards after adaptations at the requirement level.*

3.5   Evaluation of the Different Approaches

Regarding the approaches described above, they obviously build upon each other. This means that a HRA@Runtime requires V&V-Models@Runtime, which in turn require SafetyCases@Runtime and so on. So it is necessary to decide to which extent we want to shift the safety lifecycle to runtime. This results in a trade-off decision. From a safety point of view, it is certainly preferable to leave as much responsibility as possible with a human expert. Consequently, it would be reasonable to have only SafetyCertificates@Runtime. From an adaptation point of view, however, it is preferable to have as much flexibility as possible in order to tap the full potential of dynamic adaptation. In consequence, this would require shifting elements of the complete safety lifecycle to runtime.

In order to further illustrate this trade-off, Figure 6 shows the relations of the different approaches to their acceptance on the one hand and to their flexibility on the other hand. Acceptance in this case refers to the probability of acceptance by safety authorities and legislation. Since there is no practical experience available, this is a qualitative estimation. First, we assume that acceptance is inversely proportional to the responsibility and intelligence given to the system. Second, the acceptance of an approach is usually inversely proportional to its complexity. Or vice versa: The simpler an approach can be realized, the more probable is its acceptance. For obvious reasons, it is very probable that the required intelligence as well as the resulting complexity will grow with the number of safety assurance steps that are shifted to runtime. Consequently, in our opinion, SafetyCertificates@Runtime have the best chances of being accepted, whereas the acceptance of an HRA@Runtime (i.e., shifting all safety assurance activities to runtime) is quite improbable. As a further aspect, acceptance will be higher if the Safety-Models@Runtime are reconfigured at runtime to predefined variants only, whereas acceptance will rapidly decrease if the safety models themselves are adapted more flexibly at runtime.

Flexibility, on the other hand, represents the degree of which different types of adaptations are supported. More precisely, in this case we refer to the type of adaptation used to adapt the system itself and not to the type of adaptation used to adapt the safety models, since different adaptation approaches might be used for the system itself on the one hand and the safety models on the other hand. In order to classify the supported flexibility of system adaptations, we differentiate between three basic classes. We first differentiate between 'known unknowns' and 'unknown unknowns'. In the former case, we assume that the system can only adapt to a runtime context that has been anticipated at design time. In the latter case, we assume that the system needs to flexibly adapt to situations not anticipated at design time. In consequence, the system structure or behavior is hard or even impossible to predict. We have further subdivided the 'unknown unknowns' into adaptations at the design level on the one hand and at the requirements level on the other hand. In the former case, we assume that the requirements can remain unchanged and an adaptation of the realization (e.g., at the architecture level) is sufficient to adapt to the context given. In the latter case, the adaptation also includes the adaptation of existing and/or the definition of new requirements.

SafetyCertificates@Runtime can only be used to address 'known unknowns' since an adaptation of certificates to an unpredicted context is not possible without considering the underlying safety case, which forms the indispensable basis for a sound argumentation of a certificate's validity. But even for 'known unknowns' the configuration space might be too large to be covered completely by variants at the certificate level. Therefore, it might be reasonable to use SafetyCases@Runtime already to efficiently support 'known unknowns'.

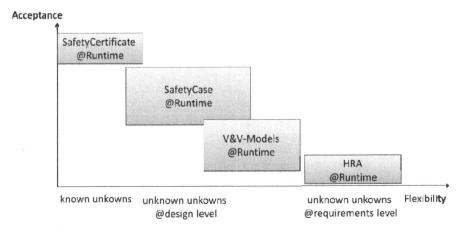

Fig. 6. Qualitative relations between acceptance and flexibility

If we consider 'unknown unknowns' at the design level, this means especially that the requirements and thus the safety goals remain unchanged. Depending on the degree of system modifications required for the adaptation, SafetyCases@Runtime or V&V-Models@Runtime are therefore sufficient. While SafetyCases@Runtime are limited to running predefined validation and verification activities at runtime, V&V-Models@Runtime additionally support the modification of V&V models, e.g., the modification of test cases or pass/fail criteria. The more flexible the system adaptations must be, the more likely it is that V&V-Models@Runtime approaches will be required in addition to SafetyCases@Runtime.

As soon as the adaptation to 'unknown unknowns' also requires an adaptation of requirements, it is additionally necessary to adapt the hazard and risk analysis and the resulting safety goals at runtime. As described above, it is not sufficient to identify new hazards or to re-assess the associated risk at runtime. In fact, the system must be able to appropriately create or adapt all affected artifacts along the complete safety lifecycle.

3.6   Conceptual Safety Assurance Framework for Open Adaptive Systems

Models@Runtime obviously provide a wide range of possible approaches for the safety assurance of Open Adaptive Systems and it is certainly not possible to pick out one particular approach that leads to the best trade-off between flexibility and acceptance in general. In fact, we believe that it will be necessary to integrate different approaches into an assurance framework in order to use the advantages and compensate for the disadvantages of the different approaches.

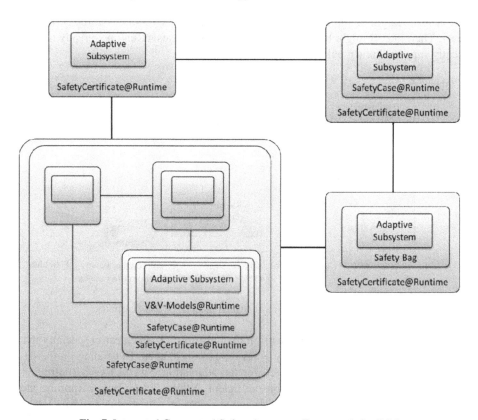

Fig. 7. Integrated Conceptual Safety Assurance Framework for OAS

Some ideas for such a framework are shown in Figure 7. Learning from traditional safety engineering, we recommend using modularity as the basic ingredient for a safety assurance framework from the very beginning. First, this obviously reduces complexity. Second, this enables us to use different assurance approaches for different modules. In this context, we use the term module very flexibly to express a modularized entity that can range from a complete system in a system of systems to a single software component. Since the required types of adaptation usually differ widely across the different modules, it reasonable to limit more complex assurance approaches to those modules that actually have to adapt very flexibly.

Following the idea of modular certification, it seems to be reasonable to use SafetyCertificates@Runtime as the basic building blocks to enable the modularization and runtime integration of different subsystems. In this case, SafetyCertificates@Runtime are the common denominator enabling the combination of a wide range of different assurance approaches used for the single modules.

Assume, for example, that we have a module that adapts to 'known unknowns' only, as shown in the upper left corner of Figure 7. Then it might be sufficient to perform the major safety assurance activities at development time and limit the runtime models to SafetyCertificates@Runtime only. If we have a module that has too large a configuration space or that also adapts to 'unknown unknowns', it might be necessary to have SafetyCases@Runtime as well, as shown in the upper right corner of Figure 3-5. As described above, SafetyCases@Runtime are an extension of SafetyCertificates@Runtime, so a runtime certificate is still available at the module's interface, facilitating the safe integration of the components. In some cases, a module might adapt so flexibly that we will need V&V-Models@Runtime or even an HRA@Runtime. However, realizing this is very complex, so it seems reasonable to keep the complexity of such modules very small. To this end, it is helpful that the modularization of the framework can be applied recursively to achieve hierarchical decomposition, as illustrated in the lower left corner of Figure 7. This decomposition additionally illustrates an alternative way of composing SafetyCertificates@Runtime. If we assume systems of systems for example, each providing a SafetyCertificate@Runtime, the single systems are usually sufficiently independent from each other that composition at the certificate level is likely to be sufficient. If we assume the runtime integration of different software modules running on the same platform, there are usually tight interdependencies. Merely the fact that they share the same resources, for example, creates a safety-relevant dependency. For this reason, it is likely that additional evidences will be required for proving that the integration of the single modules is safe as well. Therefore, it might also be reasonable to have SafetyCases@Runtime at the integration level.

The acceptance of sophisticated assurance approaches, in particular, is very low. An alternative way to ensure the safety of highly adaptive systems is given by different traditional approaches, particularly in the field of fault tolerance. So-called safety bags (cf. e.g., [47]), for example, are a typical concept for monitoring a function to detect anomalies and trigger counter-reactions. Assuming that it would be possible to define a safety bag that can detect and handle any safety-related failure of an adaptive module, it would not be necessary to provide further assurance of that module. Though such approaches are based on traditional mechanisms rather than Models@Runtime, they would nonetheless fit into our conceptual framework as shown in the lower right corner of Figure 7.

Summarizing, this conceptual framework has been created based on a prognostic evolution of state-of-the-practice safety engineering lifecycles using the idea of Models@Runtime as a catalyst, which it uses to build a conceptual bridge between the world of safety engineering on the one hand and Models@Runtime on the other hand. Being based on safety engineering principles makes acceptance of the approach more likely. Yet it provides sufficient flexibility to integrate various different solution approaches based on Models@Runtime. Therefore, in the subsequent chapters we will analyze the state-of-the-art with respect to the suitability of the different approaches to fit into specific parts of the framework. We will further identify 'white spots' and interfaces for future research.

4   State-of-the-Art from the Safety Engineering Community's Point of View

As already discussed above, Open Adaptive Systems have long been beyond the scope of the safety engineering research community. However, the work that has been done in the direction of modular certification might well prove to be a sound foundation for tackling the safety-related challenges posed by Open Adaptive Systems. Moreover, there are some first approaches advocating the introduction of runtime measures. The state-of-the-art presented in this chapter consequently focuses on approaches from the safety engineering community that either belong to the aspiring research field of modular certification, or that advocate certain runtime measures for the context of OAS.

In general, modular certification can be characterized as a means for the modularization of safety cases. The safety case is modularized such that components developed by different suppliers, and components that are likely to be replaced or reused, specify a self-contained modular safety case. These modular safety cases, specified by the module developer, are connected on the system level by the integrator to build the system safety case. In order to be able to assemble the system safety case, each module must provide an interface specification containing the module's guaranteed behavior and the behavior demanded of other interacting modules. Demands are necessary since the behavior of the module at hand depends on the behavior of the other modules it is interacting with. Therefore, the module at hand is only able to give guarantees under the premise of a certain behavior of the interacting modules. These premises are called demands and, together with the afore-mentioned guarantees, shape demand/guarantee contracts.

The idea to use contracts as a metaphor for describing the interaction of components with mutual obligations and benefits can also be found in approaches that do not specifically focus on safety, such as those presented in Section 5.1.1. These approaches do, however, focus on specifying the nominal behavior and/or specific quality characteristics of components and do not consider a component's failure behavior (how does the component fail, what failures of other components can the component tolerate), which is essential for safety-related modularization.

4.1   Foundational Work on Modular Certification

To enable modularization of safety cases, it is crucial to formalize the relevant information in an appropriate way. As a first step, it is necessary to enable modular safety analyses. A corresponding starting point is given by techniques from the class of failure logic modeling (FLM) [48], where the failure logic is modeled separately for each component and the failure logic model defines how deviations at the input of a component propagate to deviations at the outputs of the component. Architecture models, which are (should be) available anyway, define how the components are connected. Based on the architecture, it is therefore possible to also connect the failure logic models of the component, and the failure propagation throughout the overall system can be analyzed automatically. Prominent solutions in this regard are the 'Hierarchically Performed Hazard Origin and Propagation Studies' – HiP-HOPS [49] and the 'Failure Propagation and Transformation Notation' – FPTN [50]. Another approach that is based on safety contracts has been proposed by Hawkins and McDermid[51]. Moreover, component fault trees [52] provide an extension for the well-known technique of fault trees that supports the modular, component-based definition of fault trees [53]. Fault trees and CFTs generally also enable probabilistic analyses by annotating faults with respective probabilities of occurrence. Since it is often not possible to determine concrete probabilities for a given event, Foerster and Schneider introduced an approach that uses intervals of probabilities to efficiently deal with such uncertainties during development [54].

4.2   Modular Certification as Represented by Current Standards

Some concepts related to modular certification have already been adopted by current standards and thus found their way into the state of the practice. This is particularly true for the fields of automotive systems and avionic systems because the trend towards modularized architectures has been particularly strong in these fields. The following paragraphs provide a brief overview of the corresponding standards and the modularization concepts they advocate.

4.2.1   ISO 26262

The international standard ISO 26262 for the functional safety of street vehicles contains the so-called concept of Safety Element out of Context (SEooC) [55]. A SEooC is defined as a component for which there is no single predestinated application in a specific system. Therefore, the SEooC developer does not know the concrete role the product has to play in the safety concept. Subsystems, hardware components, and software components may be developed as SEooCs. Typical software SEooCs are reusable, application-independent components such as operating systems, libraries, or middleware in general.

For SEooC development, the standard suggests specifying assumed safety requirements and developing the system according to these requirements. When the SEooC is to be used in a specific system, the system developer has to specify the demanded requirements, which can subsequently be checked against the assumed requirements. If there is a match between the demanded and the guaranteed (assumed) requirements, system and component are compatible. The standard does not provide any suggestions or methods on how to identify safety requirements such as to increase the chance that assumed and real requirements match. Neither does the standard provide information on how to perform the verification of the assumed requirements during integration of the SEooC. The standard specifies a relatively coarse-grained process for embedding a SEooC development into the standard's safety lifecycle. In general, SEooC integration is expected to be done at development time and thus there is no explicit support for open systems where components are to be integrated dynamically. Moreover, there is no explicit support with respect to the management of variabilities, be it at development time or at runtime.

4.2.2   DO-297

The DO-297 [56] standard regulates the modular certification of components in an Integrated Modular Avionic (IMA) system. The terminology of the standard talks of incremental acceptance instead of modular certification. Acceptance is defined as the confirmation of a certification body that a module of an IMA system (a general-purpose execution platform or an application) fulfills its specification. This acceptance can be achieved for an IMA system and is one building block of the final certification, with the latter always being in the context of a specific airplane or engine. The wording incremental has been chosen because the process of the DO-297 allows step-wise acceptance of single modules of a system and because it allows incrementally extending a system with new applications, without having to re-certify all the modules in the system.

4.3   State-of-the-Art for Modular Certification Approaches

This section briefly describes a selection of prospective modular certification approaches. All these approaches are briefly described and their applicability in the context of Open Adaptive Systems is considered.

4.3.1   Concepts for Modular Certification by Rushby

Rushby provides some theoretical considerations on the use of modular certification for software components in IMA architectures. The goal is to enable the certification of software components in order to allow them to perform their functions in a given (aircraft) context based solely on assumptions about other related software components. Three key elements were identified as the potential backbone of a corresponding approach [60]:

1. *Partitioning* creates an environment that enforces the interfaces between components; thus, the only failure modes that need be considered are those in which software components perform their function incorrectly, or deliver incorrect behavior at their interfaces.

2. *Assume-guarantee reasoning* is a technique that allows one component to be verified in the presence of assumptions about another, and vice versa.
3. *Separation of properties into normal and abnormal properties.* Abnormal properties capture behavior in the presence of failures.

To ensure that the assumptions are closed and the system is safe, three classes of properties that must be established using assume-guarantee reasoning were identified:

1. *Safe function* ensures that each component performs its function safely under all conditions consistent with its fault hypothesis;
2. *True guarantees* ensure that each component delivers its appropriate guarantees;
3. *Controlled failure* is used to prevent a 'domino effect' where the failure of one component causes others to fail, too.

It is important to note that the publication presents conceptual foundations but does not provide concrete solutions. Still, the presented concepts are clearly relevant and likely to be of avail for future work in the context of the envisioned framework.

4.3.2   Modular Goal Structuring Notation

The Goal Structuring Notation (GSN) [61] is a graphical notation for modeling a safety argument, which is the core part of every safety case. A safety case has been defined in the context of the GSN as follows:

'A safety case communicates a clear, comprehensive and defensible argument that a system is acceptably safe to operate in a particular context.'

Therefore, a safety case serves the purpose of specifying a comprehensive argument to prove the safety of a system. To this end, the GSN allows modeling tree-like arguments beginning with safety goals, and iteratively connecting them through chains of logical argumentation and sub-goals, with the evidences created during system development. Evidences can be performed tests or analysis reports from an FMEA or an FTA that are used for underpinning the fulfillment of the goals.

In order to deal with modular systems and modular certification, there is an extension to GSN that allows modularizing safety cases [62]. The interface of a safety case module is defined by a set of public items that are available for use in other safety case modules and a set of items that the safety case module at hand demands from other modules. Those items can be goals, evidences, and context.

A strategy for the construction of a modular safety case architecture is given in [63]. These guidelines are based upon the guidelines for general modular system design and comprise the following requirements:

- Modules must be as independent as possible.
- Modules must exhibit high cohesion and low coupling.
- Modular safety cases and safety case architectures must be constructed top-down.
- Modules must have well-defined interfaces.
- All modular dependencies must be captured.

In summary, modular GSN is a graphical notation that allows modeling modular safety arguments. As described above, there are also product-related guidelines for the specification of modular safety arguments. Openness and adaptivity are not explicitly addressed, whereas the modularization concepts would at least provide a starting point for corresponding augmentations. Apart from that, it has been shown that the GSN can be utilized in conjunction with a software product line approach [64]. Considering SafetyCases@Runtime, a GSN-like notation might be a possible starting point. Usually, however, the single elements of a GSN-based safety case are described in natural language. Using GSN at runtime will require an appropriate means for formalizing the notation in order to enable runtime evaluation and adaptation.

4.3.3   The Generic Safety Case in DECOS

The DECOS (Dependable Embedded Components and Systems) project [65] was a European Integrated Project in the FP6 Embedded Systems area which ran from 2004 to 2007. The main objective of the project was to make a significant contribution to the safety of dependable embedded systems by facilitating the systematic design and deployment of integrated systems [66]. In order to reach this objective, a generic safety case approach for incremental certification was developed, which improves the efficiency of the certification process and thus shall facilitate significant cost savings during the development of safety-critical systems.

According to [66] and [67], modularity is achieved by separating the certification of core services and architectural services from applications (enabling generic application safety cases (for the class of applications) and individual (specific) safety cases by supporting independent safety arguments for different distributed application subsystems).

1. *Separating certification of architectural services from certification of applications:* The clear interfaces between the platform and the applications provided via the platform interface are a prerequisite for the separation of the certification of architectural services from the certification of applications.

2. *Separating certification of different distributed application subsystems:* The integrated architecture allows the independent certification of different application subsystems, instead of considering the system as an indivisible whole in the certification process. The safety argument for each subsystem is provided to the integrator by the suppliers along with the compiled application code of the jobs in the corresponding subsystem. In order to construct the safety argument for the overall system, the system integrator combines the safety arguments of the independently developed subsystems and acquires additional evidence, such as the results of a formal verification of the architectural services. The decomposition of the overall system into encapsulated subsystems with different criticality levels reduces the overall certification efforts and allows focusing on the most critical parts. Furthermore, the separate certification of subsystems is beneficial if functionality is reused in different systems. In this case, the safety argument for the functionality needs to be constructed only once.

Like the approaches above, DECOS supports the modularization of development time safety artifacts. Openness and adaptivity are not explicitly supported and all certification activities are to be conducted at development time. However, the incremental approach adopted by DECOS seems to be well suited to handling variability at development time, maybe in conjunction with an adequate software product line approach as it has already been explored for the GSN.

4.3.4   Vertical Safety Interfaces

The goal of the VerSaI (*Vertical Safety Interfaces*) method is to assist the integrator of an integrated architecture in checking whether the application software components are able to run safely on the execution platforms of the system, and if so, provide assistance in generating appropriate evidence [72].

Before *safety compatibility* between the application and the platform can be checked with the VerSaI approach, demands and guarantees have to be specified. Demands are typically used to express all the properties a platform needs to have for an application to be executed safely, whereas guarantees represent the safety-related properties the platform possesses. A compatibility check is successful if a sound argument for the fulfillment of the demands with the available guarantees can be established. To enable tool-supported integration, the VerSaI approach offers a semiformal language for modeling these demands and guarantees. The language consists of a number of elements, each representing a certain type of demand or guarantee exchanged by an application and a platform. This implies the noteworthy fact that there is a finite number of language elements and, therefore, also a finite number of dependencies that can be expressed with the language. First evaluations have shown that this is suitable, because the typical service relationships between an application and a platform are finite and regular, too, which is also the reason why platforms have been standardized in the first place.

The final step of the method is to check whether each demand can be met with the guarantees identified as relevant in the previous step. In contrast to conventional interfaces, it is usually not possible to simply match demands and guarantees, respectively. In fact, it is necessary to generate an additional fragment in the safety case providing the arguments and evidences that the demands of the platform are met by the guarantees given by the platform. To this end, this step is supported by a so-called strategy repository. The repository contains expert strategies that are selected and presented to the integrator and describe what guarantees are needed to fulfill the current type of demand and how to generate a piece of evidence containing a sound argument.

Like the other modular certification approaches, Versa focuses on development time integration. However, it provides some interesting aspects that could be of relevance for SafetyModels@Runtime. First, it already provides a formalization of the interface language, thus facilitating automated checks of interface consistency. Second, it introduces first ideas of how missing fragments of a safety case could be generated automatically. Though this is currently not possible without human interaction, some ideas could be a starting point for extending/modifying safety case argumentations at runtime. However, VerSaI is limited to the vertical interface between application and platform software. This has the advantage that the typical safety requirements concerning this vertical interface are quite limited - thus simplifying the formalization of the interface language. For OAS, this approach would have to be extended to horizontal interfaces as well. However, those interfaces are usually application dependent so that the formalization approach used in VerSaI cannot be easily extended to support horizontal interfaces as well.

4.4   Runtime Certification

First ideas with respect to runtime certification have been introduced by Rushby[68], [69]. In contrast to most of the other approaches presented in this section (which are already quite mature and have partly even been proven in use), Rushby`s work remains on a rather conceptual level. However, considering its motivation and the solution concepts presented, it is very important in the context of safety assurance of OAS.

In the first publication, Rushby presents the general idea that certain elements of a conventional certification case could be transferred to runtime. The focus is on those elements that apply formal analyses (e.g., automated verification) to representations of a software component and its local safety or other critical requirements. Formal analyses are usually employed at development time to formally verify that a component follows a certain prescribed behavior. At runtime it would be possible to employ monitors to control the component's behavior during execution and to trigger adequate measures when deviations occur. Such monitors might be synthesized from the model that specifies the component's behavior using very similar—and equally trustworthy—techniques as those used in formal verification.

In the second publication, Rushby outlines a framework in which the basis for certification is changed from compliance with standards to the construction of explicit goals, evidences, and arguments (generally called an 'assurance case'). He then describes how runtime verification can be used within this framework, thereby allowing certification to be partly performed at runtime. The core of this approach is again the usage of runtime monitors, which have been defined outside the context of an assurance case in order to dynamically monitor assumptions, anomalies, and safety, respectively.

Overall, the presented work is still very conceptual but nevertheless provides a good starting point for future work in the context of the envisioned framework. One of the main ideas advocated by Rushby, namely to shift parts of the safety assurance measures into runtime to cater to the specific challenges within OAS, has also been adopted by us in the framework presented here.

4.5   Discussion

From the state-of-the-art in safety engineering approaches that support modularization it becomes apparent that openness and adaptivity have been largely out of scope and thus are not explicitly supported by most approaches. Moreover, even though the umbrella term 'modular certification' seems to suggest otherwise, all of the considered approaches and standards rather focus on the modularization of pre-certification safety artifacts, particularly safety cases. The only exceptions are the approaches on runtime certification, which build on pre-certification of the system. Since most approaches have been designed to support engineers during their development time activities, they lack an adequate degree of formalization, which would be required for automated runtime evaluations. All of these approaches nevertheless provide sound conceptual starting points for new safety engineering approaches for Open Adaptive Systems. As for supporting adaptivity, some of the presented modular certification approaches (such as the GSN) have at least been used in conjunction with software product lines. Others, such as the approach introduced by Rushby, DECOS and Ver-SaI, seem to be well-suited in this regard as well.

As the considered approaches are more or less established in the safety engineering community, using them as a starting point for Models@Runtime certainly increases the probability of acceptance. Since the approaches are mainly based on safety cases, they would provide a good starting point for research in the direction of SafetyCertificates@Runtime or for SafetyCases@Runtime.

Apart from the modular certification approaches discussed above, the runtime certification approach presented by Rushby builds on dynamic monitoring (and repair) of the systems'/components' behavior. This approach could fit into the category of V&V-Models@Runtime. Based on the conceptual descriptions, however, it seems that mainly predefined verifications can be executed at runtime. So depending on the concrete realization of these concepts, they will rather support the re-validation of evidences as part of SafetyCases@Runtime.

5   State-of-the-Art from the Adaptive Systems Community's Point of View

Some of the first significant research efforts for adaptive systems emerged from the middleware community, where adaptive middleware platforms have been designed to meet the new demands of flexible, distributed heterogeneous systems. Examples in this regard are the solutions proposed by Blair et al. [4], Kon et al. [5], Capra et al. [6], and Truyen[7]. These solutions were mainly designed to enable adaptability (i.e., reconfiguration of the middleware or platform to fit a given setting) or even self-adaptation (i.e., an adaptive middleware or platform that dynamically adapts itself to provide optimized service functionality and quality in any situation). A related field of research, where the topic of self-adaptivity also gained momentum quite early, is the field of adaptive quality of service (QoS) assurance. Corresponding research has mostly focused on communication systems and end-to-end consideration of QoS. The results have been platforms, middleware, and frameworks enabling adaptive QoS.

It was soon recognized that quality assurance for adaptive systems is an important topic with significant scientific challenges. Initial corresponding research efforts have mostly focused on the issues of validation and verification (V&V) of adaptive systems. First results were based on development time V&V, but recently we have seen that V&V measures are being increasingly shifted into runtime. The upcoming topic of Models@Runtime seems to be a catalyst in this regard. Thus, even more capable Models@Runtime-based approaches for runtime V&V can be expected in the future.

In recent years, one main research focus of the community has been to investigate sound engineering methodologies for adaptive systems. Such methodologies ideally span all typical phases of software development (from requirements engineering to the validation of the final product) and explicitly consider important non-functional properties. This methodological research focus has been pushed by community research roadmaps [1]and has been advocated strongly by conferences in the area of adaptive systems, e.g., the SEAMS symposium [8] and the SASO conference [9]. In the context of engineering frameworks, the different fields of adaptive systems research are growing together ever more. The current Models@Runtime research landscape underlines this trend, since researchers from the fields of adaptive middleware, V&V, and engineering methodologies are working together to develop seamless approaches combining all these important aspects under the umbrella of the Models@Runtime topic[2][3]. Relatedly, Baresi and Ghezzi argue that the clear separation between development-time and run-time is blurring and is probably doing so even further in future [74].

From the perspective of the envisioned safety assurance framework, there are consequently two categories of approaches that will be considered in more detail in the following:

1. Approaches concentrating on V&V in the context of adaptive systems. V&V is here not necessarily aimed at safety assurance. Nevertheless, the approaches can be valuable input for future approaches in the context of the envisioned framework. A short overview of the state-of-the-art will be provided and the assurance scope of the different approaches will be considered. Note that completeness cannot be a goal for this article, thus we rather tried to identify a representative set of approaches covering the most important different classes.

2. Frameworks and approaches for adaptive systems that enable the utilization of Models@Runtime for different relevant concerns. Such approaches provide a possible technological basis and therefore define the frame the envisioned safety assurance framework would have to be integrated into. The approaches will be briefly presented and analyzed with respect to their runtime assurance capabilities and their usage of Models@Runtime. Again, completeness was not the goal. For this part of the state of the art we also compiled a possibly representative set of approaches to indicate the current status quo of Models@Runtime approaches in relation of assurances – and safety in particular.

5.1   Approaches Using Validation and Verification as a Means for Assurances

The approaches considered in this section focus on ensuring certain properties through the application of adequate V&V techniques. Some approaches rely on development time measures alone, whereas others utilize runtime measures or a combination of both. For both cases, this section will provide an overview of the respective state-of-the-art. Prior to that, however, there will be a paragraph on contract-based design, since this is an enabling technology for efficient V&V. Moreover, safety contracts and assume-guarantee reasoning are likely to be enabling technologies for important parts of the envisioned framework.

5.1.1   Design by Contract

About twenty years ago, Meyer introduced a set of basic principles of Design by Contract in the context of his Eiffel language [23]. Since then, a wide range of related approaches have been developed for the specification and utilization of different kinds of functional and non-functional contracts. Beugnard et al. provide a recent overview of the general use of Design by Contract concepts in the domains of embedded systems, component architectures, and service oriented architectures [24]. The work in the respective domains is classified according to a scheme introduced in an earlier publication by the authors [25]. Essentially, the types of contracts are classified into four levels:

1. Syntactic (or basic): The goal is to make the system work. It is generally specified with Interface Definition Languages (IDLs), as well as typed object-based or object-oriented languages. It ensures the components can be assembled.
2. Behavioral: The goal is to specify each operation. It is generally specified with a couple of assertions: a precondition and a post-condition. It ensures the operations offered and required are not only syntactically compatible but also semantically.
3. Synchronization: The goal is to specify the coordination of operations. It can be specified with an automaton labeled with operations. It ensures the operations are used in the proper order.
4. Quality of Service: The goal is to quantify a few features associated with operations. Performance, availability, and quality of result can be specified and negotiated at that level.

An interesting and widely recognized approach for contract-based design (even though not specifically addressing adaptive systems) is the Rich Component Model (RCM). The RCM is the backbone of the embedded systems design approach developed in the SPEEDS project (Speculative and Exploratory Design in Systems Engineering) [26]. One primary goal of the RCM is to optimize the reuse of embedded applications. Safety-relevant applications are explicitly included. The main ideas forming the foundation of the approach are described in [28].

The language typically used to describe such contracts is hybrid automata as shown in [27], [28] and [29]. There are formal definitions for the semantics of the hierarchical and horizontal composition of the contracts, which allows checking the fulfillment of system-level requirements after the system has been integrated, using a model checker for example. The formality of the approach increases the achievable degree of automation while equally increasing the upfront effort for modeling the system. The RCM is therefore a modeling paradigm that allows specifying the contract interface of a modular safety argument.

In relation to assurances and adaptable systems, Inverardi et al. recently presented a theoretical assume-guarantee framework for adaptable systems [30] that can be used as a basis for establishing runtime contracts and thus also for V&V in adaptive systems. The major aim of this framework is to define efficient conditions to be proved at runtime to guarantee the correctness of the adaptation of a composed adaptive system.

Conditional Safety Certificates (ConSerts) are a means for facilitating safety certification in the context of OAS [70] [71] [76]. This is one of the approaches explicitly addressing Open Adaptive Systems. There are three main differences between ConSerts and standard certificates that are owed to the nature of open systems: A ConSert is not static but conditional; it usually comprises a number of variants; and it must be available in an executable (and composable) form at runtime. Conditions within a ConSert manifest in relations between potentially guaranteed safety requirements (denoted as guarantees for the remainder of this article) and the corresponding demanded safety requirements (i.e., demands). The demands always represent safety requirements relating to the environment of a component, which consequently cannot be verified yet at design time. A ConSert therefore certifies that the guarantees will hold with acceptable probability under the precondition that the specified safety demands are fulfilled by the environment. Variants come into play because ConSerts usually comprise not only one but a series of different potential guarantees. Eventually, the ConSerts must be available at runtime in an executable representation and the systems need to possess mechanisms for composing and analyzing these runtime models. Using these means makes it possible to establish and maintain safety contracts at runtime that span all levels of a composition hierarchy through pairs of ConSert-based guarantees and demands.

In the same way as standard certificates, ConSerts shall be issued by safety experts, independent organizations, or authorized bodies after a stringent manual check of the system. To this end, it is mandatory to prove all claims regarding the fulfillment of safety requirements by means of suitable evidence. The guarantees that can be provided by a system usually depend on the fulfillment of demands. On the one hand, these demands might directly relate to the required functionalities of other systems. In other cases, some evidences must be acquired at the integration level, since safety is not completely composable. To this end, ConSerts support the concept of so-called runtime evidences. The resulting variability (of the fulfillment of demands) ultimately leads to variants and conditions within the safety case, which are the basis for the definition of ConSerts.

In terms of the conceptual assurance framework, ConSerts belong to the class of SafetyCertificates@Runtime. But they also support single elements of SafetyCases@Runtime through the instrument of runtime evidences.

5.1.2   Approaches Utilizing Development Time V&V for Assurances

In [31], Zhang and Cheng introduce a method for constructing and verifying adaptation models using Petri nets. In [32], linear temporal logic is extended with an 'adapt' operator for specifying requirements that a given system must match before, during, and after adaptation. An approach for ensuring the correctness of component-based adaptation was presented in [33], where theorem proving techniques are used to show that a program is always in a correct state in terms of invariants. [34]introduces a formal model of reconfiguration and an associated set of high-level system dependability properties that can be verified. Giese and Tichy introduced a development-time hazard analysis approach for analyzing all configurations a self-adaptive system can reach during runtime [35]. In [75], Becker et al. present a further development time verification technique for the invariant verification of structural properties. This technique has been designed to be appropriate for large multi-agent systems that are subject to structural adaptations at runtime.

Mohammad and Alagar recently introduced a formal approach for the specification and verification of trustworthy component-based systems [36] that advocates formal specifications and dedicated safety properties as a basis for V&V. The properties can be defined as constraints (such as time or data constraints) at the component level and are to be understood as invariants over the component behavior. The behavior can be defined using timed automata. Eventually, the specifications enable automated analysis and verification (through model checking) of the considered properties.

All of the above approaches have in common that they try to analyze (with respect to safety or other specific properties) all possible variants that a given system might assume during runtime. Based on the analysis results, engineers can implement adequate measures to improve or ensure the considered properties.

5.1.3 Approaches Utilizing Runtime V&V for Assurances

Runtime V&V measures are typically applied in a complementary way together with corresponding development-time activities. On the one hand, there are runtime verification techniques that utilize runtime monitoring to record software execution traces that can then be analyzed [37]. On the other hand, there are approaches that employ quantitative model checking at runtime as an assurance technique for the context of adaptive systems (e.g., [38], [39], and [40]). In [43], Goldsby et al. present AMOEBA-RT, a run-time monitoring and verification technique that provides assurance (based on dynamic model checking) that dynamically adaptive software satisfies its requirements. Calinscu and Grunske introduced the QoSMOS (QoS Management and Optimization of Service-based systems) framework for the development of adaptive service-based systems that are able to manage their QoS adaptively and predictably [44]. QoSMOS utilizes probabilistic model checking at runtime to evaluate if the system satisfies the given QoS requirements. In the traditional development-time versions of these kinds of approaches, the analysis of temporal-logic properties (including probabilities, costs, and rewards) is commonly used to assess relevant nonfunctional properties of a system. At runtime, such analyses can be performed on a model base that is continually updated as the underlying system evolves. In general, this introduction of runtime measures for the context of adaptive systems is particularly promising since traditional development-time techniques do not scale sufficiently well. Moreover, at runtime, detected issues can be addressed directly with adequate adaptations (i.e., countermeasures). A short related survey (which is not limited to V&V) considering runtime assurance techniques for adaptive systems has recently been published by Calinescu[42]. A further approach that is particularly focused on safety has been proposed by Priesterjahn et al. in [41]. The main idea of this approach is to ensure the safety of adaptive systems during runtime by checking whether recon-figuration is allowed based on associated hazard probabilities and potential damage that would be imminent after the reconfiguration. To this end, adapted hazard and risk analysis techniques are applied during runtime.

5.2   Frameworks for Adaptive Systems and Models@Runtime

5.2.1   MADAM and MUSIC

The MADAM (Mobility and Adaptation Enabling Middleware) European project and its follow-up MUSIC (Self-Adapting Applications for Mobile USers In Ubiquitous Computing Environments) aimed at providing techniques and tools for reducing the time and effort needed to develop self-adaptive mobile applications [10][11]. To this end, these projects propose an architecture-centric approach where dynamic adapta-tion is realized in an application-independent adaptation middleware. Architectural models of the applications are made available at runtime and serve as a basis for rea-soning about and controlling the adaptation. Meta-models for the specification of these models are provided by means of a dedicated component framework.

In order to realize runtime adaptation, MADAM and MUSIC employ an applica-tion-independent adaptation middleware that is implementing a typical adaptation control loop with the following responsibilities:

1.   Monitor both system and user context. The system context consists of system resources such as battery level, CPU utilization, memory usage, and network resources. The user context subsumes information on the environment and on the user's (maybe correlated) needs.
2.   Analyze the context and the context changes that occur and plan reasonable changes of the system. To this end, utility functions are used to assess which implementation variant of a certain component type would fit the given adap-tation goals best. On the system level, global utility functions are used (which can aggregate the component-level utility functions) to compute the overall utility of an application. This allows evaluating all the different configuration possibilities (i.e., it is a brute-force approach) and the most useful one in the given circumstances can be chosen at the end.
3.   Implement the changes – preferably without noticeably interrupting the opera-tion of the system.

Regarding assurances, MADAM and MUSIC explicitly address the management of functional and non-functional properties. However, the properties are only addressed in a generic way and managed via 'best-effort' without 'hard' guarantees.

5.2.2   DiVA – Dynamic Variability in Complex, Adaptive Systems

The European DiVA project can be considered as a predecessor of the MADAM/MUSIC series. In detail, the project had the following main research objec-tives [45]:

- To provide both build-time and runtime management of the adaptive system (re)configuration of co-existing, co-dependent configurations that can span across several administrative boundaries in a distributed, heterogeneous environment.
- To provide efficient management of the number of potential configurations that may grow exponentially with each new variability dimension.
- To increase the quality and productivity of adaptive system development and help the designers to model, control, and validate adaptation policies as well as the trajectory from one safe configuration to another.

DiVA tackles these challenges by applying and combining techniques from the fields of software product lines (SPL), model-driven engineering (MDE), and aspect-oriented modeling (AOM). Moreover, DiVA has a strong focus on utilizing such Models@Runtime, in accordance with the Models@Runtime paradigm. In [46], the DiVA contribution is summarized as follows:

At design time, engineers can avoid manually designing all of the system's possible configurations and transitions by explicitly defining an adaptive system as a Dynamic Software Product Line (DSPL). At runtime, the system analyzes the context and explicitly constructs a suitable configuration using AOM techniques. It also validates this configuration using traditional MDE techniques: invariant checking, simulation, and so on. Finally, the system automatically generates a safe reconfiguration script to actually adapt the running business system. If the produced configuration is not consistent, the system simply discards the configuration and derives a new one. Since the running business system has not been adapted yet, it is not necessary to perform a rollback. This process is open to evolution—designers can make the DSPL evolve by seamlessly adding or removing variants, constraints, rules, and so on.

Note that assurances were not the focus of DiVA and non-functional properties were only considered in a generic way. Still, the management of generic properties through models at runtime and runtime self-adaptation was foreseen.

5.2.3   Robocop, Space4U and Trust4ALL

The main goal of the ROBOCOP, Space4U, and Trust4ALL [12][13][14] series of European projects was to establish an adequate component-based architecture and middleware for OAS. According to [15], Robocop introduced a component-based framework for high-volume embedded devices with a focus on robust and reliable operation, upgrading, and component trading, while the focus of Space4U was on the validation, maturation, and extension of the Robocop architecture by introducing fault management, power management, and terminal management. Trust4All essentially extended the component-based middleware developed in the course of its two predecessors with respect to a trust management framework.

Correspondingly, according to the Trust4All innovation report [16], the project 'has defined, designed and developed a middleware software architecture specifically targeted at embedded systems that require a predefined level of trust, due to the nature of the services they provide. The project focuses on the trustworthiness-related aspects of the middleware software architecture in domains such as home medical care, security and automation, as well as on-the-move applications, for which dependability is particularly important'. A further important result of the project is the ISO/IEC 23004 standard on middleware, where seven of the eight parts of the standard were contributed by Trust4All (Architecture, Component Model, Resource and Quality Management, Component Download, Fault Management, System Integrity Management, and Reference Software).

In essence, the main scientific contribution of Trust4All, the trustworthiness management approach, is enabled through a trustworthiness model and a trust management framework model. The assurance scope of Trust4All can be classified as 'assurance of trust-related properties', although the reputation- and recommendation-based approach is not compatible with safety assurance in a traditional sense (i.e., certification would not be possible on that basis). Trust4All explicitly supports self-adaptation for assurance purposes, utilizing a runtime configurable fault management mechanism [14].

5.3   Discussion

Adaptive systems and Models@Runtime frameworks and approaches contribute the technological basis and knowledge for representing and utilizing runtime models for different concerns. Regarding the assurance and management of non-functional properties, however, these approaches remain very generic and are not designed to provide 'hard' guarantees. Accordingly, these approaches do not provide a sufficient methodological backbone, which is indispensable for safety assurance and certification.

Due to reasons of complexity, development time V&V as the sole measure for ensuring important properties of an adaptive system is only really feasible for closed adaptive systems. In contrast to OAS, for closed adaptive systems it is generally possible (although potentially very complex, depending on the applied adaptation concepts) to conduct sufficient safety analysis based on holistic system models already at development time. Therefore, one commonality of these approaches is that they focus on closed systems and on specific adaptation concepts that facilitate controlling the size of the adaptation space.

The runtime V&V approaches provide specific concepts for dynamically obtaining and evaluating V&V-related information in an adaptive systems context. These techniques would obviously be well suited for tackling challenges related to the runtime V&V parts of the envisioned framework. However, there is no conceptual integration with existing safety engineering approaches up to now. Nor is there support with respect to variability within the certificates, the safety case, and correspondingly the dynamic V&V measures. In other words, there can only be one 'static' certificate that is to be validated and verified, which consequently limits the flexibility of the open adaptive system, as elaborated before in this article. Nevertheless, in conjunction with a sound and comprehensive safety engineering backbone, these approaches would be a good starting point for future research and could play a vital role in safety assurance for OAS.

An approach that has an explicit focus on safety and is thus particularly relevant for this article has been proposed by Priesterjahn et al. in [41]. This approach is well suited to exemplify what has been stated above. The main idea of this approach is to ensure the safety of adaptive systems during runtime by checking whether reconfiguration is allowed based on associated hazard probabilities and potential damage that would be imminent after the reconfiguration. To this end, a compositional hazard and risk analysis technique is applied during runtime. However, all the safety engineering activities that are typically applied in addition to the safety analyses in order to get a system certified are omitted. Under the premise that safety-critical applications need to be certified, these steps would still be required. Assuming that corresponding safety engineering and certification were done at development time already, this would constrain the flexibility of the approach since a given system would need to be pre-analyzed comprehensively with respect to the acceptability of the failure probabilities of its configurations. A further potential problem of the approach is that emergent safety properties within a system of systems, such as common cause failures, feature interactions, and emergent dysfunctions, are not addressed.

The ConSerts approach directly addresses the idea of SafetyCertificates@Runtime. It is therefore one possible starting point for a safety assurance framework. Additional ConSerts support runtime evidences, which are a first step towards SafetyCases@Runtime. The approach has been successfully applied in different industry applications, which underscore the principal applicability of the idea of SafetyCertificates@Runtime.

6   Evaluation

6.1   Status Quo

Obviously, there are different kinds of approaches that address different aspects of safety assurance at runtime. The following tables summarize the main findings in the different communities.

| Approach | Safety Engineering | | | |
	supported	foundation	status quo	open issues
Certificate @Runtime	∅	[60]	- no established approach - modular certification provides a sound basis	- formalization - variability - runtime representation
SafetyCase @Runtime	([68], [69])	[60], [61], [62], [64], [65], [66], [67], [VerSaI]	- many design approaches supports modular safety cases - safety case models available - assumes human interaction (no formalization) - first ideas on runtime certification at conceptual level only	- formalization - runtime representation - adaptation of argumentations - realization of runtime evidences
V&V @Runtime	∅	∅	not considered	
HRA @Runtime	∅	∅	not considered	

For the safety engineering community, it is obvious that runtime assurance has not been in the focus of research. Actually, there is no approach that deals with modular certificate models. The reason for this could be that certificates as such do not play an important role at development time. In fact, they are not more than a piece of paper issued at the end of an assessment, which can be used as evidence in a super-ordinate safety case. This means that certificates are not direct working artifacts for safety engineers. The importance of certificate models mainly arises from the need to dynamically compose systems, which requires formal representation at the information level of the certificates (and an explicit specification of the variation points) that can be evaluated at runtime.

Nonetheless, there is a series of approaches that provide valuable starting points and that could be extended to SafetyCases@Runtime. Most of these approaches need to be further formalized in order to be used at runtime. Many safety case notations are still based on informal textual information as they are intended to be used by a human safety expert. Based on such formalization, it would be possible to evaluate Safety-Cases@Runtime and identify invalidated evidences, for example. In order to use the full potential of SafetyCases@Runtime, appropriate approaches are required to dynamically adapt the line of argumentation used in the safety case at runtime. However, there are currently no approaches that consider doing that.

There exist first ideas on how to use runtime verification to support certification at runtime [68], [69]. However, these approaches still remain at the superficial level of concepts and ideas. The dynamic adaptation of V&V models, such as test cases or pass/fail criteria, or even adaptation of the hazard analysis and risk assessment (HRA) is completely outside the scope of the safety engineering community. In other words, the V&V measures that are shifted into runtime are always completely predefined at development time already.

Approach	Models@Runtime			
	supported	foundation	status quo	open issues
Development-Time Assurance of Adaptive Systems	[31], [32], [33], [34], [35], [36]		- promising results available - limited to few groups	- maturing approaches towards applicability and acceptance - integration with concepts like SafetyCertificates@Runtime to support open systems as well
Certificate @Runtime	[ConSert]	∅	- a first approach is available, utilizing variable certificates and Models@Runtime	- could provide a good add-on to design time assurance approaches for supporting open systems

SafetyCase @Runtime		[37], [38], [39], [40], [41], [42], [43], [44]	- some research has focused on runtime execution of predefined V&V steps - currently independent solutions that can hardly be combined - no complete coverage of safety assurance	- integration of different approaches to support complete safety assurance - currently no direct support to SafetyCases@Runtime
V&V @Runtime	∅	∅	- currently no approaches available	
HRA @Runtime	∅	∅	- currently no approaches available	

Regarding the adaptive systems community, a lot of work has been done regarding the development time verification of adaptive systems and runtime execution of predefined verification steps. Also from a safety point of view, a focus on development time verification is certainly preferable. Regarding the typical characteristics of OAS, however, such an approach appears not to be sufficient. Therefore, the idea of having runtime verification is a good extension. However, the different approaches seem to be quite independent from each other. Each of the single approaches covers only one aspect of runtime safety assurance, and it is mostly unclear how the different approaches could be combined into an integrated framework. Nonetheless, they provide a very good basis for providing evidences in the context of SafetyCases@Runtime. Some work is also available on SafetyCertificates@Runtime, which already considers aspects such as runtime evidences. Obviously, there seems to be a good basis and a lot of potential could be tapped by a more efficient combination and integration of the different approaches.

6.2   A Possible Roadmap to Safety Assurance for OAS Using Models@Runtime

Summarizing the status quo, there is already a lot of work available that directly or indirectly supports the safety assurance of OAS. However, most approaches seem to be quite independent from each other. None of the approaches alone is sufficient and complete to assure safety in OAS, but all of them provide individual puzzle pieces for a safety assurance approach. Since they have been developed in isolation, it is however not possible to simply combine them. Nonetheless, the efficient combination of existing approaches would already lead to significant progress.

From our point of view, a first step towards an efficient safety assurance approach for OAS therefore seems to be to consider the big picture of safety assurance instead of regarding single elements in isolation. To this end, a safety assurance framework, comparable to the one used in this article would be required, but it certainly needs to be more mature. Such a framework would provide the big picture the single puzzle pieces have to fit into – thus simplifying classification and combination of the different approaches. Moreover, it would define a principal understanding of what safety assurance for OAS could look like. Such a commonly accepted foundation is a prerequisite to obtaining acceptance of the assurance approaches by certification bodies and safety assessors.

Taking the framework defined in this article as a starting point, a possible roadmap to safety assurance is illustrated in Figure 8.

From an industry point of view, the most urgent need for safety assurance is certainly for open systems in which the single systems only adapt to anticipated situations. Therefore, assurance of the single systems could be achieved using available assurance approaches applied at development time. If these approaches are tightly integrated into traditional safety engineering lifecycles, safety assurance could happen completely at development time. All remaining assumptions and variabilities that must be resolved at runtime could be modeled using SafetyCertificates@Runtime, which would also enable safe composition of systems of systems at runtime.

Such an approach is also very likely to be accepted by safety assessors. Design time assurance of adaptive systems is in some sense already considered in safety standards. For example, ISO26262 explicitly defines how assurance has to deal with large configuration and parameter spaces. Alternatively, from a safety engineering point of view, adaptation is nothing but an indistinguishable part of the functionality extending the system's state space, which must be completely covered by all safety assurance activities. The available development time assurance approaches tackle the resulting challenges. SafetyCertificates@Runtime are very similar to modular certification approaches. Definition and assurance of the certificates take place at development time, and only the composition of certificates is shifted to runtime. In order to be accepted, the verification of the composition mechanisms must become an additional element of the development time verification activities. This is of course also true in general for all runtime mechanisms that are introduced as part of the safety assurance framework. As described in the previous chapter, this scenario can also be extended with alternative approaches, such as extended safety bags.

If we regard open systems that require more flexible adaptations including adaptations to unanticipated situations, or if the dynamic composition happens at the level of software components instead of systems, it is additionally necessary to provide SafetyCases@Runtime. To this end, approaches facilitating the modular specification of safety cases, as they exist in the safety engineering community, could be used as a starting point. As mentioned above, this requires formalization of the notations in the first step. For many application scenarios, however, the capability to dynamically adapt the line of argumentation could be optional. Instead, it might be sufficient to integrate different variants into the safety case at design time and to reduce runtime responsibility to the resolution of these variabilities. This would require further extension of existing safety case approaches. As an additional aspect, it is necessary to provide evidences at runtime. This step can be supported by different existing runtime V&V approaches as described above. Nonetheless, some extensions are required in order to transfer the existing approaches from the idea of a stand-alone solution to an integrated part of SafetyCases@Runtime.

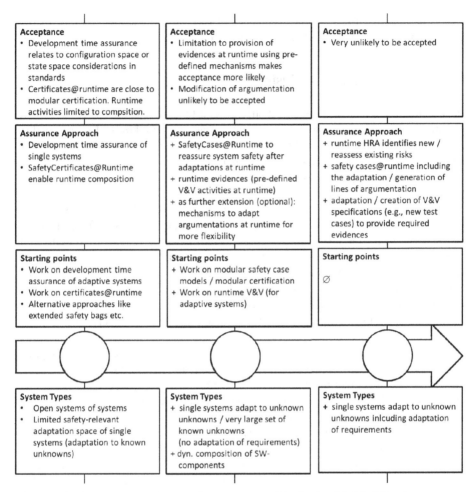

Fig. 8. Possible roadmap to safety assurance of OAS using Models@Runtime

The main aspect in this approach that complicates acceptance is the runtime provision of evidences. However, assuming that the verification activities are already defined at development time and 'only' executed at runtime, this is likely to be accepted. In order to argue the appropriateness of the runtime V&V approaches, the similarity to established concepts like built-in tests could be used as a starting point.

As soon as requirements are to be adapted as well, there are no established approaches available that could be used as a starting point. The required V&V-Models@Runtime and HRA@Runtime are currently neither supported by existing work nor is a good basis available. Moreover, it is very unlikely that such approaches will be accepted in the near future. So obviously, a significant gap exists here in the state-of-the-art. In the long run, we expect that adaptations of requirements will enable new business cases – also for safety-critical systems. Therefore, we recommend reasoning about possible assurance approaches right from the beginning.

This is particularly true since the acceptance of such an approach will require a sufficiently long history of experience and empirical evidence.

7   Summary and Conclusion

In recent years, we have witnessed a strong trend towards open adaptive systems in research and industry. Meanwhile it is quite clear that new kinds of corresponding applications promise huge benefits for end-users and for businesses. The lack of suitable safety assurance approaches for OAS is increasingly turning out to be a limiting factor in this development. Models at runtime, however, could well prove to be a potent means for overcoming these problems.

Although the approaches available were not developed with an integrated safety assurance framework in mind, a promising foundation already exists. The main application scenario for the near future is characterized by open systems of systems with subsystems that only adapt to anticipated situations. Combining and advancing existing work on SafetyCeritificates@Runtime, development time assurance, and runtime V&V could already provide a sound basic solution for this scenario.

Existing safety case models in the field of safety engineering provide a sound basis for further extending the idea to SafetyCases@Runtime in order to support more flexible system adaptations. SafetyCases@Runtime appear to be sufficient to support the assurance of a wide range of application scenarios of OAS in safety-critical applications. The largest gap obviously exists if the adaptation includes the requirements. However, we expect that the application of Requirements@Runtime in safety-critical applications will only happen in the long run – leaving sufficient time to mature the safety assurance approaches in parallel.

Summarizing the results, we can safely state that Models@Runtime seem to have great potential for being successfully used as a basis for safety assurance of OAS. Since they provide a means for creating a clear trace to established safety assurance approaches, the resulting assurance approaches are likely to be accepted by safety assessors. Regarding the current state-of-the-art, there is already a good basis providing first evidence that a safety assurance framework (comparable to the one used in this article) is technically feasible.

References

[1] Cheng, B.H.C., et al.: Software engineering for self-adaptive systems: A research roadmap. In: Cheng, B.H.C., de Lemos, R., Giese, H., Inverardi, P., Magee, J. (eds.) Software Engineering for Self-Adaptive Systems. LNCS, vol. 5525, pp. 1–26. Springer, Heidelberg (2009)

[2] Blair, G., et al.: Models@Run.Time. IEEE Computer (November 2010)

[3] Dagstuhl Seminar on Models@run.time,
http://www.dagstuhl.de/en/program/calendar/semhp/?
semnr=11481 (last visited June 2012)

[4] Blair, G., Coulson, G., Robin, P., Papathomas, M.: An architecture for next generation middleware. In: S.J. Davies, N.A.J., Raymond, K. (eds.) IFIP International Conference on Distributed Systems Platforms and Open Distributed Processing, Middleware 1998 (1998)

[5] Kon, F., Roman, M., Liu, P., Mao, J., Yamane, T., Magalhaes, L., Campbell, R.: Monitoring, security, and dynamic configuration withthe dynamic tao reflective orb. In: 2nd ACM/IFIP International Conference on Middleware, New York, pp. 121–143 (2000)

[6] Capra, L., Blair, G., Mascolo, C., Emmerich, W., Grace, P.: Exploiting reflection in mobile computing middleware. ACM SIGMOBILE Mobile Computing and Communications Review 6, 34–44 (2002)

[7] Truyen, E.: Dynamic and Context-Sensitive Composition in Distributed Systems. Ph.D. thesis, K.U.Leuven (2004)

[8] http://www.self-adaptive.org/ (last visited in June 2012)

[9] http://www.saso-conference.org/ (last visited in June 2012)

[10] Floch, J., Hallsteinsen, S., Stav, E., Eliassen, F., Lund, K., Gjorven, E.: Using Architecture Models for Runtime Adaptability. IEEE Software 23, 62–70 (2006)

[11] Rouvoy, R., Barone, P., Ding, Y., Eliassen, F., Hallsteinsen, S., Lorenzo, J., Mamelli, A., Scholz, U.: MUSIC: Middleware Support for Self-Adaptation in Ubiquitous and Service-Oriented Environments. In: Cheng, B.H.C., de Lemos, R., Giese, H., Inverardi, P., Magee, J. (eds.) Software Engineering for Self-Adaptive Systems. LNCS, vol. 5525, pp. 164–182. Springer, Heidelberg (2009)

[12] Muskens, J., Chaudron, M.: Integrity Management in Component Based Systems. In: Proc. of 30th EUROMICRO Conference (EUROMICRO 2004), pp. 611–619 (2004)

[13] Lenzini, G., Tokmakoff, A., Muskens, J.: Managing Trustworthiness in Component-based Embedded Systems. Electron. Notes Theor. Comput. Sci. 179, 143–155 (2007)

[14] Su, R., Chaudron, M.R.V., Lukkien, J.J.: Adaptive runtime fault management for service instances in component-based software applications. IET Software 1(1), 18–28 (2007)

[15] http://www.hitech-projects.com/euprojects/trust4all/results.htm (last visited in June 2012)

[16] http://www.itea2.org/project/result/download/result/5585 (last visited in June 2012)

[17] http://ercim-news.ercim.eu/adaptable-and-context-aware-trustworthiness-evaluation (last visited in June 2012)

[18] Wang, Y., Vassileva, J.: A review on trust and reputation for web service selection. In: Proceeding of the 1st Int. Workshop on Trust and Reputation Management in Massively Distributed Computing Systems (2007)

[19] Alnemr, R., Quasthoff, M., Meinel, C.: Taking Trust Management to the Next Level. In: Handbook of Research on P2P and Grid Systems for Service-Oriented Computing: Models. IGI Global, Hershey (2010)

[20] https://swt.informatik.uni-augsburg.de/tsos/ (last visited in June 2012)

[21] Avižienis, A., Laprie, J., Randell, B., Landwehr, C.: Basic concepts and taxonomy of dependable and secure computing. IEEE Transactions on Dependable and Secure Computing 1, 11–33 (2004)

[22] Schneider, D., Becker, M., Trapp, M.: Approaching Runtime Trust Assurance in Open Adaptive Systems. In: Proceeding of the 6th International Symposium on Software Engineering for Adaptive and Self-Managing Systems (SEAMS 2011), pp. 196–201. ACM, New York (2011)

[23] Meyer, B.: Applying 'design by contract'. IEEE Computer 25(10), 40–51 (1992)

[24] Beugnard, A., Jézéquel, J.-M., Plouzeau, N.: Contract aware components, 10 years after. Electronic Proceedings in Theoretical Computer Science, 1–11 (2010)

[25] Beugnard, A., Jezéquel, J.-M., Plouzeau, N.: Making components contract aware. IEEE Computer 32(7), 38–45 (1999)

[26] Website of the SPEEDS project, http://www.speeds.eu.com/ (last visited June 2012)

[27] Benveniste, A., Caillaud, B., Ferrari, A., Mangeruca, L., Passerone, R., Sofronis, C.: Multiple viewpoint contract-based specification and design. In: de Boer, F.S., Bonsangue, M.M., Graf, S., de Roever, W.-P. (eds.) FMCO 2007. LNCS, vol. 5382, pp. 200–225. Springer, Heidelberg (2008)

[28] Damm, W., Metzner, A., Peikenkamp, T., Votintseva, A.: Boosting Re-use of Embedded Automotive Applications Through Rich Components. In: Proceedings of the Workshop on Foundations of Interface Technologies 2005, FIT 2005 (2005)

[29] Benvenuti, L., Ferrari, A., Mangeruca, L., Mazzi, E., Passerone, R., Sofronis, C.: A Contract-Based Formalism for the Specification of Heterogeneous Systems. In: Proceedings of the Forum on Specification, Verification and Design Languages (FDL 2008), pp. 142–147. IEEE (2008)

[30] Inverardi, P., Pelliccione, P., Tivoli, M.: Towards an assume-guarantee theory for adaptable systems. In: ICSE Workshop on Software Engineering for Adaptive and Self-Managing Systems, SEAMS 2009 (2009)

[31] Zhang, J., Cheng, B.H.C.: Model-based development of dynami-cally adaptive software. In: International Conference on Software Engineering (ICSE 2006), Shanghai, China, pp. 371–380. ACM (2006)

[32] Zhang, J., Cheng, B.H.C.: Specifying adaptation semantics. In: Workshop on Architecting Dependable Systems (WADS 2005), St. Louis, USA, pp. 1–7. ACM (2005)

[33] Kulkarni, S.S., Biyani, K.N.: Correctness of Component-Based Adaptation. In: Crnković, I., Stafford, J.A., Schmidt, H.W., Wallnau, K. (eds.) CBSE 2004. LNCS, vol. 3054, pp. 48–58. Springer, Heidelberg (2004)

[34] Strunk, E.A.: Reconfiguration Assurance in Embedded System Software, Ph.D. thesis, University of Virginia

[35] Giese, H., Tichy, M.: Component-based hazard analysis: Optimal designs, product lines, and online-reconfiguration. In: Górski, J. (ed.) SAFECOMP 2006. LNCS, vol. 4166, pp. 156–169. Springer, Heidelberg (2006)

[36] Mohammad, M., Alagar, V.: A formal approach for the specification and verification of trustworthy component-based systems. J. Syst. Softw. 84(1), 77–104 (2011)

[37] Leucker, M., Schallhart, C.: A brief account of runtime verification. Journal of Logic and Algebraic Programming 78(5), 293–303 (2009)

[38] Calinescu, R., Kwiatkowska, M.: CADS*: Computer-Aided Development of Self-* Systems. In: Chechik, M., Wirsing, M. (eds.) FASE 2009. LNCS, vol. 5503, pp. 421–424. Springer, Heidelberg (2009)

[39] Calinescu, R., Kwiatkowska, M.: Using quantitative analysis to implement autonomic IT systems. In: Proceedings of the 31st International Conference on Software Engineering (ICSE 2009), pp. 100–110 (2009)

[40] Epifani, I., Ghezzi, C., Mirandola, R., Tamburrelli, G.: Model evolution by runtime adaptation. In: Proceedings of the 31st International Conference on Software Engineering (ICSE 2009), pp. 111–121 (2009)

[41] Priesterjahn, C., Heinzemann, C., Schäfer, W., Tichy, M.: Runtime Safety Analysis for Safe Reconfiguration. In: IEEE International Conference on Industrial Informatics Proceedings of the 3rd Workshop Self -X and Autonomous Control in Engineering Applications, Beijing, China (2012) (accepted)

[42] Calinescu, R.: When the requirements for adaptation and high integrity meet. In: Proceedings of the 8th Workshop on Assurances for Self-Adaptive Systems (ASAS 2011), pp. 1–4. ACM, New York (2011)

[43] Goldsby, H.J., Cheng, B.H.C., Zhang, J.: AMOEBA-RT: Run-Time Verification of Adaptive Software. In: Giese, H. (ed.) MODELS 2008. LNCS, vol. 5002, pp. 212–224. Springer, Heidelberg (2008)

[44] Calinescu, R., Grunske, L., Kwiatkowska, M., Mirandola, R., Tamburrelli, G.: Dynamic QoS Management and Optimization in Service-Based Systems. IEEE Transactions on Software Engineering, 387–409 (May/June 2011)

[45] http://www.ict-diva.eu/DiVA/results/diva-promo-material/DiVA-Overview-Feb2009.pdf (last visited June 2012)

[46] Morin, B., Barais, O., Jezequel, J.-M., Fleurey, F., Solberg, A.: Models@ Run.time to Support Dynamic Adaptation. Computer 42(10), 44–51 (2009)

[47] IEC 61508: Functional safety of electrical/electronic/programmable electronic safety related systems, International Electrotechnical Commission (1999)

[48] Lisagor, O., McDermid, J.A., Pumfrey, D.J.: Towards a Practicable Process for Automated Safety Analysis. In: 24th International System Safety Conference, pp. 596–607 (2006)

[49] Papadopoulos, Y., McDermid, J.: Hierarchically Performed Hazard Origin and Propagation Studies. In: Swierstra, S.D., Oliveira, J.N. (eds.) AFP 1998. LNCS, vol. 1608, pp. 139–152. Springer, Heidelberg (1999)

[50] Fenelon, P., et al.: Towards Integrated Safety Analysis and Design. ACM Applied Computing Review 2(1), 21–32 (1994)

[51] Hawkins, R., McDermid, J.A.: Performing Hazard and Safety Analysis of Object oriented Systems. In: Proc. of ISSC 2002. System Safety Society, Denver (2002)

[52] Kaiser, B., Liggesmeyer, P., Mäckel, O.: A New Component Concept for Fault Trees. In: Lindsay, P., Cant, T. (eds.) Proc. Conferences in Research and Practice in Information Technology. ACS, vol. 33, pp. 37–46 (2004)

[53] Domis, D., Trapp, M.: Integrating Safety Analyses and Component-Based Design. In: Harrison, M.D., Sujan, M.-A. (eds.) SAFECOMP 2008. LNCS, vol. 5219, pp. 58–71. Springer, Heidelberg (2008)

[54] Förster, M., Schneider, D.: Flexible, any-time FTA with component logic models. In: International Symposium on Software Reliability Engineering, ISSRE (2010)

[55] ISO/CD 26262: Road vehicles, Functional Safety Part 6: Product development at the software level, Part 10 – 'Guidelines' (2011)

[56] DO-297: Integrated Modular Avionics (IMA) Development Guidance and Certification Considerations, Radio Technical Commision for Aeronautics (RTCA) SC-200, (2005)

[57] Eveleens, R.L.: Integrated Modular Avionics - Development Guidance and Certification Considerations. In: RTO-EN-SCI-176 Mission Systems Engineering (2006)

[58] AC 20-148: Reusable Software Components, AC 20-148 (2004)

[59] Software Consideration in Airborne Systems and Equipment Certification, DO-178B (1993)

[60] Rushby, J.: Modular Certification. NASA Contractor Report CR-2002-212130, NASA Langley Research Center (2002)

[61] Kelly, T., Weaver, R.: The Goal Structuring Notation – A Safety Argument Notation. In: Proceedings of the 34th International Conference on Dependable Systems and Networks, DSN 2004 (2004)

[62] Kelly, T.: Concepts and Principles of Compositional Safety Case Construction. University of York, sfh (2001)

[63] Bate, I., Bates, S., Hawkins, R., Kelly, T., McDermid, J.: Safety case architectures to complement a contract-based approach to designing safe systems. In: Proceedings of the 21st International System Safety Conference (ISSC 2003): System Safety Society, pp. 182–192 (2003)

[64] Habli, I., Kelly, T.: A Safety Case Approach to Assuring Configurable Architectures of Safety-Critical Product Lines. In: The Proceedings of the International Symposium on Architecting Critical Systems (ISARCS), Prague. Czech Republic (2010)

[65] DECOS: Dependable Embedded Components and Systems, Inte-grated Project within the EU Framework Programme 6, http://www.decos.at (last visited June 2012)

[66] Kopetz, H., Obermaisser, R., Peti, P., Suri, N.: From a Federated to an Integrated Architecture for Dependable Embedded Real-Time Systems. TU Vienna University of Technology, Austria, and Darmstadt University of Technology, Germany (2004)

[67] Althammer, E., Schoitsch, E., Sonneck, G., Eriksson, H., Vinter, J.: Modular certification support — the DECOS concept of generic safety cases. In: 6th IEEE International Conference on Industrial Informatics (INDIN), pp. 258–263 (2008)

[68] Rushby, J.: Just-in-Time Certification. In: Proceedings of the 12th IEEE International Conference on the Engineering of Complex Computer Systems (ICECCS), Auckland, New Zealand, pp. 15–24 (2007)

[69] Rushby, J.: Runtime Certification. In: Leucker, M. (ed.) RV 2008. LNCS, vol. 5289, pp. 21–35. Springer, Heidelberg (2008)

[70] Schneider, D., Trapp, M.: A Safety Engineering Framework for Open Adaptive Systems. In: Proceedings of the Fifth IEEE International Conference on Self-Adaptive and Self-Organizing Systems, Ann Arbor, Michigan, USA, October 3-7 (2011)

[71] Schneider, D., Trapp, M.: Conditional Safety Certificates in Open Systems. In: Proceedings of the 1st Workshop on Critical Automotive applications: Robustness & Safety (CARS), pp. 57–60. ACM, New York (2010)

[72] Zimmer, B., Bürklen, S., Knoop, M., Höfflinger, J., Trapp, M.: Vertical Safety Interfaces - Improving the Efficiency of Modular Certification. In: Proc. of the 30th International Conference of Computer Safety, Reliability, and Security (SAFECOMP 2011) (2011)

[73] Fenn, J.L., Hawkins, R.D., Williams, P.J., Kelly, T.P., Banner, M.G., Oakshott, Y.: The Who, Where, How, Why And When of Modular and Incremental Certification. In: 2007 2nd Institution of Engineering and Technology International Conference on System Safety, October 22-24, pp. 135–140 (2007)

[74] Baresi, L., Ghezzi, C.: The disappearing boundary between de-velopment-time and run-time. In: Proceedings Workshop on Future of Software Engineering Research (FoSER 2010), pp. 17–22. ACM (2010)

[75] Becker, B., Beyer, D., Giese, H., Klein, F., Schilling, D.: Symbolic invariant verification for systems with dynamic structural adaptation. In: Int. Conf. on Software Engineering (ICSE). ACM Press (2006)

[76] Schneider, D., Trapp, M.: Conditional Safety Certification of Open Adaptive Systems. ACM Trans. Auton. Adapt. Syst. 8(2), Article 8, 20 pages (July 2013)

Author Index